CHILD
WELFARE
RESEARCH
REVIEW

Volume 1

CHILD
WELFARE
RESEARCH
REVIEW

Volume 1

Richard Barth,
Jill Duerr Berrick,
and Neil Gilbert,
editors

Columbia University Press
New York

Columbia University Press
New York   Chichester, West Sussex
Copyright © 1994 Columbia University Press
All rights reserved

Library of Congress Cataloging-in-Publication Data

Child welfare research review / Richard Barth, Jill Duerr Berrick, and
    Neil Gilbert, editors.
       p.   cm.
    Includes bibliographical references and index.
    ISBN 0–231–08074–3 (cloth).   —ISBN 0–231–08075–1 (paper)
       1. Child Welfare—United States.   I. Barth, Richard P.
    II. Berrick, Jill Duerr.   III. Gilbert, Neil
    HV713.C3953   1994   94–1252
    362.7'0973—dc20   CIP

Printed in the United States of America

c 10 9 8 7 6 5 4 3 2 1
p 10 9 8 7 6 5 4 3 2 1

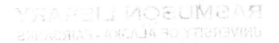

Contents

PART THREE
FOSTER CARE CASELOAD DYNAMICS

PART FOUR
ADOPTION RESEARCH

PART FIVE
OUTCOMES OF CHILD WELFARE SERVICES

Acknowledgments

Numerous students and colleagues helped bring about the publication of this volume. First and foremost, we are grateful to Susan Katzenellenbogen and Renee Robinson, the office staff at the Child Welfare Research Center who painstakingly sewed the work of many authors into this volume. The Family Welfare Research Group, which is part of the School of Social Welfare at the University of California at Berkeley, is the gracious host for the Child Welfare Research Center. We thank all our colleagues there for sharing their ideas, offices, and computers with us. We are especially indebted to Cecelia Sudia who provided us with much up-to-date information on child welfare research efforts around the country. Her dedication to this field inspires us in this work. We also thank Penny Maza for her deep commitment to the development of effective child welfare services through research. We benefited from Fred Wulczyn, Bob Goerge, Kristine Nelson, Mary Berry, and Duncan Lindsey's visits to the Berkeley Child Welfare Research Center. Dean Harry Specht has always provided effective leadership in support of social research, particularly research bearing on the School's mission to improve the publicly supported social services. In myriad ways, Jim Steele, Judy Ambrose, Stephanie Smith, Carol Welsh, Sharon Ikami, and Loretta Dodson all devoted substantial time and talent to the completion of this project. We would also like to thank Gioia Stevens, associate executive editor at

Columbia University Press, for her encouragement and friendly support of this project.

Richard P. Barth
Jill Duerr Berrick
Neil Gilbert

Berkeley, California
January, 1994

Introduction

The child welfare system in the United States is responsible for investigating nearly three million reports of child maltreatment each year, for determining when families require services and when children need to be removed from the home, for arranging the placement of children at risk, and for monitoring the legal and developmental status of more than 400,000 children in foster care. This daunting charge demands a firm commitment to the well-being of children and compassion for families. But to ensure the protection of children, commitment and compassion must be joined with sound judgment and reliable decision making based on knowledge. Ultimately, professional efforts to promote child welfare rest on the humane application of good social science. Under mounting reports of maltreatment and increasing caseloads, child welfare professionals face a persistent challenge to improve the scientific knowledge that guides practice and policy in this field.

Responding to this challenge, the Children's Bureau and the Office of Policy and Evaluation of the U.S. Department of Health and Human Services, Administration for Children, Youth, and Families created three national research centers in 1990 as focal points for the development and dissemination of scientific knowledge on practice and policy in child welfare. The establishment of these centers extends the Children's Bureau's longstanding commitment to social policy research. Recounting the history of social welfare in the U.S., Leiby (1978) notes that as far back as the 1920s one found, in addition to concerns for standards of professional service, a broader view in the Children's Bureau "that included social legislation and administration and the research necessary for well-founded judgments on such matters." In support of this continuing mission, the *Child Welfare Research Review* was launched under the auspices of the Berkeley Child Welfare Research Center at the University of California, Berkeley. The *Review* seeks to bring a core of exemplary studies—representing the most recent and rigorous works in child welfare—to the attention of child welfare researchers, policymakers, practitioners, administrators, and students. Some of the chapters in this volume are drawn from already published sources, but most of them are the result of work currently being done in the forefront of the field.

Divided into five parts, this inaugural volume presents a range of studies that frame major issues in current areas of concern, employ advanced research methods, and contribute notable findings that have implications for policy and practice. The first part addresses the broad parameters of one of the central problems that child welfare workers have to come to grips with daily: How to define maltreatment? This definition has tremendous implications for reporting, intake, service, and placement decisions. The essays in this section examine the way different theoretical perspectives, social objectives, and cultural norms affect alternative definitions of maltreatment. They offer empirical evidence about cultural variations that need to be considered in order to develop a firmer understanding and greater sensitivity in defining abusive behavior.

Analyzing the recent trend toward the use of family-based services, the studies in part 2 report on various models of in-home and out-of-home care. These papers reveal some of the mixed outcomes of family preservation efforts, shed light on how family-based services work with different types of maltreatment, and recommend additional criteria that might be used to evaluate these programs.

In part 3, we offer several papers that push the limits of conventional child welfare research techniques. A growing body of literature is becoming available that provides an overview of the paths children take through the foster care system. These paths are not static but dynamic processes as children move in and out of various placements, as they reunify with their families, and, sometimes, as they return to foster care. Cross-sectional analyses—those conducted in most child welfare research to date—are not as useful in describing the dynamic process at work in child welfare services. Therefore the papers presented in this section provide an excellent overview of our current knowledge in the field.

Adoption is a cornerstone of permanency planning. The delicate balance and timing of permanency planning rests on the assumption that children who cannot go home can and will be adopted. Excitement about the growing practice of special needs adoptions in the 1970s provided the basis for time limits on efforts to reunify children from foster care. Although adoption is now a fundamental part of child welfare services, there is concern about its capacity to address the needs of older and more troubled children. Part 4 includes the first research on adoption seeking that uses a national probability sample and recent research on adoption of children who had been exposed to drugs.

Every day thousands of child welfare practitioners make decisions based on their understanding of the outcomes of their actions for children. Part 5 presents two papers that provide data on the results of those actions. Although factors related to the outcome of child welfare services are also informed by findings in the other sections, these studies address questions directly concerned with service outcomes. The final chapter reviews a broad array of studies conducted since permanency planning was initiated. In addition to showing likely outcomes for children depending on the service program they receive, this review conveys a sense of the vast amount of research that has been produced in the last decade and of how much more is needed to provide a firm scientific basis for our work.

This research in child welfare will enlighten readers and contribute new insights to policy and practice. The research methods described set a high standard for future research. At the same time, the research raises many additional questions. Whether on the whole this reduces uncertainty or elevates it to a higher level of sophistication is an open question. More than twenty years ago, Alfred Kadushin (1971) concluded his review of the state of child welfare research with the observation that "research may never be able to give as much as we want. But research may be able to give us some increasingly modest increment of what we need." We hope that the findings reported in this volume will satisfy the latter objective. We are confident that future use of the research methods demonstrated in this volume will lead to continued growth in knowledge about child welfare services.

REFERENCES

Kadushin, Alfred. (1971). Child welfare. In Henry Mass (Ed.), *Research in the social services: A five-year review* (pp. 13–69). New York: National Association of Social workers.

Leiby, James. (1978). *A history of social welfare and social welfare in the United States.* New York: Columbia University Press.

CHILD
WELFARE
RESEARCH
REVIEW

Volume 1

PART ONE

DEFINING CHILD
ABUSE AND NEGLECT

By the late 1960s every state in the nation had established child abuse reporting laws. Since then, both the definition of child maltreatment covered by these laws and the categories of persons required to report suspected cases of maltreatment have expanded. At first, maltreatment was defined primarily as involving serious physical injury. Today, almost all child abuse reporting laws refer not only to physical abuse but also to emotional or psychological abuse, sexual abuse and exploitation, and physical neglect. As the definitions of maltreatment broadened, the circle of mandatory reporters was enlarged from a group composed mainly of physicians to an assembly of professionals including school personnel, social workers, dentists, law enforcement officials, nurses, and child care workers. Beyond mandatory reporting by professionals, in about 40% of the states the laws require all citizens to report suspected cases of abuse (Besharov 1990; Bagley and King 1990).

These legislative developments were followed by an enormous surge in child abuse reporting across the United States. Since 1976 the number of reports has grown almost fourfold, from 669,000 to 2.5 million (Lindsey forthcoming). In recent years about 60% of these reports turned out to have been unfounded (Besharov 1990). That is, in approximately 1.5 million of the cases reported to the child welfare system the protective service workers found insufficient evidence to warrant official action. Many reports are based on the less tangible criteria of neglect. In New York State, for example, Pryor (cited in Lindsey forthcoming) found that less than 1% of child abuse allegations involved children presenting serious physical injuries, while the most frequent allegations referred to "lack of supervision." Nationwide, less than 3% of the child abuse and neglect incidents reported in 1986 involved major physical injury (American Humane Association 1988).

The increase in child abuse reporting produced tremendous strains on the system, which have reshaped the basic functions of child welfare. As Lindsey explains:

> Child welfare resources were thus, within a dozen years, redirected from providing services to needy children and families toward investigative and interventive services required to respond to the increasing number of child abuse reports. . . . The investigation might take a week, or two weeks, a month or longer, before sufficient data were collected that would permit a decision on what action should be taken. The process was difficult and expensive.

But the resources available to child welfare services did not increase to match the costs of dealing with a rising tide of child abuse reports. In light of the escalating number of reports, the high rate of unfounded cases, and the considerable expense of investigation, there is a growing concern that the definitions of child maltreatment have become too broad (Pelton 1992; Besharov 1985; Lindsey forthcoming).

Defining child maltreatment, of course, is a complex matter fraught with disagreements and normative ramifications (Gilbert 1989). Taking just one dimension of maltreatment, for example, research efforts to estimate the prevalence of child sexual abuse illustrate the wide variance in definitions of what constitutes abusive behavior. Among fifteen surveys that attempt to estimate the prevalence of this problem, the proportion of females found to be sexually abused as children ranges from 6% to 62% of the population. These differences are accounted for in large measure by the researchers' various operational definitions of child sexual abuse, which might include an array of behaviors from unwanted propositions to unwanted touches and kisses to sexual intercourse (Finkelhor et al. 1986).

The studies in this section address the challenge of defining child maltreatment from several perspectives. Hutchison's article offers an analytic framework that draws our attention to the different social aims served by definitions of maltreatment and the theoretical perspectives brought to bear in defining this problem. She identifies a range of issues arising out of these varying theories and objectives. One of the most important and timely of these issues is the question: Who shall define maltreatment? Answers to this question are related to theoretical perspectives on the nature of social problems.

As Hutchison notes: "Both the sociocultural and social labeling perspectives challenge the sovereign role of professionals in providing the definition for child maltreatment. The sociocultural approach points to the varying expectations of caregivers across cultures and over time and cautions that the definitions of maltreatment need to reflect cultural norms."

What are these cultural norms and how do they vary among different groups? Hong and Hong (1991), for example, found that Chinese were less critical of parental use of force than Hispanics and Caucasians. Comparing a broader range of groups, Ahn's study in this volume is among the most recent empirical efforts to identify some of the cultural variations that need to be considered in defining abusive behavior. The groups covered in her study include African-Americans, Cambodians, Hispanics, Koreans, Vietnamese, and whites. Ahn's findings neither resolve the issue of professional versus community definitions of child abuse nor do they furnish definitive guidelines for sociocultural definitions of child maltreatment. However, they do provide important insights into cultural differences and, as she points out, they confirm the need for sensitivity to these differences in defining child abuse.

In light of the varying cultural expectations about parent-child relations and appropriate behaviors, it may be argued that Hutchison's proposal to narrow the definition of child maltreatment to include only seriously harmful behaviors and outcomes would improve the social balance between the protection of children and respect for the cultural diversity of family life in the United States. But proposals to narrow the definition of child maltreatment form a point of contention among child welfare professionals. Those opposed to a more limited definition suggest that the breadth of protection to children provided by a broader conception of the problem is worth preserving (Barth 1992; Finkelhor 1990), while the negative consequences of unsubstantiated reports are usually negligible.

REFERENCES

American Humane Association (1988). *Highlights of official child neglect and abuse reporting, 1986.* Denver, CO: American Humane Association.

Bagley, C. & King, K. (1990). *Child sexual abuse: The search for healing.* London: Routledge.

Barth, R. P. (1992). Should child abuse laws regarding physical abuse and sexual abuse be sharply limited to discourage overreporting? In M. Mason & E. Gambrill (Eds.), *Children and adolescents:Debating controversial issues.* Thousand Oaks, CA: Sage.

Besharov, D. (1985). Doing something about child abuse: The need to narrow the grounds for state intervention. *Harvard Journal of Law and Public Policy, 8, 539–89.*

Besharov, D. (1990). Gaining control over child abuse reports. *Public Welfare, 48(2), 34–40.*

Finkelhor, D. et al. (1986). *A sourcebook on child sexual abuse.* Beverly Hills, CA: Sage Publications.

Finkelhor, D. (1990). Is child abuse overreported? *Public Welfare, 48(3), 23–29,46–47.*

Gilbert, N. (1988). Teaching children to prevent sexual abuse. *The Public Interest, 93, 3–15.*

Hong, G. & Hong, L. (1991). Comparative perspectives on child abuse and neglect: Chinese versus Hispanics and Whites. *Child Welfare, 70(4), 463–75.*

Lindsey, D. (forthcoming). *The welfare of children.* New York: Oxford University Press.

Pelton, L. (1991). Beyond permanency planning: Restructuring the public child welfare system. *Social Work, 36(4), 337–43.*

ONE

Child Maltreatment: Can It Be Defined?

Elizabeth Hutchison

In 1974 the United States Congress passed the Child Abuse Prevention and Treatment Act (CAPTA). The overall goal of CAPTA was to protect children from maltreatment through abuse (commission) and neglect (omission) by parents and other caregivers. The passage of CAPTA marked the beginning of the second "child saving" movement in the United States and ushered in an era in which protective services became a major function of the child welfare system.[1] To implement the congressional intent of CAPTA, state statutes as well as federal and state regulations have been developed for the reporting, investigation, and follow-up of child maltreatment.

One might assume that clarity exists regarding the definition of child maltreatment since child abuse and neglect are against the law and since both the legal and welfare systems actively participate in protective services. This clarity, however, does not exist. Soon after the passage of CAPTA, practitioners and scholars from several disciplines noted the absence of clear, operational, uniform definitions of child maltreatment. Speaking at the first national conference on child abuse and neglect in 1976, Edward Zigler, first director of the Office of Child Development, questioned the feasibility of investigating a phenomenon that lacks a widely acceptable definition. He suggested that "resolving [the] definitional dilemma must become the first item of business among workers in the child abuse area" (Zigler 1977).

Many child welfare leaders continue to voice this concern (Giovannoni & Becerra 1979; Kahn & Kamerman 1980; Ross & Zigler 1980; Duquette 1982; Gelles 1982; Rosenthal & Louis 1981; Biller & Solomon 1986). Most published reports lack clear, operational, and comparable definitions of maltreatment (Lamphear 1985; Stein 1984). Thus the incidence and consequences of child maltreatment cannot be determined. In addition, existing laws, which are vague regarding the conditions that constitute maltreatment, provide insufficient guidance to child welfare workers and judges (Stein & Rzepnicki 1984; Besharov 1985).

The purpose of this article is to analyze the efforts made during the last three decades to define child maltreatment, to summarize the current status of attempts to clarify the definition, and to propose future policy directions regarding definition. This analysis takes on special importance in light of the current heated attack on the child welfare system from opposing camps as a system that is either underprotective or overly intrusive.

Purposes of Maltreatment Definitions

The problem of defining child maltreatment stems in part from the fact that different groups and professions devise and use definitions for different purposes and social aims. Catherine Ross and Edward Zigler point out that "no single definition of abuse has succeeded in fulfilling all of the functions that social scientists and social service professionals would like" (Ross & Zigler 1980:294). Definitions have been developed to meet four interrelated purposes: social policy and planning, legal regulations, research, and case management.

Social Policy

The way a social problem is defined determines both the range of feasible solutions to the problem and the types of specific strategies that will be used to accomplish those solutions (Cartwright 1973). Different perceptions of a problem may lead to very different policy directions. This point is best illustrated by two definitions of child maltreatment proposed at different times by the same child welfare scholar. In 1968 David Gil defined child abuse as "non-accidental physical attack or physical injury, including minimal as well as fatal injury, inflicted upon children by persons caring for them" (Gil 1968). Writing a little over a decade later, Gil proposed the following conceptual definition: "Abuse of children is human-originated acts of commission or omission and human-created or tolerated conditions that inhibit or preclude unfolding and development of inherent potential of children" (Gil 1981).

Although both definitions require further explication, the latter definition clearly is broader and implies attention to structural arrangements of society as well as the case-specific caregiver behaviors targeted in the earlier definition. The first definition suggests a residual approach to policy development and the second definition suggests an institutional approach.[2] The choice of definition is crucial for child welfare policy and planning because it will govern such important decisions as which families are eligible for services, what kinds of services will be provided, whether the service system will emphasize voluntary or involuntary services, and what strategies will be used for case finding.

Legal Regulations

As Lawrence Aber and Edward Zigler suggest, modern cultures have come to rely heavily on law as well as on the social and health sciences to negotiate human conflicts that once were resolved by religion or folk custom (Aber & Zigler 1981). Legal definitions of child maltreatment are used to guide judicial decision making about conditions that require reporting of maltreatment, conditions that warrant coercive state intervention, and conditions that warrant termination of parental rights to custody. Legal definitions provide the mandate for enforcing society's standards for child care and have a strong impact on social work practice in child welfare. In the United States most of the statutes regarding child maltreatment are passed at the state level (Kahn & Kamerman 1980:124). All states have two sets of laws relating to child abuse and neglect: those in the penal code that define criminal maltreatment and those in the civil code that include mandatory reporting laws and spell out the grounds for making a child a ward of the court (Giovannoni & Becerra 1979:6–8).

Douglas Besharov asserts that a decade of efforts to improve on vague legal statutes has failed. In fact in the last decade there has been a broadening of legal definitions leading to even greater imprecision (Besharov 1985). The "battered child syndrome" has been expanded to include physical neglect, emotional maltreatment, and sexual abuse. Donald Duquette suggests that the current imprecision in legal statutes is a serious problem because due process of law requires that caregivers have clear definitions of expected behaviors (Duquette 1982:192).

Research

The adequacy and comparability of research definitions are important because of their effect on the development of theories about causation and because of the relationship between research and policy. As Jeanne Giovannoni and Rosina Becerra state, "social policy regarding social problems can begin to take on a rational stance only when informed by valid data as to the nature and scope of the problem" (Giovannoni & Becerra 1979:13). Without clear definitions, researchers cannot measure the incidence of maltreatment or determine its individual and societal costs.

Two methods have been used to resolve the definitional dilemma in research. The most common method is to simply adopt as the operational definition those cases that have been labeled by responsible agencies as involving maltreatment. With this method, however, it is impossible to establish exactly what behaviors and conditions are being measured because the labeling process, known to be full of inconsistencies, is poorly understood (National Study of the Incidence and Severity of Child Abuse and Neglect 1981). The other method of operationalization is for the researcher to specify the conditions and behaviors constituting maltreatment. Although this method avoids the inconsistencies of the labeling process, the lack of uniformity of definitions inhibits the comparison of research findings. Vivian Lamphear cites the absence of comparable operational definitions of child maltreatment as a major limitation in drawing reliable conclusions about effects of child maltreatment on the psychosocial development of children (Lamphear 1985:252).

Case Management

Statutory and policy definitions of child maltreatment are used by child welfare workers to make decisions about whether maltreatment has occurred, when coercive action is necessary, and what the intervention goals should be. These definitions also serve to guide professionals mandated to report suspected cases of maltreatment. The definitional dilemma currently poses both ethical and technological problems for practitioners. Child welfare workers cannot ethically engage in coercive interventions into family life without a clear sense that they represent social standards rather than individual agendas of practitioners, professionals, institutions, or administrations. Furthermore, practice ethics as well as practice technology require child welfare workers to inform involuntary clients of the thresholds at which coercive action will be initiated (Hutchison 1987). Due to their ambiguity the existing definitions provide insufficient guidance to child welfare workers for such case management activities.

In recent years, policy analysts have suggested that the lack of clear definitions has contributed to various case management problems: underreporting, overreporting, low rates of substantiation, unnecessary intrusion into family life, and unwarranted strain on the child welfare system (Stein 1984; Besharov 1985). The ambiguities of statutory definitions currently contribute to an atmosphere in which "except for extreme situations where the child's condition, the location of an injury, and the child's age interact so as to eliminate any doubt that abuse has been perpetrated, professionals agree that it is very difficult to determine what is and is not child maltreatment" (Stein & Rzepnicki 1984:10).

Theoretical Perspectives and Maltreatment Definitions

Definitions of social problems cannot be divorced from theories about their etiology, correlates, and sequelae. The many theories of child maltreatment that have been proposed in the last three decades can be categorized into medical-psychological and sociological approaches. In recent years, several theoreticians have presented the interactionist or transactional approach as a synthesis of the medical-psychological and sociological approaches.

Medical-Psychological Approach

The rediscovery of child maltreatment as a social problem and the initiation of the second "child saving" movement in the 1960s rested on a medical-psychological construction of the problem. In 1962 Henry Kempe and associates published the now famous article "The Battered Child Syndrome" in the *Journal of the American Medical Association* (Kempe, Silverman, Steele, Droegemueller, & Silver 1962). This article stimulated media attention in which child maltreatment was defined as a "disease" of the perpetrator that could be diagnosed by radiological examination of the victim. As suggested by

Aber and Zigler, "The aim of a medical diagnostic definition is to identify a pathological process or condition underlying a symptom pattern in a way that enables a therapeutic intervention" (Aber & Zigler 1981:2).

From this perspective the abusive behavior—with its medical consequences for the child—came to be viewed as a symptom of a pathological process resulting from psychological characteristics of the abuser. In fact, Kempe and associates stated that they would define abuse on the basis of the characteristics of the abuser rather than the maltreating behavior or its consequences for the child (Kempe & Helfer 1972). For approximately a decade after the publication of "The Battered Child Syndrome," leaders of the medical-psychological approach devoted their energies to developing a psychological profile that would allow the detection of abusive parents before injury to the child occurred. This effort failed to produce such a profile, however, and is no longer considered worthy of pursuit by many child welfare scholars.[3]

The medical-psychological perspective of the "battered child syndrome" eased the way for state and federal legislation regarding child maltreatment. The psychological interpretation, oriented toward the individual, of an easily diagnosable medical condition made the problem seem serious, self-contained, and noncontroversial because it did not challenge social structures or child care norms (Nelson 1984). The passage of CAPTA rested on the success of legislators like Mondale in keeping testimony focused on a very narrow definition of maltreatment as "the battered child syndrome." Although the original drafters of CAPTA intended to limit the legislation to physical abuse, a more comprehensive definition of maltreatment is included in the bill: "The physical or mental injury, sexual abuse, negligent treatment or maltreatment of a child under the age of 18, by a parent who is responsible for the child's welfare, under circumstances which indicate that the child's health or welfare is harmed or threatened."

The people who initially identify a social problem have great influence on how others will comprehend the problem. The imagery of the "battered child syndrome" survived the broadening of the definition, and the exclusive focus on psychological characteristics of caregivers continued for some time. This construction of the problem stimulated a residual response to policy development. The resulting child welfare system relies on mandatory reporting laws as the casefinding method, emphasizes involuntary rather than voluntary services, and seeks solutions to cope with the deficiencies of individual caregivers. However, adding such varied concepts as neglect, mental injury, and sexual abuse to the definition diffused attempts to develop psychological profiles, and by the middle of the 1970s a medical-psychological approach was no longer considered adequate by most scholars.

Several leaders in the field noted that the medical-psychological construction of child maltreatment wrongly assumes that society affords adequate opportunities for all parents to provide needed physical, emotional, and social resources to their children and that therefore any failure to care adequately for children is an individual or family failure, requiring an intervention aimed at changing the individual or the family in question. A variety of sociological theories were advanced to counter this psychological construction of the problem.

Sociological Approach

Sociological researchers have attempted to define child maltreatment within the context of social attitudes, social structures, and resource distribution. These views can be divided into three categories: the labeling perspective, the sociocultural perspective, and the sociositua-tional perspective. The sociological approach, which became the dominant approach for explaining maltreatment in the 1970s, lacked the unity of the medical-psychological approach dominant in the 1960s. The several strains that developed emphasized different sociological concepts and distinct variables.

Labeling Perspective. The labeling perspective, also called the social deviance perspective, is based on the assumption that particular behaviors cannot be classified apart from the social context—that the definition of any social problem arises from the social system in which it is manifested. Behavior that varies significantly from societal expectations for a particular role is judged to be "socially deviant." The amount of societal energy directed toward control of the deviant behavior depends on the perception of threat to the social order. From this perspective, no behavior toward children can be defined a priori and for all times as maltreatment; however, at any given time, specific behaviors toward children are determined by "crucial actors in the social system" to be maltreating behavior (Giovannoni &

Becerra 1979:23). Researchers operating from a labeling perspective have studied the beliefs of "crucial actors" to resolve the definitional dilemma (Dingwall, Eckelaar, & Murray 1983; Giovannoni & Becerra 1979). They have also been interested in the process by which caregivers come to be labeled as maltreaters.

The original aims of the labeling perspective were relatively modest: to enlarge the range of variables considered in the study of deviant phenomena by including actions of people other than the allegedly deviant actor (Becker 1974; Schur 1971). The labeling proponent is particularly interested in the rules and definitions that are used to label deviance as well as in the participants and mechanisms involved in the labeling process. Rules and definitions of social deviance are considered to be part of a process and "far from being immutable, are continually constructed anew in every situation, to suit the convenience, will, and power position of various participants" (Becker 1974:51). Instead of focusing on the maltreating parent, as the medical-psychological approach did, the labeling proponent directed attention to public opinion and welfare institutions to assist in resolving the definitional issue.

Sociocultural Perspective. The sociocultural approach explores how cultural values affect adult-child interactions. Theoreticians and researchers from this perspective propose that child maltreatment is related to such factors as the value placed on children in the culture, the cultural understanding of the needs of children, the cultural stance on corporal punishment, the degree to which the culture prescribes collective responsibility for the welfare of children, the availability of multiple caregivers, and the expectations regarding paternal involvement in child care (Biller & Solomon 1986; Gil 1971). Cross-cultural research suggests that the competitive, individualistic values of western cultures create a situation in which dependent persons and their caregivers are not valued and supported. In such an environment children as well as their economically dependent caregivers often become the victims of violence (Korbin 1981).

Besharov suggests that the definitional dilemma is in part due to the wide variations among subcultures and communities in the United States regarding proper child-rearing practices (Besharov 1978). In a similar vein, some scholars operating from a sociocultural perspective argue that child-protective legislation will be based inevitably on definitions that support the majority culture and undermine minority cultures: "The various arguments against uniformly applying one child abuse and neglect law tend to take one of two forms: that one law cannot account for the cultural variations in how abuse and neglect are perceived; and that the law discriminates against those groups who differ most from the majority culture, such as poor, black, Indian, and migrant families" (Hirsh, Davis, Blanchard, & Christmas 1977:109). Others suggest that an acceptable definition in a pluralistic society should respect ethnic and cultural diversity and set minimum standards that are agreeable to minority as well as majority groups (Stein & Rzepnicki 1984:37).

Sociosituational Approach. The sociosituational approach focuses on the ways in which social structures and situational stressors contribute to the maltreatment of children. Writers in this tradition note the persistent correlation between poverty and maltreatment and propose that poverty constitutes societal and institutional abuse. Gil suggests that widespread abuse of children derives from social policies as well as political and economic structures (Gil 1981:294).

Others propose that the context and constraints of contemporary parenthood lie at the root of child maltreatment (Biller & Solomon 1986; Graham 1980; Washburne 1983). James Garbarino submits that when things are bad for children, it means things are bad for adults, and child maltreatment should be viewed as a social indicator of larger problems (Garbarino 1981). Although writing from the perspective of exchange theory, Richard Gelles makes a similar argument. He suggests that much maltreatment can be attributed to the fact that under current social structures and policies the costs of parenting often outweigh the rewards, especially for adults with few resources (Gelles 1983).

Proponents of the sociosituational perspective argue for a broad definition of child maltreatment that includes societal and institutional abuse; they also argue for a service system that focuses intervention at the community or broader system level. Many propose that an improved general social service system would go further to alleviate the problem than the categorical coercive protective system that emerged from the medical-psychological interpretation of maltreatment (Dingwall, Eckelaar, & Murray 1983; Kahn & Kamerman 1980). Barbara Nelson points out, however, that the relative ease with which CAPTA and the state mandatory reporting laws passed was due to the success of policymakers and politicians in circumscribing the problem. These laws passed with minimal resistance because child maltreatment had been presented as a classless phenomenon, and protective legislation was divorced from unpopular poverty legislation (Nelson 1984).

Interactionist Approach

In the 1980s an interactionist perspective replaced the sociological perspective as the dominant approach to explaining maltreatment. This approach suggests that child maltreatment should be investigated from the combined perspectives of child, adult, and environmental characteristics. Kerby Alvy proposes that a comprehensive definition of maltreatment should include collective, institutional, and individual abuse of children (Alvy 1975).[4] Collective abuse, according to Alvy, includes such factors as racial and social class discrimination and adult attitudes about the exercise of power over children. Institutional abuse includes physical and emotional abuse by schools, correctional facilities, and other institutions that serve children. Individual abuse is abuse by primary caregivers.

Researchers in the interactionist tradition examine the ways in which environmental and social factors interact with psychological processes to contribute to individual abuse. Aspects of the medical-psychological approach are retained and are considered useful in explaining abusive situations attributed to the psychiatric impairment of the perpetrator (Gelles 1983). The interactionist perspective has contributed to the recognition of the need for research looking at multiple causation and takes an empirical approach to the question of the relative contribution of individual and social factors to maltreatment.

Proponents of the interactionist perspective, like those who support a sociological approach, suggest that the response to child maltreatment should include community and system interventions as well as individual intervention. They also recommend an improved general services system rather than a categorical protective service system (Zigler 1980:3–32). It is clear, however, that the reporting and investigative nature of the current child protection system would not be sufficient to address maltreatment if a comprehensive interactionist definition were employed.

Issues in Defining Maltreatment

Formal attempts to define child maltreatment have revealed several important and complicated issues connected with defining the phenomenon. Attempts to resolve these issues have failed to produce a clear operational definition that serves all the purposes of social scientists and child welfare practitioners. Delineation and discussion of the issues clarifies the process and the elements of the definition that must be considered if the definitional dilemma is to be resolved satisfactorily.

Who Shall Define?

The question of who shall define child maltreatment and by what mechanisms the definition is to be developed is essentially a political question. However, these considerations are related to theoretical formulations. Two views on "who shall define" have been advanced in the past three decades: one is that the definition should be supplied by professionals; the other is that child maltreatment is a matter of social definition and that the process of defining should involve a cross section of the community.

Professionals Shall Define. Suggestions that professionals should provide the definition have taken two forms. Henry Kempe and Ray Helfer's medical-diagnostic perspective was the basis of CAPTA. This perspective assumes that "maltreating parent" is a clinical condition. The clinical condition is further assumed to be one professionals can diagnose, detect early, and treat. The definition of the clinical condition, provided by professionals, is based on clinical criteria including but not limited to aspects of behavior toward children (Helfer & Kempe 1968; Helfer & Kempe 1972).

Recommendations that professionals should provide the definition also come from another group of behavioral scientists who criticize the limitations of the medical-psychological perspective. These scholars suggest that behavioral scientists, particularly developmental psychologists, have a specialized knowledge about children's needs and their responses to different child-rearing methods. This knowledge, not held by the general population, should guide the definitional process (Rizley & Cicchetti 1981). Aber and Zigler propose a developmental model for evaluating harm to children as the best approach to definition but concede that the knowledge base for such an approach is not yet available (Aber & Zigler 1981:22).

The Public Shall Define. Both the sociocultural and social labeling perspectives challenge the sovereign role of professionals in providing the definition for child maltreatment. The sociocultural approach points to the varying expectations of caregivers across cultures and over time and cautions that the definition of maltreatment needs to reflect cultural norms (Ross 1981). Professionals, in this view, come from the majority culture and represent majority interests.

The social labeling perspective proposes that the perception of child maltreatment as a social problem rests on widely held philosophies regarding the nature of childhood and the nature of the parent-child relationship. Operating from this perspective, Giovannoni and Becerra suggest that child maltreatment consists of those care-giver behaviors toward children that violate societal expectations. They propose that behavioral thresholds of maltreatment be stipulated through public survey, with all segments of the population represented (Giovannoni & Becerra 1979). In these sociological approaches, exclusive reliance on professionals to provide the definition is feared to invite problems in policy formulation as well as in policy implementation. Middle-class activists may attempt to formulate a policy that imposes child-rearing methods that they have come to value and can afford on low-income families who lack the economic, social, and emotional resources for such practices (Pelton 1981; Ross 1980). Once policy is formulated, families in the child welfare system may be held accountable to a standard of child care that, based on professional standards, is higher than the one prevailing in the community at large (Stein & Rzepnicki 1984:37).

It could be argued that professionals should take a strong advocacy stance to define the needs of children rather than simply reflect societal standards of child care. However, the knowledge base of current behavioral science does not clearly articulate the varying effects of different child-rearing practices. Social and behavioral scientists should continue to seek empirical evidence regarding the relationship between child-rearing practices and adult outcomes. Ultimately, the empirical evidence about consequences of the caregivers' actions will have to be weighed against social values regarding desired outcomes of child rearing.

Determining Factors in Definition

Attempts to define child maltreatment have focused on different sets of variables. Those having received the most attention may be dichotomized into caregiver variables and harm-to-child variables. Both sets of variables introduce obstacles to the definition of child maltreatment.

Caregiver Variables. Both the medical-psychological approach and some aspects of the sociological approach emphasize caregiver variables to define maltreatment. The medical-psychological approach was initially based on a harm-to-child criterion, the "battered child syndrome," but quickly came to focus on parental psychological pathology. In this view, a caregiver's potential for abuse, based on a psychological profile, is as important as his or her acts of abuse. Operating from different theoretical formulations, both the labeling and the sociocultural perspectives also focus on caregiver variables. The emphasis here, however, is on actual rather than potential acts of the caregiver. The failure of proponents of the medical-psychological approach to develop a psychological profile has been noted earlier, but sociological emphasis on the caregivers' behaviors also introduces several complicated issues into the definition. The first of these issues arises from the fact that maltreatment, according to the labeling and sociocultural perspectives, is determined by the degree to which the acts of the caregivers deviate from cultural norms. In reality, the caregivers' behaviors are not easily dichotomized into maltreating and nonmaltreating acts; instead, definers must make decisions about where on a continuum to place the thresholds of maltreatment. May a school-aged child be left alone for thirty minutes? Two hours? Overnight? May a parent hit a child with a hand? With a belt? With a baseball bat? Gelles attempts to resolve this issue for physical abuse by labeling all acts of physical aggression against children as abusive. This solution fails to advance definitional efforts, however, because his own research indicates a high level of physical aggression against children as part of the U.S. culture (Gelles 1980).

Another challenging issue for the definer using caregiver variables is the question of the motivation of the caregiver. It is not always easy to differentiate between intentional and accidental behavior. For example, did the mother's placement of her baby's foot in scalding water result from an intentional act to harm the baby, an accident when she slipped while testing the water, or an accident with some unconsciously intended elements? The question of chronicity of the caregivers' behavior also arises. Do isolated outbursts under stress get labeled in the same way as chronic physical aggression?

A final issue facing the definer becomes apparent in the example of the scalding incident. Because many, if not most, caregiver-child interactions occur without witnesses, it is often difficult, if not impossible, to determine who caused harm to a child and the motivations and behaviors that accompanied the harmful outcome. In view of the high value placed on family privacy in our culture, the caregivers' actions alone will not be sufficient for definitions guiding case management.

Harm-to-Child-Variables. The contrasting view holds that because societal interest in maltreatment is based on a duty to protect children, the primary element in definition should be harm to the child rather than the actions of the caregivers. This stance is explicitly stated by some scholars who attempt to define abuse for legal purposes, and it is implied by the sociosituational perspective. The harm-to-child criterion theoretically resolves issues related to the invisibility of the caregivers' actions, but it certainly is not completely free of problems.

The first question that arises when harm to the child is chosen as the focus of definition is that of seriousness. Harm to the child, like the caregivers' behaviors, falls on a continuum; the continuum ranges from hurt feelings or minor pain to death. How serious must injury to the child be before the incident is labeled maltreatment and coercive intervention is mandated? The definer must also decide whether to include potential as well as actual harm. Besharov introduces the concept of "cumulative harm" to discuss behavior of caregivers that "will cause cumulatively serious harm to the child if it continues for a sufficient length of time" (Besharov 1985:25). This is the chronicity issue again.

Gelles criticizes the use of the harm-to-child criterion for definitional purposes because of the many contingencies that intervene between the caregivers' behavior (act) and harm to the child (outcome), such as aim, size, strength, and luck (Gelles 1980:84). Gil suggests that consequences of abusive and neglectful acts are equally due to the behavior of the perpetrator and to chance (Gil 1971).

Leroy Pelton claims that inadequate supervision is more likely to lead to harm to a child in an impoverished home due to the health and safety hazards that exist in such homes (Pelton 1981). If this is accurate, who is responsible for the harm to the child?

For the case manager, once harm to child has been determined, the perpetrator must be identified. As suggested above, due to the privacy of family life this is often difficult and sometimes impossible. To compound the problem, the sociosituational perspective raises the question of the culpability of people other than the caregivers. Gil proposes a definition that holds a variety of institutions responsible for harm to children (Gil 1981). Henry Biller and Richard Solomon suggest that current approaches have a sexist bias that fails to take into account demographic realities (Biller & Solomon 1986). They express special concern about incidents of neglect in single-parent families, questioning why the noncustodial parent is not held as accountable as the custodial parent.

Many legal scholars attempt to resolve the issue of the determining factors in the definition by arguing that harm to the child must be tied to behaviors of the caregiver(s). In this view, both serious harm to the child and identifiable acts of maltreatment by caregivers are required to justify state intervention.

Narrow versus Broad Definitions

As stated earlier, current popular and professional interest in child maltreatment was stimulated by the discovery of the "battered child syndrome," a narrow interpretation of the problem. This narrow construction aided in the passage of mandatory reporting laws on the state level and of federal legislation. However, physical neglect was immediately added to the definition, and very quickly other phenomena, such as emotional abuse, emotional neglect, and sexual abuse, were added. Alvy and Gil present the broadest focus by including any failure of the environment to meet the developmental needs of children (Alvy 1975; Gil 1981). As the definition was broadened to incorporate more acts and behaviors of the caregivers, it became more and more difficult to use the conditions covered by the definition as an operational basis.

Narrow Definition. The vagueness of the definition poses a case management problem for legal and social welfare practitioners, given the categorical, coercive service system that developed in response to the earlier narrow definition. In recent years, therefore, many legal scholars have pressed for a narrower, more specific definition to guide decision making in the judicial and social work areas (Besharov 1985; Wild 1975). Policy analysts have noted that as the definition of maltreatment is broadened, the error in diagnosing incidents and the costs of screening cases increase (Gelles 1979; Besharov 1985; Stein 1984). Some suggest that this overloads the protective system with nonserious cases and undermines the ability of protective workers to respond effectively to endangered children. Narrow, specific definitions are thought to limit the discretion and therefore the biases of decisionmakers. They also provide for closer adherence to due process of law because they allow judges and social workers to be more explicit with caregivers regarding the thresholds for intervention. The goal suggested by a narrow definition is to protect children from serious harm.

Broad Definition. On the other hand, some family law scholars have argued in favor of the existing imprecision in state statutes because they provide judicial flexibility to individualize cases and greater sensitivity to local community standards (Katz 1975). A broad definition expands eligibility for social services and provides greater numbers to impress funding sources. The broad definition also focuses attention on the roots of maltreatment in the structure of society. One goal of the broad definition is to improve the quality of life for all children.

Developmental Level of the Child

Few legal or child welfare scholars have considered the developmental state of the child as a critical issue in defining child maltreatment. Joseph Goldstein, Anna Freud, and Albert Solnit focused attention on this variable in relation to custody decisions in their 1973 book *Beyond the Best Interests of the Child.* Aber and Zigler have proposed the need for a developmental model for defining maltreatment (Aber & Zigler 1981). The developmental issue becomes more important when neglect and emotional abuse are added to the definition. Pointing out that lack of supervision currently forms the basis for many reports of maltreatment, Theodore Stein and Tina Rzepnicki caution against criteria based solely on the child's age. They recommend, instead, criteria that test the child's ability to cope in an unsupervised situation (Stein & Rzepnicki 1984:67). This approach will unavoidably call for a high level of professional discretion in such situations. The developmental issue appears especially pertinent to decisions about maltreatment of adolescents. One child welfare screening supervisor was recently overheard to exclaim, "Frankly, we don't know what to do about adolescents."

Can Child Maltreatment be Defined?

Given the complexity of the issues inherent in defining child maltreatment, the question arises, "Is it feasible to resolve the definitional dilemma?" Both negative and affirmative answers to this question are presented in the literature, with some writers proposing the need for different definitions for varied purposes.

After careful examination of the definitional dilemma, Gelles concludes that the problem of defining child abuse is an impossible task—that the issue of intent as well as problems in developing objective standards for actions of the caregivers and harm to the child defy solution (Gelles 1980:82, Gelles 1982:29). Although not quite as pessimistic, Duquette also expresses reservations about the feasibility of developing precise definitions, particularly for child neglect. He suggests that the unattainability of precise definitions has led the courts to bypass the definitional problem by using the rationale that "a statute need not be more specific than is possible to draft under the circumstances" (Duquette 1982:193).

In contrast, Giovannoni and Becerra report that data from their research validate the potential for more precise definitions. In an attempt to clarify some of the definitional issues of child maltreatment, these researchers conducted a two-phase project. The first phase consisted of an opinion survey of samples of professionals and a lay population regarding definitions of maltreatment. The results of the study demonstrated "amazing similarity" in the judgments of the relative seriousness of different types of maltreatment among the professionals as a group and among the lay respondents as a group. Lay persons tended, however, to see most types of maltreatment as more serious than the professionals, with lawyers seeing maltreatment as less serious than other professionals. Consensus or near consensus existed among all groups on four types of maltreatment as being serious enough to warrant coercive intervention: sexual abuse, serious physical injury, leaving a young child unattended, and fostering delinquency (Giovannoni & Becerra 1979).

Others suggest that no one definition can meet all the purposes for definition but that "a finite number of formal definitions . . . be developed and that each definition should be tailored to the major social aims and objectives for which it is intended" (Aber & Zigler 1981:12). They propose a broad definition for policy and a narrow definition for legal purposes. Besharov indicates the need to develop a two-level definition, the lower level to determine eligibility for voluntary services and the higher level to require involuntary intervention (Besharov 1978:3).

If we choose to sanction child maltreatment, we must decide what it is and enforce that definition. Although the issues surrounding the definition of child maltreatment are complex, Giovannoni and Becerra's research provides convincing evidence that a more precise definition can be attempted. Their research indicates that public and professional surveys can be used to produce greater consensus regarding definition. With more clarity about the intent of policy and greater understanding of public and professional opinions, it should be possible to develop one definition to serve the aims of policy, legal regulations, case management, and research. Current policy states the goal negatively, to eliminate maltreatment behaviors, rather than positively, to improve the quality of nurturant resources for children. This negative policy requires a narrow definition stating what we as a society are willing to label and penalize as maltreatment. This narrow policy definition should then serve both legal and case management purposes and should be chosen for research purposes as well so as to allow for policy revision. The determining factor for this narrow definition could be serious existing or potential harm to the child. That is, after all, the imagery out of which the current policy was developed. If existing harm is determined, intent must be examined in cases of physical abuse. Harm due solely to parental lack of material resources is not parental maltreatment. To determine potential harm, the behavior of the caregiver(s), not their psychological profiles, must be examined. The definition needs to stipulate thresholds of harm, or, in the case of potential harm, it should stipulate behaviors of caregivers that are inherently seriously harmful (i.e., leaving a young child unattended). The stipulated behaviors should reflect the values of our pluralistic society. Empirical evidence about subcultural and regional differences should guide decisions about whether the definition is developed at the local, state, or national level.

Some child welfare specialists argue that increased precision in the definition will limit the discretion of social workers (Polansky, Chalmers, Buttenwieser, & Williams 1981). There will always be room for discretion in child welfare decision making, but the question of what constitutes maltreatment should be subject to minimal discretion by agencies and individual workers. Professional discretion comes into play in decisions about the types and sources of information that must be brought to bear to evaluate whether a defined condition exists, who perpetrated the condition, and, in cases of physical abuse, whether it was done intentionally.

The choice of a narrow definition does not imply that social control of child maltreatment by caregivers is the extent to which child and family welfare policy should go. Rather, it emphasizes that a coercive service system based on a negative and residual policy model is incompatible with broad definitions. There is an urgent need in the United States for a comprehensive family policy that supports rather than controls caregivers and for an improvement in general social services. Efforts must continue toward improving the precision and narrowing the scope of the definition used for coercive intervention. Besharov's suggestion of a two-level definition, one for voluntary service, the other for coercive intervention, should be considered. This would eliminate the practice of substantiating maltreatment reports in the gray or nonserious area because this is the only way to make clients eligible for certain services. The negative consequences of such labeling have not yet been tested empirically but may be substantial.

Solnit argues, and convincingly so, that "most of us would not like to live in a society that was able to prevent every single instance of child abuse" (Solnit 1980). The level of family surveillance required to accomplish such a goal would be unacceptable to all segments of society. Yet, issues of equity require that children, like adults, be protected from serious harm to the extent possible in a society that values family privacy and pluralism of lifestyles.

A comprehensive family policy and improved general social services would assist families to respond in more nurturing ways to children's needs while not eliminating the necessity for protective services. The definition of child maltreatment should include only seriously harmful behaviors and outcomes; protective policies and systems should be utilized only to enforce societal sanctions, not to enforce ideal standards of caregiving. Using residual welfare policies to attempt to accomplish institutional welfare goals leads to over-promising and, ultimately, to disillusionment with social welfare institutions and solutions. There is a pressing need for a better fit between the definition of child maltreatment and the structure of the service system responsible for addressing the problem.

NOTES

1. The first "child saving movement" emerged in the late nineteenth century and led to the development of Societies for the Prevention of Cruelty to Children (SPCCs)

2. It is common practice among social policy scholars to dichotomize approaches to welfare policy as residual or institutional approaches. A residual approach to describe the function of social welfare conceptualizes the welfare institution as a safety net institution utilized as a last resort in times of individual failure. The institutional approach to describe the function of social welfare proposes, in contrast, that the welfare institution is a normal and acceptable means to assist individuals and their collectives to fulfill social needs. In the institutional approach, need for services of the social welfare system is not based on individual deficiency. For original discussion of these two concepts of social welfare, see Wilensky and Lebeaux (1958). For more recent discussions of the concepts, see, for example, Compton (1989) and Gilbert and Specht (1974).

3. For a thorough discussion of attempts to develop psychological profiles, see Starr (1982).

4. This perspective was also presented earlier by Gil (1971).

REFERENCES

Aber III, J. L. & Zigler, E. (1981). Developmental considerations in the definition of child maltreatment. In R. Rizley & D. Cicchetti (Eds.), *New directions for child development no. 11: Developmental perspectives on child maltreatment* (pp. 1–25). Washington, D.C.: Jossey-Bass.

Alvy, K. T. (1975, September). Preventing child abuse. *American Psychologist, 30,* 921–28.

Becker, H. (1974). Labeling theory reconsidered. In P. Rock & M. McIntosh (Eds.), *Deviance and social control* (pp. 41–66). London: Tavistock.

Besharov, D. J. (1978). Child abuse and neglect: An American concern. In D. J. Besharov (Ed.), *The abused and neglected child: Multi-disciplinary court practice* (pp. 30–50). New York: Practicing Law Institute.

Besharov, D. J. (1985, Spring). Right versus rights: The dilemma of child protection. *Public Welfare, 43,* 19–27.

Biller, H. B. & Solomon, R. S. (1986). *Child maltreatment and paternal deprivation.* Lexington, MA: Lexington Books.

Cartwright, T. (1973, May). Problems, solutions, and strategies: A contribution to the theory and practice of planning. *Journal of the American Institute of Planners, 39,* 179–187.

Compton, B. R. (1980). *Introduction to social welfare & social work* (pp. 26–31). Homewood, IL: The Dorsey Press.

Day, P. J. (1989). *A new history of social welfare* (pp. 37–45). Englewood Cliffs, NJ: Prentice Hall.

DHHS. (1981). *National study of the incidence and severity of child abuse and neglect.* (DHHS Publication No. 81-30325). Washington, D.C.: Government Printing Office.

Dingwall, R., Eckelaar, J., & Murray, T. (1983). *The protection of children: State intervention and family life.* Oxford: Blackwell.

Duquette, D. N. (1982). Protecting individual liberties in the context of screening for child abuse. In R. H. Starr, Jr. (Ed.), *Child abuse prediction: Policy implications* (pp. 191–204). Cambridge, MA: Ballinger.

Garbarino, J. (1981). An ecological approach to child maltreatment. In L. H. Pelton (Ed.), *The social context of child abuse and neglect* (pp. 228–67). New York: Human Sciences Press.

Gelles, R. J. (1979). *Family violence.* Beverly Hills: Sage Publications.

Gelles, R. F. (1980). A profile of violence toward children in the United States. In G. Gerbner, C. Ross, & E. Zigler (Eds.), *Child abuse: An agenda for action* (pp. 82–104). New York: Oxford University Press.

Gelles, R. F. (1982). Problems in defining and labeling child abuse. In R. H. Starr, Jr. (Ed.), *Child abuse prediction: Policy implications* (pp. 1–30). Cambridge, MA: Ballinger.

Gelles, R. J. (1983). An exchange/social control theory. In D. Finkelhor, R. J. Gelles, G. T. Hotaling, & M. A. Straus (Eds.), *The dark side of families* (pp. 151–65). Beverly Hills, CA: Sage.

Gil, D. G. (1968). Incidence of child abuse and demographic characteristics of persons involved. In R. E. Helfer & H. Kempe (Eds.), *The battered child* (p. 20). Chicago: University of Chicago Press.

Gil, D. G. (1971, July). A sociocultural perspective on physical child abuse. *Child Welfare, 50,* 389–95.

Gil, D. G. (1981). The United States versus child abuse. In L. H. Pelton (Ed.), *The social context of child abuse and neglect* (p. 295). New York: Human Sciences Press.

Gilbert, N. & Specht, H. (1974). *Dimensions of social welfare policy* (pp. 6–8). Englewood Cliffs, NJ: Prentice Hall.

Giovannoni, J. M. & Becerra, R. M. (1979). *Defining child abuse.* New York: The Free Press.

Goldstein, J., Freud, A., & Solnit, A. (1973). *Beyond the best interests of the child.* New York: Free Press.

Graham, H. (1980). Mothers' accounts of anger and aggression towards their babies. In N. Fruse (Ed.), *Psychological approaches to child abuse* (pp. 39–51). Guilford: Billing.

Hirsh, B., Davis, B., Blanchard, E., & Christmas, J. J. (1977). One law/many child rearing cultures. In *Proceedings of the First National Conference on Child Abuse and Neglect* (pp. 109–11). DHEW.

Hutchison, E. D. (1987, December). Use of authority in direct social work practice with mandated clients. *Social Service Review, 61,* 581–98.

Kahn, A. J. & Kamerman, S. B. (1980). Child abuse: A comparative perspective. In G. Gerbner, C. Ross, & E. Zigler (Eds.), *Child abuse: An agenda for action.* (pp. 118–24). New York: Oxford University Press.

Katz, S. (1975, Spring). Child neglect laws in America. *Family Law Quarterly, 9,* 1–372.

Kempe, C. H., Silverman, F. N., Steele, B. F., Droegemueller, W. &. Silver, H. K. (1962, July). The battered child syndrome. *Journal of the American Medical Association, 181,* 17–24.

Kempe, C. H. & Helfer, R. E. (Eds.). (1972). *Helping the battered child and his family* (pp. xi–xii). Philadelphia, PA: Lippincott.

Korbin, J. E. (Ed.). (1981). *Child abuse and neglect: Cross-cultural perspective.* Berkeley and Los Angeles: University of California Press.

Lamphear, V. S. (1985). The impact of maltreatment on children's psychosocial adjustment: A review of the research. *Child Abuse and Neglect, 9,* 251–63.

Nelson, B. J. (1984). *Making an issue of child abuse: Political agenda setting for social problems.* Chicago: University of Chicago Press.

Pelton, L. H. (1981). Child abuse and neglect: The myth of classlessness. In L. H. Pelton (Ed.), *The social context of child abuse and neglect* (p. 35). New York: Human Sciences Press.

Polansky, N. A., Chalmers, M. A., Buttenwieser, E., & Williams, D. P. (1981). *Damaged parents: An anatomy of child neglect* (pp. 13–15). Chicago: University of Chicago Press.

Rizley, R. & Cicchetti, D. (Eds.). (1981). *New directions for child development: Developmental perspectives on child maltreatment.* Washington, D. C.: Jossey-Bass.

Rosenthal, M. & Louis, J. A. (1981). The law's evolving role in child abuse and neglect. In L. H. Pelton (Ed.), *The social context of child abuse and neglect* (pp. 55–89). New York: Human Sciences Press.

Ross, K. J. (1980). The lessons of the past: Defining and controlling child abuse in the United States. In G. Gerbner, C. Ross, & E. Zigler (Eds.), *Child abuse: An agenda for action* (pp. 118–24). New York: Oxford University Press.

Ross, C. & Zigler, E. (1980) In G. Gerbner, C. Ross, & E. Zigler (Eds.), *Child abuse: An agenda for action* (pp. 293–304). New York: Oxford University Press.

Schur, E. M. (1971). *Labeling deviant behavior: Its sociological implications.* New York: Harper & Row.

Solnit, A. J. (1980) Too much reporting, too little service: Roots and prevention of child abuse. In G. Gerbner, C. Ross, & E. Zigler (Eds.), *Child abuse: An agenda for action* (p. 35). New York: Oxford University Press.

Stein, T. J. (1984, June). The child abuse prevention and treatment act. *Social Service Review, 58*, 302–14.

Stein, T. J. & Rzepnicki, T. L. (1984). *Decision making in child welfare: Intake and planning*. Boston: Kluwer-Nijhoff.

Washburne, C. K. (1983). A feminist analysis of child abuse and neglect. In D. Finkelhor, R. J. Gelles, G. T. Hotaling, & M. A. Straus (Eds.), *The dark side of families* (pp. 289–92). Beverly Hills, CA: Sage.

Wild, M. (1975, April). State intervention on behalf of neglected children: A search for realistic standards. *Stanford Law Review, 7*, 985–1040.

Wilensky, H. L. & Lebeaux, C. N. (1958). *Industrial society and social welfare*. New York: Russell Sage Foundation.

Zigler, E. (1977). Controlling child abuse in America: An effort doomed to failure. In *Proceedings of the First National Conference on Child Abuse and Neglect* (p. 30). DHEW.

Zigler, E. (1980). Controlling child abuse: Do we have the knowledge and/or the will? In G. Gerbner, C. Ross, & E. Zigler (Eds.), *Child abuse: An agenda for action* (pp. 3–32). New York: Oxford University Press.

TWO

Cultural Diversity and the Definition of Child Abuse

Helen Noh Ahn

In the public mind child abuse is associated with inexpressibly bad behavior. But when professionals and the public try to mark the boundaries of this type of abuse, they do not seem to agree on where they should draw the line. The definition of child abuse encompasses an array of behaviors that falls along a continuum ranging from serious offenses that almost everyone will agree constitute abuse to mild acts that very few will label as abusive. Between these two ends of the continuum lies a gray area in which agreement about abusive behavior is more difficult to establish (Giovannoni & Becerra 1979). This realm of ambiguity is no trivial matter since definitions of child abuse form the practical basis for child welfare identification, intervention, and preventive measures.

Recently, several professional organizations, including the National Association of Social Workers, have made policy statements or resolutions opposing parental use of physical punishment as a way to prevent child abuse. Human service professionals belonging to these organizations state that physical punishment even in its mildest form lowers a child's self-esteem and that it is an act of violence that teaches a child to accept force as an appropriate way to settle conflicts (Haeuser 1990). Some even say that spanking is a form of child abuse (Jameson 1990). Increasingly, human service professionals are seeing cultural norms that sanction physical punishment of children as one cause of child abuse and are implementing campaigns to change such norms (Heuser 1990).

On the other hand, studies consistently reveal that a majority of the public views physical punishment as a necessary and effective form of discipline. In Alvy's (1987) cross-cultural study of parenting ideas and practices, 99% of low-income African-American parents, 95% of low-income Caucasian parents, and 82% of high-income Caucasian parents spanked or hit their children. The national public opinion poll commissioned by the National Committee for Prevention of Child Abuse in 1991 (Daro) found that 52% of its 1,250 randomly selected sample had spanked their children in the past year.

An English study (Christopher 1982) discovered that the professionals and public differ in their views of child abuse and that primarily the opinions of professionals are reflected in the interventions enforced. In a survey of forty-three cases of social worker intervention in England, 50% of the children showing bruising to the buttocks were removed while only 15% of those whose head was bruised were removed. On the other hand, a public attitude study revealed that parents were more opposed to impulsive punishment than to traditionally accepted methods of corporal punishment. The highest number of parents recommended removing the child from the home when presented with a vignette of "a nine-year-old's eye was blackened as the result of a misdirected blow to the cheek." Seventy percent of these same parents regarded spanking a seven-year-old on his/her bare buttocks "normal and justifiable" (Christopher 1982:438).

As these arguments and studies suggest, there is often a wide gap between the public's and the professional's definition of child physical abuse. Even professionals differ in their views regarding the point of transition at which socially sanctioned physical punishment becomes a socially deviant behavior, that is, child abuse (Kadushin & Martin 1981). A heated debate continues among experts regarding the appropriateness of physical punishment. Some believe that it is never appropriate while others think that it is appropriate under certain conditions (Lassiter 1987). While more and more professional organizations are taking a strong stand against physical punishment, a recent study found that 70% of family physicians and 50% of pediatricians supported the use of spanking (*Washington Times* 1992).

The confusion regarding "normal" and abusive methods of discipline within the dominant culture is compounded by the tremendous degree of cultural diversity in the United States, which gives rise to different patterns of discipline in family life. In her anthropological study of child rearing patterns in many different countries, Korbin (1981) shows the contextual dependence of definitions of child abuse and neglect. Child-rearing practices essentially help to develop characteristics in children that are highly valued by the culture (e.g., independence, filial piety, violence, and endurance) so that the cultural values can be perpetuated. For instance, in New Guinea initiation rites involving extreme physical pain and violence are considered absolutely necessary for the children to develop into healthy adults who can participate in and contribute to the society as warriors (Langness 1981). In the West parents isolate infants and small children in beds and rooms of their own at night and let them cry without immediately attending to their needs because they want their children to grow up to be independent and self-sufficient (Korbin 1981).

Hong and Hong's (1991) comparative study of the views of parental conduct among Chinese, Hispanics, and whites found that Chinese tended to be least critical of the use of physical force by parents and to recommend agency intervention least frequently. They interpreted this finding in light of the filial piety and familism espoused by Chinese culture. Filial piety expects children to subordinate their wishes and interests to those of their parents, while familism dictates that the success, the unity, the continuity, and the reputation of the family be maintained, if necessary at the expense of the individuals. Hong and Hong stressed that protective actions need to be culturally sensitive by pointing to the case of a Vietnamese immigrant who was arrested for alleged child abuse because he administered a folk health practice that involved scratching the child's body to make him feel better. The father committed suicide even when he was completely exonerated. The stigma and humiliation of being accused of child abuse may have been especially devastating for someone from a culture that holds parental authority and familism in high esteem.

The public opinion poll commissioned by the National Committee for Prevention of Child Abuse (Daro 1991) also found that on virtually every question examined, the responses differed according to the participants' age, race, sex, income, educational background, occupation, political preference, and geographic location. The Committee concluded the report by emphasizing the need for a diversified prevention message and specialized prevention efforts that respond to the different parenting practices and family relationships found in various racial and cultural groups.

Almost one third of the child-protective cases in the United States involves minority families (Burgdorf 1980). When considering definitions of child abuse, professionals continually caution about the need to recognize the implications of cultural diversity. As the Institute of Judicial Administration observes: "Given the cultural pluralism and diversity of child rearing practices in our society, it is essential that any system authorizing coercive state involvement in child rearing fully take these differences into account" (JJSP 1977:44).

While professionals readily acknowledge the need for "cultural sensitivity" in dealing with problems of child abuse, it is unclear what exactly this sensitivity entails and how it may be translated into policy and practice. The issue of culture, Gray and Cosgrove (1985) explain, is frequently raised but almost never dealt with. As they point out:

> The only accepted statements on the subject are that cultural issues must be considered in examining child abuse and neglect; child abuse investigators, adjudicators and treatment professionals must take culture into account in performing their role and policies should not be made strictly from the perspective of dominant cultural values and practices. We do not know how to put these sentiments into practice, however. (389)

To gain insight into cultural definitions of child abuse and the implication they hold for antispanking campaigns, cultural groups will be compared in their attitudes toward behaviors enforcing family discipline.

Patterns of Family Discipline

Are cultures really different in their views of acceptable or unacceptable forms of discipline in family life? How do the views of different groups compare with those of the professionals involved in the antispanking campaigns? To explore these questions, we will examine data on patterns of family discipline drawn from a survey of 364 mothers from six ethnic groups: the sample consists of 95 African-Americans, 30 Cambodians, 56 Caucasians, 96 Hispanics, 57 Koreans, and 30 Vietnamese. Most of the respondents were recruited from religious organizations. These institutions were chosen because they are among the few places where people of the same ethnic group regularly congregate.

TABLE 2.1
Effectiveness of Spanking/Hitting as a Method of
Discipline by Ethnic Groups

	Ethnic Groups						
	Caucasian (n = 56)[a]	Afr-American (n = 95)	Hispanic (n = 96)	Korean (n = 57)	Vietnamese (n = 30)	Cambodian (n = 30)	Total (n = 364)
Yes response to questions[b] (%)							
do you think spanking or hitting works with children as a punishment?	77.8	95.8	45.8	78.6	58.6	36.7	69.2***

[a]These sample sizes may vary slightly on different rows depending on the amount of missing data and/or responses other than yes/no.
[b]P value was obtained from X2 statistics.
***p<.001

    The interview schedule developed for this survey was translated into Cambodian, Korean, Spanish, and Vietnamese. All of the interviews were conducted by interviewers of the same ethnicity and sex as the people they were questioning. Interviews with Cambodian, Korean, Vietnamese, and Spanish-speaking Hispanic respondents were administered in their native languages. A test-retest analysis of the interview schedule with forty-one respondents randomly selected from the sample produced a reliability coefficient of .90[1].

    The areas of family discipline examined in this survey were grouped into three different realms: general views on discipline, views on appropriate methods of discipline, and views on what constitutes abuse.

Views on Discipline

Effectiveness of Spanking/Hitting. The respondents were asked whether they thought spanking or hitting worked with children as a punishment. Except for Cambodians and Hispanics, the majority of the respondents in each group answered this question affirmatively (see table 2.1). Among those who considered it an effective method of discipline, the main reason given was that children who are young or stubborn sometimes require physical punishment.

African-American respondents in this study seemed most convinced of the effectiveness of spanking or hitting as a punishment, with almost the entire sample attesting to it. Research on African-American families indicates that in general they use physical punishment and believe in it as a necessary disciplinary tool (Alvy 1987; Staples 1982; Hines & Boyd-Franklin 1982; Lassiter 1987; Wright 1982). Three reasons are frequently offered for this pattern of discipline. The first relates to the extensive influence the Christian church has had on the lives of African-Americans, encouraging them to adopt parenting attitudes derived from biblical principles such as "spare the rod, spoil the child" (Hines & Boyd-Franklin 1982). The second reason offered is the legacy of slavery. The hostile environment in which African-Americans had to raise their children during slavery demanded swift and harsh discipline. Disciplining children to be docile and submissive to authority was a key to survival. Child-rearing practices are often transmitted generation after generation without awareness of their origin (Lassiter 1987). Finally, it has also been argued that although slavery as a physical reality has been abolished, its psychological legacy has not only continued but has been reinforced by unequal opportunity and discrimination. The hostile environment of slavery has been replaced by one of poverty, unemployment, poor educational settings, and racism that is equally hostile. (Alvy 1988; Hines & Boyd-Franklin 1982; Lassiter 1987; Staples 1982; Wright 1982). Thus, in raising children many African-American parents are faced with the task of helping them resist the pull of the street culture and economy (Alvy 1988). For these reasons, discipline has always been an essential prerequisite to survival for many African-Americans. It helped their children cope with the tyranny of their masters during slavery. Today it helps them avoid the problems of teenage pregnancy, dropping out of school, drug and alcohol addiction, crime, unemployment, and welfare dependency (Alvy 1988; Lassiter 1987). In this light, it is interesting to note that in Alvy's (1988) study comparing low-income African-American and middle-income Caucasians, 6% of the former stated that they hit their children now to prevent them from being hit later in their lives by other nonfamily figures, such as the police.

African-Americans in this sample also embraced physical punishment as an important component of discipline. They believed that the pain caused by physical punishment made children remember not to repeat their misbehavior. As suggested by experts, they also tended to regard spanking children for discipline as an act of love and a critical responsibility of a caring parent (Lassiter 1987):

> *If a child is never spanked, he may feel that he's not loved. It'll register better if you spank and explain.*

The pervasive influence of Christian beliefs and traditions upon African-Americans was also reflected in some of the respondents' remarks:

> *Being a Christian, I believe that the rod of correction is one of our strongest areas to use for discipline.*
> *God tells you to discipline your children by spanking them, but not by beating.*

Interestingly, of all the ethnic groups, African-Americans had the largest percentage (18%) plainly stating that they had personal experiences with physical punishment and that it worked for them. One African-American also asserted that it was the best type of punishment while other African-Americans emphasized that spanking should be done in an appropriate manner and not in anger.

> *If it's given in a constructive way and not when you're angry. It's penalty for a wrongdoing.*

When this finding is examined in light of Alvy's (1988) work, it is interesting to note that only 3% of the African-Americans (low-income) in his study reported that they spanked in anger as compared to nearly 40% of high-income Caucasians. African-Americans in his study, like those in this, viewed spanking as a necessary method in teaching children appropriate social behaviors, obedience to authority, and the difference between right and wrong.

While about the same percentage of Koreans and Caucasians were in favor of spanking or hitting as a disciplinary method, the groups gave somewhat different explanations for their beliefs. Of all the groups, Caucasians seemed most ambivalent about corporal punishment. Almost 90% of them tempered their answers in one way or another, primarily emphasizing that it was appropriate only for young or defiant children. More than any other ethnic group, Caucasians seemed compelled to justify their use of spanking as a method of discipline. They often referred to having deliberated on the issue for a long time or having resorted to spanking only because nothing else worked or that it should be only "one swat" at a time.

These sentiments are in accord with those detected in Alvy's study (1987), which found a larger percentage of the high-income Caucasians (39%) in the sample communicating ambivalence about spanking and its effectiveness in comparison to low-income African-Americans (12%). High-income Caucasians (38%) in his study were also more likely than low-income African-Americans (19%) to say that they used spanking when nothing else worked.

Unlike other ethnic groups, quite a number of Caucasians made efforts to differentiate between hitting and spanking. They emphasized that while spanking was an effective disciplinary measure, hitting was never appropriate. They tended to equate hitting with severe spanking resulting from immaturity and anger:

> *Spanking can work. Hitting is a result of your own anger.*
> *Spanking yes. A very quick way of effectively making a situation serious. It works for direct disobedience and safety orientation.*

Although a smaller percentage of Vietnamese (58.6%) than Koreans (78.6%) viewed spanking or hitting as effective, when considering only those mothers who regarded it as a useful disciplinary measure, Vietnamese seemed more like Koreans than like Caucasians. Although about half of the Vietnamese and Koreans also qualified their answers, asserting that spanking worked only sometimes and only for certain children, they were much more certain about its efficacy than Caucasians. Vietnamese who believed that corporal punishment worked primarily emphasized its role in making children obey rules. One mother also remarked that it was a Vietnamese custom:

> *This is a Vietnamese custom, not sure about American.*
> *Children need to be punished hard sometimes to keep them in rule.*

Several Koreans expressed similar sentiments but also resembled African-Americans in other aspects. One mother referred to the emotional pain that parents feel when they have to spank their children. She remarked:

> *Parents and children are of the same blood and flesh. It's my blood getting in contact with my own blood. It's disciplining with love. You feel affection even though you feel pain. I feel so much pain while I am spanking the child too. Some people say that they wish their parents*

*spanked them while they were growing up because it is a sign of love
and caring.*

In this statement one encounters a vivid portrayal of the concept of
oneness between parent and child detected in some Asian cultures.
Hitting one's child for discipline is equated with hitting oneself. It is
considered a task that results in greater pain to the parents not only
because they sympathize with their children but also because each
misbehavior of their children that necessitates spanking reminds them
of their failure as parents. To many Koreans, the concept that spanking or hitting children for discipline is violence inflicted by one person
on another would be an affront to the essence of the parent-child
relationship. One Korean explained, "Spanking children is not done
to control them with power and strength; it is done to help a child
control his/her bad behavior."

Even more than African-Americans, Koreans were concerned
about the impropriety of spanking children on impulse. They felt that
children would be able to accept spanking as a punishment that they
deserve when parents set a rule in advance and administer it in a
manner appropriate for discipline:

*As long as parents don't do it out of impulse, if they have made a
promise with the child that s/he would get a spanking if s/he does a
certain thing, s/he will accept the spanking.*

It was also interesting to observe a Korean remark "I don't know
about American children, but Korean children need to be spanked if
you want them to have good habits. They can be raised as their
parents desire." Such an assertion contradicts one value of the dominant culture, the importance of respecting rights, opinions, and
wishes of children. Her statement did not give consideration to what
the child might want. While such thinking may appear repressive
to many mothers of the dominant culture, once again it should be
understood in the specific cultural context. In many Asian cultures
parents perceive children as extensions of themselves, and thus it
seems that children's rights do not become an issue. It is assumed that
parents always know and decide what is best for their children. In
this light, it is interesting to note how the following three sayings
from China, Korea, and Vietnam, respectively regard physical punishment as an expression of love: "To hit is to love, to scold is to be
affectionate" (Ying 1988); "one raises his/her rod more for the child

you love," "when you hate your children, give them sweetness: when you love them, give them (physical) punishment" (Gray & Cosgrove 1985).

It appears that in general physical punishment is accepted and used more in cultures that tend to expect children to obey and conform to certain rules. In this study, African-Americans, Koreans, and Vietnamese seemed to place the most value on obedience but for different reasons. In this light, the ambivalence Caucasians expressed toward corporal punishment is not surprising. Instilling obedience and conformity in children is typically not the prime goal of child rearing in the dominant culture.

The uncertainty that Caucasians manifested toward corporal punishment should also be understood in the context of the recent historical development of increased public campaigns against the use of corporal punishment, mainly resulting from movements to prevent child abuse. Today, educated parents frequently encounter books and other parenting materials that advise against the use of corporal punishment. For instance, a book on parenting entitled *Discipline Without Shouting or Spanking* describes spanking as the earliest model of violence for children (Wychoff & Unell 1984). Dr. Spock (1988), the doyen of parenting advisers, also asserts that an effort toward a kindlier and safer society can be initiated by halting the physical punishment of children. He claims that physical punishment "teaches that might makes right, [and] that it encourages some children to be bullies" (173). Thus, more than at any other time in history, parents who now rely on professional advice are more likely to feel guilty if they use spanking as a method of discipline. Yet, it is remarkable that despite such campaigns and expert advice a large majority of the Caucasians in the study, although ambivalent, still believed that spanking worked. This finding should be interpreted with the nature of the Caucasian sample in mind, however. Being church-going Christians, the Biblical teaching of "spare the rod, spoil the child" may have influenced the respondents' beliefs regarding physical discipline. In Alvy's (1988) study, too, 82% of the high-income Caucasians reported having used spanking with their preschool children.

In contrast to the other ethnic groups, the majority of Cambodians and Hispanics did not think spanking or hitting worked with children as a punishment. Cambodians suggested that parents should talk to their children while many Hispanics recommended taking away privileges. What accounts for the difference between Cambodians and Hispanics and the rest of the ethnic groups in their views of physical punishment?

Although a country in southeast Asia like Vietnam, Cambodia has been much more strongly influenced by Indian than by Chinese tradition. The Cambodian lifestyle has also been more thoroughly guided by Buddhism than the Vietnamese lifestyle. Cambodian Buddhism follows the Theravada tradition that originated in Sri Lanka and contrasts with the Mahayana tradition, the Chinese school of Buddhism that dominated Vietnam. The influence of Buddhism on Cambodians seems to have provided an attitude toward life that is fundamentally pacific, emphasizing tolerance and respect for the destiny of each person. Everyone is on a personal path toward his/her ultimate destiny that is unique. Thus, it is no one's affair to interfere with such a course of life. In Cambodian families, individuals are not considered subordinate to the family or social group as they are in Vietnamese families. Although the family structure is patriarchal, fathers are not all-powerful as Confucian fathers often are (Garry 1980). Such traditions and beliefs may influence the general lack of support for corporal punishment among Cambodians. If each child is born with a destiny, it is beyond parental power to change that destiny. An old Cambodian saying goes "If you plant a seed on a rock and that plant grows, you don't have to fertilize." A good plant will grow naturally, while a bad plant will die, no matter how much water and fertilizer one may provide. In the same way, if a child is bad, she or he will always remain bad, no matter how much the parents may spank. Cambodian parents tend to believe that they must accept the child as fate begotten by them because of something they have done in their past lives (Siv 1989). All of these interpretations must be viewed in terms of the relatively small number of Cambodians in the study sample ($n = 30$), however.

With respect to Hispanics, on the other hand, studies have consistently found that Hispanic parents report requiring high standards of discipline from their children but are relaxed about the actual implementation of punishment. Threats of physical punishment, though they may be used often, are not always followed by actual punishment. Mothers, in particular, are considered to "overprotect" their children and frequently allow them to do as they wish. Mexican-American parents have also been found to have a willingness to "give in" to their children (Bartz & LeVine 1978; Carillo 1982; Escovar & Escovar 1985; LeVine & Bartz 1979). Hispanic mothers' relatively low support for physical punishment may be a reflection of such lenient tendencies toward children.

Those mothers from other ethnic groups who did not consider spanking/hitting to be effective as a disciplinary method, like Cambodians and Hispanics, felt that talking or other types of punishment worked better. It is interesting to note that Caucasians and Hispanics, more than any other group, tended to believe that physical discipline resulted from anger and that it was a form of violence toward children:

> *It builds up a fear in the kids that their parents will get out of control. It also teaches children that it's okay to strike out in frustration or anger.*
>
> *It teaches them that violence is acceptable. That bigger people can have more power over smaller people by force.*

In interpreting these findings, however, it is important to recognize that differences between ethnic groups can be complicated by other variables, such as socioeconomic status and degree of acculturation. Although socioeconomic status is often defined as a composite measure of occupation, education, and income, education has been found to be among the strongest predictors of parental values (Wright & Wright 1976). It is also the best predictive measure of future socioeconomic status, particularly among students whose occupational status and income are temporarily diminished. Education was used as an indicator of socioeconomic status in this study since many of the subjects were graduate students or spouses of graduate students.

Virtually no difference was observed across educational levels within the African-American and the Hispanic groups of respondents with respect to their attitude toward the effectiveness of spanking/hitting. However, analysis across levels of acculturation within the Hispanic group revealed that in comparison to 33.3% of the Hispanics who have lived less than half of their lives in the U.S.A., 61.7% of the American-born Hispanics viewed corporal punishment as effective ($X^2 = 9.34$, $p = .00224$). Moving in the direction of the dominant Caucasian group response, the more acculturated Hispanics were more inclined to view physical punishment as an effective disciplinary measure than their less acculturated counterparts.

TABLE 2.2

Boundaries of Discipline by Ethnic Groups: Hitting on Hand with a Wooden Stick for Cheating

	Ethnic Groups						
	Caucasian (n = 56)[a]	Afr-American (n = 95)	Hispanic (n = 96)	Korean (n = 57)	Vietnamese (n = 30)	Cambodian (n = 30)	Total (n = 364)
Yes response to vignettes[b] (%)							
parents punish 9-yr. old son for cheating in school by hitting him on his hand with a wooden rod	7.1	19.4	2.1	70.2	50.0	23.3	23.8***

[a]These sample sizes may vary slightly on different rows depending on the amount of missing data and/or responses other than yes/no.

[b]P value was obtained from X^2 statistics.

***$p < .001$

Appropriate Methods of Discipline

Hitting on the Hand with a Wooden Stick. As summarized in table 2.2, over 70% of the Koreans and half of the Vietnamese in the sample approved of parents punishing a nine-year-old son for cheating in school by hitting him on his hand with a wooden rod. In contrast, almost 80% or more of the other groups disapproved, with Hispanics and Caucasians being most opposed. Koreans who approved of this disciplinary method generally considered cheating a serious transgression on the part of the child that needed to be stopped immediately with firm punishment. They considered it a parent's duty to help control the behavior when the child is not able to do it himself. The Confucian tradition in these societies has historically strongly emphasized that people had to pass civil service examination to move up the social ladder (Min 1988). Moreover, since hitting a child with a wooden rod on his/her hands is a standard method of discipline in Korea (Pan Asian Parent Education Project n.d.), such a positive response to the appropriateness of this method of disciplining a child is not surprising:

Of all things, cheating is the worst.

If the child has done it knowing that it's bad—you should do it to convey the message that the parents think that cheating is a serious problem, hitting on the palm of the child's hands with a ruler is one way of doing it.

The strong Confucian influence in Vietnam has also made the people underscore the importance of education in child rearing (Tran 1988). The practice of hitting with a wooden stick also appears to have been an accepted form of discipline in Vietnam (Nguyen & Nguyen 1985). Probably for these reasons, Vietnamese who approved of the practice, like the Koreans, tended to emphasize that hitting a child on his hand with a wooden rod for cheating was a normal disciplinary measure to prevent the child from repeating the behavior:

It's just a normal way to discipline children.
The child needs a hard punishment so he won't do that again.

Most often, those respondents who disagreed with this method of disciplining stated that a parent hitting a child on his hand with a wooden stick for cheating is too severe or ineffective and/or suggested alternative methods. Of the mothers who disapproved, many Hispanics (18.5%) and Caucasians (13.7%) asserted that this type of punishment was wrong or abusive. They seemed to be most ardent in their indignation about this practice:

That is not a place to hit a child. A child should not be hit at all. That is child abuse.
It's going to hurt his hands for a start. A form of abuse. Emotional and physical. It doesn't do any good.

Interestingly enough, 21.7% of the African-Americans, 16.3% of the Hispanics, and 14.7% of the Caucasians in the study also specifically mentioned the real dangers of hitting a child on his hand with a wooden stick. Generally, these mothers seemed to consider spanking acceptable but not in the way described in the vignette. Many suggested that the child should be spanked somewhere else and/or with something else:

You should use a switch or belt, but not a stick. Don't discipline humans with sticks. Sticks are for animals.
It's cruel. It could break bones. Trauma is really bad.

> *I believe that when a parent has to resort to physical punishment, it should be done with an open hand on the child's behind.*

Such concerns may in part reflect the fact that this method of disciplining is completely unfamiliar to these three ethnic groups. Since this is not a common practice in these ethnic groups, the vignette may conjure up images, some of which may seem terribly dangerous. On the other hand, as discussed previously, hitting a child on the palm of his hand with a wooden stick is considered a standard method of disciplining in Korean and Vietnamese cultures. These ethnic groups are confident that there is little danger involved if this method is implemented appropriately. Thus, unlike these three groups, those Koreans and Vietnamese who disapproved of this disciplinary measure mainly communicated concern about the effectiveness of using such a method with the problem of cheating rather than about the possible physical risks involved. Respondents in each ethnic group seemed to have their own criteria for deciding on the types of punishment called for by different types of misconduct and on how they should be implemented.

A theme distinctive to Caucasians emerged that appeared to reflect the "psychological mindedness" of this middle-income group. Only among the Caucasians in the study were there mothers who specifically referred to the cheating as a symptom of a deeper problem. Moreover, only the Caucasian mothers precisely referred to hitting a child on his/her hand with a wooden stick for cheating as a discipline that does not address the real issue and does not relate directly to the misdeed. Such a view parallels that of an expert explaining that "a chronic misbehavior is a child's way of telling you that something is awry in [his/her] life" and that it must be dealt with at its source to eliminate it (Briggs 1970:260). These mothers seemed more inclined to believe in the presence of underlying reasons for behaviors and to assume that an effective punishment should be logically related to the misbehavior:

> *If a son has cheated, the cheating is a symptom. What was the cause? He was not prepared for the test. Talk about cheating.*
>
> *The punishment should be related to the infraction. It doesn't give a good message.*

Again, controlling for education and acculturation did not alter the patterns of ethnic differences and similarities observed in the original analysis. comparisons across educational levels among african-Americans and Hispanics and acculturational levels among Hispanics also did not reveal any significant differences.

What Constitutes Abuse?

Is a Bruise Evidence of Physical Abuse? Table 2.3 traces the great divergence among ethnic groups in their views on whether an incident where a child is bruised from physical punishment is considered abusive, particularly in relation to a nine-year-old son. Of the six groups, the two southeast Asian groups deviated most from each other. Consistently, almost 90% of the Vietnamese did not perceive a child bruised from spanking as a case of physical abuse while Cambodians almost unanimously thought otherwise.

About half of the African-Americans and of the Koreans did not judge such an incident child abuse for nine- and fifteen-year-old children. For three-year-olds, however, almost 80% of both groups viewed it as abusive. In general, the three groups that tended to be most confident about the effectiveness of physical discipline (African-Americans, Koreans, and Vietnamese) were also less inclined to assess bruises as evidence of child abuse.

Caucasians and Hispanics were the most similar to one another with a clear majority in both groups regarding such discipline as abusive. However, about 15% fewer Hispanics (77.8%) than Caucasians (91.7%) thought that an incident where a fifteen-year-old son is bruised from spanking was abusive.

Bruises on a child are often used as evidence of physical abuse calling for intervention. However, it is remarkable to note that only about 10% of the Vietnamese respondents considered it child abuse when a son was bruised by his parents' spanking. Their responses were similar for all three age groups. Moreover, of those who did not perceive bruises on a child as physical abuse, not one Vietnamese qualified her answer while 100% of the Caucasians, 46.7% of the Hispanics, 35.3% of the Koreans and 34.1% of the African-Americans did. Most of the Vietnamese respondents who did not think a child bruised from spanking was physically abused explained that parents never want to hurt or abuse their own children. They believed that sometimes parents spank their children hard because they need to be punished for having done something very bad:

TABLE 2.3
"Is a Bruise Evidence of Physical Abuse?" by Ethnic Group

	Ethnic Groups						
	Caucasian (n = 56)[a]	Afr-American (n = 95)	Hispanic (n = 96)	Korean (n = 57)	Vietnamese (n = 30)	Cambodian (n = 30)	Total (n = 364)
Yes response to questions[b] (%)							
For a 3-year-old boy							
is it physical abuse if a 3-year-old boy got bruised because his parents spanked him for doing something very bad?	89.6	78.5	88.3	75.4	14.8	100.0	79.1***
For a 9-year-old boy							
is it physical abuse if a 9-year-old boy got bruised because his parents spanked him for doing something very bad?	89.1	48.2	83.7	40.4	6.9	100.0	63.1***
For a 15-year-old boy							
is it physical abuse if a 15-year-old boy got bruised because his parents spanked him for doing something very bad?	91.7	53.3	77.8	53.6	6.7	96.7	64.8***

[a]These sample sizes may vary slightly on different rows depending on the amount of missing data and/or responses other than yes/no.
[b]P value was obtained from X^2 statistics.
***p<.001

In Asian culture parents never want to hurt their children. They do this because the child needs to be punished for something he has done wrong.
Parents spank the child because they want their child to be good.

They seemed unable to entertain the notion that any parent would abuse his/her own child.

Similar themes were detected among Koreans who did not believe that a child bruised from spanking would represent a case of child abuse. Many Koreans underscored that it was a parent's duty to punish a child out of love for him, that the parent had no intention to bruise the child, and that if it were for punishment of a wrongdoing, it could not be abuse:

A parent spanking a child is not physical abuse. It probably happened unintentionally. The parent hit him because he did something wrong. She did not spank to have fun.

Song (1986) found in her study of Korean-Americans in Los Angeles that 56% of her subjects regarded the law concerning physical abuse to be in conflict with Korean child-rearing practices. In the same vein, it was apparent in the study reported here that many Koreans were aware that physical punishment was frowned upon by the dominant culture. One respondent went on at length explaining why children needed spanking, that it was good for them and that the children felt less guilty that way. A few also remarked in an emphatic tone: "What parent would abuse his/her own child?" This reflected their complete faith in parents to always act in the best interests of their children.

African-Americans who did not regard a child bruised from physical punishment as an incident of child abuse also underscored the fact that the parent's intention was not to harm but to discipline the child. Compared to the Koreans and the Vietnamese, more African-Americans in the study also stated that bruises cannot be equated with abuse because some children bruise easily.

Some African-Americans also expressed that such discipline may be necessary to get one's point across and to maintain control:

If you spank him, you'll get your point across. You're not trying to kill him, but he may be bruised.
He needed a reminder, a proof that what he did was really bad.

All of the Caucasians and the majority of the Hispanics who did not think the incident was physically abusive qualified their answers. Most of them stated that the definition of physical abuse depends on a number of factors, such as the frequency of the incident and the severity of the bruise:

> *Physical abuse should be defined by the severity and amount of bruises. Not if it's one bruise that was left. Children bruise easily.*
> *In this situation, I would call the spanking a form of discipline, not abuse. There is, although, a fine line.*

On the other hand, when taken as a whole, the majority of respondents who viewed the circumstances reported in the vignette as abusive stated that leaving a bruise on a child implied that the punishment was too severe. A few subjects from the total sample also remarked that a bruise on a child indicated that the parent was angry, emotional, or out of control while disciplining the child:

> *An effective spanking doesn't have to leave a bruise. We've spanked our kids, but they've never been marked by it. There might be a bruise if a parent is spanking with anger.*
> *You can punish with a few spankings. If a child is bruised, it's a sign that the parent was emotional.*

It is interesting to note that 12% of the Cambodians and 8.7% of the Koreans who viewed the incident as abusive remarked that this was against the law in the U.S.:

> *Because parents can be responsible for their actions and it is against the law in the U.S.*
> *A teacher will tell the police and will cause trouble to the parent.*

The Cambodians in particular seemed to be well aware of the problems that can result from being reported for child abuse. Such remarks from people who have been in the U.S. for less than five years on the average suggest that the Cambodians may have indeed been informally or formally educated about child abuse when they arrived in the U.S.

In general, more respondents considered bruises from spanking on a three-year-old child abusive than bruises on a nine-year-old. The main reason for perceiving such discipline as unacceptable for a three-year-old was that it was too severe for so young a child. On the other hand, the overall percentage of those who considered it abusive to bruise a fifteen-year-old remained similar to the one regarding the bruising of a nine-year-old as abusive.

Comparisons across educational levels within the African-American and the Hispanic respondent groups revealed statistically significant differences in both groups but only for the assessment of bruises on a nine-year-old. Interestingly enough, this is the only significant difference observed across educational levels with respect to attitudes toward family discipline. Among the African-Americans, 66.7% of those in the low education level considered the incident abusive in contrast to 41.0% of those in the high education level ($X^2 = 4.55$; $p = .03292$). Similarly, among Hispanics, 92.9% of those in the low education level perceived such discipline as physical abuse compared to 69.4% of those in the high education level ($X^2 = 8.80$; $p = .00301$).

This is in contrast to one's expectation. Since families of low socioeconomic status have often been linked to a more frequent use of corporal punishment (Bronfenbrenner 1958; Havighurst & Davis 1955; Maccoby & Gibbs 1954; Waters & Crandall 1964; White 1957), it seems easier to surmise that they would also be more likely to accept bruises as one of the inevitable consequences of the punishment. However, similar to the research results of Giovannoni and Becerra (1979), African-American and Hispanic respondents in the low education group in this study seemed to have a more stringent definition of abuse than those in the group with high education.

This finding also seems to contradict the common assumption that families of lower socioeconomic status appear to be more accepting of child abuse since more cases are found in these groups. Environmental pressures, such as poverty and social isolation, may be more responsible for such a phenomenon (Giovannoni & Becerra 1979). The national public opinion poll of 1990 commissioned by the National Committee for Prevention of Child Abuse also found that while fewer parents with higher incomes reported the use of physical punishment, those who hit their children appeared to use more serious forms of physical punishment (Daro 1991).

Another explanation for the contradiction may lie in child abuse reporting patterns. Regardless of actual child abuse incidence, families of lower socioeconomic status may possibly be reported for abuse more frequently than those of higher socioeconomic status for social reasons such as class-bound judgments made by middle-income professionals. Such a tendency has been observed in research findings especially when minority families were involved (Gelles 1982; Hampton & Newberger 1985).

One other factor may also be at play. Giovannoni and Becerra (1979) observed in their study that the higher educated subjects had a greater willingness to admit their potential for being abusive and had a higher level of awareness of the problem of child abuse in general. They had also been more exposed to the current thinking of experts that child abusers are in need of treatment because they were themselves victims of abuse as children. In the current study, too, the higher educated respondents may have been more cautious in arriving at a conclusion (i.e., designating someone as a child abuser) that may involve serious consequences.

Across levels of acculturation, Hispanics who have lived less than 50% of their lives in the U.S. (93.3%) were more likely to perceive bruises from physical discipline on a nine-year-old as a case of child abuse than American-born Hispanics (76.7%). However, the difference between the two groups was not statistically significant.

Implications for Defining Child Abuse

The findings cited above reveal a number of significant variations among cultural groups in their views of acceptable forms of discipline. To observe that cultural differences exist is not necessarily a justification for accepting all sorts of behavior. One can imagine behaviors that different groups might practice that would be physically harmful to children and simply unacceptable in light of the prevailing standards of the majority community. Addressing the problem of child abuse is of prime importance. But it is also essential to recognize that the different views expressed in the study reflect a deeper, more basic, disagreement about the nature of children and the parent-child relationship.

Such recognition of the cultural diversity in values and beliefs related to child rearing is particularly important since studies have consistently identified concerns about differential treatment of minority families and lack of cultural competency among professionals working in the field (Close 1983; Jenkins, Diamond, Flanzraich, Gibson, Hendricks, & Marshood 1983). Children of color are also removed from their families more often than Caucasian children, and many receive less comprehensive and possibly inferior services (Close 1983; Jenkins et al. 1983).

Studies have also found professional bias in reporting individuals for child abuse. In a study of 157 physicians, Gelles (1982) found that when these professionals made a report of child abuse, they considered not only the child's physical condition but also the caregiver's occupation, education, race, and ethnicity. Five percent of the physicians surveyed stated that the caregiver's race and ethnicity were so important that when faced with a case of suspected child abuse they would file a report on the basis of those characteristics alone.

A sample of cases ($n = 17,645$) from the National Study of Incidence and Severity of Child Abuse and Neglect has also shown that hospitals tend to overreport African-Americans and Hispanics and underreport Caucasians. For African-American and Hispanic families, the recognition of signs of possible child maltreatment almost ensured their being reported to child protective services (Hampton & Newberger 1985).

How should child abuse be defined then? As cultures come into contact with one another, varying child-rearing practices and beliefs create a situation ripe for cultural conflict in the definition of child abuse (Korbin 1980). When the issue of physical abuse is involved, however, the disparity between professionals and parents seems even more evident than cultural differences. As reviewed in the beginning of this essay, a study of parents and professionals in England revealed that the criteria social workers used to remove children from their homes did not reflect social norms (Christopher 1982). While regular incidents of physical punishment were considered serious enough to warrant removal of a child by the social workers, explosive blows made in the heat of anger were considered more serious by parents. The parents were reluctant to suggest removal of a child when traditionally accepted methods of corporal punishment were used. In the same vein, it is interesting to observe that many respondents of the current study who believed in the effectiveness of physical discipline mentioned the importance of being in control of one's anger when spanking.

Recently the antispanking movement has taken a strong hold among some professional organizations. For instance, the National Association of Social Workers has openly taken a firm position against parental use of physical punishment, declaring that all physical punishment of children has some harmful effects and should be stopped (NASW 1989). Although physical punishment is generally considered to be less effective and less equitable as a disciplinary method (Kadushin & Martin 1981), no study has yet proven that physical punishment *by itself* is harmful to children (Giovannoni & Becerra 1979).

Moreover, Trickett and Susman's (1988) comparative study of physically abusive and nonabusive families found that the use of or belief in corporal punishment cannot necessarily be associated with child abuse. With respect to child-rearing practices and beliefs, they found that abusive parents significantly differed from a matched sample of nonabusive parents in many aspects (abusive parents were less satisfied with their children and perceived child rearing to be more difficult than the nonabusive parents) but not in their belief in spanking. On a scale of 5 (1 = strong belief that spanking should never be used, 5 = strong belief in importance of spanking), abusive parents scored on the average 2.33 while nonabusive parents scored 2.44. In another study, the abusive parents did not use physical punishment more frequently than the nonabusive parents but used more severe forms of punishment such as striking the face, hitting with an object, or pulling the child's hair (Trickett & Kuczynski 1986).

Social workers have launched the antispanking movement as a genuine effort to prevent child abuse because they are deeply concerned with the welfare of children. Physical abuse generates grave problems, and abuse in every form must be avoided. Laying down absolute rules such as "physical punishment is always inappropriate," however, does not seem to address the complexity that surrounds the problem of child abuse nor the diverse meaning cultures give to physical discipline in family life. Findings from this study suggest that it is too simplistic to take physical discipline in a vacuum, isolated from all other variables, and declare it harmful.

One of the fundamental principles of the helping professions is the necessity of starting where the client is. To start where the client is, one has to first understand where the client is. Movements such as antispanking campaigns will continue to broaden the definition of abuse, calling for intervention for behaviors previously tolerated or ignored. More and more, disciplinary methods that were regarded as normative in the past will be defined as deviant. The problem is that a large percentage of the population targeted for interventions, the parents, have not made the same shift in defining their own behaviors (Kadushin & Martin 1981). Professionals should remember that the majority of the "normal" parents in this study and others (Alvy 1988) believed in spanking as an effective disciplinary method. Moreover, many of the African-Americans, Koreans, and Vietnamese in the current study regarded it an act of love that parents should consider their responsibility. Even among the Caucasians, although they were ambivalent, almost 80% viewed physical punishment as an effective method of discipline. In their actual family life, 63% of the African-Americans and almost half of the Caucasians in this study used spanking to discipline their children. Not all cultures emphasize a child's ability to reason and communicate as much as middle-income Caucasians do. Equating physical punishment with violence is a modern concept that is certainly not the norm among many ethnic groups, including a large number of Caucasians. Professionals may disagree with the parents' attitudes toward physical discipline, but unless they understand the behavior from the parents' point of view, they cannot discuss this behavior with them with any hope of effecting change (Kadushin & Martin 1981).

In their study of parents who were identified as abusive, Kadushin and Martin (1981) found that in most cases parents have tried to deal with their children's behavioral problems in a less punitive manner, and when such interventions succeeded, abuse did not take place. The abuse was a testimony to the failure of other disciplinary procedures. For antispanking campaigns to be effective, it is essential that parents be educated about alternative disciplinary strategies first. Disarming them of one of few disciplinary methods they know can only lead to frustration and feelings of inadequacy as parents.

The most important element linked with physical abuse has been found to be the caregivers' stress (Hampton 1987). This was found to be true to an even greater extent in minority families (Daniel, Hampton, & Newberger 1987). Substantiated cases of maltreatment among African-Americans from the National Study of the Incidence and Severity of Child Abuse and Neglect mainly included families who were poor, on public assistance, and in father-absent households (Hampton 1987). The presence of potential bias in the field leading to overreporting minority and low-income families should not be overlooked (Gelles 1982; Hampton & Newberger 1985). At the same time, environmental pressures, such as the stresses of poverty, especially when compounded with racial discrimination, may precipitate reactions leading to physical mistreatment of children.

The public also seems to believe that child abuse is closely linked to poverty but not so much to parents spanking their children. Forty-five percent of the respondents of the public opinion poll commissioned by the National Committee for Prevention of Child Abuse (Daro 1991) reported that child abuse was caused by poverty while only 19% thought that parental spanking could contribute a "great deal" to child abuse rates. A disproportionately high number of minority respondents, particularly African-Americans, were also concerned with racism as one of the causes of child abuse. Thus it seems that the prevention of and intervention against child abuse should be targeted at stress reduction in family life rather than at formulating absolutes against something that many people consider normative.

Lytton and Zwiner (1975) found in their observational study of parent-child disciplinary interaction of two- to three-year-old Caucasian boys that physical control (slapping or physically restraining or restricting) had a more powerful effect on the child than other kinds of interventions ("command," "reasoning," etc.), both for compliance and noncompliance. The physical interventions did have potency for immediate accomplishment of parental disciplinary objectives. Although it is difficult to accept the idea, professionals may need to recognize that for some parents physical punishment has helped to achieve their objectives as parents. They experience firsthand that physical punishment gets behaviors changed in their children. The professionals' denial of this reality will only lead to the further loss of their credibility in the eyes of the public (Kadushin & Martin 1981). The professionals' declaration that all physical punishment is wrong may only alienate the very public they are trying to serve. Human service professionals' sincere wish to care for and help children cannot be effective if they fail to work with parents. Unless they first become allies with the parents through genuine acceptance and respect, they will not be trusted as helping professionals.

Who then decides what is and is not acceptable with respect to family discipline? To what extent should this be determined by individual families or by professionals or by society at large? These are questions that do not have simple answers. Yet the present study makes one point obvious. This country cannot sensitively address the issue of child abuse without recognizing that different ethnic groups have different norms regarding parent-child relationships. Any action to prevent or treat child abuse should be undertaken with this in mind: families differ in their goals for child rearing and in their beliefs about the nature of children, about children's rights, and about discipline.

NOTES

1. For a more detailed explanation of the survey methods see: Helen Noh Ahn, Intimacy and Discipline in Family Life: A Cross-Cultural Analysis with Implications for Theory and Practice in Child Abuse Prevention (Ph.D. diss., University of California, Berkeley, 1990).

REFERENCES

Alvy, K. (1987). *Black parenting: Strategies for training.* New York: Irvington .

Ahn, H. N. (1990). Intimacy and discipline in family life: A cross-cultural analysis with implications for theory and practice in child abuse prevention. Ph.D. diss., University of California, Berkeley.

Bartz, K. W. & LeVine, E. S. (1978). Childrearing by black parents: A description and comparison to Anglo and Chicano parents. *Journal of Marriage and the Family, 40,* 709–19.

Bronfenbrenner, U. (1958). Socialization and social class through time and space. In E. E. Maccoby, T. M. Newcomb, & E. L. Hartley (Eds), *Readings in Social Psychology* (pp. 400–24). New York: Henry Holt.

Burgdorf, K. (1980). Recognition and reporting of child maltreatment: Findings from the national study of the incidence and severity of child abuse and neglect. Rockville, MD: Westat. As cited in Alfaro, J. (1981). Child neglect and cultural tradition. *Human Ecology Forum, 12,* 26–30.

Carillo, C. (1982). Changing norms of Hispanic families: Implications for treatment. In E. E. Jones & S. J. Korchin (Eds.), *Minority mental health* (pp. 250–66). New York: Praeger.

Christopher, R. J. (1982). Public perception of child abuse and the need for intervention: Are professionals seen as abusers? *Child Abuse and Neglect, 7,* 435–42.

Close, M. (1983). Child welfare and people of color: Denial of equal access. *Social Work Research and Abstracts, 19*(4), 13–20.

Daniel, J., Hampton, R., & Newberger, E. (1987). Child abuse and accidents in black families: A controlled comparative study. In R. Hampton (Ed.), *Violence in the black family: Correlates and consequences.* Massachusetts: Lexington Books.

Daro, D. (1991). *Public attitudes and behaviors with respect to child abuse prevention, 1987–1991.* The National Committee for Prevention of Child Abuse.

Dreikurs, R. with Soltz, V. (1987). *Children: The challenge.* New York: Dutton.

Escovar, L. & Escovar, P. (1981). Child-rearing practices among Hispanic groups. Manuscript, Florida International University, Miami. As cited in Escovar, L. & Escovar, P. (1985). Retrospective perception of parental

child-rearing practices in three culturally different college groups. *International Journal of Intercultural Relations, 9,* 31–49.

Garry, R. (1980). Cambodia. In E. Tepper (Ed.), *Southeast Asian exodus: From tradition to resettlement: Understanding refugees from Laos, Kampuchea, and Vietnam in Canada.* Ottawa: The Canadian Asian Studies Association.

Gelles, R. (1982). Child abuse and family violence: Implications for medical professionals. In E. H. Newberger (Ed.), *Child abuse.* Boston: Little, Brown.

Giovannoni, J. & Becerra, R. (1979). *Defining child abuse.* New York: The Free Press.

Gray, E. & Cosgrove, J. (1985). Ethnocentric perception of child-rearing practices in protective services. *Child Abuse and Neglect, 9*(3), 389–96.

Haeuser, A. (1990). Ending physical punishment of children. *A Common Ground.* 6(3), 1, 9–10.

Hampton, R. (1987). Race, class, and child maltreatment. *Journal of Comparative Family Studies, 13,* 126–33.

Hampton, R. & Newberger, E. (1985). Child abuse incidence and reporting by hospitals: Significance of severity, class, and race. *American Journal of Public Health, 75*(1), 56–60.

Havighurst, R. J. & Davis, A. (1955). Comparison of the Chicago and Harvard studies of social class differences in child rearing. *American Sociological Review, 20,* 438–42.

Hines, P. M. & Boyd-Franklin, N. (1982). Black families. In M. McGoldrick, J. K. Pearce, & J. Giordano (Eds.), *Ethnicity and family therapy* (pp. 84–107). New York: Guildford Press.

Jameson, D. (1990). It's not ok to hit children. *A Common Ground, 6*(3), 1, 9–10.

Jenkins, S., Diamond, B. E., Flanzraich, M., Gibson, J. W., Hendricks, J., & Mashood, N. (1983). Ethnic differentials in foster care placements. *Social Work Research and Abstracts, 19*(4), 41–45.

Juvenile Justice Standards Project (1977). *Standards relating to abuse and neglect: Tentative draft.* Cambridge: Ballinger.

Kadushin, A. & Martin, J. (1981). *Child abuse: An interactional event.* New York: Columbia University Press.

Korbin, J. (1980). The cross-cultural context of child abuse and neglect. In C. Kempe & R. Helfer (Eds.), *The Battered Child* (3d edition) (pp. 21–35). Chicago: University of Chicago Press.

Korbin, J. (1981). (Ed.). *Child abuse and neglect: Cross-cultural perspectives.* Berkeley & Los Angeles: University of California Press.

Langness, L. (1981). Child abuse and cultural values: The case of New Guinea. In J. Korbin (Ed.), *Child abuse and neglect: Cross-cultural perspectives.* Berkeley: University of California Press.

Lassiter, R. (1987). Child rearing in black families: Child abusing discipline? In R. Hampton (Ed.), *Violence in the black family: Correlates and consequences* (pp. 39–53). Massachusetts: Lexington Books.

LeVine, E. S. & Bartz, K. V. (1979). Comparative child-rearing attitudes among Chicano, Anglo, and Black parents. *Hispanic Journal of Behavioral Sciences, 1,* 165–78.

Lytton, H. & Zwiner, W. (1975). Compliance and its controlling stimuli observed in a natural setting. *Developmental Psychology, 11*(6), 769–79.

Maccoby, E. E. & Gibbs, P. K. (1954). Methods of child rearing in two social classes. In W. E. Martin & C. Stendler (Eds.), *Readings in child development* (pp. 380–96). New York: Harcourt Brace.

NASW News. (1989). Anti-spanking campaign gets support. *NASW News, 34*(4), 13.

Nguyen, P. H. & Nguyen, A. F. (1985, June). Southeast Asian refugees: Cultural issues in child abuse/neglect. In *Multicultural Child Abuse Prevention Symposium.* Los Angeles: Multicultural Coordinating Council.

Pan Asian Parent Education Project. (n.d.). *Pan Asian child rearing practices: Filipino, Japanese, Korean, Samoan, Vietnamese.* San Diego: The Pan Asian Parent Education Project.

Salisbury, B. (1990). Personal communication.

Schumacher, W. (1990). Physical discipline is different from corporal punishment. *A Common Ground, 6*(3), 1, 9–10.

Siv (1989). Personal Communication.

Song, K. (1986). Defining child abuse: Korean community study. Ph.D. diss., University of California, Los Angeles.

Spock, B. (1989). *Dr. Spock on parenting.* New York: Pocket Books.

Tran, T. V. (1988). The Vietnamese family. In C. Mindel, R. Habenstein, & R. Wright (Eds.), *Ethnic families in America: Patterns and variations* (3d ed.) (pp. 276–99). New York: Elsevier.

Trickett, P. & Kuczynski, L. (1986). Children's misbehavior and parental strategies in abusive and nonabusive families. *Developmental Psychology, 22,* 115–23.

Trickett, P. & Susman, E. (1988). Parental perceptions of child-rearing practices in physically abusive and nonabusive families. *Developmental Psychology, 24* (2), 270–76.

Waters, E. & Crandall, V. (1964). Social class and observed maternal behavior from 1940 to 1960. *Child Development, 35,* 1021–32.

White, M. S. (1957). Social class, child rearing practices, and child behavior. *American Sociological Review, 22,* 704–12.

Wright, K. (1982). Sociocultural factors in child abuse. In B. A. Bass, G. E. Wyatt, & G. J. Powell (Eds.), *Afro-American family: Assessment, treatment, and research issues.* New York: Grune & Stratton.

Wright, J. & Wright, S. (1976). Social class and parental values for children: A partial replication and extension of the Kohn thesis. *American Sociological Review, 41,* 527–37.

Wychoff, J. & Unell, B. (1984). *Discipline without shouting or spanking.* New York: Meadowbrook Books.

Ying, Y. (1988). Personal Communication.

PART TWO

FAMILY-BASED IN-HOME AND OUT-OF-HOME SERVICES

In recent years, family-based services have developed rapidly across the country. These programs have an immediate appeal because they are grounded in the recognition of the family as the most vital resource for raising children. Although the state has become increasingly involved in child rearing with escalating numbers of children in foster care, most acknowledge the primary role parents play in caring for and rearing their own children.

Permanency planning initially resulted in a reduction of children in foster care. Yet, by the mid-1980s the foster care caseload began to rise across the country. This led some analysts to suggest that significant numbers of children were being removed from their homes unnecessarily (Edna McConnell Clark Foundation 1985). At the same time, practitioners had begun the careful work of program development, monitoring the amount, intensity, and duration of services necessary to support and strengthen families while ensuring the protection of children within the home. Although it was once commonly held that the best interests of children at imminent risk of harm would be realized with placement outside of the home, early family preservation efforts focused on changing the home environment so that parents could reestablish their protective role for children (Fraser, Pecora, & Haapala 1991).

Today, family-based services programs vary considerably. Intensive family preservation services are designed to shore up the family system in the hopes of avoiding placement in out-of-home care. Most family preservation programs are provided in-home; they are intensive, and they generally rely upon a short-term model. Other distinguishing features include a small caseload, twenty-four-hour availability, and assistance with concrete services (Pecora, Whittaker, & Maluccio 1992). Most programs are crisis-oriented and build on the strengths families initially bring with them.

With the unfolding of various family-based services models has come a flurry of research activity. The majority of evaluations to date have focused on intensive family preservation services, and most studies have reviewed outcomes relating to a particular model of services (for a review of these studies see: Feldman 1990; Fraser, Pecora, & Haapala 1991; Nelson & Landsman 1992; Yuan 1990). Rossi's (1990) review of family preservation evaluations and directions for future research offers guidance for the design of careful research strategies. More recent studies of family-based services programs and those offered in this section have incorporated many of his suggestions for (1) randomized experimental or case overflow designs; (2) the use of behavioral measures in addition to placement outcomes as criteria for evaluating program success; (3) services provided to a heterogeneous population of families; (4) multisite program implementation; and (5) adequate sample size.

Although initial studies in the field of family preservation showed remarkably positive results, more recent evidence points to rather mixed outcomes with regard to placement prevention. Preliminary results from a statewide effort to prevent out-of-home placement in Illinois suggest no difference in placement rates between the randomly assigned treatment and control groups (Littell & Rzepnicki 1992). Rzepnicki and associates suggest that the ambiguity of these findings emphasizes the importance of using criteria such as parent satisfaction to shed light on other relevant outcomes that have not heretofore been examined. Their study is the most extensive study of client reactions to family preservation.

Nelson also reports on a study conducted in various sites including several program models. Her research is designed to determine the relative effectiveness of different types of interventions using varying lengths of time. The study is particularly important as it provides new insights into the role of family-based services in working with families reported for different types of maltreatment.

Finally, Walker and associates provide evidence about the impact of parental substance abuse on outcomes for children in foster care. Substance abuse is a major contributor to rising foster care caseloads (Besharov 1989); yet it is unclear whether the family characteristics, needs, services, or outcomes for children in these families differ from those of other children placed in out-of-home care. The study, which is exploratory in nature, provides a useful contribution to our knowledge of children in out-of-home care. As substance abuse continues to plague communities across the country, it is important to gain a clear view of the needs of the children affected by this debilitating condition.

REFERENCES

Besharov, D. (1989). The children of crack: Will we protect them? *Public Welfare, 47,* 13–15, 42–43.
Edna McConnell Clark Foundation. (1985). *Keeping families together: The case for family preservation.* New York: Author.
Feldman, L. H. (1991). Evaluating the impact of intensive family preservation services in New Jersey. In K. Wells & D. E. Biegel (Eds.), *Family preservation services* (pp. 47–71). Newbury Park, CA: Sage.
Fraser, M. W., Pecora, P. J., & Haapala, D. A. (1991). *Families in crisis: The impact of intensive family preservation services.* New York: Aldine de Gruyter.
Littell, J. & Rzepnicki, T. (1992, September). Paper presented at the International Congress on Child Abuse and Neglect. Chicago, Illinois.
Nelson, K. & Landsman, M. (1992). *Alternative models for family preservation: Family-based services in context.* Springfield, IL: Charles C. Thomas.
Pecora, P. J., Whittaker, J. K., & Maluccio, A. N. (1992). *The child welfare challenge: Policy, practice, and research.* New York: Aldine de Gruyter.
Rossi, P. H. (1991). *Evaluating family preservation programs: A report to the Edna McConnell Clark Foundation.* Amherst, MA: Social and Demographic Research Institute.
Yuan, Y-Y. T. (1990). *Evaluation of AB 2562 in-home care demonstration projects.* X^2 = Volumes I and II. Sacramento: MacDonald and Associates.

THREE

An Experimental Study of Family Preservation Services: Early Findings from a Parent Survey

Tina L. Rzepnicki, John R. Schuerman,
Julia H. Littell, Amy Chak, and Marva Lopez

Like many other states, Illinois offers intensive family preservation services to reduce out-of-home placement of abused and neglected children while maintaining them safely in their own homes. A state-wide evaluation of these services was undertaken to examine their effectiveness and to identify the characteristics of families who benefit most and least from these services. A randomized experiment was conducted with a sample of more than sixteen hundred families to assess the effects of the family preservation program compared with the services these families would ordinarily receive. Preliminary findings suggest that overall the program has had no significant effect on placement rates: within one month of referral, only 6% of the family preservation cases and 8% of the control group cases experienced a placement. The likelihood of placement increased to approximately 20% for both groups within six months and 30% within one year. The program also appears to have no effects on subsequent child maltreatment (measured by substantiated reports of maltreatment). As with placement, the risk of subsequent maltreatment appears to be fairly low: 7% of the cases in both groups had one or more substantiated reports of maltreatment within one month of referral. By six months, the figure was about 17% for both groups (Littell 1991).

Family preservation programs are concerned with more than placement rates and further maltreatment, however. Ultimately, these programs attempt to improve the health and well-being of children and their families. If family preservation services are more successful than regular services in reducing the problems that lead to maltreatment, then we might expect family preservation cases to close more quickly in the public child welfare system.[1] Some families might also benefit by leaving the child welfare system in which they may be subject to intrusive interventions. Our examination of case closing rates in the public child welfare system found significant differences favoring the experimental group—the likelihood of case closing for family preservation cases was 46% greater than for the control group (Littell & Fong 1992).

Child and family functioning, including child and parent behaviors and conditions of the home, are probably best measured more directly through observation (an exceedingly difficult task) or through a variety of instruments designed to tap into areas of life relevant to the concerns of child welfare. Although several family preservation evaluations have included measures of child and family functioning (AuClaire & Schwartz 1986; Feldman 1990; Fraser, Pecora, & Haapala 1991; Yuan et al. 1990), only one study collected data on the control group. Results of this study favored the experimental group on five of eighteen measures (Feldman 1990).

The Illinois evaluation is also concerned with the impact of family preservation services on client behaviors and living conditions. Data were collected from the workers and a sample of families from both groups under study. This paper presents initial findings from a survey of families who provided information about their situation at three points in time.

Program and Evaluation Overview

Family First Program

The intensive family preservation program, Family First, is administered by the Illinois Department of Children and Family Services (DCFS) and operates through contracts with sixty private child welfare agencies throughout the state. Families are eligible for services after a finding of abuse or neglect. Over six thousand families have been served since the program was initiated in 1988. Services are designed to be home-based and time-limited (90 days), although 40% of the families receive services for more than 90 days and 24% for more than 120 days (Rzepnicki June 1991). The range of services includes various forms of counseling, resource linkage, advocacy, cash and material assistance, and parenting skills training. Families typically receive multiple services. Many of the agencies use service teams composed of caseworkers and homemakers. Caseloads are quite small, typically under ten families per worker. The large scale of the program and variations in its content and structure across agencies offer an opportunity to identify the characteristics of families who benefit from different kinds of programs.

The Experiment

As part of the statewide evaluation, an experiment was begun in April 1990 to assess the effects of the family preservation program compared to those of services these families would ordinarily receive. In seven locations throughout the state (twenty agencies), eligible families were randomly assigned by computer to the Family First program or to regular services.[2] Random assignment continued for two years and involved a total of 1,677 families. The study is the largest experiment on family preservation services conducted to date.

Data on family characteristics, services, and outcomes were collected on both groups. Data were obtained from state computer files; qualitative interviews with program administrators, social workers, and case aides; and case instruments completed by providers. Recognizing that client perceptions are also important in understanding program effects, a survey of parents was launched in May 1991.

Parent Survey Methods

In-person interviews were conducted with randomly selected families in both the Family First program and regular DCFS services groups. Data were collected on parental views of child and family well-being and of the services received. The survey is longitudinal in design: initial interviews were conducted at least three months after the random assignment to services, and follow-up interviews were conducted approximately nine months later. Additional follow-up interviews are planned for up to two years. These data will help determine whether the Family First program benefits clients in the ways intended, and they will provide a more complete picture of the effects of family preservation services in Illinois.

Sampling Methods. Initial interviews were conducted with families living in an area of Chicago and families from two other areas of the state were subsequently added to the sample. This report is based on the Chicago sample with which two rounds of interviews have been completed. The area is among the poorest in Chicago. It includes six of the ten communities in Chicago with the highest poverty rates (*The Chicago Sun-Times,* June 4, 1992); the percentage of abandoned or boarded up housing units in the neighborhoods where respondents live is six times higher than in the city as a whole (U.S. Census Bureau 1990).

The sampling frame for this study included all cases in the selected area randomly assigned to the experimental or control group between October 1, 1990, and March 31, 1991. The sampling frame included 123 Family First cases and 79 regular services cases. Random samples of 61% of the Family First cases and 95% of the regular services cases were drawn (75 families in each group). Five cases were excluded from the sample in the course of interviewing.[3]

Instrumentation. We developed a structured interview guide for the parent survey.[4] This instrument was adapted in part from the Parent Outcome Interview designed by Stephen Magura and Beth Silverman Moses (1986) for recipients of child welfare services. Information was elicited from parents regarding changes in the problems for which services were provided and other problems that may pose risks for children. The nine life domains that were addressed were housing, economic conditions, physical child care, discipline and emotional care of children, children's academic adjustment, children's conduct, children's symptomatic behavior, victimization of children, and parental coping. Additional information was obtained on the referral situation, out-of-home placements, and the parent's relationship with the primary social worker. Finally, Family First and regular services clients also provided their views on various aspects of the services they received. Questions covered the hallmarks of family preservation services, such as the use of time-limits, worker availability, service intensity, and the location of sessions.

Other sections of the instrument include questions about the occurrence of major life events (adapted from Cochrane & Robertson 1973), the availability and use of social support (adapted from Barrera 1981), and further service utilization. Data from these sections are presented elsewhere (Chak 1992) or are not yet analyzed.

Interviewers. In the first wave, eleven field staff conducted interviews. During the course of data collection, six of the original eight interviewers left the study and three replacement staff were hired.[5] They were residents of the region in which the sample families lived and were familiar with the geography of the area. On average, interviewers had five years of experience, and most had worked on a number of local and national studies. Nine had experience with in-person interviews, and two had only done telephone interviews.

The second wave of interviews was conducted under a subcontract with NORC (National Opinion Research Center) with their interviewers. Fifteen interviewers were trained; two quit after training, and one was added later. Of the fourteen interviewers who worked on the project, all but two had prior experience with in-person interviewing.

Two days of training preceded each wave of interviews. Training consisted of a review of procedures for finding the correct respondent, obtaining informed consent, and the questionnaire, administrative procedures, case assignments, and mock interviews.

Staff turnover was a problem, particularly in the first round of interviews. Turnover may have been related to the content of the interview (questions covered topics such as drug use, family violence, and a broad range of other problems) and to the conditions of poverty in which most of the interviews took place. Field staff reported that the interviews were more stressful and emotionally draining than other surveys on which they had worked in similar geographic areas.

Informed Consent and Data Collection Procedures. Parents were notified by mail that they had been selected for the survey. The letter provided a brief description and rationale for the survey and addressed the issues of voluntary participation and confidentiality. A monetary incentive ($15) was offered to respondents for completing the interview. Parents had an opportunity to refuse to participate by returning a postcard.

When there was more than one adult in the family, the person selected for the interview was the adult who had the most contact with DCFS or Family First during the service period. Informed consent was obtained from the parent at the time of the interview as well as detailed information to help us locate the family in the future. All interviews were conducted in-person. On average, the questionnaire took approximately one and one-half hours to administer, but interviewers spent an average of eleven hours on each case (much of this time was spent locating families, preparing for interviews, and reviewing the interviews to make sure they were complete).

We are more confident of the results of some sections of the survey than we are of others. Respondents may have been reluctant to describe the full extent of their problems, especially conditions that may have been reportable to child protective services. Our experience was, however, that most participants appeared eager to express their opinions, to describe their problems, their successes, and their frustrations. Most showed no noticeable reluctance to express their views about either the Family First program or regular services of DCFS.

Locating Families. Addresses were obtained from DCFS administrative records and from several state agencies' computer files. Multiple addresses were given to the interviewer if these were available. Initial contact with the respondent was almost always in person. If no one was home, the interviewer returned later.

Locating families in the sample was very difficult. Some families did not live at any of the addresses provided. People living at these addresses and others in the neighborhood were asked whether they knew where the family lived. In several cases, this led the interviewer to the family. If the family still could not be located, additional measures were taken to find the family. A postal search produced correct address information in a few cases. In addition, DCFS and Family First workers cooperated with requests for information, but sometimes the information they had was no more recent than the outdated information in the administrative records.

Once families were located, there were often delays in completing the interview. In some cases the correct respondent lived at another location (a few were in in-patient drug treatment or jail). In many cases interviewers found respondents but were asked to return at another time for the interview.

Parents who completed the interviews provided considerable information for further locating efforts (e.g., names, addresses, and phone numbers of friends and relatives). We expected that this group would be relatively easy to locate for the second round. However, by the time of the second interview, some of these families had moved, and their whereabouts were not known to friends and family members.

Completion of the first two rounds of interviews was slower than expected due to a combination of staff turnover and locating problems. A major factor that contributed to staff retention problems was our underestimation of the physical stamina and motivation required to track the study sample. For many families, incorrect addresses were provided, and little or no other locating information was available. Given the difficulties encountered, it is understandable that we obtained a lower response rate than we had hoped.

The extended field periods produced data that do not fit neatly into the time frames we had established for interviewing families three months and nine months following their random assignment. Instead we found that in the first round the interval was stretched to as much as fourteen months (with a median of seven months). In the second round it was extended to up to twenty months (with a median of sixteen months).

Preliminary Results

This section describes data from two rounds of interviews with parents who received Family First placement prevention or regular DCFS services.[6] Findings in twelve of the fifteen sections of the Parent Survey are reported. These sections include information regarding changes in problems in the life areas listed above. We also report parents' perceptions regarding the referral situation, their relationship with the primary social worker, and the services they received.

Sample Characteristics. Of the 144 cases in the sample, initial interviews were completed with 97 (67%), 49 in Family First and 48 in the regular services group. Interviews were not conducted with 48 clients (33%), primarily because they could not be located.[7] In the second round, eighty-one interviews were completed, a response rate of 56%, forty-two from the Family First group and thirty-nine from the regular service group.

Administrative data and information collected from workers on individual cases allowed us to examine differences between the families interviewed and those selected for the sample but not interviewed. Very few differences between respondents and nonrespondents were found in either the experimental or the control group.[8] Similarly, few differences were observed in background characteristics of Family First clients and regular service clients who were interviewed.

Nearly all respondents in this survey were female (99%) and black (95%). Primary caretakers averaged twenty-nine years of age. Only 5% of the primary caretakers were adolescents, 54% were single adults. Nearly one-third of the households (30%) were multigenerational. Major family problems identified most frequently by workers were substance abuse (49% of the families), poverty (33%), and inadequate supervision of children (25%). Prior to random assignment, very few clients had contact with the court (12%) or had experienced protective custody of a child (9%).

A comparison of families in the Family First and regular service groups who were interviewed suggests that Family First clients may have been worse off in two respects.[9] A significantly larger percentage of Family First cases was reported for severe physical injury of a child (33% compared to 8% of the regular service respondents)[10] and had been investigated more than once prior to referral (57% of Family First clients interviewed compared to 21% of the regular service cases interviewed).[11]

Parents' View of Problems and Perception of Change over Time

In the nine domains of functioning, parents were asked about the presence or absence of a number of specific problems. At the first interview (approximately seven months after the random assignment), more parents reported problems in housing than in other domains (table 3.1). In all problem domains, however, Family First parents tended to report that they had fewer problems than at the time of referral. By the second interview (approximately sixteen months after the random assignment), the number of families reporting problems increased in every domain, although significantly fewer Family First parents than regular services parents reported problems with physical child care.[12]

Parents were asked whether they perceived that any changes had occurred in the problems they reported in each domain. At the time of the first interview, parents who reported problems in specific domains were asked to compare their situation at the time of the interview with their situation at the time of referral. Significant differences were found between Family First and regular services parents (favoring the Family First group) in housing, economic conditions, physical child care, and children's conduct (see table 3.2).[13] We observed that more parents receiving regular services reported that their situation had worsened in these four domains. In the other domains, over three-quarters of Family First parents reported that their situations

TABLE 3.1

Percentage of Parents Citing At Least One Problem (by Point in Time and Group[a])

Domains	At referral Family first %	At referral Regular services %	First interview Family first %	First interview Regular services %	Second interview Family first %	Second interview Regular services %
Housing	78	79	50	71	73	74
Economic Conditions	53	58	33	47	48	47
Physical Child Care	43	37	20	21	40*	68*
Discipline and Emotional Care of Children	50	45	28	16	53	50
Children's Academic Adjustment (> = 5 years old)	45	25	14	17	38	52
Children's Conduct (> = 5 years old)	56	46	31	35	66	50
Children's Symptomatic Behavior (> = years old)	44	30	32	19	36	63
Victimization of Children	23	13	0	3	10	13
Parental Coping	80	74	30	34	65	74

[a]This table only includes the seventy-eight parents who participated in both interviews. Of these, children's academic adjustment was relevant for fifty-three families, children's conduct were relevant for fifty-eight families, children's symptomatic behavior was relevant for sixty-one families.
NOTE: Asterisks indicate significant differences between groups: * = $p < 0.05$. The difference between Family First and regular services groups were not statistically significant with one exception. Significantly fewer Family First parents reported problems with physical child care at the time of the second interview ($p = 0.01$).

had improved while fewer regular services parents reported improvement, but the differences were not significant.

In the second round of interviews the question about perceptions of change over time was different. All parents, not just those who reported problems in a particular area, were asked to compare their situation at the time of the interview with their situation three months ago. In all domains, there were more families reporting that their situation had improved than families reporting deterioration (table 3.3). None of the differences between the Family First group and the regular services group in any of the domains were significant. With the single exception of parental coping, however, a higher percentage of Family First parents reported improvement. One-half or more of the parents in both groups reported that their situation had remained the same in all domains except for their children's academic adjustment (where the majority of respondents thought things had im-

TABLE 3.2
Parents' Views of Change in Problem Areas in the First Interview (by Group[a]

| | Family first | | | | Regular services | | | |
Domains	Valid N	Better %	Same %	Worse %	Valid N	Better %	Same %	Worse %
Housing	36	75**	14**	11**	37	38**	32**	30**
Economic Conditions	26	62*	23*	15*	28	25*	46*	29*
Physical Child Care	20	80*	20*	0*	20	40*	35*	25*
Discipline and Emotional Care of Children	24	83	17	0	20	80	20	0
Children's Academic Adjustment (> = 5 years old)	14	86	14	0	8	75	13	13
Children's Conduct (> = 5 years old)	23	78*	22*	0*	14	57*	29*	14*
Children's Symptomatic Behavior (> = 4 years old)	17	71	29	0	12	67	33	0
Victimization of Children	10	100	0	0	7	71	14	14
Parental Coping	38	87	11	3	36	75	17	8

[a] In the first interview, these questions were asked of families who received services for problems in these domains.
NOTE: Asterisks indicate significant differences between groups: * = $p < 0.05$, ** = $p < 0.01$, *** = p < 0.001. Significantly more Family First parents reported doing better in the following domains: housing ($p = 0.005$), economic conditions ($p = 0.03$), physical child care (P = 0.01), and children's conduct ($p = 0.028$).

proved). The domains in which the parents more often reported that their situation had worsened were housing, economic conditions, and parental coping.

Change in Mean Proportion of Problems Reported. A second measure of change was also computed: the number of problems reported by the parent in each domain divided by the total number of problem items in that domain.[14] In the initial interview respondents were asked about the presence of problems at the time of referral as well as at the time of the interview. Hence, we have data on problems at three points in time. The proportion was computed at each point in time, and the change over time in this proportion was determined for each case. Only parents interviewed in both the first and second round of interviews were included in this analysis.

Table 3.4 summarizes the mean proportion of problems reported

TABLE 3.3
*Parents' Views of Change in Problem Areas in the Second Interview
(by Group[a])*

	Family first			Regular services		
Domains	Better %	Same %	Worse %	Better %	Same %	Worse %
Housing	38	50	12	36	46	18
Economic Conditions	33	48	19	23	51	26
Physical Child Care	48	50	2	39	59	2
Discipline and Emotional Care of Children	55	45	0	39	56	5
Children's Academic Adjustment (> = 5 years old)	71	26	3	58	29	13
Children's Conduct (> = 5 years old)	44	53	3	41	52	7
Children's Symptomatic Behavior (> = 4 years old)	31	69	0	23	71	7
Victimization of Children	33	64	2	26	64	10
Parental Coping	29	52	19	41	46	13

[a]Eighty-one families participated in the second interview. Of these, children's academic adjustment was relevant for fifty-five families, children's conduct was relevant for sixty-one families, children's symptomatic behavior was relevant for sixty-six families. These questions were asked regardless of whether families said they had problems in these domains.
NOTE: None of the differences between the Family First and regular services groups were statistically significant.

in each domain at the time of referral, the first interview, and the second interview. Repeated measures analysis of variance was used to test whether changes in the mean proportion of problems over the three time periods were significant and whether those changes were different in the two groups. For both groups and across all domains, the mean proportions of problems were higher at the time of referral, dipped at the time of the first interview, and increased again at the time of the second interview. In all domains these changes over time were significant.

Significant differences between Family First and regular services groups over time were found in the domains of physical child care, children's academic adjustment, and parental coping.[15] In these domains, the Family First group reported slightly higher mean proportions of problems at referral, the two groups' mean proportions were about the same at the time of the first interview, and at the time of the second interview, the regular services group reported a higher mean proportion of problems (see figures 3.1, 3.2, and 3.3).

TABLE 3.4

Mean Proportion of Problems Reported in Each Time Period
(by Group[a])

Domains	At referral Family First	At referral Regular services	First interview Family First	First interview Regular services	Second interview Family First	Second interview Regular services
Housing	0.26	0.27	0.12*	0.23*	0.23	0.26
Economic Conditions	0.21	0.18	0.12	0.15	0.18	0.19
Physical Child Care	0.13	0.09	0.04	0.03	0.07	0.15
Discipline and Emotional Care of Children	0.16	0.11	0.07	0.02	0.12	0.13
Children's Academic Adjustment (> = 5 years old)	0.19	0.11	0.07	0.07	0.1	0.20
Children's Conduct (> = 5 years old)	0.15	0.20	0.08	0.15	0.16	0.16
Children's Symptomatic Behavior (> = 4 years old)	0.18	0.08	0.08	0.06	0.11	0.16
Victimization of Children (> = 2 years old)	0.05	0.05	0	0.01	0.02	0.04
Parental Coping	0.36	0.25	0.1	0.1	0.24	0.32

[a]The proportion of problems is the number of problems reported by the parent in each domain divided by the total number of problem items applicable in that domain.
NOTES: This table only includes the seventy-eight parents who participated in both interviews. Of these, children's academic adjustment was relevant for fifty-two families, children's conduct was relevant for fifty-seven families, children's symptomatic behavior was relevant for sixty-one families, victimization of children was relevant for seventy families.
Asterisks indicate significant differences between groups: * = $p < 0.05$. The difference between Family First and regular services groups were not statistically significant with one exception. The mean proportion of problems reported at the first interview was significantly lower for Family First parents ($p = 0.03$).

Parents' Views of Services Provided. Parents were asked if they received any services to help them with the problems they reported in each domain. At the time of the first interview Family First parents indicated that they had received significantly more services than regular services parents in seven of the nine domains (see table 3.5). Family First parents confirmed earlier findings from other data sources[16] that the program provided significantly more services than were provided to the families receiving regular services. At the time of the second interview, there were no differences in reports of services received by Family First parents and regular services parents during the previous three months in any of the domains. At the second interview, in each domain (with the exception of victimization of children)[17] less than 20% of the parents in either group who said they had problems received services to address these problems.

Physical Child Care Problems

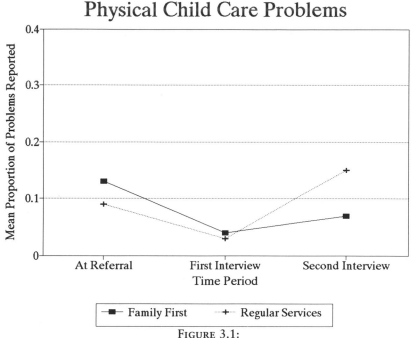

FIGURE 3.1:
*Mean Proportion of Physical Child Care Problems Reported in Each Time
Period (by group)*

Of those who reported that they still had problems in particular areas at the time of the parent survey, both Family First and regular services groups wanted more concrete services: of fifty-six respondents
who had problems with housing 79% wanted help with these problems; of thirty-five respondents who had problems with their economic
condition 86% wanted help with that. Fewer families wanted help
with child care issues: of the twenty families who reported problems
with children's physical care 55% wanted help in this area; of twenty-
five families reporting problems with discipline and the emotional care
of their children 24% wanted help in that area.

In addition to questions about services in particular problem areas,
parents were asked whether they had received any of a list of concrete
and counseling services. In the first interview, Family First parents
reported significantly more services received during program involvement than did regular services parents (an average of 2.1 concrete
services and 1.1 counseling services in the Family First group com-

Children's Academic Adjustment Problems

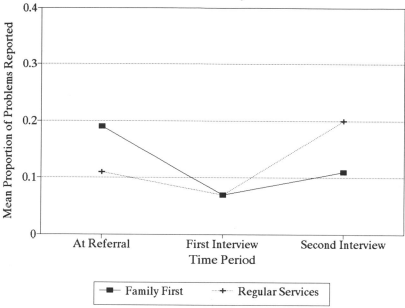

FIGURE 3.2:
*Mean Proportion of Children's Academic Adjustment Problems Reported in
Each Time Period (by Group)*

pared to an average of 0.5 concrete services and 0.5 counseling services for regular service cases).[18] Concrete services most often received by Family First parents were: furniture or other household goods (31%), food (29%), clothing (27%), transportation (25%), and financial assistance (22%). The service most often received by regular services parents was transportation (8%) and less than 5% of the families received other kinds of concrete services. Significantly more Family First parents received clothing, financial assistance, food, furniture, or other household goods, and toys or other recreational equipment. Family First and regular services parents received similar kinds of counseling services; these included drug or alcohol treatment (Family First 27%, regular services 15%), family counseling (Family First 25%, regular services 8%), and individual counseling (Family First 22%, regular services 13%). When asked to identify services they were currently receiving, less than 5% of the parents from each group reported receiving any concrete services. About 10% of the

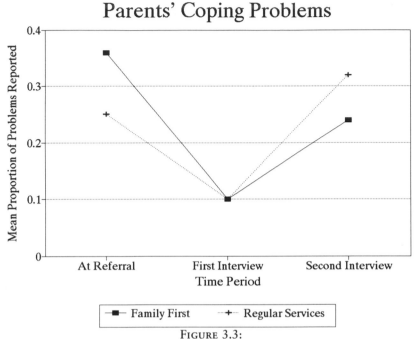

Parents' Coping Problems

FIGURE 3.3:
*Mean Proportion of Parents' Coping Problems Reported in Each Time
Period (Group)*

parents (12% of the Family First parents and 8% of those receiving
regular services) reported drug or alcohol treatment, 10% of the
regular services parents received individual counseling, and 7% of
these parents received family counseling.

Parents in the Family First group were considerably more satisfied
with services than those receiving regular services.[19] This difference
may be partially explained by the additional time workers spent with
families, which was made possible by lower caseloads,[20] the broad
array of services provided by the Family First program, and the
quality of the casework relationship.

In the second interview, parents were asked to identify services
they had received from any provider in the past three months. Family
First and regular services parents did not differ significantly in their
reports (an average of 2 concrete and 0.5 counseling services for
Family First cases and an average of 1.6 concrete and 0.7 counseling
services for regular service cases). Similar kinds of concrete and counseling services were identified most frequently by both groups. In-

TABLE 3.5
Comparison of Services Received (by Group[a])

	First interview				Second interview			
	Family First		Regular services		Family First		Regular services	
Domains	N	%	N	%	N	%	N	%
Housing	36	36*	37	11*	30	17	28	11
Economic Conditions	26	58***	28	0***	20	20	18	11
Physical Child Care	20	30	20	20	17	12	26	19
Discipline and Emotional Care of Children	24	63***	20	5***	21	14	19	11
Children's Academic Adjustment (> = 5 years old)	20	35*	10	0*	12	8	13	15
Children's Conduct (> = 5 years old)	23	30*	14	0*	22	9	13	0
Children's Symptomatic Behavior (> = 4 years old)	17	35	12	0	14	7	18	11
Victimization of Children	10	20*	7	0*	4	50	5	0
Parental Coping	38	42**	36	14**	28	7	28	14

[a]In this table, N represents the number of cases with problems in these domains, on which percentages are based. Percentages are the number of cases that received services for these problems divided by the total number of cases with problems in these domains.
NOTE: Asterisks indicate significant differences between groups: * = $p < 0.05$, ** = $p < 0.01$, *** = $p < 0.001$. Significant differences between groups were found in services received in all but two domains at the time of the first interview. There were no significant differences between groups at the time of the second interview.

cluded were financial assistance (Family First 41%, regular services 33%), food (Family First 41%, regular services 26%), medical and dental care (Family First 36%, regular services 23%), drug or alcohol treatment (Family First 19%, regular services 18%), and babysitting (Family First 19%, regular services 15%).

Parents' Views of the Relationship with the Primary Social Worker. Parents were asked a number of questions regarding the quality of their contacts with the social worker. Fifteen percent (seven) of the families receiving regular services reported that they did not have a DCFS caseworker between the time of referral and the time of the interview. They were excluded from this analysis.

During the service period, parents from both groups reported that the preponderance of the contact was with their caseworkers (82% in Family First and 85% in regular services) rather than with a homemaker or a caseworker from another agency. Although the majority

TABLE 3.6
Parents' View of the Relationship with Their Caseworkers[a]

Worker's empathy	Significance of difference between Family First and regular services (*p*-value)	
Concerned about you as a person	.128	
Understood your opinions, even if she/he didn't always agree with you	.261	
Made you feel everything wrong was your fault	.287	
Assured you that progress could be made in solving your problem	.414	
Asked how you felt about problems and the kinds of help you wanted	.006	(+)

Worker's skills or professionalism	Significance of difference between Family First and regular services (*p*-value)	
Explained what she/he was trying to do and why she/he was doing it	.259	
Helped you better understand your feeling and behavior	.003	(+)
Fought or stuck up for you with other agencies or people	.003	(+)
Well organized and competent	.080	
Helped you to talk about issues that were not easy to talk about	.013	(+)
Helped you see your good points as well as your problem areas	.006	(+)

Client's level of comfort (trust) toward worker	Significance of difference between Family First and regular services (*p*-value)	
Felt comfortable talking with your caseworker	.141	
Felt you could depend on your caseworker when you ran into a problem	.008	(+)
Caseworker was open or "straight" with you	.239	

Worker's availability	Significance of difference between Family First and regular services (*p*-value)	
Caseworker visited or kept in touch with you	.002	(+)
Caseworker was available when you needed her/him	.009	(+)

Worker's expectations	Significance of difference between Family First and regular services (p-value)	
Let you know when she/he thought you weren't working hard enough on your problems	.001	(+)

[a]Parents rated each item on a scale of "never" to "always" (scored 1 to 4). The (+) indicates significantly more Family First parents rated higher on the scale than regular services parents. Regular services parents did not rate higher on any item.

N O T E : The *p*-value is the probability that differences between groups are due to chance alone. A *p*-value of less than 0.05 is considered significant here.

of the families in both groups (76% in Family First and 66% in regular services) felt their contact with the caseworker was frequent enough,[21] Family First parents reported that they took greater initiative[22] and were more willing to contact their caseworker[23] than did parents receiving regular services.

Questions on the parents' relationships with their caseworkers were asked only in the first interview. Overall, Family First parents reported much more satisfaction with their relationships with their caseworkers than did parents receiving regular services.[24] Compared to regular services parents, Family First parents rated their relationships with their caseworker significantly more positively on a number of dimensions (the mean rating on a four-point scale was 3.4 for Family First parents compared to 2.8 for regular services parents).[25] Family First parents rated their caseworkers higher on nine of seventeen items (see table 3.6), particularly on those related to skills and professionalism, the availability of the worker, and his or her expectations.

Summary

Findings from the first round of the parent survey in Chicago suggest that at the time of referral, experimental and regular services families faced similar problems in living. Parents described severe environmental pressures and coping difficulties, which may have affected their ability to provide a minimal standard of care for their children.

Family First parents reported that they had received more services than regular service parents in seven of the nine life areas surveyed. This difference in services is corroborated by data obtained from workers. Parents in the experimental group also received a greater range of services, both directly from their caseworkers and indirectly through community providers. Their workers had much smaller caseloads and spent more time with the families they served. Not surprisingly, Family First parents expressed more satisfaction with their relationship with the primary caseworker and with the services provided.

Compared to regular service clients, more Family First parents reported improvements in housing, economic conditions, physical child care, and children's conduct at the time of the first interview. The first three problem areas represent basic survival needs that must be met before other changes are likely to occur. They are conditions that are frequently improved through the provision of concrete resources (which were in greater supply in the Family First program). Moreover, problems in these areas may be amenable to change within the brief time limits of the program. Of parents who identified problems with their children's behavior, only Family First parents indicated that they had received services for this problem area and attributed improvements to services received or to better housing.

At the time of the second interview, a median interval of sixteen months had passed after the random assignment. There were a few differences between Family First and regular services families on the problems they identified and the services received. In an analysis of the change between the time of referral and the second interview, the Family First group differed significantly from the regular services group on the mean proportion of problems in physical child care, children's academic adjustment, and parental coping. In each of these domains, Family First parents reported more problems at the time of referral, similar proportions of problems at the first interview, and fewer problems at the second interview than regular services cases. In the six other domains, the mean proportions of problems at the time of the second interview had increased to approximately the levels reported for the time of referral. It appears that in this sample families may have experienced greater problem reduction in three out of nine domains as a result of Family First services and these improvements were relatively durable. These findings should be interpreted cautiously, however. We are not convinced that respondents were able to accurately recall some details of their experience that may have taken place as much as one year ago (when reporting on their situation at the time of referral).

Preliminary findings from the parent survey component of an evaluation of intensive family preservation services have been reported. The survey is being administered within the context of an experimental design. As one of several data sources, the parent survey improves our ability to determine the impact of the family preservation program. Most important, the survey taps the client's point of view, a perspective often missing in social service research. Furthermore, it will permit us to identify discrepancies in the perceptions of parents and caseworkers and to monitor family functioning over time.

The survey has been expanded to two other areas of the state. The larger survey will add geographic and program diversity to the sample. In addition, follow-up interviews will be conducted so that the long-term effects of services can be observed. Future analyses will focus on open-ended responses in the parent survey, the life events inventory, the use of social support, and long-term effects of the Family First program on child and family well-being. Also examined will be comparisons of the parents' and caseworkers' views of problems, services, and outcomes.

Examination of changes in the clients' problems and living situation are becoming increasingly a focus of family preservation research. Programs are, after all, not only interested in keeping children out of foster care but also seek to improve conditions in the home. While improvements in family well-being are desirable, program effects in this area are likely to be modest at best. Increasing social problems that affect families' lives cannot be solved by child welfare services; they require sweeping changes in social policy. Many people believe that family preservation programs provide good things to families and should not be abandoned, even in the face of evidence that programs do not prevent placement. The basis upon which family preservation programs are sold, therefore, may soon have to change. As the major objectives shift to a greater focus on family and child well-being, research needs to uncover specific program benefits.

NOTES

The research reported here was funded by the Illinois Department of Children and Family Services. The parent survey is also supported by the U.S. Department of Health and Human Services, Administration for Children and Families. This paper is largely adapted from interim reports submitted to the state.

1. In Illinois family preservation services are provided by private agencies to cases that are referred by the public child welfare agency as a result of a protective service investigation that has uncovered child maltreatment.

2. Regular services included in-home services, foster care, and reunification services provided directly by DCFS staff or through purchase of service contracts with private agencies. Data from workers suggest that families in the regular services group received far fewer services than Family First cases. Workers reported that they spent one-tenth the number of hours in face-to-face contact with these families and that their caseloads were ten times larger than those of the Family First workers (Rzepnicki September 1991).

3. One Family First case was assigned to a service provider in a nonexperimental site, in another Family First case the primary caretaker died, two regular services cases had received Family First services in the past (thus, they should not have been considered for inclusion in the experiment), and one regular service case was ordered into the Family First program by the court.

4. Copies of the parent survey instrument are available from the authors.

5. The interviewing staff included ten females and one male ranging in age from twenty-nine to fifty-four.

6. Most of the findings in this section were originally reported in Chak 1992.

7. Many (forty) had moved from the addresses provided to us by DCFS or the Family First provider. Two parents seemed to be avoiding our interviewers. Six refused to participate.

8. For this analysis, data provided by workers on family characteristics, major problems, prior court contact, and services were available on seventy-six of the ninety-seven families interviewed in the first round and on thirty-four of the forty-eight families who were not interviewed. Administrative data on founded reports of abuse and neglect and out-of-home placements were also available on ninety-four of the families interviewed and on all nonrespondent families. On nearly every measure, respondents and nonrespondents were found to be similar. In the regular service group, workers reported poverty as a major problem significantly less often for respondents than for nonrespondents (29% versus 55%, $p = 0.044$).

9. We would expect some differences due to chance even when groups are formed by random assignment.

10. $p = 0.003$.

11. $p < 0.001$.

12. $p = 0.012$.

13. $Tau\text{-}b = 0.0345, p < 0.001$
$Tau\text{-}b = 0.328, p = 0.002$
$Tau\text{-}b = 0.374, p = 0.003$
$Tau\text{-}b = 0.287, p = 0.028$.

14. Because the number of items varied across domains, proportions are more meaningful and are comparable across domains.

15. Multivariate tests of interaction between experimental group and time:
$F = 3.59, d.f. = 2,75, p = 0.033$
$F = 3.42, d.f. = 2,44, p = 0.042$
$F = 3.46, d.f. = 2,75, p = 0.037$.

16. Analysis of data obtained from workers reported in Rzepnicki (September 1991), an update of findings originally reported in Schuerman, Littell, and Johnson, (June 1991).

17. This domain includes violent and criminal behaviors that victimize children. Parents reported problems in this domain least often and also reported the lowest mean proportion of problems. Because the consequences of problems in this domain are likely to involve injury to the child or lead to court involvement, families may be more likely to receive services for them.

18. Values are: $t = 5.75, d.f. = 95, p < 0.001$ $t = 4.18, d.f. = 95, p < 0.001$.

19. $p < 0.001$.

20. Family First workers reported an average caseload of five, whereas DCFS workers reported an average of fifty-two families (Rzepnicki September 1991).

21. Data from the workers indicated that Family First workers had almost ten times more hours of contact with the families than regular services workers (Rzepnicki September 1991).

22. $p < 0.001$.

23. $p = 0.04$.

24. $p = 0.008$.

25. Values are: $t = 3.56, d.f. = 87, p = 0.001$.

REFERENCES

AuClaire, P. & Schwartz, I. M. (1986). *An evaluation of intensive home-based services as an alternative to placement for adolescents and their families*. Minneapolis: University of Minnesota, Hubert Humphrey School of Public Affairs.

Barrera, M., Jr. (1981). Arizona social support interview schedule. In B. H. Gottlieb (Ed.), *Social networks and social support*. Beverly Hills, CA: Sage Publications.

Chak, A. (1992, June). Recent findings from the parent survey. In J. R. Schuerman, T. L. Rzepnicki, & J. H. Littell, *An interim report from the evaluation of the Illinois Family First Placement Prevention Program*, Chicago: Chapin Hall Center for Children at the University of Chicago.

Cochrane, R. & Robertson, A. (1973). The life events inventory: A measure of the relative severity of psycho-social stressors. *Journal of Psychosomatic Research, 17,* 135–39.

The Chicago Sun-Times (June 4, 1992). Poverty deepens in city, pp. 1 and 12.

Feldman, L. H. (1991). Evaluating the impact of family preservation services in New Jersey. In K. Wells & D. E. Biegel (Eds.), *Family preservation services: Research and evaluation* (pp. 47–71). Newbury Park, CA: Sage Publications.

Fraser, M. W., Pecora, P. J., & Haapala, D. A. (1991). *Families in crisis: The impact of intensive family preservation services.* Hawthorne, NY: Aldine de Gruyter.

Littell, J. H. (1991, September) Preliminary findings regarding program outcomes. In J. R. Schuerman, T. L. Rzepnicki, & J. H. Littell (Eds.), *An interim report from the evaluation of the Illinois Family First Placement Prevention Program,* Chicago: Chapin Hall Center for Children at the University of Chicago.

Littell, J. H. & Fong, E. (1992, June). Recent findings on selected program outcomes. In J. R. Schuerman, T. L. Rzepnicki, & J. H. Littell (Eds.), *An interim report from the evaluation of the Illinois Family First Placement Prevention Program,* Chicago: Chapin Hall Center for Children at the University of Chicago.

Littell, J. H., Schuerman, J. R., Rzepnicki, T. L., & Johnson, P. (1992, June). Evaluation activities. In J. R. Schuerman, T. L. Rzepnicki, & J. H. Littell (Eds.), *An interim report from the evaluation of the Illinois Family First Placement Prevention Program,* Chicago: Chapin Hall Center for Children at the University of Chicago.

Magura S. & Moses, B. S. (1986). The parent outcome interview. In S. Magura & B. S. Moses, *Outcome measures for child welfare services.* Washington, D.C.: Child Welfare League of America.

Rzepnicki, T. L. (1991, June). Changes in Family First services over time. In J. R. Schuerman, T. L. Rzepnicki, & J. H. Littell (Eds.), *An interim report from the evaluation of the Illinois Family First Placement Prevention Program,* Chicago: Chapin Hall Center for Children at the University of Chicago.

Rzepnicki, T. L. (1991, September). Services received by Family First and regular services families. In J. R. Schuerman, T. L. Rzepnicki, & J. H. Littell (Eds.),,, *An interim report from the evaluation of the Illinois Family First Placement Prevention Program,* Chicago: Chapin Hall Center for Children at the University of Chicago.

Schuerman, J. R., Littell, J. H., & Johnson, P. (1991, June) Services received by Family First and regular services families. In J. R. Schuerman, T. L. Rzepnicki, & J. H. Littell (Eds.), *An interim report from the evaluation of the Illinois Family First Placement Prevention Program,* Chicago: Chapin Hall Center for Children at the University of Chicago.

U.S. Census Bureau (1990). Summary Tape File STF1A. Indices compiled by Gunnar Almgren, University of Washington.

Yuan, Y. Y., McDonald, W. R., Wheeler, C. E., Struckman-Johnson, D., & Rivest, M. (1990). *Evaluation of AB 1562 in-home care demonstration projects: Volumes I and II.* Sacramento, CA: Walter MacDonald and Associates.

FOUR

Family-based Services for Families and Children at Risk of Out-of-home Placement

Kristine E. Nelson

There is a growing recognition of the need for services to preserve families and provide a safe alternative to placement. The Children's Bureau of the Department of Health and Human Services took an early lead in funding program development, research, and resources for the expansion of family-based services (Maybanks & Bryce 1978; Fraser, Pecora, & Haapala 1991; Nelson & Landsman 1992). The Adoption Assistance and Child Welfare Act of 1980 (Public Law 96–272) built on innovative family-based and family preservation programs begun in the early 1970s and accelerated the spread of family-based services among both public and private providers by requiring "reasonable efforts" to prevent out-of-home placement.

In the 1980s other organizations began to advocate for and disseminate family preservation services. The Edna McConnell Clark Foundation has been instrumental in promoting one model, the crisis intervention approach of the Homebuilders program in Washington State, also called Intensive Family Preservation Services (Kinney, Haapala, & Booth 1991). By developing standards of practice for different levels of family-based intervention, the Child Welfare League of America has also helped to establish prevention and reunification as necessary parts of the service continuum (Child Welfare League of America 1989).

Three Models of Family Preservation Services

Although intensive family preservation services based on the Home-builders model have been the most widely disseminated, three distinct practice models were identified in a comparative analysis of place-ment prevention programs operating in the mid-1980s (Nelson, Landsman, & Deutelbaum 1990). The crisis intervention model, typi-fied by Homebuilders, employs very brief interventions (thirty to forty-five days) with low caseloads (two to four), intensive family contact (at least eight to ten hours a week), and an emphasis on skill building and concrete services. Based on social learning theory, the interventions aim to stabilize the family and teach new coping skills (Kinney et al. 1991).

The home-based model, which was developed in the 1970s in the Midwest, provides comprehensive services to alter both dysfunctional interactions within the family and the family's relationships within the community. Services last longer (four to six months or more) and caseloads are higher (six to ten) than in the crisis intervention model (Nelson et al. 1990). Grounded in family systems theory, the home-based model emphasizes assessment and intervention with the family as a whole, but interventions from a variety of treatment paradigms as well as concrete services are also provided (Leverington & Wulff 1988).

The family treatment model is similar in theoretical orientation and interventions to the home-based model, but concrete services are usually coordinated by a case manager outside the program. In this model, families can be seen in the office as well as in their homes depending on the program structure, the needs of the family, and the preference of the worker (Hartley, Showell, & White 1989). Services are on average briefer than in the home-based model, and when families are seen in the office, caseloads are higher since workers do not spend time traveling to families' homes (Nelson et al. 1990). The research reported in this essay included home-based and family treatment programs. A companion study of intensive family preserva-tion services, which was also funded by the Children's Bureau, is available elsewhere (Fraser et al. 1991).

The Family Systems Approach

All the programs described and analyzed in this study employ a family systems approach. Family systems theory places individual problems within the context of the family and family problems within the context of the larger community and social system (Carter & McGoldrick 1980; Lloyd & Bryce 1984; Napier & Whitacker 1978). Assessment aims at understanding the family as an entity composed of interacting parts in terms of its history, current behavior, and interactions with larger systems. Interventions based on a systemic assessment may focus on individuals, dyads, the whole family, or the social environment. Depending on the level of intervention, a variety of theories may inform practice, from psychoanalytic and social learning theories at the individual level to conflict and consensus theories at the community level (Hartman & Laird 1983; Henggeler & Borduin 1990).

Some interventions that have been developed by family therapists and that are identified with family systems therapy include genograms, reframing, unbalancing, and various interventions based on communications theory (Hartman 1978; McGoldrick & Gerson 1985; Minuchin 1974; Minuchin & Fishman 1981; Satir 1982). These interventions focus primarily on the relationships between people rather than on the behavior or feelings of individuals (Janzen & Harris 1986; Minuchin 1985). Thus, they avoid attributing blame or placing the burden of change on one individual, which is useful in getting the cooperation of all family members in the change effort. However, therapists also employ interventions such as active listening (Rogerian), role modeling (learning theory), and homework (cognitive theory) based on other constructs useful in understanding human behavior and change (Ellis 1973; Gambrill 1977; Rogers 1942).

Recent research has provided some support for the use of family systems theory in assessing and planning interventions in cases of child maltreatment. Dysfunctional family relationships seem to play a larger part in sexual abuse than in neglect, which is more often associated with individual problems in functioning or with environmentally induced stress (Nelson & Landsman 1992). In particular, problematic relationships between spouses and between mothers and daughters who have been victimized have been implicated in the etiology of sexual abuse (Glaser & Frosh 1988:42–47; Gomes-Schwartz, Horowitz, & Cardarelli 1990:115–27, 143–45; Sirles & Lofberg 1990). Indeed, the mother's role is pivotal in determining the outcome and effects of sexual abuse. If she sides with the perpetrator, the child is more likely to be placed and to suffer psychological damage (Everson, Hunter, Runyan, Edelsohn, & Coulter 1989;

Hunter, Coulter, Runyan, & Everson 1990; Pellegrin & Wagner 1990).

Due to an influx of research funds in the mid 1970s, more attention has been given to the treatment of sexual abuse than to that of physical abuse or neglect (Kaufman & Rudy 1991). In spite of the importance of dyadic relationships in the etiology and treatment of sexual abuse, most research has been focused on treating victims and survivors of sexual abuse in isolation from the rest of their family. There is considerable controversy, however, about when and if specific family members should be included in conjoint treatment (Coleman & Collins 1990).

Although there has been less research on the treatment of physical abuse, what research there is focuses on relationship issues including marital and parent-child conflicts. In particular, multisystemic therapy has been found to be more effective in improving parenting than parent education groups (Brunk, Henggeler, & Whelan 1987). In one of the few studies of family preservation services that analyzed the different types of child maltreatment separately, researchers in Oregon found the family treatment model to be most successful with physical abuse. Specifically, multiple impact therapy was rated as very effective in physical abuse cases (Hartley et al. 1989).

Although Daro (1988) found family interventions to be effective with neglecting families, little research has been done on the treatment of neglect. As with physical abuse, with neglecting families multisystemic therapy has been found to be more effective than parent education alone (Brunk, Henggeler, & Whelan 1987). Studies of family preservation services that have analyzed subtypes of maltreatment, however, have found placement rates to be higher in neglect cases than in physical or sexual abuse cases (Berry 1990; Nelson & Landsman 1992; Yuan & Struckman-Johnson 1991).

The lack of an adequate definition of child maltreatment is one of the persistent problems hindering the development of research, policy, and practice in the field of child welfare (Giovannoni 1989). Many studies either fail to specify the population under consideration or combine two or more of the subtypes of child maltreatment. Since there is growing evidence that physical abuse, sexual abuse, and neglect are distinct in etiology and treatment (Daro 1988:58), they will be examined separately in this study.

In addition to discussing the services provided to maltreating families at risk of placement, differences between families referred for physical abuse, sexual abuse, and neglect will be explored using Belsky's (1981) ecological model of child maltreatment as a base. The contribution of individual level, family level, and service variables to an outcome of placement or nonplacement will be assessed using both bivariate and multivariate methods. Not all of the causal factors proposed by Belsky will be considered in the following review, since for the most part historical and contextual data were not available in the case records studied. The information available for analysis consists primarily of the characteristics of the caregiver and family, the services provided, and short-term outcomes.

Method

The data in this paper are from nine of eleven family-based child welfare programs included in a two-year, exploratory study undertaken by the National Resource Center on family-based services in conjunction with the Regional Research Institute for Human Services at Portland State University in 1985 (Nelson, Emlen, Landsman, & Hutchinson 1988). The purpose of the study, which was funded by the Children's Bureau of the Department of Health and Human Services, was to gather descriptive information and analyze factors contributing to success or failure in preventing placement.

Although the family-based programs in the study provided a broad array of services and used different service delivery models, they had several characteristics in common. First, they were committed to maintaining children in their own homes whenever possible. Second, they focused on the whole family rather than on the "problem child." Third, services were time-limited and based on goal-oriented treatment plans established with the active participation of the families. Finally, the programs provided comprehensive services delivered either directly by the family-based worker or in coordination with other providers.

The original study included family-based preplacement programs in six states: Colorado, Iowa, Minnesota, Ohio, Oregon, and Pennsylvania. The programs were well established and were selected to represent a variety of treatment populations and organizational and community contexts. With further analysis, it was found that two of the programs were not typical of most family-based placement prevention programs, and therefore they were excluded from the sample. The remaining programs are described in detailed case studies in Nelson

TABLE 4.1
Type of Maltreatment by Site

Programs	Neglect $n = 67$	Physical abuse $n = 91$	Sexual abuse $n = 50$	Total $n = 208$
Franklin County Children Services, OH	28.4	17.6	6.0	18.3
SCAN, Philadelphia, PA	32.8	11.0	6.0	16.8
Iowa Department of Human Services	3.0	15.4	18.0	12.0
Dakota County Human Services, MN	4.5	15.4	8.0	10.1
Iowa Children & Family Services	10.4	11.0	6.0	9.6
Intensive Family Services Multnomah County, OR	4.5	5.5	24.0	9.6
Oregon Children's Services Division	7.5	4.4	20.0	9.1
Boulder County Social Services, CO	4.5	8.8	8.0	7.2
Lutheran Social Services, MN	4.5	11.0	4.0	7.2

N O T E : Unweighted; *n*'s vary in subsequent tables due to weighting and missing data. Percentages may not total 100 due to rounding.

and Landsman (1992). Brief descriptions are provided below to establish the broad programmatic outlines within which study findings should be interpreted.

Sample

For the maltreatment sample, cases were classified according to the reason for which they were referred. If more than one type of maltreatment was reported, the most important (the first one listed) was used to classify the case. Using this method, sixty-nine neglect, ninety-one physical abuse, and fifty sexual abuse cases were identified. Although cases were classified in only one category of maltreatment, there was some overlap. According to referral sources, in 9.1% of the 210 maltreatment cases both physical abuse and neglect had recently occurred; in 4.1% of the cases physical abuse coincided with sexual abuse, and in 2.3% there was both neglect and sexual abuse.

Most of the *neglect* cases came from three agencies, all following a home-based model (see table 4.1). Over a third were from the Supportive Child/Adult Network (SCAN), a private agency that contracts with the Philadelphia County Children and Youth Agency to provide child protective and placement prevention services to an inner-city catchment area. Another quarter of the neglect cases were from Franklin County Children Services, a public child welfare agency serving Columbus, Ohio. A third agency that provided services to more than 10% of the neglect cases in the study was Iowa Children and Family Services, a private agency serving at-risk families in rural southeastern Iowa (ICFS).

Almost half of the *sexual abuse* cases came from the Children's Services Division of the Oregon Department of Human Services. Within Oregon, the majority of sexual abuse cases were seen in Multnomah County Intensive Family Services (IFS), a private agency offering in-home services in the Portland area. The others were from five publicly administered IFS programs that offer both in-office and in-home services. A third agency contributing more than 10% of the sexual abuse cases was an office-based program in the Ottumwa district office of the Iowa Department of Human Services (Iowa DHS).

The *physical abuse* cases were spread across a wider range of agencies. Of the programs with the most cases, the top three were in public agencies, and four out of five of them were home-based. The most physical abuse cases came from Franklin County Children Services, described above. Iowa DHS and the Dakota County Human Services Department, Minnesota, a county-administered social service agency that also served a large proportion of status offenders, had the second highest number of physical abuse cases. Iowa Children and Family Services and SCAN both contributed 11% of the physical abuse cases as well as having large numbers of neglect cases. Overall, Franklin County (thirty-eight) and SCAN (thirty-five) had the most child maltreatment cases and Lutheran Social Services (fifteen), a private agency in rural western Minnesota, had the fewest.

Procedures

Data were collected in three phases: through on-site interviews with agency administrators and family-based program administrators, supervisors, and workers; through a survey of past and current family-based service workers who carried cases selected for the sample; and through a review by case readers (mostly graduate and undergraduate social work students) of fifty closed case records in each agency. To be eligible for the sample, the primary child(ren) of concern could not have been continuously out of the home for more than thirty days preceding or following referral to the family-based program. Also excluded were cases that were seen for assessment only. Most cases were opened between 1982 and 1985.

Data in this analysis are primarily from the case record review. The on-site case readers had two days of training in data collection from National Resource Center (NRC) or Regional Research Institute staff and were supervised by agency-based project liaisons. Cases were selected by NRC staff using a table of random numbers from deidentified lists of preplacement prevention cases seen during the study period; twenty-five cases that ended in placement and twenty-five where the family remained intact were selected at each site.[1] All the eligible placement and/or nonplacement cases were used in some agencies serving small numbers of families.[2] Case coding took place in the agency and averaged one and a half hours per case. Because the data collected included information about reasons for closure, type of and reason for placement, and restrictiveness of placement, coders were not blind to the outcome of the case. For further detail on methodology and copies of research instruments, please refer to Nelson et al. (1988), chapter 2 and appendices.

Reliability analyses were conducted on two levels: interrater reliability of key variables tested on a sample of twenty cases, two from each agency in which a second coder was available, and interitem reliability of additive scales tested using Cronbach's *alpha*. Three-quarters of the tested variables demonstrated levels of reliability acceptable for outcome research in child welfare (Magura & Moses 1986:185, 187). Low reliability reduces the size of relationships and the significance of the variables affected and, therefore, leads to underestimating rather than overestimating effects (Magura & Moses 1986:192–3). Since they were unlikely to produce falsely positive results, variables with low reliability were not excluded from the analyses (see Nelson & Landsman 1992, Appendix B for reliability statistics).

Results

The Families

In many ways the problems of child neglect, physical abuse, and sexual abuse reflect different stages and phases during the family life cycle, compounded by disadvantages relating to race and social class

TABLE 4.2
Family Characteristics by Type of Maltreatment

Characteristics		Neglect $n = 67$	Physical abuse $n = 101$	Sexual abuse $n = 52$	Total $n = 219$
Below poverty level[a]	%	89.4	60.7	69.9	72.6**
Second adult in household employed[b]	%	20.6	64.2	47.1	48.0**
Primary caregiver					
Age	m	27.9	32.2	35.4	31.6**
	sd	8.1	7.4	6.4	7.9
Non-white	%	35.6	16.6	9.0	20.4**
Married	%	21.2	55.4	33.5	39.7**
Employed	%	13.8	43.6	35.5	32.6**
Low functioning		23.0	2.3	2.8	8.7**
Parental disposition subscale[c]	m	69.5	73.7	75.7	72.9*
	sd	13.7	13.8	11.5	13.4

[a]$n = 161$.
[b]$n = 147$.
[c]Child Well-Being Scales (Magura & Moses, 1986).
*$p < .05$. **$p < .001$.

(Kreppner & Lerner 1989). Although the different kinds of child maltreatment, particularly physical abuse and neglect, are often treated as a single entity, the only family characteristic consistent across all the maltreatment groups was the average size of the family—four people, including 2.6 children. Beyond this, a different demographic pattern prevailed for each type of maltreatment, in part due to differences among study sites.

Families referred for child *neglect* were at the earliest stage of the family life cycle, with younger children, averaging 5.3 years (*s.d.* = 4.7), and younger mothers. In terms of family characteristics this was the most distinctive group, since it included significantly more poor families, more nonwhite families, more unemployed adults, and lower-functioning caregivers than the other two groups (see table 4.2). Neglecting families also had the largest number of children at risk of placement (table 4.3).[3] Their multiple problems included social isolation, inadequate housing, health or mental health problems, and a lack of stable parenting (table 4.4).

Physical abuse cases included families in different circumstances. Primary caregivers were older, more often white, and more often married to an employed spouse. More than a quarter of the families were remarried with at least one stepchild in the household. The

TABLE 4.3
Child Characteristics by Type of Maltreatment

Characteristics		Neglect $n = 67$	Physical abuse $n = 101$	Sexual abuse $n = 52$	Total $n = 219$
Number at risk of imminent placement[a]	m	1.2	.9	.6	.9*
	sd	1.4	1.0	.7	1.1
Highest risk child					
Female	%	56.2	53.6	64.8	57.1
Age[b]	m	6.1	9.7	12.6	9.3**
	sd	5.4	4.4	4.1	5.2
Prior placement	%	17.3	17.6	34.5	21.6*
At least one stepchild[c]	%	4.8	28.6	9.0	16.4**

[a]Ranges: 0–5, 0–5, 0–3, 0–5.
[b]$n = 192$.
[c]Ranges: 0–17, 0–17, 0–19, 0–19.
* $p < .05$. ** $p < .001$.

TABLE 4.4
Adult Problems by Type of Maltreatment

Problems		Neglect $n = 67$	Physical abuse $n = 101$	Sexual abuse $n = 52$	Total $n = 219$
Marital	%	43.8	62.7	58.0	55.9*
Health/mental health	%	54.4	39.6	25.2	40.7**
Discontinuity in caregivers[a]	%	40.7	25.6	29.6	31.4
Social isolation	%	36.3	15.1	27.6	24.5**
Substance abuse	%	32.5	21.8	19.1	24.4
Housing	%	40.0	8.8	11.9	19.0***
Total number[b]	m	6.2	4.6	4.4	5.0***
	sd	2.7	3.2	2.8	3.0

[a]$n = 196$.
[b]Range: 0–14, 0–13, 0–11, 0–14.
* $p < .05$.
** $p < .01$.
*** $p < .001$.

children were also older (average age 7.8, *s.d.* = 4.3), and usually only one was at imminent risk of placement. Nearly two thirds of the physically abusing families presented marital problems and nearly 40% contained adults with health or mental health problems.

Sexual abuse cases represented still another family constellation with the oldest caregivers and children (*m* = 11.3 years, *s.d.* = 4.3).

Nearly a third had experienced a divorce within the previous year, and a third of the children at highest risk had been in placement before. Children in sexual abuse cases were the least likely to be at imminent risk of placement, primarily because the perpetrator was not in the home. With the exception of marital problems, most of the issues presented by these families had to do with the children: parent-child conflict, peer relationships, or juvenile offenses (table 4.5).

Despite these differences, some problems were reported consistently by families in the three groups. For nearly 80%, family-child relationships were problematic, and almost half contained children with behavior problems. Although reported more frequently in neglecting families, around a third of *all* maltreating families experienced discontinuities in parenting in the year before receiving services, and more than a third of the families had children with health or mental health problems. In a quarter of the families substance abuse was identified as a problem.

Services and Outcomes

Case objectives and services tended to reflect the families' differing needs (see tables 4.6 and 4.7). With the main objective of changing the behavior of the adults in the family, *neglect* cases received the most intensive and comprehensive services, including parent education, paraprofessional services, and transportation, as well as family and individual counseling. Nearly three quarters of the neglecting

TABLE 4.5
Child Problems by Type of Maltreatment

Problems	Neglect $n = 67$	Physical abuse $n = 101$	Sexual abuse $n = 52$	Total $n = 219$
Poor family relationships	72.4	82.4	82.1	79.7
Child behavior	39.9	50.8	56.8	48.9
Parent-child conflict	25.0	50.7	62.8	45.8**
Peer/school	37.2	32.7	53.5	39.0*
Health/mental health	46.5	33.6	35.2	37.9
Status offense or delinquency	10.0	9.7	47.9	18.8**

NOTE: Percentages.
*$p < .05$.
**$p < .001$.

TABLE 4.6
Services by Type of Maltreatment

Services	Neglect n = 67	Physical abuse n = 101	Sexual abuse n = 52	Total n = 219
Case Objectives				
Use counseling	44.0	22.5	60.7	38.1***
Adult behavior	45.6	31.9	9.7	30.8***
Marital relations	21.0	37.7	22.0	28.9*
Services				
Family counseling	83.7	89.7	96.7	89.5
Individual counseling	73.4	68.7	55.9	67.1
Information/ referral	69.6	52.5	50.0	57.1*
Protective services	71.7	54.0	43.2	56.8**
AFDC	72.0	37.9	39.1	48.6***
Parent education	54.1	35.3	25.7	38.8**
Marital counseling	16.8	39.6	40.1	32.8**
Role modeling	42.3	27.7	19.6	30.2*
Accompanied to appointment	38.1	18.9	36.5	28.9**
Paraprofessional	44.7	22.6	13.5	27.1***
Mental health	32.0	21.1	29.1	26.3
Self help/volunteer	20.0	21.0	41.1	25.5*
Transportation	37.9	21.8	14.9	25.1**
Money management	40.1	15.3	4.8	20.4***

NOTE: Percentages.
*$p < .05$.
**$p < .01$.
***$p < .001$.

families received AFDC, were referred to other services, and were simultaneously receiving child protective services. Role modeling techniques were used to help change the adults' behavior. While all the maltreatment cases were open for an average of about six months, neglect cases received substantially more services and more different kinds of services than physical or sexual abuse cases during this time.

In *physical abuse* cases both objectives and services were directed more toward marital problems although most families also received family and individual counseling, child protective services, and information and referral services. *Sexual abuse* cases were oriented toward helping the families use other counseling services. They were also distinctive in receiving more office-based and volunteer services and in participating more in self-help groups and activities. Sexual abuse cases were the least likely to receive paraprofessional and child protective services concurrently with family-based services.

In light of the differences in family characteristics and services, the different types of cases were surprisingly similar in outcome. Only 22.1% of the families were reported for child maltreatment while their cases were still open, substantially fewer than the 30–47% reported in other treatment programs (Daro and Cohn 1988). More than 50% improved in behavior, family relations, emotional climate, perception of their problems, and use of services as measured by the Family Systems Change Scale.[4] Only neglect cases improved significantly in material resources—X^2 (2, $n = 159$) = 17.31, $p < .001$— a particularly important finding since these families were the most economically disadvantaged.

Placement rates did not differ significantly among the three types of maltreatment—X^2 (2, n = 219) = 3.67, $p = .16$—even though 24.2% of the neglect cases terminated in placement, a rate nearly 10% higher than that for physical (13.1%) or sexual (15.0%) abuse.

TABLE 4.7
Intensity of Service by Type of Maltreatment

Intensity		Neglect $n = 67$	Physical abuse $n = 101$	Sexual abuse $n = 52$	Total $n = 219$
Total number of services[a]	m	15.8	11.4	10.3	12.5***
	sd	8.9	7.6	6.6	8.1
Home visits in first month[b]	m	5.2	4.0	2.6	4.1**
	sd	4.8	4.0	3.2	4.2
Office visits in first month[c]	m	.3	.7	1.2	.7***
	sd	.8	1.3	1.7	1.3
Total contacts in first three months[d]	m	18.1	14.3	11.5	14.8*
	sd	13.4	10.8	7.9	11.3
Length of service (months)[e]	m	7.6	6.1	6.5	6.6
	sd	6.1	4.9	3.5	5.0

[a]Range: 1–40, 0–45, 1–28, 0–45.
[b]Range: 0–20, 0–21, 0–12, 0–21.
[c]Range: 0–4, 0–5, 0–10, 0–10.
[d]Range: 3–67, 1–56, 1–42, 1–67.
[e]n = 190; Range: 35–893, 0–740, 0–463, 0–893.
*$p < .05$.
**$p < .01$.
***$p < .001$.

TABLE 4.8
Participation by Type of Maltreatment

Services	Neglect $n = 67$	Physical abuse $n = 101$	Sexual abuse $n = 52$	Total $n = 219$
Primary caregiver	60.3	76.5	87.4	74.1*
Second adult[a]	33.3	51.9	22.6	39.9*
Target child[b]	45.3	56.8	58.7	53.9

NOTE: Percentages.
[a] $n = 150$.
[b] $n = 203$.
*$p < .01$.

The only significant difference in outcome was the programs' differential success in engaging caregivers in service. Less than two-thirds of the neglecting caregivers attended most or all the scheduled sessions compared to more than three quarters of the caregivers in physical and sexual abuse cases (table 4.8).

Factors Related to Placement

Several characteristics associated with placement were found across all three maltreatment types (table 4.9).[5] Lack of positive change in family functioning, having at least one child at risk of imminent placement, lower functioning of caregivers, and, for the children, poor family relationships were consistently related to higher placement rates. Lack of cooperation and less participation in treatment by the primary caregiver and having at least one child with a prior placement foreshadowed an outcome of placement in two of the three types of maltreatment. In neglect cases, the failure to involve the child at highest risk in most sessions was also related to placement.

In order to determine the most important factors in avoiding placement in child abuse and neglect cases, a series of multivariate discriminant analyses were performed (see Nelson & Landsman 1992, Appendix E for methodology). Seven analyses covering different domains—family demographics and history, characteristics of second adults, resource problems, adult problems, child problems, interventions, and involvement in treatment—were performed separately for physical abuse, sexual abuse, and neglect cases. Overall, differences between placement and nonplacement cases were explained more effectively by demographics and history than by resource problems.

Family characteristics were the best predictors, accurately identifying 30% of the placement cases. Lack of material resources only predicted 3% of the placements.

Overall, the separate discriminant analyses revealed strong predictors in each domain for *neglect* cases: demographics, involvement in services, child problems, resource problems, adult problems, and interventions. Only variables concerning a second adult had little predictive value, since so few families contained a second adult. A single discriminant model that combined significant predictors of placement in this study with those found in other studies identified the primary caregiver's attendance at most sessions and stability of

TABLE 4.9

Factors Related to Placement by Type of Maltreatment

		Neglect $n = 38$	Physical abuse $n = 36$	Sexual abuse $n = 24$
Number of areas of				
Positive change[a]	m	1.9***	2.4*	1.6***
	sd	2.2	2.9	2.2
Negative change[b]	m	1.2***	.7	1.5**
	sd	1.4	1.2	1.8
Child Well-Being Scales				
Parental disposition	m	59.4***	65.7**	67.0**
	sd	12.9	13.4	12.9
Caregiver's				
compliance[c]	m	60.6**	66.8[t]	65.3***
	sd	14.0	17.5	13.6
Child's family				
relations	m	57.3***	61.7*	57.9*
	sd	23.7	19.6	22.1
Prior placement of				
highest-risk child	%	41.6*	37.4*	47.7
Number of children				
at high risk[d]	m	1.9**	1.4*	1.2***
	sd	1.3	1.0	.8
Attended most sessions				
Primary caregiver	%	23.0***	54.3*	71.4
Highest risk child	%	16.7**	44.9	40.4

NOTE: Significance tested with two-tail t-tests and chi-square. Scores for placement families only.
[a] Range: 0–8, 0–10, 0–8.
[b] Range: 0–4, 0–4, 0–6.
[c] Motivation, recognition, and cooperation subscales.
[d] Range: 0–4, 0–5, 0–3.
[t] $p < .10$.
* $p < .05$.
** $p < .01$.
*** $p < .001$.

caregiving as the factors most predictive of placement prevention. Paraprofessional services also contributed to placement prevention. The most important predictors of placement were the number of children at risk of imminent placement, prior placements, and the total number of problems in the family. Together the eight variables in the model correctly classified 94.7% of the nonplacement cases and 73.4% of the placement cases (see Nelson & Landsman 1992, Table E-I).

Placement in *physical abuse* cases was not dominated by any single domain. However, this may be the result of combining cases involving the abuse of adolescents with those concerning the abuse of younger children. Since there were too few cases to enable separation of these two groups, predictors were combined in a single discriminant analysis.[6] The resulting statistical model revealed that the primary caregiver's score on the Parental Disposition Subscale of the Child Well-Being Scales was the most important indicator of whether a child would be placed or not. This scale measured the caregiver's capacity for child care; acceptance, approval, and expectations of the children; recognition of problems, motivation, and cooperation; and family relationships.[7] Placement prevention in physical abuse cases was also associated with several service characteristics, including marital counseling, caregiver's participation in most treatment sessions, and role modeling. Continued receipt of child protective services and additional reports of abuse foreshadowed placement. Several other variables, including adult substance abuse, made less important contributions to predicting placement. Together the eleven variables in the model correctly classified 96.6% of the nonplacement cases but only 48.1% of the placement cases (Nelson & Landsman 1992, Table E-II).

In terms of the different domains, the presence of a second adult in *sexual abuse* cases was also important—in predicting an outcome of placement. Although the primary caregivers in sexual abuse cases were the most motivated and compliant at the outset of services, assisting them to protect their children and to obtain further counseling was most important for placement prevention. Simply referring the families to other services was not an effective preventive measure. Employed mothers with an employed spouse who was involved in treatment were the most likely to have a child placed. The specific problems presented by the adults or the children had little impact on the outcome.

In combining these characteristics into a single predictive model for sexual abuse cases, having a child at imminent risk of placement, a noncompliant primary caregiver, a second adult at most or all of the sessions, and an employed primary caregiver contributed almost equally to an outcome of placement. Placement prevention, on the other hand, was associated with a case objective of increasing the family's use of outside counseling services. All together the eleven characteristics included in the sexual abuse model correctly classified all the nonplacement cases and 75.3% of the placement cases (Nelson & Landsman 1992, Table E-III).

Discussion

These findings confirm the importance of poverty, large families, and multiple problems in child neglect. In one sense, placement in neglect cases is overdetermined (Daro 1988:34), with significant differences between placement and nonplacement cases in all areas except those relating to a second adult in the family. While preexisting characteristics, such as instability in caregiving in the year before referral, previous placements, the number of children facing imminent placement, and multiple problems, all contribute to placement, successfully engaging the caregiver in services is of the utmost importance in preventing placement. This is a most challenging task, but one that is more likely to succeed with families who benefit from the comprehensiveness of family-based services, including parent education, transportation, counseling, and, most important in the predictive model, paraprofessional services (Ayoub & Jacewitz 1982; Kagan & Schlosberg 1989, ch. 3; Kaplan 1986; Colon 1980). Still, as has been found in other studies of family preservation services (Berry 1990; Yuan & Struckman-Johnson 1991), in this study neglecting caregivers participated least and had the highest placement rates among the child maltreatment cases.

Although they included more employed and married caregivers, families referred for physical abuse were also more likely to contain stepparents and to have marital problems, both risk factors identified in previous research (Garbarino, Schellenbach, & Sebes 1986; Garbarino 1989). Health and mental health problems also appeared to create additional stress in these families. While placement is less predictable in cases involving physical abuse (Cicchetti & Carlson 1989:140 ff.), it is also less determined by historical factors and more

amenable to preventive interventions, especially marital counseling and role modeling. These interventions relate directly to the marital conflict and lack of parenting skills that have been associated with physical abuse in earlier studies (Gelles & Maynard 1987; Reid, Taplin, & Lorber 1981). The level of parental functioning and the degree to which caregivers are engaged in services, however, remain important determinants of case outcome (Justice & Justice 1982 & 1990; Ory & Earp 1980).

Families referred for sexual abuse presented a strikingly different profile, with high rates of divorce and prior placement, perhaps related to the abuse itself (Gomes-Schwartz et al. 1990:52, 143, 118; Sever & Janzen 1982). Due to the absence of the perpetrator from the home, most of the children were not at risk of imminent placement; nevertheless, they did have considerable behavioral problems. Most caregivers were very motivated and cooperative with services, and successful cases were directed toward engaging families in longer-term treatment (Daro 1988:105–8; Gomes-Schwartz et al. 1990:163–65; Keller, Cicchinelli, & Gardner 1989). However, a distinctive subset of characteristics was identified that made placement more likely. As in other studies, this research found that less compliant caregivers, especially if they were seen conjointly with their spouses and both were employed, were more likely to have their child placed (Daro 1988:38; Garbarino 1989:699; Glaser & Frosh 1988:140–53; Green 1988).

Some of the differences observed among types of maltreatment emanated from differences between specific programs in the study. The programs for neglecting families were the most alike, with the exception that SCAN served the greatest number of black families. Since most of the sexual abuse cases were seen in the Oregon sites, directly or indirectly under the auspices of the Children's Services Division, there were also many similarities between these programs. The greatest differences were observed in the treatment of physical abuse. At one extreme were the agencies that also saw a large number of neglect cases (Franklin County, SCAN, and ICFS). They served poorer families with younger children and more problems, especially with substance abuse. At the other extreme were programs in public agencies (Iowa DHS, Boulder County, and Dakota County) that served families with older children and more relationship problems but fewer problems overall.[8]

Despite the differences among sites, several of the predictors of placement or nonplacement cut across maltreatment types. The risk to the child, the functioning and cooperation of the primary caregiver, and a history of prior placements have all been found to correlate with placement in past studies of child protective (Meddin 1984) and family preservation services (Fraser et al. 1991; Yuan & Struckman-Johnson 1991). This consistency, however, should not lead to the conclusion that some " 'hard core' parents . . . are virtually untreat-able" (Green, Power, Steinbook, & Gaines 1981), since placement remains a rare event that is hard to predict. In each maltreatment group the predictive models were more accurate in identifying successful cases than in predicting placements. That is, it is easier to tell who will succeed in family-based services than to identify families who will not remain together even when the outcome is known in advance, as it was in this retrospective study.

While definitive treatment models have not yet emerged, there are encouraging developments in each area of child maltreatment that deserve further testing. A recent survey of program characteristics found that two-thirds of sexual abuse treatment programs focused on treating the family and the victim together, excluding from treatment perpetrators who deny responsibility for the abuse (Keller et al. 1989). The specifics of interventions within a family systems model have been less fully developed for cases involving neglect and physical abuse. Research and demonstrations involving prevention and intervention with families identified as at-risk have replaced earlier efforts to identify effective interventions in known cases of physical abuse (Kaufman & Rudy 1991), and until very recently little attention was given to the treatment of child neglect (Wolock & Horowitz 1984). Kaufman and Rudy (1991) identify four promising approaches— social learning, ecobehavioral, family-centered and home-based, and multisystemic—that merit more research and development. The programs in this study were eclectic, reflecting a multisystemic approach (Henggeler & Borduin 1990).

While useful, traditional family therapy techniques need to be modified in working with severely dysfunctional families. In more serious and chronic cases of physical abuse, sexual abuse, and neglect, accepting the family's goals, working slowly to gain their trust, and only carefully challenging their perceptions and functioning may require working with subsystems, avoiding interventions that increase conflict and disequilibrium, and providing a strong model of positive parenting (Weitzman 1985). This seems particularly true with neglecting families who are more often headed by low-income single parents and face multiple problems.

Whatever the treatment modality or the reason for referral may be, engaging the primary caregiver in the treatment process is of utmost importance (Dale & Davies 1985; Green et al. 1981; Orenchuk-Tomiuk, Matthey, & Pigler-Christensen 1990; Weitzman 1985). Motivation is a complex but important construct that has received little attention in social work research (Gold 1990). Partly a predisposition of the client and partly a result of the success of the therapist in engaging the family in treatment, motivation and cooperation are keys to success in family-based services as well as in other types of therapy. In encouraging families to set their own goals, acknowledging their strengths, and instilling hope for positive change, family-based workers are supported by psychological research on motivation. Finding out how best to use information, recognition, and material reinforcers to support individual families is part of the larger task of identifying which of the wide range of interventions used in family-based services is most effective with families having different strengths and problems.

NOTES

Funding for this research was provided by a grant from the Children's Bureau of the U.S. Department of Health and Human Services (Grant No. 90-CW-0732).

1. Placements included emergency shelter, supervised independent living, foster family homes, group homes and halfway houses, institutions for mentally retarded/developmentally disabled, residential treatment, or psychiatric hospitalization, incarceration, adoptive homes, and formal or informal placement with a friend or relative if it was in response to the family's problem and not a routine visit (e.g., during a holiday or with a noncustodial parent). To be classified as a placement case, at least one child in the family had to be in placement or to have placement planned or imminent at termination of the case from family-based services. A temporary placement from which a child was transferred or returned home before the termination of services was not counted as an outcome of placement.

2. Two weighting systems were used in analyzing the data. Since Franklin County and Lutheran Social Services both had fewer than twenty-five codable placement cases, both placement and nonplacement cases were weighted to

represent the equivalent of twenty-five each in analyses that involved placement as the dependent variable. When frequencies are reported or programs are compared to each other, the case data are weighted by the estimated incidence of placement in each agency so as to present a more accurate picture of family and service characteristics than is provided by equal numbers of placement and nonplacement cases, since in reality the latter are much more frequent.

3. Case readers assessed the risk of placement using four categories: low risk: no indication of possible placement in the case record; moderate risk: discussion of possible placement, but not imminent; high risk: placement imminent without family-based services, or just returned from placement; temporary placement: child to be returned to family within thirty days of intake into family-based services. To assess a case as being at imminent risk for placement, some action must have been taken toward making a placement and must have been recorded.

4. The Family Systems Change Scale was developed by the National Resource Center on Family-based Services to detect systemic change not captured by individually oriented measures. On each of ten items, the case reader rated the family as having improved, made no change, or gotten worse between intake and case closure. The scale demonstrated a high degree of interrater (r = .74) and interitem (*alpha* = .94) reliability. A copy of the scale is reprinted in Nelson & Landsman 1992, Appendix D).

5. Placement status was assessed at the termination of family-based services. A child was not counted among the placements if he or she moved from a temporary placement back home before the termination of services. On the other hand, children living with relatives and friends at the time of termination were counted as placements. Other outcome measures were highly related to placement or nonplacement, including both the percentage of case goals achieved or partially achieved and changes in family functioning from intake to case closure measured by the Family Systems Change Scale (see Nelson & Landsman 1992, Appendix A for further discussion of outcome measures).

6. Separating the families by age of the child at highest risk (zero to eleven and twelve to eighteen) identified caregiver functioning as the most important factor in placement of younger children and the involvement of child protective services as most important for older children. Although the involvement of the primary caregiver was essential to placement prevention in both groups, role modeling was the most effective intervention for younger families and marital counseling for families of older children.

7. The Child Well-Being Scales have many strengths, including behavioral indicators that leave little room for bias, high interrater reliability, and desirable psychometric properties that are enhanced by the seriousness weights when used with child welfare populations. They have been extensively tested for reliability and validity in relevant populations. Response categories, which are normally rated by a social worker, consist of rank-ordered, descriptive

paragraphs for each of the forty-two scales (Magura & Moses 1986). In this study, interitem reliability was high (*alpha* = .73), but interrater reliability was low (*r* = .51) due to the difficulty of coding the scales from case record data. See Nelson (1991) for a further discussion of interrater reliability of the Child Well-Being Scales.

8. Variations between sites were especially high for variables included in the discriminant models that did not significantly differentiate between placement and nonplacement at the bivariate level. Regarding differences between sites in neglect cases, previous placements were most frequent in Franklin County, and families served by SCAN had the most problems. Paraprofessional services were most effectively used for placement prevention in SCAN, where placement was also more frequent among families with more children. Mothers in nonplacement cases were one year older at the birth of the child at highest risk than mothers in placement cases in Franklin County.

In physical abuse cases, ICFS and SCAN had the highest rates of substance abuse in placement cases, and Iowa DHS and SCAN were the most likely to accompany placement cases to appointments. Franklin County and Dakota County were most successful in using parent education to prevent placement. In sexual abuse cases, a second employed adult was significantly related to placement in Multnomah County but not in the other sites. Referring out contributed most to placement in the other CSD site. Prior placement was most frequent in Multnomah County. An objective to increase the family's ability to use outside counseling was most frequent in the Oregon programs, which were also the most effective in involving the child at highest risk in services. Role modeling, however, was not offered as a service in any of the sites that served larger numbers of sexual abuse cases.

REFERENCES

Ayoub, C. & Jacewitz, M. M. (1982). Families at risk of poor parenting: A descriptive study of sixty at-risk families in a model prevention program. *Child Abuse and Neglect, 6,* 413–22.

Belsky, J. (1981). Child maltreatment: An ecological integration. In S. Chess & A. Thomas (Eds.), *Annual progress in child psychiatry and child development* (pp. 637–65). New York: Brunner-Mazel.

Berry, M. (1990). Keeping families together: An evaluation of an intensive family preservation program. Ph.D. diss., School of Social Welfare, University of California, Berkeley.

Brunk, M., Henggeler, S. W., & Whelan, J. B. (1987). Comparison of multisystemic therapy and parent training in the brief treatment of child abuse and neglect. *Journal of Consulting and Clinical Psychology, 55,* 171–78.

Carter, E. & McGoldrick, M. (Eds.). (1980). *The family life cycle: A framework for family therapy.* New York: Gardner.

Child Welfare League of America. (1989). *Standards for services to strengthen and preserve families with children.* Washington, D.C.: Child Welfare League of America.

Cicchetti, D. & Carlson, V. (1989). *Child maltreatment: Theory and research on the causes and consequences of child abuse and neglect.* New York: Cambridge.

Coleman, H. & Collins, D. (1990). Treatment trilogy of father-daughter incest. *Child and Adolescent Social Work, 7,* 339–55.

Colon, F. (1980). The family life cycle of the multiproblem poor family. In E. Carter & M. McGoldrick (Eds.), *The family life cycle: A framework for family therapy* (pp. 343–77). New York: Gardner.

Dale, P. & Davies, M. (1985). A model of intervention in child-abusing families: A wider systems view. *Child Abuse and Neglect, 9,* 449–55.

Daro, D. (1988). *Confronting child abuse.* New York: Free Press.

Daro, D. & Cohn, A. H. (1988). Child maltreatment evaluation efforts: What have we learned? In G. T. Hotaling, D. Finkelhor, J. T. Kirkpatrick, & M. A. Straus (Eds.), *Coping with family violence: Research and policy perspectives* (pp. 275–87). Newbury Park, CA: Sage Publications.

Ellis, A. (1973). *Rational emotive therapy.* New York: Springer.

Everson, M. D., Hunter, W. M., Runyan, D. K., Edelsohn, G. A., & Coulter, M. L. (1989). Maternal support following disclosure of incest. *American Journal of Orthopsychiatry, 59,* 197–207.

Fraser, M., Pecora, P., & Haapala, D. (1991). *Families in crisis.* New York: Aldine de Gruyter.

Gambrill, E. D. (1977). *Behavioral modification: Handbook of assessment, intervention, and evaluation.* San Francisco: Jossey-Bass.

Garbarino, J. (1989). The dynamics of adolescent maltreatment. In D. Cicchetti & V. Carlson (Eds.), *Child maltreatment: Theory and research on the causes and consequences of child abuse and neglect* (pp. 685–706). New York: Cambridge.

Garbarino, J., Schellenbach, C. J., Sebes, J., & Associates (1986). *Troubled youth, troubled families.* New York: Aldine de Gruyter.

Gelles, R. J. & Maynard, P. E. (1987). A structural family systems approach to intervention in cases of family violence. *Family Relations, 36,* 270–75.

Giovannoni, J. (1989). Definitional issues in child maltreatment. In D. Cicchetti & V. Carlson (Eds.), *Child maltreatment: Theory and research on the causes and consequences of child abuse and neglect* (pp. 1–37). New York: Cambridge.

Glaser, D. & Frosh, S. (1988). *Child sexual abuse.* London: Macmillan.

Gold, N. (1990). Motivation: The crucial but unexplored component of social work practice. *Social Work, 35,* 49–56.

Gomes-Schwartz, B., Horowitz, J. M., & Cardarelli, A. P. (1990). *Child sexual abuse: The initial effects.* Newbury Park, CA: Sage Publications.

Green, A. H. (1988). Child maltreatment and its victims: A comparison of physical and sexual abuse. *Psychiatric Clinics of North America, 11,* 591–610.

Green, A. H., Power, E., Steinbook, B., & Gaines, R. (1981). Factors associated with successful and unsuccessful intervention with child abusive families. *Child Abuse and Neglect, 5,* 45–52.

Hartley, R., Showell, W., & White, J. (1989, September). Outcomes of Oregon's family treatment programs: A descriptive study of 1752 families. Paper presented at the Intensive Family Preservation Services Research Conference, Cleveland, OH.

Hartman, A. (1978). Diagrammatic assessment of family relationships. *Social Casework, 59,* 465–76.

Hartman, A. & Laird, J. (1983). *Family-centered social work practice.* New York: Free Press.

Henggeler, S. W. & Borduin, C. M. (1990). *Family therapy and beyond: A multisystemic approach to treating the behavior problems of children and adolescents.* Pacific Grove, CA: Brooks/Cole.

Hunter, W. M., Coulter, M. L., Runyan, D. K., & Everson, M. D. (1990). Determinants of placement for sexually abused children. *Child Abuse and Neglect, 14,* 407–17.

Janzen, C. & Harris, O. (1986). *Family treatment in social work practice* (2d. ed.). Itasca, IL: Peacock.

Justice, B. & Justice, R. (1982). Etiology of physical abuse of children and dynamics of coercive treatment. *Family Therapy Collections, 3,* 1–20.

Justice, B. & Justice, R. (1990). *The abusing family* (Rev. ed.). New York: Plenum Press.

Kagan, R. & Schlosberg, S. (1989). *Families in perpetual crisis.* New York: Norton.

Kaplan, L. (1986). *Working with multiproblem families.* Lexington, MA: Lexington Books.

Kaufman, K. L. & Rudy, L. (1991). Future directions in the treatment of physical child abuse. *Criminal Justice and Behavior, 18,* 82–97.

Keller, R. A., Cicchinelli, L. F., & Gardner, D. M. (1989). Characteristics of child´sexual abuse treatment programs. *Child Abuse and Neglect, 13,* 361–68.

Kinney, J., Haapala, D., & Booth, C. (1991). *Keeping families together: The Homebuilders model.* New York: Aldine de Gruyter.

Kreppner, K. & Lerner, R. M. (1989). *Family systems and life-span development.* Hillsdale, NJ: Lawrence Erlbaum.

Leverington, J. & Wulff, D. (1988). Home-based family therapy. *Social Work, 33,* 211–14 (erroneously attributed to L. Woods).

Lloyd, J. C. & Bryce, M. E. (1984). *Placement prevention and family reunification.* Iowa City: The University of Iowa School of Social Work, National Resource Center on Family-based Services.

Magura, S. & Moses, B. S. (1986). *Outcome measures for child welfare services: Theory and applications.* Washington, D.C.: Child Welfare League of America.

Maybanks, S. & Bryce, M. (1978). *Home-based services for children and families: Policy, practice, and research.* Springfield, IL: Charles C. Thomas.

McGoldrick, M. & Gerson, R. (1985). *Genograms in family assessment.* New York: Norton.

Meddin, B. (1984). Criteria for placement decisions in protective services. *Child Welfare, 63, 367–73.*

Minuchin, P. (1985). Families and individual development: Provocations from the field of family therapy. *Child Development, 56, 289–302.*

Minuchin, S. (1974). *Families and family therapy.* Cambridge: Harvard University Press.

Minuchin, S. & Fishman, C. (1981). *Family therapy techniques.* Cambridge: Harvard University Press.

Napier, A. & Whitacker, C. (1978). *The family crucible.* New York: Harper & Row.

Nelson, K. E. (1991). Populations and outcomes in five in-home placement prevention programs. In K. Wells & D. A. Biegel (Eds.), *Family preservation services: Research and evaluation* (pp. 92–118). Newbury Park, CA: Sage Publications.

Nelson, K., Emlen, A., Landsman, M., & Hutchinson, J. (1988). *Factors contributing to success and failure in family-based child welfare services.* Iowa City: The University of Iowa, National Resource Center on Family-based Services.

Nelson, K. & Landsman, M. (1992). *Alternative models of family preservation: Family-based services in context.* Springfield, IL: Charles C. Thomas.

Nelson, K., Landsman, M., & Deutelbaum, W. (1990). Three models of family-centered placement prevention services. *Child Welfare, 69, 3–21.*

Orenchuk-Tomiuk, N., Matthey, G., & Pigler-Christensen, C. (1990). The resolution model: A comprehensive treatment framework in sexual abuse. *Child Welfare, 69, 417–31.*

Ory, M. & Earp, J. (1980). Child maltreatment: An analysis of familial and institutional predictors. *Journal of Family Issues, 1, 339–56.*

Pellegrin, A. & Wagner, W. G. (1990). Child sexual abuse: Factors affecting victims' removal from home. *Child Abuse and Neglect, 14, 53–60.*

Reid, J. B., Taplin, P. S., & Lorber, R. (1981). A social interactional approach to the treatment of abusive families. In R. B. Stuart (Ed.), *Violent behavior: Social learning approaches to prediction, management, and treatment* (pp. 83–101). New York: Brunner-Mazel.

Rogers, C. R. (1942). *Counseling and psychotherapy: Newer concepts in practice.* Boston: Houghton-Mifflin.

Satir, V. M. (1982). *Conjoint family therapy* (3d. rev. ed.). Palo Alto, CA: Science and Behavior Books.

Sever, J. & Janzen, C. (1982). Contradictions to reconstitution of sexually abusive families. *Child Welfare, 61, 279–88.*

Sirles, E. A. & Lofberg, C. E. (1990). Factors associated with divorce in intrafamily child sexual abuse cases. *Child Abuse and Neglect, 14, 165–70.*

Weitzman, J. (1985). Engaging the severely dysfunctional family in treatment: Basic considerations. *Family Process, 24,* 473–85.

Wolock, I. & Horowitz, B. (1984). Child maltreatment as a social problem: The neglect of neglect. *American Journal of Orthopsychiatry, 58,* 91–103.

Yuan, Y. T. & Struckman-Johnson, D. L. (1991). Placement outcomes for neglected children with prior placements in family preservation programs. In K. Wells & D. A. Biegel (Eds.), *Family preservation services: Research and evaluation* (pp. 92–118). Newbury Park, CA: Sage Publications.

FIVE

Parental Drug Abuse and African-American Children in Foster Care

Clarice Dibble Walker, Patricia Zangrillo, and Jacqueline Marie Smith

The impact of parental substance abuse on children continues to be studied and documented by researchers and practitioners from a variety of disciplines. Problems in parental functioning among substance abusers have been described as profoundly affecting their ability to provide consistent and protective care concerning the basic physical and emotional needs of their children. Increasingly, the outcome for these children is detection by the child welfare system and, in many cases, out-of-home placement in the foster care system.

Data from a National Black Child Development Institute (NBCDI 1989) study that profiled 1,003 African-American children who entered foster care in 1986 in five cities provided clear evidence of the trend toward foster care. A significant finding was that drug abuse of the parent was a major contributing factor in a child's placement in care for 36% of the children. In two of the cities, New York and Miami, where crack cocaine was reported to be widely available in 1986, parental drug abuse was reported in 52 and 50% of the foster care cases respectively. Crack was identified as the primary drug used by the group of parents studied in these two cities. The study also found indications that the concurrent use of several drugs was likely.

Reporting these findings led to questions about this population: What are the characteristics of children who have been placed out of their homes due to parental drug abuse? Are they and their families different from others in the foster care system? How have agencies responded to these children and their families? And what policies and services, if any, need to be developed or changed to meet the needs of these children and their families?

Methodology and Sample

This analysis utilized data from the referenced NBCDI (1989) study. Those data were collected by trained volunteers who reviewed case records of African-American children aged eighteen or younger, who were placed in state-designed, state-supervised foster care living arrangements for at least twenty-four hours. In New York and Detroit, a sample of cases was randomly selected from child age and gender strata in order to proportionately approximate these distributions in the population of eligible children.

Data collection began and ended at various times in the different cities. Houston had the smallest mean and median case review period of twenty-one months. The review period is the amount of time from the child's entry into foster care until his or her case record was reviewed and data collected from it. The mean and median case review period for the entire sample was twenty-six months.

The Children

Children from families with parental drug abuse were younger than the other children. The mean age for the children in the parental drug abuse group for the total sample was 5.6 years (median 4.7 years). In contrast, the mean age for children in the group not using drugs was 7.6 years (median 7.5 years). This finding of younger children coming into care as a result of parental drug abuse corroborates findings from other studies as well (Subcommittee on Human Resources 1990; Office of Inspector General 1990).

A serious attempt was made to collect as much information as possible regarding the children in the case record. Unfortunately, this information was often missing from the record. In particular, documentation of the psychological, emotional, and social needs of the child and of the child's behavior was missing. Even school assessment and health assessment data on the child were found to be missing from the record. This finding has serious implications in light of the special health and educational needs of this population, which have been cited in numerous studies in the last decade (Barth 1991;

TABLE 5.1
Primary Reason for Placement By Parental Drug
Abuse as A Contributing Factor (In Percent)

	Perinatal Drug Abuse	
Primary Reason for Placement	Yes	No
Abandonment	9.2	8.0
Neglect	60.6	29.3
Abuse	14.7	32.5
No One Willing or Able	4.4	5.8
Voluntary Placement	10.0	21.8
Missing	1.1	2.6
N of Cases	360	624

Chasnoff 1987; U.S. House of Representatives, Select Committee CYF 1989).

Reason for Placement

The reasons for placement shed some light on the experiences the children encountered before their placement and on the kinds of service needs these families had. Table 5.1 illustrates the primary reasons why the children came into care. It should be noted that for the parental drug abuse cases the primary reason for placement tended to be neglect and not abuse. In most cities abandonment, abuse, and neglect together comprised roughly three quarters of the reasons for placement.

The finding of neglect as the principal reason for placement for the parental drug abuse group runs counter to the view that mothers using crack, according to Besharov, are violent perpetrators of abuse to their children: "Crack children are also at great risk of physical battering. Crack is a mean drug that seems to induce some parents to great violence. Cases of crack-crazed battering of children are becoming more common." Yet the data from the analysis tell a different story, one of children neglected rather than abused. The following three vignettes from the data collection instrument were chosen randomly from New York to illustrate typical cases:

- The child (an eight-year-old girl) was kept home from school because of the mother's addiction to drugs. She was unable to prepare the child for school. The mother is addicted to cocaine and

TABLE 5.2
Types of Abuse or Neglect By Parental Drug
Abuse as A Contributing Factor (In Percent)

| | Parental Drug Abuse | |
Type of Abuse or Neglect	Yes	No
Malnourishment	20.8	5.8
Poor Hygiene	21.1	12.2
Physical/Needs Unmet	30.8	9.7
Physical Abuse	20.6	35.6
Sexual Abuse	8.8	9.7
Emotional Abuse	15.0	14.9
Unattended/Unsupervised	40.5	21.0
Uncertain Return of Parent	36.4	17.8
Kept Home from School	12.0	6.8
N of Cases	341	589

NOTE: This is a multiple response table.

heroin. She fails to provide adequate care or supervision for the child. She uses drugs in the child's presence.

· The natural mother often let the children (including this ten-year-old girl) parent each other. She would go off with friends for days, leaving them without food and supervision. On 1/3/86 the father of one of the siblings reported to SSC that the natural mother was using drugs and leaving the five children alone.

· The mother had lost her AFDC grant at the time of placement. Her drug habit interfered with her cooperating with the AFDC office. The mother was on the drug "crack." She had lost her AFDC and could not feed or clothe her children (including this ten-year-old boy). Neighbors and others reported that the mother was very neglectful of the children. The child's school reported a very poor attendance record. The caseworker visited and found the children to be dirty and without food, and she could not find the mother. The children were placed.

A more detailed identification of the types of abuse or neglect is presented in table 5.2. Malnourishment, poor hygiene, and physical/medical needs unmet were significantly more common in the group of parents that abused drugs than in the one that did not in New York and Miami. The severity of each type of abuse or neglect was not measured in the study.

Children from the group not using drugs were more likely than those from the parent group using drugs to be in foster care, at least in part because of their own emotional, behavioral, and other problems. It should be noted that although there were not many boarder babies at the time of the study, the majority of their parents belonged to the group abusing drugs.

Family

Consistent with other studies of children who enter the foster care system, parents who abuse drugs are more often single parents (53.4%) as opposed to women living in nuclear or extended families (39.0%). It was also found that mothers who abused drugs were significantly more likely to have less than a high school education (67.2%) than parents who were not identified as drug abusers (49.3%).

Table 5.3 illustrates that the primary means of financial support for families with parental drug abuse prior to placement was AFDC rather than employment. In every city except Houston this was the case for 80% or more of the group of parents abusing drugs. In New York City, the incidence of AFDC recipients among the drug-abusing parents in the sample reached the highest rate, at 93%. In families without parental drug abuse, on the other hand, there was significantly more employment and less AFDC use prior to placement.

The Role of the Environment: Poverty and Poor Housing

For every variable indicating poverty or poor housing, the finding was the same: families with substance-abusing parents were significantly

TABLE 5.3
Primary Financial Support of Family Before Placement (In Percent)

	Parental Drug Abuse	
Primary Financial Support	Yes	No
Employment	11.0	37.6
AFDC	85.0	58.1
Other	4.0	4.3
N of Cases	246	444

more likely to be poor and have inadequate housing than other families whose children were placed in foster care.

Poverty as a contributing reason for placement was found significantly and twice as often for families with parental drug abuse (38.6%) than for those without it (17.5%). Poverty as a factor in placement indicates that poverty was mentioned in the child's case record as an obvious condition in the child's household when the child was placed in foster care. This variable does not necessarily reflect all of those cases with family incomes below the poverty line. In New York and Miami, where crack was most prevalent, the incidence of poverty being reported as a contributing factor in placement was higher than in the other cities or in the total sample (45% in Miami and 52% in New York).

Inadequate housing was reported as a contributing factor in placement significantly more often in the drug-abusing part of the parent sample (44.2%) than in the group not using drugs (22.5%).

It is not possible to reach any ultimate conclusions from the data on whether poverty caused or promoted the drug abuse of these parents or whether the drug abuse caused or contributed to the poverty. Both of these premises are certainly plausible. Without knowing which came first—the poverty or the drug abuse—causality cannot be proven for these particular cases. However, the data strongly suggest that these parents' poverty was long term and enduring because many of the indicators normally associated with poverty and normally occurring in the long term were present (NBCDI 1989). For example, it is unlikely that mothers dropped out of high school, became single parents, and became AFDC recipients all in the time since crack became available.

Parental Service Needs, Services Offered, and Discharge Outcomes

The types of services offered to parents during placement should ideally be addressing all of the reasons that brought the child into placement. If the parent with the help of the agency accomplishes each of the parental responsibilities as described in the case plan, then reunification should occur.

In reality, the goals of reunification were unfulfilled for many of the children in this study. The data show that many African-American children were not discharged by the close of the study, approximately twenty-six months after entering foster care. The data further show that there were needs identified for which no services were provided, either directly or indirectly, by the agency or through referrals to other agencies.

Additional problems for families with drug abuse, in decreasing order of their magnitude were: housing (44.2%), poverty (38.6%), alcohol abuse (34.3%), incarceration (16.6%), homelessness (13.4%), and mental illness (9.49%). The parent group abusing drugs had twice the proportion of reported housing problems and poverty problems as the group that did not use drugs. There also was more than twice the incidence of incarceration for the drug-abusing group as for the group not using drugs. The data do not identify the type of crime or whether it was related to drugs, child abuse, or another type of violation of the law.

The data suggest that these families have significant needs for a range of services in addition to drug treatment, as do many other families with children in placement. It should be noted that the case files also identify one-third of the families with drug abuse problems as alcohol abusers. Use of several drugs was considered common among drug users in 1986 and is consistent with current reports.

Of services offered or referred to parents, drug treatment was noted in the case files for only 60% of the parents abusing drugs. Of the parents in the study, 48% were offered or referred to parenting skills education. Reasonable efforts requirements would seem to imply that all of the parents from the group abusing drugs should have been provided with these services.

The lack of housing assistance services is a glaring service gap for the parents who abuse drugs. The need for housing assistance was identified in 44% of the cases in the group using drugs, but housing services were offered or referrals made in only 12% of these cases.

Although poverty was also an issue in 39% of the placements in the group abusing drugs, employment services (training or job placement) were available in only 7% of these cases and financial services in only 12%. Miami was exceptional in that there 25% of the parents who abused drugs were offered or referred to employment services. Financial assistance services were offered much more consistently than employment training in all the cities in the study; probably these services primarily involved casework assistance regarding application for AFDC or other forms of public assistance.

The extent to which the lack of available and accessible resources

TABLE 5.4
Barriers to Reunification for Cases Still in Care At
Study End (In Percent)

| | Parental Drug Abuse | |
Barriers to Reunification	Yes	No
Lack of Cooperation of Parent	49.5	43.0
Inadequate Housing	43.2	25.6
Drug Addiction of Parent	62.8	3.6
Parenting Skills Lacking	25.6	25.9
Lack of Finances	29.9	15.7
Parent Whereabouts Unknown	9.0	8.5
N of Cases	301	363

NOTE: This is a multiple response table.

to address parental needs was responsible for the gaps in services is not known. However, it is believed that for problems related to drug treatment, housing, and employment services, this gap was a significant factor. These services are not directly provided by child welfare agencies although they are noted in case plans as responsibilities the parents must fulfill in order to achieve reunification. Parents are also known to be subject to long waiting lists because of an inadequate supply of these resources and to face other obstacles of eligibility. A prime example is the wait for public housing, which in some cities can be many years.

It is possible that some cases involved mothers who could not have received services based on their circumstances. These cases would include: (1) mothers who were unknown to the child welfare agency because of total abandonment of their children (including boarder babies), (2) those whose whereabouts were unknown during placement, (3) those who were incarcerated for the entire duration of the child's placement, and (4) mothers who voluntarily relinquished their children for adoption upon placement. The data could not reveal the exact magnitude of these types of mothers, but they strongly suggest that these mothers are a very small minority.

The barriers to reunification identified in the case record for those children still in foster care by the study's conclusion are summarized in table 5.4.

Many of the needs identified at the beginning of these cases were still present at the end of the study: inadequate housing, drug abuse of the parent, inadequate parenting skills, and lack of finances. In nearly half of the cases, the caseworker partly blames the parent by indicating "Lack of Cooperation from Parent." It is interesting to note that in this regard there is little difference between the group abusing drugs and the group not using drugs. The preceding discussion suggests that a lack of services offered or referred to the parent by the agency is probably also responsible for the failure to reunify these cases.

By the end of the study, more than two years after these children had entered foster care, only 28% of the children of parents abusing drugs had been discharged—in contrast to 51% of the children of the parents in the group not using drugs.

Of the children who were discharged, there was comparatively and significantly more reunification for the parent group not using drugs (60.6%) than for the group abusing drugs (36.6%) and more placements with relatives for the children from the parent group abusing drugs (33.7%) than for the other group (19.1%).

In the total sample, the length of time spent in foster care until the case was reviewed was significantly shorter for the children from the group not using drugs than for those from the group of drug-abusing parents. By the time the case was reviewed (an average of twenty-six months), the mean length of placement for the children of parents in the drug-abusing group was twenty-two months; for children of parents in the other group it was seventeen months. Length of time refers to the time in months between the day the child was placed in foster care and either the day of trial or final discharge, or, if he or she was not discharged, the day the child's foster care case record was reviewed.

The Role of Relatives

The role of relatives in formal foster care is a critical issue as kinship placements have multiplied in recent years. The *New York Times* (Daley 1989) reported: "In less than three years, the number of children in (relative foster care) has grown to 19,000 more children than were in the city's entire foster care system two years ago." In 1990 New York City reported 22,000 placements with relatives— more than half of the total foster care population.

Relatives have successfully established the right under federal law to be chosen and reimbursed as a foster parent (Miller vs. Youakim).

Yet there are wide variations and interpretations related to type of payments and monitoring requirements. Advocates have stressed the importance of placing children in kinship homes as the most appropriate alternative when children are unable to remain with their parents. When children must be separated from their families, federal law mandates that children be placed in the least restrictive, familylike setting.

In this study the cities varied in the extent to which they considered relatives a potential resource during placement. Except for Miami and Seattle, relatives were considered a resource significantly more often in cases of parental drug abuse than in cases not involving drug abuse. For the total sample, relatives were regarded as placement resources in 85% of the cases involving drug abuse and in 72% of the other cases. In 60% of the cases involving drug abuse when relatives were considered, they were a resource ultimately used for placement; in 55% of the cases not involving drug abuse these relatives were used as resources.

The usual form of assistance from relatives in the cases involving parental drug abuse was taking the children into their homes. In addition, 12% of these relatives became legal guardians of the children, and 17% provided other assistance, such as housing, for the parent. In the majority of cases the relative willingly responded and identified the needs of the children. An example of this is the fact that one-third (33.1%) of the placements in the cases involving parental drug abuse were initiated through a referral by a relative of the child.

When relatives did not offer assistance, it was usually because they were overburdened financially or had other child care responsibilities. The most common reason why a relative did not offer to help was lack of financial support. Other reasons given were that the relative was too old or already had to care for too many children. The agency rejected 9% of the relatives because they were considered to be substance abusers themselves or because there was a potential for further child neglect or abuse.

Discussion of the Findings

Prolonged Stays in Foster Care

Child welfare agencies are not achieving permanency for children, particularly those with parents who abuse drugs. Despite mandated Public Law 96–272 goals and guidelines, long-term foster care appeared common among African-American children placed in foster care in 1986. This was particularly true of children from families with drug-abusing parents. Even after twenty-six months, 72% of the children of drug abusers in the total sample were still in foster care. By contrast, 51% of the children whose parents did not abuse drugs had been discharged from foster care. Reunification with the biological parent was almost twice as frequent for cases involving parents who did not abuse drugs as for those with parents abusing drugs. Adoptions, guardianships, and other nonreunification discharge options were generally rare for cases with parental drug abuse; however, placements with relatives were more frequent in these cases than in the others.

It is indisputable that not every child benefits from reunification with his or her biological parents. The study's findings show, however, that only 9% of the children of drug-abusing parents had been adopted within twenty-six months after placement. Adoption in the formal child welfare system has traditionally been difficult to achieve for older African-American children and particularly for those with emotional, physical, or behavioral problems. Legal adoptions as well as nontraditional options, such as legal guardianship by a relative or open adoptions should be actively pursued by the agencies.

Child abuse and neglect prevention programs and services (including components reaching out to at-risk families such as those with parental substance abusers) are also needed to reduce the number of children coming into foster care in the first place. Many of the families with children entering foster care are known to service agencies well before any abuse or neglect allegations.

Inadequacy of Services

Services to address the problems contributing to placement in foster care are either unavailable or insufficiently brokered and coordinated with other organizations. When the family characteristics prior to placement in the total sample of children were compared, it became obvious that the families with parental drug use had greater poverty and more inadequate housing than the group not using drugs. Of the mothers in the drug-abusing families, 67% had not completed high school, 53% were single parents, and 85% received AFDC. Inadequate housing and poverty were cited as placement factors twice as often among these cases as for families without drug-abusing parents.

Agencies did not provide adequate assistance in remedying these factors. The case plans gave the mothers responsibility to provide adequate housing and financial support, for instance—then kept the children in care when the mothers could not do so, making such factors important barriers to reunification.

It may be unrealistic for foster care agencies to expect poor families to provide affordable, decent housing when that is not available. It is even more unlikely that these families can find adequate housing when one considers that mothers whose children are in foster care lose their AFDC payments, which for many were their sole source of financial support. Since they may only be employable for low-paid jobs, such parents are more likely to lose or retain their previous housing during the child's placement than to become able to upgrade it.

Another major barrier to reunification was the continued drug abuse of the parent. Drug abuse of the parent was a barrier to reunification in 63% of the cases involving parental drug abuse that were not discharged by the end of the study. Yet drug treatment referrals were made by the agency for only 60% of all drug-abusing parents at some time during foster care.

The literature strongly suggests that drug treatment programs were probably not in adequate supply or accessible to provide all of these mothers with the treatment they needed. Many of the treatment slots available in a city may also not have been suitable for them. For example, New York's Mayor Dinkins (1990) reported that there was only one residential drug treatment program in that city that served young mothers with their children. Half of the programs did not accept pregnant women; only one-third treated pregnant women with Medicaid, and only 13% of the programs provided detoxification from crack for pregnant women with Medicaid.

Parenting education, a service that is frequently provided directly by the child welfare agency, was offered to only 48% of the drug-abusing parents and to 34% of the other parents in the study even though the need was much greater considering that 85% of the drug-abusing parents and 70% of the parents not using drugs abandoned or neglected their children prior to placement.

Child welfare agencies must form closer partnerships with other service providers utilizing an integrated service delivery approach, both public and private, in their communities in order to assure that families receive the services they need to achieve reunification. In addition, child welfare staff need training in order to recognize and understand drug abuse and to be knowledgeable about the various types of drug treatment available in their communities.

Relatives as Resources

Relatives were often available as foster parent resources and represent a significant resource for children. Relatives were able and willing to provide help to the children 60% of the time when the agency considered them. When relatives did not assist, the reason was usually a lack of personal financial resources. Indeed, relatives demonstrated their concern prior to placement in at least one-third of the cases involving parental drug abuse because they were the source of the initial child protective services (CDP) referrals.

Since many jurisdictions cannot find enough qualified foster parents to provide homes and care for all of the children coming into care, especially since the beginning of the drug crisis, relatives have become an essential resource. However, there are many controversial and unresolved issues concerning kinship foster placements.

Critics question whether foster care payments should be made to relatives. They fear disincentives for reunification with biological parents given that the reimbursement rate for foster care is higher than what is paid under AFDC. Additional concerns arise over the propriety of governmental intervention in potential intrafamily disputes regarding the disposition of children.

When a placement with a relative is appropriate and is supported by the agency, it promotes an uninterrupted relationship for the child with the parent and relative, which is vital to a child's physical, social, and emotional well-being. Therefore agencies should encourage strengthened familial bonds, which may also continue to function to the benefit of the family after reunification.

Although the study itself found no conclusive data on the stability or length of foster care placements with relatives, Goerge (1990) found that these placements were the most stable of all placements. Though not a panacea, placements with relatives should certainly be explored if reunification with the biological parents seems impossible.

NOTE

Permission for reprinting this material has been obtained from the National Black Child Development Institute (NBCDI) in Washington, D.C., the original publisher of this study. Funding for this study was provided by the U.S. Department of Health and Human Services, Office of the Assistant Secretary for Planning and Evaluation. A grant from the Skillman Foundation in Detroit, Michigan, provided support for the NBCDI study "Who will care when parents can't? A study of black children in the foster care systems" (1989).

REFERENCES

Barth, R. P. (1991). Adoption of drug-exposed children. *Children and Youth Services Review, 13,* 323–42.

Besharov, D. (1989). The children of crack: Will we protect them? *Public Welfare, 47,* 7–11.

Chasnoff, I. J. (1987). *A first: National hospital incidence study.* Chicago: National Association for Perinatal Addiction Research.

Daley, S. (October 23, 1989). Treating kin like foster parents strains a New York child agency. *The New York Times,* B4.

Dinkins, D. (February 5, 1990). Testimony before the Subcommittee on Children, Family, Drugs, and Alcoholism. In *Children of Substance Abusers.* Washington, D.C.: Government Printing Office.

Goerge, R. (1990). The reunification process in substitute care. *Social Service Review, 64,* (3), 422–57.

Maluccio, A. & Fein, E. (1983). Permanency planning: A redefinition. *Child Welfare, 62*(3), 195–201.

National Black Child Development Institute. (1989). *Who will care when parents can't? A study of black children in the foster care system.* Washington, D.C.: Author.

N.B.C.D.T. (1991). *Parental drug abuse and African-American children in foster care: Issues and study findings.* Washington, D.C.: Author.

U.S. Congress, Subcommittee on Human Resources. (June 12, 1990). *The enemy within: Crack-cocaine and America's families.* Washington, D.C.: Government Printing Office.

U.S. Department of Health and Human Services, Office of the Inspector General. (June 1990). *Crack Babies.* Washington, D.C.: Government Printing Office.

Select Committee on Children, Youth, and Families, U.S. House of Representatives. (November 1989). *No place to call home: Discarded children in America.* Washington, D.C.: Government Printing Office.

PART THREE

——

FOSTER CARE CASELOAD DYNAMICS

The number of children whose lives are touched by the foster care system is increasing annually. After the adoption of Public Law 96–272 the size of the foster care caseload dipped to a low of approximately 270,000 (Pelton 1989). Yet, since that time the caseload has been rising steadily, and some estimate that there will soon be almost half a million children in out-of-home care (Kamerman & Kahn 1989).

Cross-sectional descriptions of the foster care caseload tell a one-dimensional story about what is occurring and what is expected to occur for children in the child welfare services system. These numbers say little about the careers of children in foster care. Some children enter foster care and stay for a few short months; others enter care and stay for several years, whereas some may enter and exit foster care several times throughout their childhood years. Cross-sectional data cannot distinguish them. A few researchers have recently captured the diversity of these experiences and have characterized the foster care experience as a fluid process (Goerge 1990; Wulczyn 1991). Others have tried to articulate the meaning of this process for the individual lives of children (Fanshel, Finch, & Grundy 1989).

The papers in this section offer some of the most advanced methodological procedures now in use in the social sciences to measure foster caseload dynamics. Most of the studies are based upon longitudinal data bases rather than the more typical cross-sectional studies used frequently in the field of child welfare. Until recently, few researchers had the technological resources (e.g., powerful computer systems and advanced statistical procedures) at their disposal. With the simultaneous development of computer systems and statistical methods, a handful of researchers across the country are now attempting to answer several questions about the foster care system that could not be addressed previously.

Tatara provides important information about the out-of-home care population from a national perspective. His study examines rates of entry into and exits out of substitute care on an aggregate basis using the Voluntary Cooperative Information System (VCIS). Although entry rates increased significantly during the past decade, recent exit rates point to the increased length of stay for many children, a factor contributing profoundly to the overall growth in the foster care population.

Courtney examines the factors that contribute to placement in group care. Although some children placed in out-of-home care have always resided in congregate care facilities, the enthusiasm for the use of this placement type has shifted over the years. Today, group care is seen by most practitioners as a unique placement for children with special medical or emotional needs. Using logit analyses, Courtney describes the effect of specific variables, such as gender, age, and AFDC eligibility, on the odds that a child's first and subsequent foster care placements will be in a group home.

Goerge takes a unique approach to the examination of factors contributing to family reunification. Using event-history techniques, his paper reviews the effect of social worker turnover on the probability of reunification. While the results are somewhat counter-intuitive, Goerge provides some interesting interpretations of their meaning and points to the need for further work in this area.

Wulczyn provides definitive evidence for the link between foster care and poverty. Using data provided by the census and vital statistics on birth and death records, he geo-codes out-of-home care data and examines child welfare use by census tract. The analysis focuses on the infant placement rate, and his findings are startling. Writing about the dramatic increase in foster care placement rates in some of the poorest communities in New York City he notes: "If these [growth] trends develop into secular changes in the pattern of parent/child relations, then we may well have to ask ourselves whether single-parent families are giving way to 'no-parent families.' " His findings shed light on our understanding of foster care, but they are more important, perhaps, as they relate to the cohesion and strength of the family during times of severe stress.

Finally, in the last paper in this section, Albert uses time series analysis to predict the growth in the foster care population based upon a series of exogenous variables thought to contribute to foster care use. Time series is a statistical procedure largely used in studies of welfare use. The translation of this methodology to the field of child welfare is warranted as researchers refine the variables necessary to predict diverse child welfare outcomes.

REFERENCES

Fanshel, D., Finch, S., & Grundy, J. (1989). Foster children in a life-course perspective: The Casey Family Program experience. *Child Welfare, 68*(5), 467–78.

Goerge, R. (1990). The reunification process in substitute care. *Social Service Review, 64*, (3), 422–57.

Kamerman, S. & Kahn. A. J. (1990). Social services for children, youth, and families in the United States. *Children and Youth Services Review, 1/2*, 1–181.

Pelton, L. (1989). *For reasons of poverty: A critical analysis of the public child welfare system in the United States.* New York: Praeger.

Wulczyn, F. (1991). Caseload dynamics and foster care reentry. *Social Service Review, 65*(1), 133–56.

The Recent Rise in the U.S. Child Substitute Care Population: An Analysis of National Child Substitute Care Flow Data

Toshio Tatara

The U.S. child substitute care[1] population reached 429,000 at the end of fiscal year (FY) 1991 and apparently has increased since then. Preliminary estimates from states suggest that it rose by at least 4% to 5% between FY 1991 and FY 1992. If these estimates are accurate, nearly 450,000 children[2] nationwide are currently residing in out-of-home care. Because there were about 280,000 children in substitute care in the country at the end of FY 1986, the current figure of 450,000 represents an increase of 60.7% over a period of six years. Moreover, along with the recent rise in the point prevalence of child substitute care, there have been substantial increases in the volume of substitute care caseloads that are served by the nation's public child welfare system. For example, during FY 86, a total of about 456,000 children spent at least one day in substitute care, but the number of children served by the system rose to 636,000 during FY 91, an increase of 39.5% from FY 86.

On the surface, it appears to make sense to attribute the recent rise in the size of the child substitute care populations largely to an increase in the count of entrants into care. Indeed, there has been a considerable increase in the number of children coming into care in the past several years. Experts cite rising "parental drug problems" along with factors generally associated with the worsening of the economy (e.g., unemployment, poverty, homelessness) as major causes of this rapid increase in the number of substitute care entrants. For example, one researcher observed that children's various risks for being placed in out-of-home care were greatly increased by recent "changes in children's family life" and identified several specific risks closely associated with children's substitute care placements (Testa 1992). These risks included: (1) rising numbers of teenage mothers and never-married parents, (2) high child poverty rates, (3) child abuse and neglect, (4) parental substance abuse, and (5) AIDS (Testa 1992:35). Similarly, a recent study of children and families receiving foster care and preventive services by the New York State Department of Social Services found that such problems as parental substance abuse, child abuse and neglect, poverty, domestic violence, and parental mental illness are greatly related to the growing foster care caseloads in the state of New York (New York State Department of Social Services 1992). In particular, the study discovered that 61% of the foster care cases in the study sample that were opened during 1990 had come from families with problems of parental drug abuse or alcoholism (New York State Department of Social Services 1992). Studies from a number of other states also showed that "parental drug and alcohol problems" and other "parental reasons" (e.g., economic hardship, absence, illness) significantly contributed to an increase in the count of substitute care entrants in these states (Tatara 1991).

Several questions still remain unanswered by the existing explanations about the recent rise in the U.S. child substitute care population. Some of the unanswered questions are: Can the recent increases in the child substitute care population be fully explained by the increases in the counts of entrants into care? Were there any recent changes in substitute care exits or in the length of time children stay in substitute care? What are some of the major factors associated with substitute care exits? Using the national aggregate data on substitute care children that were gathered by the Voluntary Cooperative Information System (VCIS) operated by the American Public Welfare Association (APWA), along with some anecdotal information obtained from a number of states, this study explores the possible answers to these questions. Although the main focus of the study is an analysis of the substitute care population trends, based on the substitute care "flow" data for the period between FY 86 and FY 91 the statistics from previous years are also examined as needed.

VCIS Child Substitute Care Flow Data

One of the unique features of the VCIS substitute care data is that they are organized in accordance with a "population flow paradigm," a framework for analyzing the child substitute care data that was developed in the early 1980s (Gershenson 1984). The population flow paradigm permits an analysis of the movement (and the characteristics) of children coming into and out of the substitute care system. Through the application of a "population flow analysis algorithm," it also helps generate a wide variety of evaluation indicators that may be used to monitor the performance of the substitute care system. For example, using this algorithm, a researcher designed the Child Welfare Management Self-Evaluation Technology (CWMSET), a computerized self-evaluation tool for child welfare agencies capable of computing a total of thirty-seven performance indicators for substitute care and adoption services (Tatara 1985). Some of these indicators related to substitute care include: the point prevalence rate, the incidence rate, the overall entry and exit rates, the new entry and reentry rates, the multiple placement rate, the turnover rate, the movement ratio, the service trend rate, the reunification exit rate, the age of majority/emancipation exit rate, the median length of time in care, and the median age of children in care.

The great advantage of the population flow paradigm and the analytic tools designed on the basis of the population flow analysis algorithm (e.g., CWMSET) is that they can be used to analyze substitute care aggregate data that may be readily available at *any* level of government. For example, a population flow analysis can be performed, with the use of the appropriate statistics, at the agency level as well as at the state or national levels. For the purpose of this study, however, the population flow paradigm is applied to the national aggregate data on substitute care children that VCIS has collected from states.

Since its inception in 1981, VCIS has gathered, in aggregate form, the child substitute care flow data (along with adoption statistics) from state child welfare agencies. These data are composed of four basic items: (1) the count of children who were in care at the start of each fiscal year; (2) the count of children who entered care during each fiscal year; (3) the count of children who left care during each fiscal year; and (4) the count of children who were still in care at the end of each fiscal year. These four sets of data represent the core data for the substitute care population flow paradigm. In addition, VCIS has also gathered information about various characteristics of children included in each one of these core data items. For example, for the count of children who entered care during each fiscal year, VCIS obtained statistics for the following items: (1) the Title IV-E eligibility status of children, (2) the ages of children, and (3) the race/ethnic characteristics of the children entering care. Similarly, for the count of children who left care during each fiscal year, VCIS collected data on the discharge outcomes of these children and the length of continuous time these children spent in care as well as statistics for the ages and race/ethnic characteristics of these children. For the count of children who were still in care at the end of each fiscal year, the list of items was even longer and included: (1) the sex of the children, (2) the living arrangements of the children, (3) the number of children who were placed in unlicensed/unpaid relatives' homes, (4) the legal placement status of the children, (5) the disabling conditions of children, (6) the number of placements the children experienced while in the system, (7) the permanency plan goals for the children, and (8) the length of continuous time the children spent in care. Data on the ages and race/ethnic characteristics and the Title IV-E eligibility status also were collected for the children who were still in care at the end of each fiscal year. Finally, a summary of the analysis of these flow data and detailed "breakout" data was released each year in the publication, *Characteristics of Children in Substitute and Adoptive Care*.[3]

Substitute Care Entrants and Children Who Left Care Between FY 86 and FY 91

The algorithm for the flow analysis suggests that the size of the substitute care population at the end of a given fiscal year is determined by the following formula:

$$(a + b) - c,$$

where a represents the "count of children who were in care at the start of the fiscal year," while b is the "count of children who entered care during the fiscal year," and c signifies the "count of children who left care during the fiscal year." Given that for a given year, a is constant, the size of the substitute care population is the function of both the count of children entering care and the count of children

TABLE 6.1
U.S. Child Substitute Care Population With Flow Data
FY 86 through FY 91

Year	Start	Entered Care	Total Served	Left Care	End	% Difference from end of FY 86
FY 86	273*	183	456	176	280	—
FY 87	280	222	502	202	300	+ 7.1%
FY 88	312	199	511	171	340	+21.4%
FY 89**	343	222	565	182	383	+36.8%
FY 90***	379	238	617	210	407	+45.4%
FY 91***	412	224	636	207	429	+52.9%

SOURCE: The Voluntary Cooperative Information System (VCIS), the American Public Welfare Association (APWA).
* All figures are in thousands.
** The figures for FY 89 are final. Any previous estimates released by VCIS now must be corrected.
*** The figures for FY 90 and FY 91 are highly reliable but are still tentative. Final figures will be confirmed when VCIS completes its collection of more detailed data. Finally, the figure at the end of a given fiscal year and the figure at the start of the next fiscal year are close to one another but are rarely the same. The discrepancy between the two figures is caused mainly by the fact that states make adjustments to the count of children in care at the end of each fiscal year by correcting reporting and system errors.

leaving care. In other words, it is important to examine both "entry" and "exit" statistics (as well as the factors influencing these statistics) when explanations for any changes in the child substitute care population are sought. The VCIS estimates of the U.S. child substitute care population, along with the essential flow data for FY 86 through FY 91, are presented in table 6.1.

As can be seen in table 6.1, there was a sizable increase in the number of entrants to care from FY 86 to FY 87 (an increase of 21.3%), but the number of substitute care entrants declined considerably from FY 87 to FY 88 (a drop of 10.4%). Interestingly enough, this number rose again between FY 88 and FY 89 (an increase of 11.6%) and went back to the FY 87 level in FY 89. Then, the number of entrants to care grew again and reached the highest point in FY 90 (an increase of 7.2% from FY 89) but went down to the FY 89 level in FY 91.

From FY 86 to FY 87, there was a significant rise in the number of substitute care exits (an increase of 14.8%), but this gain totally disappeared when the number of exits reached the lowest point during FY 88 (a drop of 15.3% from FY 87). While the number of entrants to care kept growing after FY 88, the number of substitute care exits rose only slightly from FY 88 to FY 89 (an increase of 6.4%), and a sizable increase in the number of exits did not happen until FY 90 (an increase of 15.4% between FY 89 and FY 90). There was a small decrease in the number of children who left care from FY 90 to FY 91. Notice that between FY 86 and FY 91, there was no fiscal year in which the number of substitute care exits exceeded the number of substitute care entries. The cumulative result of this fact was a steady, continued increase in the size of the child substitute care population during this five-year period.

Child Substitute Care Entry and Exit Rates, FY 86 Through FY 91

An analysis of the *raw* estimated numbers in table 6.1 presents only a partial picture of what happened to the U.S. child substitute care population in recent years. The use of the above-mentioned "population flow analysis algorithm" provides further insight into the relationships between substitute care entries and exits as well as into trends in the nation's substitute care population from FY 86 to FY 91. Accordingly, using the flow data included in table 6.1, both the national substitute care entry and exit rates are calculated and presented in table 6.2.

TABLE 6.2
National Child Substitute Care Entry and Exit Rates
FY 86 through FY 91

Year	Entry Rate(a)	Exit Rate (b)	b-a*
FY 86	0.401**	0.386***	−0.015
FY 87	0.442	0.402	−0.040
FY 88	0.389	0.335	−0.054
FY 89	0.393	0.322	−0.071
FY 90	0.386	0.340	−0.046
FY 91	0.352	0.325	−0.027

SOURCE: Based on the data presented in Table 6.1.
  * The result of *b-a* determines the extent of gain or loss in the substitute care population for a given fiscal year. If the figure is positive, there was a *decrease* in the population. But if the figure is negative, there was an *increase* in the number of substitute care children. Generally, the difference of 0.01 represents several thousands of children.
  ** The figure can be interpreted as follows: 40.1% of the children served by the substitute care system during FY 86 were those who entered care during that year.
  *** On the other hand, this figure means that 38.6% of the children served by the system during FY 86 left care during the same year.

The entry rate represents the proportion of the number of children who entered care during a given fiscal year in relation to the total number of children served by the substitute care system during the same fiscal year. It can be obtained through the use of the following formula:

$$a \div (a + b),$$

where *a* represents the count of substitute care entrants, and *b* stands for the count of the children who were in care at the start of the fiscal year. The denominator of this formula, *a* + *b*, represents the total number of children served by the substitute care system during the fiscal year. The entry rate is an indicator of the volume of substitute care entries in proportion to the total volume of care provided by the system during a given period.

On the other hand, the exit rate is the proportion of the number of children who left care during a given fiscal year in relation to the total number of children served by the system during the same year. It can be calculated using the following formula:

$$c \div (a + b),$$

where *c* represents the count of substitute care exits during the fiscal year, and *a* + *b* signifies the total number of children who spent at least one day in substitute care during the same year, as illustrated in the description of the entry rate. The exit rate is a measure of the total exits from care in proportion to the total volume of care provided by the substitute care system during a given year.

Because of the way the formulas for the entry and exit rates are structured, the relationship between the two rates is obvious: when the entry rate is larger than the exit rate in a given reporting period, the result is an increase in the number of substitute care children at the end of the same period. On the other hand, if the entry rate is smaller than the exit rate, a decrease in the size of the substitute care population is the net result. Finally, it is important to note that only a small difference between the two rates amounts to a large gain or loss in the number of children at the end of the reporting period. What the difference of 0.01 between the rates means in the actual number of children depends on the numbers used in the calculation of these two rates. But such a difference usually signifies several thousands of children. For example, during FY 86, the entry rate was greater than

TABLE 6.3
National Child Substitute Care Entry and Exit Rates
FY 82 through FY 85*

Year	Entry Rate(a)	Exit Rate (b)	b-a*
FY 82	0.371	0.396	+0.025
FY 83	0.412	0.398	−0.014
FY 84	0.404	0.395	−0.009
FY 85	0.413	0.400	−0.013

SOURCE: The Voluntary Cooperative Information System (VCIS), the American Public Welfare Association (AWPA).

* The interpretations of the figures presented in this table are the same as those shown in Table 6.2.

the exit rate by 0.015 (0.401 − 0.386), resulting in an increase of 7,000 children at the end of that year (280,000 − 273,000).

The rates presented in table 6.2 clearly show that *both* the entry and exit rates went down noticeably from FY 86 to FY 91. Although there was a similar pattern of decline in the two sets of rates, the exit rate dropped somewhat more than the entry rate during the five-year period (a drop of 12.2% for the entry rate and 15.8% for the exit rate). During FY 86, 38.6% of the children served by the substitute care system left care, but this percentage dropped to 32.5% in FY 91, showing that the rate of children leaving care has become significantly smaller in recent years than it had been several years ago. Additionally, it is also clear from the table that between FY 86 and FY 91 there was not one year in which the exit rate was larger than the entry rate, indicating that the nation's substitute care population continued to grow during this period.

Child Substitute Care Entry and Exit Rates, FY 82 Through FY 85

To show that the trends in the entry and exit rates (as well as the relationship between the two sets of rates) in the early 1980s were somewhat different from those between FY 86 and FY 91, the entry and exit rates for FY 82 through FY 85 were calculated, using the national aggregate data on substitute care children. These rates are presented in table 6.3.[4]

The fact that the exit rate was slightly larger than the entry rate (a difference of 0.025) during FY 82 indicates a net decrease in the substitute care population during that year. In all other years, however, there was an increase in the number of children in care. Nonetheless, when the differences in the entry and exit rates are compared between table 6.2 and table 6.3, it is clear that these differences widened more in recent years than in the early 1980s. This signifies that the rate of growth in the child substitute care populations was much greater during the period after FY 86 than it was before that year. In the early 1980s both rates were very similar, suggesting that there was only a small change in the substitute care population from one year to another.

Furthermore, a comparison of the exit rates presented in the two tables shows that these rates were considerably larger during the period between FY 82 and FY 85 than they have been in recent years. In other words, in relation to the total number of children in care greater numbers of children left care before FY 86 than after that year. For example, during FY 85, 40.0% of the children served by the nation's substitute care system exited care, but only 32.5% of these children left the system during FY 91 (a drop of 18.8%). Nevertheless, the fact that the difference between the entry and exit rates again became smaller after FY 89 may be an indication of some decline in the rate of growth in the child substitute care population after that year.

An Additional Analysis of Data from Twenty-two States

The analyses presented earlier were performed with the use of national aggregate data, which were "national estimates" developed on the basis of statistics reported by fewer than all states. In particular, the national estimates for substitute care entries and exits were made using the figures gathered from fewer than forty states. In an attempt to obtain a more accurate picture of trends in the substitute care entry and exit rates in the past several years, an additional analysis was conducted with the use of *actual* data from twenty-two states[5] that provided all the statistics needed for the calculations of both entry and exit rates for the entire period between FY 86 and FY 91. The substitute care entry and exit rates from these twenty-two states are summarized in table 6.4.

On the whole, the analysis of the actual statistics from the twenty-two states presented in table 6.4 confirms what was displayed in table 6.2 and gives high credibility to the use of national aggregate data. As

TABLE 6.4
*Child Substitute Care Entry and Exit Rates in 22 States,
FY 86 through FY 91**

Year	Entry Rate(a)	Exit Rate (b)	b-a*
FY 86	0.386	0.364	−0.022
FY 87	0.400	0.343	−0.057
FY 88	0.380	0.308	−0.072
FY 89	0.372	0.287	−0.085
FY 90	0.338	0.292	−0.046
FY 91	0.305	0.285	−0.020

SOURCE: The Voluntary Cooperative Information System (VCIS), the American Public Welfare Association (AWPA).
* The interpretations of the exit and entry rate are presented along with Table 6.2.

the national data indicated, the data from these twenty-two states show steady downward trends in both the substitute care entry and exit rates from FY 86 to FY 91. Specifically, the entry rate went down gradually from 0.386 in FY 86 to 0.305 in FY 91 (a drop of 21.0%). Similarly, the exit rate also declined considerably during the same period (a drop of 21.7%). The exit rate of 0.285 for FY 91 was the lowest during the period between FY 86 and FY 91 and indicates that only 28.5% of the children served by the substitute care system left care during FY 91.

Additionally, the differences between the entry and exit rates in the twenty-two states became noticeably wider in FY 87, FY 88, and FY 89, with the entry rates growing markedly higher than the exit rates. The national aggregate data showed essentially the same trend. However, the clear downward trend in the differences between the two rates after FY 89 (which was also seen in the national aggregate data) may be an indication that the extent of growth in the substitute care population became somewhat smaller in the past few years than it had been in previous years.

Additional Explanations for the Recent Rise in the National Child Substitute Care Populations

The substantial increases in the size of the U.S. child substitute care population in the past several years must be explained by changes in *both* substitute care entries and exits. The review of the VCIS data for FY 86 through FY 91 reveals that there was indeed a considerable increase in the actual number of children coming into care during this five-year period. In addition, there are no reasons to dispute the commonly accepted explanation that such factors as "parental drug and alcohol problems" and "other parent-related reasons" caused by a combination of social and individual reasons (e.g., unemployment, poverty, homelessness, abandonment, mental illness) have made the number of substitute care entrants grow.

However, a noticeable drop in the substitute care entry rates after FY 87, as shown in table 6.2, indicates that there was an overall decline in the proportion of substitute care entrants to the total number of children served by the nation's substitute care system in recent years. In fact, as mentioned earlier, there was a minor downward trend in the substitute care entry rates after FY 87, and nationally there were no major changes in the actual number of children coming into care after FY 87 (except for FY 88, when the number of substitute care entrants decreased by 10.4% compared to the number for FY 87).

On the other hand, the trend in substitute care exits was somewhat confusing, as discussed earlier. There were ups and downs in the actual counts of children leaving care between FY 86 and FY 91, with a pattern in which the "poor performance year" (i.e., FY 86) was generally followed by the "good performance year" (i.e., FY 87) throughout this period. However, the count of substitute care exits appeared to be on the rise after FY 89. Despite this recent trend in the actual number of exits, the rate of exits continued to drop after FY 87, as shown in the earlier analyses. In fact, the steady decline in the substitute care exit rate began after FY 85 but was interrupted in FY 87, an exceptional year in which the exit rate as well as the entry rate reached their highest points in the ten years between FY 82 and FY 91. Overall, however, it is clear that the proportion of children exiting the substitute care system became continually smaller in recent years, highlighting the fact that the number of substitute care exits has *not* kept pace with the growing number of children in care. In programmatic terms, this finding is very important to the public child welfare community because it suggests that there has been a decline in the child welfare system's effectiveness in helping achieve permanency of care for substitute care children. The recent decline in substitute care exit rates is a troubling sign that children are no longer leaving substitute care at the same rates as they were in the early 1980s. Clearly, ways must be found to further strengthen efforts (e.g., family reunification and adoption services) aimed at expediting the return of substitute care children to permanent caregivers.

The Length of Time Children Spend in Substitute Care

The above finding that children are not leaving care at the same rates as in previous years implies that the period of time children spend in substitute care has become longer. The relationship between the length of stay in care of the children and the probability of their exits from care has intrigued researchers from time to time since the late 1950s, but to date only a small number of empirical studies on this topic have been conducted (Maas & Engler 1959; Fanshel & Shinn 1976; Shapiro 1976; Goerge & Wulczyn 1990; Goerge 1990). Existing data generally suggest that the likelihood of children leaving substitute care declines considerably after a certain period of time spent in care, but there still is some debate as to what may be the critical point in time that decreases the statistical probability of children exiting care. This paper is not intended to provide any new information about substitute care duration and its effect on substitute care exits. But it attempts to show, with the use of the VCIS data, that while exit rates were declining in recent years (as illustrated by the earlier analysis), the period of time children remained in care was becoming somewhat shorter.

VCIS has been collecting aggregate state statistics for the length of continuous time children spend in care on two groups of children: on children who were discharged from substitute care each fiscal year and on children who were still in care at the end of each fiscal year. The data on the first group of children have been available since FY 85, and the data on the second group have been gathered since FY 82. The intent of VCIS was to develop the *national* estimates for substitute care durations for these two groups of children, but because data were available from only about one-half of the states, the development of true national estimates has not been possible. The median length of time in care for the children who left care each year (until the time of their exits) from FY 85 to FY 88 is indicated in table 6.5 (Tatara 1992:75).

The median length of stay in substitute care for the children who exited care went down from 8.9 months in FY 85 to 7.9 months in FY 88, indicating that overall children spent a somewhat shorter amount of time in care during FY 88 than they did during FY 85. The earlier analyses on exit rates show a decline in the substitute care exit rate from 0.400 in FY 85 to 0.308 in FY 88, suggesting that the rate of children leaving care dropped considerably during this three-year

TABLE 6.5
Median Length of Time Spent in Substitute Care (FY 85 to FY 88)

For Children Who Left Care

	FY 85	FY 86	FY 87	FY 88
Median length of time in care*	8.9 mos.	9.5 mos.	9.1 mos.	7.9 mos.
No. of states included in calculations	28	25	22	24
For Children Still in Care				
	FY 85	FY 86	FY 87	FY 88
Median length of stay in care*	1.5 years	1.5 years	1.3 years	1.4 years
No. of states included in calculations	31	32	23	23

SOURCE: The Voluntary Cooperative Information System (VCIS), the American Public Welfare Association (APWA).

* Because these figures were developed using data reported from fewer than fifty-one states, they may not be nationally representative. It is not possible to determine how the difference in the numbers of states included in the calculations affected these medians.

period. In other words, the overall time spent in care for substitute care children became shorter, but the rate of children leaving care did not improve.

Separate data from the VCIS child welfare data base reveal that the median age of children who left the nation's substitute care system became slightly lower between FY 85 and FY 88 (i.e., 12.7 years of age in FY 85 and 11.1 years of age in FY 88) (Tatara 1992:78). The same downward trend was also found among the children who entered care during this period (i.e., 10.2 years old in FY 85 to 8.2 years old in FY 88) (Tatara 1992:78). It is indeed tempting to suggest that the ages of children coming into care have an effect on the length of stay in substitute care. However, findings from a recent study in Illinois and New York on the relationship between these two variables are mixed and inconclusive. For example, in Illinois, older entrants into care spent more time in care than younger ones, while in New York older entrants were in care for a shorter time than younger entrants (Goerge & Wulczyn 1990:27).

It is puzzling that the rate of substitute care exits was not rising when the duration in care became shorter and the ages of children coming into care became lower. It is true that the dynamics of substitute care exits are very complex and cannot be fully explored with the use of aggregate data alone. After analyzing a sample of nearly twelve hundred substitute care children in Illinois, one researcher noted that "the median duration in care does not show whether the probability of reunification is increasing, decreasing, or remaining constant over time" (Goerge 1990:454). As this researcher suggests, a declining rate of substitute care exits is caused by a combination of a large number of factors. An investigation of these factors clearly requires detailed "case-level" data collected from diverse geographic locations, but aggregate data (such as those of VCIS) may also be useful in terms of depicting overall trends and identifying broad research questions, as this paper attempts to do.

Major Factors Associated with a Decline in Substitute Care Exits

The earlier analysis of the VCIS data leaves no doubt that the stymied progress in efforts to increase substitute care exits has greatly contributed to the recent rise in the child substitute care population. What are some of the factors associated with the seeming lack of positive results from these efforts? A number of factors can be considered, but because most of these factors have not been validated through empirical research, they are offered in the form of broad research questions to be further refined and tested. It would also be beneficial to those concerned with the well-being of the nation's children if these and other factors are debated in professional forums and classrooms. In this author's view, the major factors that have hampered efforts to expedite substitute care exits in recent years include the following:

Greater Emphasis on Placement Prevention. In the past decade the nation's public child welfare system has continually placed greater emphasis on efforts to prevent the placement of children in substitute care than on efforts to move children out of care. The view that out-of-home placements should be avoided unless absolutely needed was not only the dominant philosophy of child welfare professionals, but it was also the nation's law. The Adoption Assistance and Child Welfare Act of 1980 (Public Law 96–272), which guided child welfare practices in the 1980s, made it clear that substitute care placements must be limited to only those cases that are at "imminent risk of placement," and it required that public child welfare agencies made "reasonable efforts" to keep abused or neglected children with their parents. This federal law also stipulated that the stay of children in substitute care must be brief and that efforts must be made to reunify children with their families or to find other permanent arrangements (e.g., adoption) if reunification was not possible. However, it appears that throughout the 1980s a disproportionately greater amount of resources has been spent on programs for placement prevention (e.g., family preservation programs) than on programs for reunifying substitute care children with their families. Many communities have developed home-based, intensive service programs to help prevent the placement of children into substitute care. Targeted to families at risk of dissolution, these programs sought to ensure that unnecessary placements are avoided and that the placement of children in out-of-home care is the last resort. Although data are still inconclusive on the true effectiveness of many placement prevention programs, a number of jurisdictions report that these programs were quite successful.[6] In the meantime, this emphasis on placement prevention by the child welfare community is now taking its toll at a time when greater success in reunification of substitute care children with their parents is needed.

More Difficulty In, and Higher Cost of, Reunification. Empirical data on the comparative costs of placement prevention and reunification efforts are almost nonexistent. One of the reasons for the lack of these data is that the child welfare community has not yet clearly defined what reunification programs are and how such programs must be implemented. Nonetheless, experts appear to agree that reunification programs generally are more costly and pose more difficulties in achieving the desired outcomes than placement prevention programs. This is true particularly when "multiproblem families" are to be served by reunification programs, because the kinds of programmatic resources needed to help alleviate the problems of these families are extremely costly and are always scarce. For example, a family with parental mental health and drug problems and without steady incomes, living in a deteriorated house, requires an enormous amount of resources (e.g., family therapy, drug counseling, employment, housing programs) to help achieve an adequate level of "self-sufficiency" needed to receive its child back from substitute care. However, most of these resources are not generally available within the public child welfare system and must be found elsewhere. In fact, a recent survey of state child welfare agencies by APWA has revealed that only three types of services (i.e., child protective services, foster care, and adoption) are available statewide in all states, but the availability of services aimed at assisting families with children placed in substitute care is very limited across the country (National Commission on Child Welfare and Family Preservation 1990:3). The current lack of programmatic resources necessary to adequately address the multiple problems of many families with children in out-of-home placement is not an encouraging sign for the prospect of reunification between these families and their children.

Recent Rise in the Number of Severely "Damaged" Families and Children. Data show that families from which children were removed in recent years are more severely "damaged" and have more complex multiple problems than families in past years. Additionally, there is evidence that many recent entrants into substitute care themselves have more difficult problems than did the entrants of some years ago. The VCIS data on "reasons for children entering care" indicate that the percentage of children entering care because of parental conditions or absence (e.g., substance abuse, unemployment, homelessness, illness, imprisonment) increased substantially from 17.0% in FY 84 to 22.3% in FY 88 (Tatara 1992:55). Moreover, as mentioned earlier, a recent study by the New York State Department of Social Sciences found that 61% of the children entering substitute care came from families with parental substance abuse problems and that over one-third of the families of these children had "four or more serious problems" (e.g., child abuse and neglect, poverty, domestic violence, mental illness, inadequate housing) (New York Department of Social Services 1992:i–ii). It does not take great imagination to assume that the children coming from these backgrounds have difficult problems of their own and are often in need of highly specialized care. Effectively serving these families and children with severe multiple problems requires more expertise and time (not to mention programmatic resources) than are currently available within the public child welfare system.

Stiffer Criteria for Reunification. Criteria for returning substitute care children to their families vary considerably from one state to another and from one locality to another within the same state. A number of jurisdictions uses some decision support tools (e.g., risk assessment, protocols) to assess the readiness of families to receive their children back from substitute care, but most of them rely largely on professional judgments of case workers and their supervisors to determine when to reunite children with their parents. Out of fear that children may be harmed again after they return home, many states appear to have stiffened their criteria for making reunification decisions through legislation, agency policy, or procedural changes. It is assumed that the growing number of child deaths in home settings has caused many public child welfare agencies to "play it safe" and practice "defensive social work." The fact that nationwide more than twelve hundred children died from abuse or neglect in 1990, as estimated by the National Committee for the Prevention of Child Abuse (Daro & McCurdy 1991:16), must have influenced these agencies' defensive posture in making reunification decisions. As a result, fewer children have been reunified with their families than have been removed from their homes in recent years.

Unrealistic Societal Expectations About the Public Child Welfare System. Historically, this country has relied almost totally (and perhaps unrealistically) on the public child welfare system to ameliorate all the problems of children and families. Yet, as discussed earlier, it is clear that most of these problems are deeply rooted in very difficult societal problems (e.g., poverty, joblessness, inadequate housing, poor education), which are far beyond the ability of any one social welfare program alone to solve. In addition to a reassessment of the role of the public child welfare system in society (as has recently been done by APWA's National Commission on Child Welfare and Family Preservation and other groups), an examination of what *other* social and economic institutions must contribute to combat these larger societal problems is needed. Clearly, it is unrealistic to expect that the public child welfare system alone can solve all of these difficult societal problems.

It is not unreasonable to assume that a combination of these factors has caused a recent overall decline in substitute care exits. It is hoped that future research and intellectual debate will focus on these and other factors to further clarify their significance in relation to reunification efforts.

The recent dramatic rise in the U.S. child substitute care population was not caused primarily by increases in the number of children coming into care. The actual number of entrants into care did not increase greatly after FY 87. Data clearly show that a continual decline in the rate of children leaving substitute care in the past several years has caused the substitute care population to grow. Using both national aggregate data and specific state data, this paper analyzed both substitute care entry and exit rates, briefly explored the relationship between exit rates and the length of the children's stays in care and finally identified some of the major factors that may be closely associated with the recent lack of progress in efforts to expedite the reunification of children with their families. In sum, the nation's public child welfare system has begun to show signs of "strain" as it is faced with a growing number of children coming into the system from families with extremely difficult problems, a decline in the amount of resources available to effectively address these problems, and the somewhat unrealistic societal expectations that the public child welfare system must help alleviate all the problems of families and children.

NOTES

This paper is the revised version of the author's original study, "Some Additional Explanations for the Recent Rise in the U.S. Child Substitute Care Population," distributed in the VCIS Research Notes, *5 (November 1991). The original study was supported in part by a grant (No. 90–0J-2015) awarded to the American Public Welfare Association (APWA) to operate the Voluntary Cooperative Information System (VCIS) and by the U.S. Department of Health and Human Services (HHS). New information was added to the original study. Views expressed in this paper are those of the author and do not reflect the policies of the federal government or APWA.*

1. For the purpose of this paper, the term "child substitute care" is defined as a living arrangement in which children are residing outside of their own homes under the case management and case planning responsibilities of public child welfare agencies or of private/voluntary child placing agencies under contract to public child welfare agencies. Substitute care is synonymous with "out-of-home care" and includes living arrangements such as foster family homes (both homes of relatives and of nonrelatives), foster homes, group homes, child care facilities, emergency shelters, supervised living arrangements, institutions, and other living arrangements regarded by public child welfare agencies as twenty-four-hour substitute care.

2. APWA's Voluntary Cooperative Information System (VCIS) plans to collect national child substitute care flow data for FY 92 sometime in 1993. Until then this figure should be viewed as tentative.

3. The most recent VCIS data on substitute and adoptive care analyzed and released to the public were those from FY 88. VCIS is currently analyzing the FY 89 data with an expected publication date of spring 1993. VCIS is also collecting the FY 90 data on both substitute care and adoption services. The collection of detailed FY 91 data will not begin until sometime in 1993.

4. Both the entry and exit rates for FY 82 through FY 85 were calculated, using the following substitute care flow data:

Year	Start	Entered Care	Total Served	Left Care	End
FY 82	273*	161	434	172	262
FY 83	263	184	447	178	269
FY 84	272	184	456	180	276
FY 85	270	190	460	184	276

SOURCE: The Voluntary Cooperative Information System (VCIS), The American Public Welfare Association (APWA).
* All figures are in thousands.

5. These twenty-two states are: Alabama, California, Connecticut, Florida, Idaho, Kentucky, Maine, Massachusetts, Mississippi, Missouri, New Jersey, New York, North Carolina, North Dakota, Puerto Rico, South Dakota, Tennessee, Texas, Utah, Vermont, Virginia, and Wisconsin. Several urban states with large substitute care populations are included, but other large states are not included in the group (e.g., Georgia, Illinois, Michigan, Ohio, Pennsylvania, and Washington).

6. Many published and unpublished evaluation studies of family preservation programs exist. For a review of the major evaluations of these programs, see: Rossi 1992:77–97.

REFERENCES

Daro, D. & McCurdy, K. (1991). *Current trends in child abuse reporting and fatalities: The results of the 1990 Annual Fifty State Survey*. Chicago: The National Committee for Prevention of Child Abuse.
Fanshel, D. & Shinn, E. B. (1976). *Children in foster care: A Longitudinal investigation*. New York: Columbia University Press.
Gershenson, C. P. (1994, March). Child welfare population flow theory and method. *Child Welfare Research Notes, 5*.
Goerge, R. M. & Wulczyn, F. H. (1990). *Placement duration and foster care reentry in New York and Illinois* (Volume One: A Report Prepared for the U.S. General Accounting Office). Chicago: The Chapin Hall Center for Children at the University of Chicago.
Goerge, R. M. (1990, September). The reunification process in substitute care. *Social Science Review*, 423–57.

Maas, H. S. & Engler, R. E. (1959). *Children in need of parents.* New York: Columbia University Press.

National Commission on Child Welfare and Family Preservation. (1990). *Factbook on public child welfare services and staff.* Washington, D.C.: APWA.

New York State Department of Social Services. (1992). *Families in the child welfare system: Foster care and preventive services in the nineties—An executive summary* (pp. i–vii). New York: Author.

Rossi, P. H. (1992). Assessing family preservation programs. *Children and Youth Services Review* (A Special Issue: Reforming Child Welfare Through Demonstration and Evaluation), *14*(1/2), 77–97.

Shapiro, D. (1976). *Agencies and foster children.* New York: Columbia University Press.

Tatara, T. (1991). *Children of substance abusing and alcoholic parents in public child welfare.* Washington, D.C.: APWA.

Tatara, T. (1992). *Characteristics of children in substitute and adoptive care: Based on FY 82 through FY 88 data.* Washington, D.C.: APWA.

Tatara, T. (1991, September). Parental drug problems and child substitute care: A review of VCIS data on children who entered care during FY 88. *VCIS Research Notes, 4.*

Tatara, T. (1985). *Child welfare management self-evaluation technology (CWMSET): Self-instructional manual.* Washington, D.C.: APWA.

Testa, M. F. (1992). Conditions for risk for substitute care. *Children and Youth Services Review* (A Special Issue: Reforming Child Welfare Through Demonstration and Evaluation), *14*(1/2), 27–35.

SEVEN

Status at Birth and Infant Placements in New York City

Fred Wulczyn

I. Background

In the middle of 1986 New York City experienced its first sustained increase in the number of first admissions to foster care in more than a decade. Over the next three years, first admissions more than doubled, from 9,270 children in 1986 to 19,709 in 1989. For much of that same period, the number of children leaving foster care actually declined. Not until 1989 did the number of children discharged from foster care surpass the number reported during the preceding year by a significant margin. According to summary reports, about eleven thousand children were discharged from New York City's foster care system in 1989, which was 25% more than in 1988 but still far below the number of admissions. The net result of this unprecedented growth in admissions and the decline in children discharged pushed the total number of children in placement in New York City from 18,793 in 1986 to 47,145 in 1989.

Caseload changes of this magnitude rarely go unnoticed, and there have been a number of hypotheses offered to help explain the growth that took place during the latter part of the 1980s. Above all, the years between 1986 and 1989 were marked by a shift in risk patterns related to substance abuse, especially among pregnant women, leading some experts to conclude that drug and alcohol use must account for some of the pressure on child welfare services (Phibbs, Ciaran, Bateman, & Schwartz 1991; Kaye 1989).[1] More recently, observers of New York's foster care system have started to look at policy changes that may have stimulated the surge in placement activity. In particular, the practice of placing children with relatives who receive full foster care reimbursement is coming under increased scrutiny (Link 1990; Gallagher 1991). In 1986, the year before the policy of approved placement with relatives was adopted in New York City, only 872 children started placement in the home of a relative who was reimbursed for foster care.[2] By the end of 1989, the third full year of placements with relatives, the number of admissions to the homes of relatives in New York City had climbed to 6,211. Data for April of 1991 indicate that more than half of the children in foster care spent some time in the home of a relative. In fact, the population in the homes of relatives in New York City is now considerably larger than the city's entire foster care population was in 1987.

While the growth of placements in the homes of relatives is a striking example of how much has changed in New York City's foster care population over the last six years, it is unlikely that this or any other single factor account's for the rapid pace of change. In a previous paper, Robert Goerge and I explored three related measures of caseload activity in an effort to describe and compare changes in the foster care populations in New York and Illinois more concisely (Wulczyn & Goerge 1992). Our analysis started with a simple description of the admissions and discharges over time. The results showed that caseloads in both states started growing during 1986. In addition, the analysis highlighted the need to weigh the combined impact of admissions and discharges on caseload growth. The tendency to focus on admissions understates the dynamic nature of the foster care population and the role discharges can play in caseload changes over time.

Our study also looked at changes in caseload demographics. Both states reported a sharp influx in the number of infant admissions that was accompanied by a decline in the number of adolescents. Since past research has shown that infants move through the foster care system more slowly, some portion of the drop in the number of children leaving foster care must be attributed to basic demographic changes, at least over the short term. We also examined placements with relatives. Illinois has placed children with relatives since 1979, so changes in the utilization of homes of relatives in that state serve as a good baseline for judging the impact of New York's policy change in 1987. Among other similarities, the findings indicated that both states experienced an increase in the use of placements in the homes of relatives that started around 1987 (Wulczyn & Goerge 1990). The fact that Illinois witnessed a similar pattern of growth in placements in the homes of relatives diminishes the likelihood that New York's policy change per se was responsible for the marked increase in admissions.

II. The Present Study

It is somewhat easier to understand how New York's foster care population grew to its present size knowing that Illinois experienced many of the same changes. Still, foster care trends like those described above raise any number of basic questions that have yet to be answered. The purpose of this study is to bring some additional clarity to the changes in foster care utilization by looking more closely at the impact of infant admissions on New York City's foster care population. When the caseload first started to grow in 1986, infants accounted for just 15% of all first admissions; by 1990, 30% of New York City's first admissions involved a child under the age of one. Indeed, no other group of children affected the foster care population in New York City more profoundly during the late 1980s than children under the age of one at the time of admission.

The evidence gathered to judge the impact of infant admissions on the foster care population and the impact of foster care placement on infants takes several forms. The foster care placement data is taken directly from the Department of Social Services' Child Care Review Service (CCRS) and is used to describe both the number and the rate of infant placements in New York City. In addition, the placement data have been compiled by New York City zip codes in an effort to describe those areas of New York City where the risk of placement is highest.

The placement data are supplemented with vital statistics data from the New York State Department of Health. These data are incorporated in two ways. First, birth and mortality data produced by the Department of Health have been used to reveal those areas in New York City where birth outcomes tend to be poorest. These areas are then compared with the placement data to determine the extent to which birth outcomes correspond to foster care placement of infants.

Second, a link between CCRS placement records and the vital statistics records for individual infants was established with the cooperation of the Department of Health. In essence, the data link enables us to study directly the relationship between birth status and foster care outcomes such as placement duration. With this capacity, the presentation shifts between aggregate and individual levels of analysis in order to pinpoint changes in birth status and placement outcome more precisely.

Although the goal of this paper is to understand infant foster care placements, it is important to consider the broader context into which these findings may ultimately fit. In our previous research, Robert Goerge and I used birth data to calculate infant placement rates to compare changes in the basic risk of placement over time (Wulczyn & Goerge 1992). For New York City, the placement rate more than tripled between 1986 and 1989, reaching forty-four per thousand live births in 1989, or 4.4% of all the children born in New York City that year. Further analysis, presented here, revealed that in some of New York City's poorest neighborhoods, the rate of infant foster care placement in 1988 exceeded 12% of total live births, four to five times the rate reported in 1985 (Wulczyn 1991).

The high rate of infant placement found in the city's impoverished neighborhoods draws foster care closer and closer to the debate over poverty's coercive influence on family structure. While child welfare experts have always believed that poverty and foster care placement are intertwined, the epidemiological data needed to establish such relationships firmly have never been available widely. Moreover, researchers studying the relationship between poverty and family structure have tended to ignore child placement as a basic indicator of familial breakdown even though the separation of parents and children represents a fundamental break in the continuity of traditional family relations. This may be due to the fact that at any one time the number of children in foster care rarely exceeds 1% of the total child population, a relatively small figure when compared to the number of children living in single-parent families. Nevertheless, trends that have developed over the past five to seven years suggest that the likelihood that a child will spend some portion of his or her childhood in foster care may have increased substantially. Already, slightly more than 4% of all the children born in New York City between 1984 and 1989 have been in foster care at least once. The cumulative placement rate in communities where the infant placement rate reached levels in excess of 10% may well be approaching 20%. If these recent trends develop into secular changes in the pattern of parent-child relations, then we may well have to ask ourselves whether single-parent families are giving way to "no-parent families."[3]

It is difficult to anticipate the direction in which placement trends will move, and it is equally difficult to gauge how child placement will shape what we learn about poverty and family structure in the near future. Of more immediate concern is that the data make it abundantly clear that the time between the onset of pregnancy and a child's first birthday is quite perilous. For mothers who avail themselves of prenatal care, birth outcomes tend to be more positive. It now appears that children whose mothers receive prenatal care spend less time in foster care if they enter placement at all. At the community level, the fact that placement is so common in impoverished areas raises questions about how communities can help families develop and sustain permanent attachments to individual members when parents and their children live in the midst of urban hardship. Child welfare policy accepted the psychological dimensions of permanency planning long ago. It may now be time to explore how the attributes of a community influence permanency plans.

III. Infant Placements in New York City

As indicated, the data prepared for this paper come from two primary sources. The placement data was extracted from the Child Care Review Service (CCRS), a data system used by the Department of Social Services to track the placement careers of children admitted to publicly financed foster care. Although CCRS tracks all children, infant placements were selected as the initial indicator for a number of reasons, each of which is designed to narrow and thereby sharpen the focus. Of all possible measures of placement activity, the infant placement rate is probably the most easily measured. The Department of Health annually produces population data (the number of births) for several relevant geographical units so that historical placement rates can be computed easily. As a result, there is little need to rely on decennial census data to produce a reliable measure of family stability.

The contextual data come largely from the Department of Health and include traditional measures of birth outcomes: infant mortality, birth weight, prenatal care utilization, and births to teenagers. These

TABLE 7.1

Number of Children Placed for the First Time by Age at Placement:
New York City, 1984–89

Age at Placement	Number					
	1984	1985	1986	1987	1988	1989
Age at Placement	7,981	8,642	8,386	13,862	16,306	19,072
Infants, total	1,226	1,472	1,381	3,331	4,486	5,598
Less than 1 month	593	641	398	1,123	2,072	2,793
1 to 6 months	365	520	644	1,547	1,692	1,978
6 to 12 months	268	311	339	661	722	827
Children older than 1 yr.	6,755	7,170	7,005	10,531	11,820	13,474
	Percent of all placements					
	1984	1985	1986	1987	1988	1989
All ages, total	100%	100%	100%	100%	100%	100%
Infants, total	15.4%	17.0%	16.5%	24.0%	27.5%	29.4%
Less than 1 month	7.4%	7.4%	4.7%	8.1%	12.7%	14.6%
1 to 6 months	4.6%	6.0%	7.7%	11.2%	10.4%	10.4%
6 to 12 months	3.4%	3.6%	4.0%	4.8%	4.4%	4.3%
Children older than 1 yr.	84.6%	83.0%	83.5%	76.0%	72.5%	70.6%

SOURCE: New York State Department of Social Services, Child Care Review (CCRS) Event History File, June, 1990.

data are presented by zip code for each of New York's five boroughs and reveal a pattern of risk that is concentrated in a few geographic areas. In addition to the data aggregated by zip code, the placement records of individual foster children (infants) were matched with their birth record to provide a direct measure of birth outcome and placement history. Since these data cover the period from 1984 to 1988, the CCRS/Vital Statistics link provides the most complete record of the relationship between birth status and placement history currently available.

The Foster Care Baby-boom

The so-called foster care baby-boom refers to a dramatic increase in the number of infants admitted to foster care that substantially altered caseload demographics in New York City. The data from CCRS, summarized in table 7.1, indicate that infant admissions climbed from 1,226 in 1984 to 5,598 in 1989 if placements with approved relatives are included. The data in table 7.1 further indicate that the increase

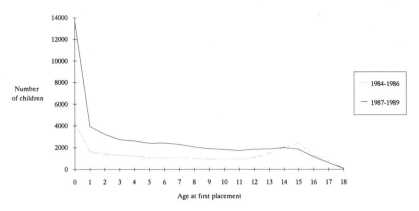

FIGURE 7.1:
*First Admissions to Foster Care by Age and Year: New York City,
1984–1989*

in admissions was most pronounced among children who were less than six months of age at the time of placement. In 1984 New York City recorded 958 placements involving children under six months of age. The figure for 1989 was 4,771, nearly five times the number reported in 1984.

The surge in infant placements was not the only change to affect the basic profile of New York City's foster care population. Historically, the age distribution of children admitted to foster care in New York City has been bimodal: large numbers of infants and large numbers of adolescents with relatively fewer children between the ages of one and twelve. When the number of infant placements increased in the mid-1980s, the age distribution flattened noticeably, a trend captured clearly in figure 7.1. Over the three-year period between 1987 and 1989, the number of infant admissions in New York City was three times higher than the number reported during the previous three-year period while admissions of children between the ages of fourteen and eighteen actually declined by 13%. By 1989 almost one-third of all first admissions to New York City's foster care programs involved an infant compared with just 15% of first admissions in 1984.

By far the most critical measure of placement activity for this study is the infant placement rate. Because the rate adjusts for the number of eligible children, the infant placement rate measures changes in the actual risk of placement over time. For this study, the infant place-

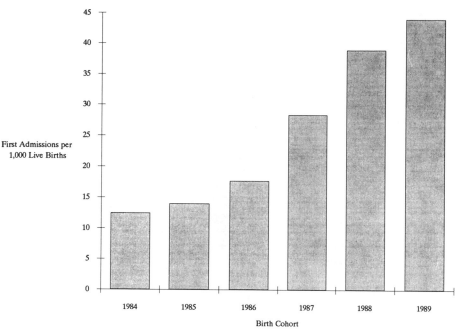

FIGURE 7.2:
Infant Placement Rate: New York City, 1984–1989 Birth Cohorts

Note: Includes approved placements with relatives.

ment rates were calculated for six consecutive birth cohorts based on the number of children who were placed prior to their first birthday.[4]

As displayed in figure 7.2, the risk of placement increased moderately from 1984 to 1986, just before a dramatic increase was reported in 1987. At that time the rate of infant placement jumped from 17.7 placements per 1,000 live births in 1986 to 28.1 per 1,000 live births in 1987. This latter figure is equivalent to just under 3% of the live births in 1987. By 1988, the placement rate reached thirty-nine per thousand births. The rate of infant placement jumped again to forty-four per thousand births in 1989 or to just under 4.5% of all births in New York City.

The Distribution of Infant Placements

New York is a socially and economically diverse city where symbols of affluence and urban hardship are often neighbors. It comes as no

FIGURE 7.3:
Infant Foster Care Placements: New York City, 1984–1989.

Source: CCRS Event History File, 9/89.

real surprise then to find that placement rates in some portions of
New York's inner city are substantially higher than the rates reported
for the city as a whole. Nevertheless, the actual pattern of placement
concentration is striking. The data displayed in figure 7.3 reveal the
pattern of infant placements in New York's five boroughs. Each point
on the map identifies the approximate location of at least one infant
who entered foster care (based on the address of the parents) between
January 1, 1984, and September 30, 1989.

The available data demonstrate clearly that infant foster care admissions are clustered in a few geographic areas within each New
York borough. In fact, the data indicate that the highest concentra-
tions of infant placement tend to be found within one or two geographic areas (or neighborhoods) in each borough. For example,

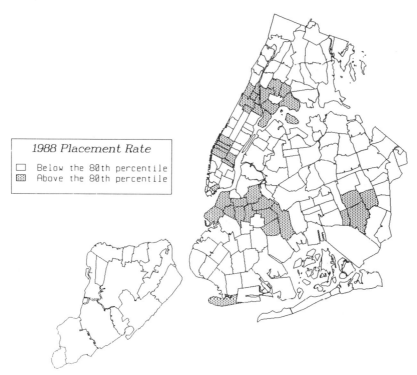

1988 Placement Rate

☐ Below the 80th percentile
▦ Above the 80th percentile

FIGURE 7.4:
Number of Infants Placed per 1,000 Live Births: 1988 Birth Cohort

Source: CCRS Event History File, 9/89.

the highest placement activity in Brooklyn can be found along the northeastern edge of the borough, areas encompassed by the neighborhoods of Bedford Stuyvesant and East New York. To a lesser extent, placement activity was also concentrated in the Sunset Park and Coney Island neighborhoods.

Although the concentration of infant placements is readily apparent, the lack of a standard unit of measure in figure 7.3 limits the interpretation of the data, a problem treated most directly by computing placement rates for common geographic units, such as zip codes. Figure 7.4 presents the estimated number of infant placements in 1988 per thousand live births for each zip code area in New York City. The shading pattern distinguishes between zip codes above and below the 80th percentile.

TABLE 7.2
Infant Foster Care Admissions by New York City Neighborhood: 1988

Borough/Neighborhood/ Zip Code	Infant placements 1988	Births 1988	Placement rate* 1988
Brooklyn	750	10,716	70.0
Bedford Stuyvesant			
11212	125	2,210	59.0
11213	76	1,561	48.7
11216	130	1,180	110.2
11221	129	1,804	71.5
11233	127	1,472	86.3
11238	66	1,001	65.9
Downtown/Heights/ Slope			
11201	49	594	82.5
11205	41	784	52.3
11217	41	580	70.7
Greenpoint/Williamsburg			
11206	97	1,578	61.5
Bronx	413	7,283	56.7
Crotona Tremont			
10457	75	1,719	43.6
10460	54	1,084	49.8
High Bridge/Morrisania			
10451	64	913	70.1
10452	79	1,634	48.3
10456	141	1,933	72.9
Hunts Point/Mott Haven			
10454	53	875	60.6
10455	33	750	44.0
10473	39	887	44.0
Queens	149	2,207	67.5
Jamaica			
11412	35	574	61.0
11433	51	495	103.0
11434	41	800	51.3
11436	22	338	65.1
Rockaway			
11691	33	900	36.7
11692	15	345	43.5
Manhattan	434	4,085	106.2
Central Harlem/M'side Heights			
10026	77	609	126.4
10027	107	1,021	104.8
10030	94	538	174.7
10031	92	1,454	63.3
10039	64	406	157.6
Chelsea/Clinton			
10018	9	44	204.5
10019	18	351	51.3
10036	36	227	158.6

East Harlem			
10029	65	1,375	47.3
10035	541	619	87.2
10037	30	281	106.8

SOURCE: New York State Department of Social Services, CCRS Event History File, September, 1990. New York State Department of Health, Bureau of Production Systems Management, unpublished data, October, 1990.

* Number of placements per 1,000 live births. Borough totals include only those areas listed separately.

Number of placements by zip code based on an address and zip code cross reference.

The geographic comparison of 1988 placement rates found in figure 7.4 highlights the pattern of concentration within each borough. The areas with the highest rates are virtually the same as those depicted in figure 7.3: Bedford Stuyvesant, Park Slope, and Greenpoint/Williamsburg in Brooklyn; the South Bronx; Harlem and Chelsea in Manhattan; and Jamaica in Queens. In each of these areas, one or more zip codes reported a placement rate in excess of 6% of the births in 1988, more than twice the level recorded for the city as a whole.

Table 7.2 contains the specific placement rates for many of the heavily shaded zip code areas shown in figure 7.4. Nine zip code areas, seven in Manhattan and one each in Brooklyn and Queens, had placement rates that exceeded 10% of the live births in 1988. For the eleven Manhattan zip codes listed separately in table 7.2, the composite placement rate was 106.2 placements per 1,000 births, or just above 10% of the births in those zip codes combined. This figure was three times as high as the rate citywide. In Brooklyn, the borough with the second highest composite placement rate, the estimated rate of placement in the ten zip codes displayed was seventy per thousand births.

IV. Birth Outcomes and Infant Placements in New York City

Regardless of their numbers, the infants who enter foster care pose a unique set of challenges to the child welfare system. Even healthy babies require special care and attention. Since most infants enter foster care within three months of birth, establishing and maintaining a bond with the birth parents is both critical and difficult. Infants tend to remain in foster care longer than older children, so termination of parental rights and adoption become increasingly important options as time passes.

Although infants may require special attention once they enter placement, the path taken to foster care is the same for all children, regardless of age. There are no special statutes or regulations governing eligibility for preventive services, defining maltreatment, or regulating the judicial process that apply exclusively to infants.[5] In short, infants are covered by the same standards of intervention that protect the welfare of all children who are at risk.

These administrative similarities notwithstanding, the circumstances just prior to the placement of an infant are themselves unique. Unlike older children, much if not all of the time leading up to placement is spent in utero. During this time, abandonment in the traditional sense is impossible, and maltreatment takes the form of maternal substance abuse, poor nutrition, and inadequate prenatal care. From a preventive service perspective, any mandated preventive services to which the family is entitled must be rendered in the form of prenatal care and/or drug treatment and must be designed to improve birth outcomes.

To demonstrate the crucial link between birth outcomes and the foster care experience of infants, the following section will examine the birth status indicators introduced previously to profile birth outcomes in New York City for the years 1987 through 1989. As before, the data are presented for each zip code in New York City and then compared with the placement data to show how areas with poor birth outcomes also tend to have the highest placement rates. The analysis continues with a closer look at how the birth outcomes of the infants who entered foster care declined between 1984 and 1988, the period when infant admissions increased most significantly. Last, a multivariate analysis examines the impact of birth status on the length of foster care placements.

Birth Outcomes in New York City

The first data presented in this section provide an overall context for interpreting the changes in birth outcomes among the infants who entered foster care. In table 7.3, four birth status indicators for New York City are compared to national data. Except for births to teenage mothers, birth status indicators for New York City tend to be lower than the national averages. In particular, the percentage of mothers with late or no prenatal care is considerably higher than in the nation as a whole. According to New York State vital statistics data, 12.4%

TABLE 7.3
Birth Outcomes: United States and New York City, 1988

Birth Status Indicator	Percent, N.Y.C.			Percent	
	1987	1988	1989	U.S.	N.Y.C.
Total	100.0%	100.0%	100.0%	100.0%	100.0%
Births to teenage mothers	10.7%	10.7%	10.6%	12.5%	10.7%
Late or no prenatal care	10.4%	12.4%	14.8%	6.0%	12.4%
Birthweight under 2,500 grams	9.5%	9.8%	9.6%	6.9%	9.8%
Infant deaths	1.3%	1.3%	1.3%	1.0%	1.3%

SOURCE: National Center for Health Statistics. Advance report of final natality statistics, 1988. Monthly vital statistics report; vol. 39, no. 4, supp. Hyattsville, Maryland; Public Health Service, 1990. National Center for Health statistics. Advance report of final mortality statistics, 1988. Monthly vital statistics report; vol. 39, no. 7 supp. Hyattsville, Maryland; Public Health Service, 1990. New York State Department of Health, 1988, unpublished data, Vital Statistics, Bureau of Production Systems Management, Information Systems and Health Statistics.

of the mothers who gave birth in 1988 reported late or no prenatal care compared with just 6% nationwide.[6] Babies born in New York City during 1988 tended to be smaller at birth and were also somewhat more likely to die in the first year than babies born elsewhere in the country. While the disparities between New York City and the rest of the nation have attenuated somewhat over the past twenty years, current conditions reflect longstanding patterns.

The data in table 7.3 reflect changes in birth status in New York City over a three-year period, from 1987 to 1989. In general, birth status changed little, but prenatal care utilization did decline. About 15% of the women who gave birth in 1989 reported late or no prenatal care compared with slightly more than 10% in 1987. Infant mortality, birthweight, and births to teenagers were largely unchanged even though substance abuse among pregnant women escalated during this period.

The Distribution of Birth Outcomes

Just as infant placements tend to be concentrated in a few areas of the city, poor birth outcomes as measured by the indicators discussed above are also most common in one or two areas within each borough. Each of the maps presented in this section are designed to show the extent to which this is true. The data, which were compiled by the New York State Department of Health, represent composite rates or percentages calculated on the basis of recorded vital statistics for the

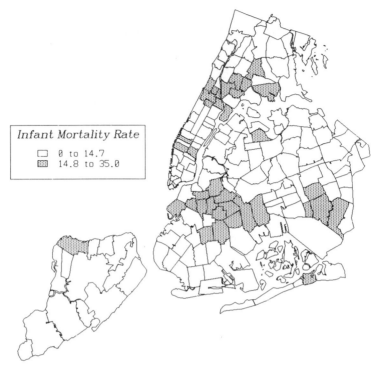

FIGURE 7.5:
Infant Mortality Rate per 1,000 Live Births, New York City: 1987–1989

Source: Office of Public Health, New York State Department of Health.

years 1987 through 1989. Furthermore, each map has two shading patterns. The darker shaded areas represent those zip codes found in the upper quintile (80th percentile). Figure 7.6 displays the infant mortality rate for each zip code; figure 7.7 shows how prenatal care utilization varied across the city; figure 7.8 presents the distribution of birthweight; and figure 7.9 reveals the concentration of births to teenagers in New York's boroughs.

The maps leave little doubt about the pattern or distribution of birth outcomes in New York City and the extent to which birth outcomes are worst in the very same neighborhoods where foster care placements are most common. With a few exceptions, Central Harlem, East Harlem, and Chelsea in Manhattan; Jamaica in Queens; areas in and around the South Bronx, and zip code areas along the

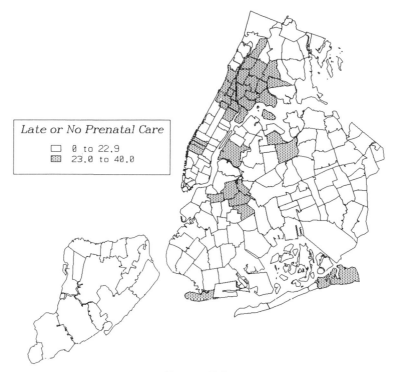

Late or No Prenatal Care

☐ 0 to 22.9
▦ 23.0 to 40.0

FIGURE 7.6:
Late or No Prenatal Care as a Percentage of All Live Births: 1987–1989

Source: Office of Public Health, New York State Department of Health.

northern rim of Brooklyn can be found consistently among those areas reporting the poorest birth outcomes.

The data in table 7.4 offer a more precise indication of how birth outcomes in the shaded areas depart from those in the city as a whole. Displayed are the four birth status indicators summarized for the period between 1987 and 1989. Although most of the zip codes displayed in table 7.4 correspond to the maps, there are some minor differences. The data reveal areas where more than 30% of the mothers reported late or no prenatal care (some sections of the Bronx and Harlem); more than 20% of the babies where born weighing less than 2,500 grams (Harlem); births to teenagers exceeded 20% (sections of each borough except Staten Island), and infant mortality reached 2%

FIGURE 7.7:
Low Birthweight Babies as a Percentage of All Live Births: 1987–1989

Source: Office of Public Health, New York State Department of Health.

or more (portions of Bedford Stuyvesant, Jamaica, and Harlem and Chelsea in Manhattan).

The Birth Status of Infant Foster Children

The close correlation between placement rates and birth outcome leaves little doubt about the relationship between health at birth and placement, at least at the aggregate level. What these data do not say, however, is to what extent birth outcomes can be implicated directly in the surge of infant placements observed in New York City. For example, did the health of infant foster children as measured by birthweight change during the period of rising admissions, and how do these changes influence the time children spend in foster care?

In this section of the paper, data are reported that show the birth

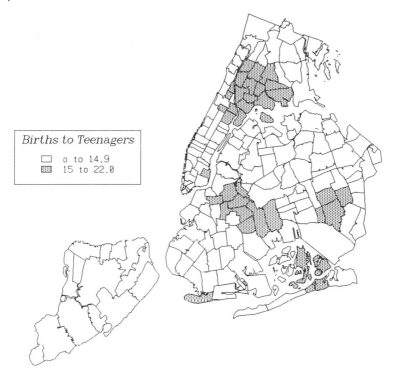

FIGURE 7.8:
Births to Teenagers as a Percentage of All Live Births: 1987–1989

Source: Office of Public Health, New York State Department of Health.

status of infant foster children during the period between 1984 and 1988. The analysis is divided into two parts. The first section demonstrates the extent to which the birth status of children who entered foster care differed from that of other children born in New York City during the same year. The analysis then examines the birth status of infant foster children over the five-year period from 1984 to 1988. Across all indicators of birth status, the data reveal a marked decline in the health of children who were admitted to foster care as infants. The second phase of the analysis examines how birth status influences the length of placement. Again, one question at the center of the analysis concerns relationships over time and whether patterns observed in earlier periods become more or less important as time passes.

The data in table 7.5 represents a comparison of birthweight,

T A B L E 7.4

Number of Infants by Birth Status Indicator and New York City Neighborhood: 1987–89.

Borough/Neighborhood/Zip Code	Birth Status Indicators					Percent of Live Births				
	Births*	Late/No Prenatal Care	Low Birthweight	Teen Births	Infant Deaths	Births	Late/No Prenatal Care	Low Birthweight	Teen Births	Infant Deaths
New York City, total	372,078	58,017	35,665	39,565	4,525	100.0%	15.6%	9.6%	10.6%	1.2%
Brooklyn										
Bedford Stuyvesant										
11212	6,264	738	898	1,095	121	100.0%	11.8%	14.3%	17.5%	1.9%
11213	4,759	816	606	587	79	100.0%	17.1%	12.7%	12.3%	1.7%
11216	3,517	633	513	601	63	100.0%	18.0%	14.6%	17.1%	1.8%
11221	5,443	1,202	758	1,110	97	100.0%	22.1%	13.9%	20.4%	1.8%
11233	4,391	924	722	880	95	100.0%	21.0%	16.4%	20.0%	2.2%
11238	2,935	574	433	432	66	100.0%	19.6%	14.8%	14.7%	2.2%
Downtown/Heights/Park Slope										
11201	1,851	232	178	209	21	100.0%	12.5%	9.6%	11.3%	1.1%
11205	2,230	539	302	421	25	100.0%	24.2%	13.5%	18.9%	1.1%
11217	1,769	274	187	240	36	100.0%	15.5%	10.6%	13.6%	2.0%
Greenpoint/Williamsburg										
11206	4,786	1,085	547	1,012	85	100.0%	22.7%	11.4%	21.1%	1.8%
Bronx										
Crotona/Tremont										
10457	5,268	1,348	647	920	77	00.0%	25.6%	112.3%	17.5%	.5%
10460	3,310	736	402	566	55	00.0%	22.2%	12.1%	17.1%	1.7%
High Bridge/Morrisania										
10451	2,737	836	357	516	43	00.0%	30.5%	13.0%	18.9%	1.6%
10452	4,998	1,526	600	780	72	00.0%	30.5%	12.0%	15.6%	1.4%
10456	5,733	1,585	802	1,120	109	00.0%	27.6%	14.0%	19.5%	1.9%

Hunts Point/Mott Haven										
10454	2,743	920	386	573	40	00.0%	33.5%	14.1%	20.9%	1.5%
10455	2,375	781	301	453	45	00.0%	32.9%	12.7%	19.1%	1.9%
10473	2,665	508	311	414	40	00.0%	19.1%	11.7%	15.5%	.5%
Queens										
Jamaica										
11412	1,786	196	242	274	26	00.0%	11.0%	13.5%	15.3%	1.5%
11433	1,505	177	217	284	36	00.0%	11.8%	14.4%	18.9%	2.4%
11434	2,404	262	298	362	51	00.0%	10.9%	12.4%	15.1%	2.1%
11436	1,048	138	161	187	19	00.0%	13.2%	15.4%	17.8%	.8%
Rockaway										
11691	2,983	548	333	432	40	00.0%	18.4%	11.2%	14.5%	1.3%
11692	1,044	221	136	228	18	00.0%	21.2%	13.0%	21.8%	.7%
Manhattan										
Central Harlem/ M'side Heights										
10026	1,906	512	334	346	37	00.0%	26.9%	17.5%	18.2%	1.9%
10027	2,912	723	490	433	61	00.0%	24.8%	16.8%	14.9%	2.1%
10030	1,679	522	347	257	33	00.0%	31.1%	20.7%	15.3%	2.0%
10031	4,406	1,008	549	563	66	00.0%	22.9%	12.5%	12.8%	1.5%
10039	1,289	381	229	205	18	00.0%	29.6%	17.8%	15.9%	.4%
Chelsea/Clinton										
10018	116	28	10	6	0	00.0%	24.1%	8.6%	5.2%	0.0%
10019	1,040	181	103	75	7	00.0%	17.4%	9.9%	7.2%	0.7%
10036	683	182	103	72	16	00.0%	26.6%	15.1%	10.5%	2.3%
East Harlem										
10029	4,249	810	624	760	58	00.0%	19.1%	14.7%	17.9%	1.4%
10035	1,967	468	331	376	45	00.0%	23.8%	16.8%	19.1%	2.3%
10037	854	214	198	125	29	100.0%	25.1%	23.2%	14.6%	3.4%

SOURCE: New York State Department of Health, Office of Public Health, unpublished data, 1990.
* Number of live births per zip codes area, 1987–1989. Birth Outcomes of New York State Department of Health, Office of Public Health, March 1990.

TABLE 7.5.

Number of Live Births by Birthweight and Onset of Prenatal
Care, 1988: United States, New York City, and New York City
Infant Foster Care Population.

Birthweight	Percent		
	U.S.	N.Y.C.	N.Y.C. Foster Care*
Total	100.0%	100.0%	100.0%
below 1000 gms	0.6%	0.9%	1.7%
1000 to 1499 gms	0.6%	1.0%	4.1%
1500 to 1999 gms	1.3%	1.9%	9.6%
2000 to 2499 gms	4.4%	5.9%	21.4%
2500 gms and above	93.1%	90.2%	63.1%
Onset of Prenatal Care Total	100.00%	100.00%	100.00%
1st Trimester	75.9%	52.7%	27.0%
2nd Trimester	18.0%	33.4%	28.5%
3rd Trimester	4.2%	9.9%	14.6%
No Care	1.9%	3.9%	29.8%
Age Total	100.0%	100.0%	100.0%
Under 20	12.5%	10.7%	12.1%
20 to 24	27.3%	24.5%	32.7%
25 to 29	31.7%	30.3%	31.9%
30 to 34	20.6%	22.7%	17.1%
35 to 39	6.9%	9.6%	5.4%
40 and above	1.0%	2.0%	0.7%

SOURCES: National Center for Health Statistics. Advance report of final natality statistics, 1988. Monthly vital statistics report; vol. 39, no. 4, supp. Hyattsville, Maryland; Public Health Service, 1990. National Center for Health Statistics. Advance report of final mortality statistics, 1988. Monthly vital statistics report; vol. 39, no. 7 supp. Hyattsville, Maryland; Public Health Service, 1990. New York State Department of Health, 1988, unpublished data, Vital Statistics, Bureau of Production Systems Management, Information Systems and Health Statistics.

NOTE: Number of births does not include cases with missing data about onset of prenatal care.

* N.Y.C. foster care is a nonrandom sample of the infants born in 1988 and placed in foster care prior to their first birthday.

prenatal care, and mother's age for infants born in 1988 and admitted to foster care as infants and those of the entire 1988 birth cohort. In each instance, the birth status of infant foster children differs markedly from the status reported for the general population of babies. Particularly striking are the differences in birthweight and prenatal care utilization. The vital statistics data indicate that about 37% of the infants admitted to foster care from the 1988 cohort weighed less than 2,500 grams, an incidence three times higher than the figure reported for all children born in New York City and about five times as high as the national average.

Data that describe prenatal care utilization are also provided in table 7.5. From these data, it is clear that the mothers with infants in foster care appeared much less likely than other mothers to use prenatal care. According to our data, of the mothers responding, about 44% reported either late or no prenatal care. This compares with just under 14% of mothers in New York City and 6% of the mothers across the nation. Even in those areas of New York City where prenatal care utilization in 1988 was lowest, the reported level of prenatal care was still well above the rate reported among the mothers of infant foster children (see table 7.3).

When compared with the entire 1988 birth cohort, mothers of infant foster children also tended to be younger (see table 7.6). Specifically, 12% of the mothers were under the age of twenty, a percentage that is somewhat higher than city data and comparable to the national figure. About 64% of the mothers were between the ages of twenty and twenty-nine compared with 54% for New York City.

The trend data for the years 1984 and 1988 reveal changes in birth

TABLE 7.6

Number of Live Births by Mother's Age, 1988: United States, New York City, and New York City Infant Foster Care Population.

Age	Number of births			Percent		
	U.S.	N.Y.C.	N.Y.C. Foster care*	U.S.	N.Y.C.	N.Y.C. Foster care*
Total	3,909,510	127,128	2,479	100.0%	100.0%	100.0%
Under 20	488,941	13,665	301	12.5%	10.7%	12.1%
20 to 24	1,067,472	31,206	811	27.3%	24.5%	32.7%
25 to 29	1,239,256	38,575	792	31.7%	30.3%	31.9%
30 to 34	803,547	28,913	425	20.6%	22.7%	17.1%
35 to 39	269,518	12,265	133	6.9%	9.6%	5.4%
40 and above	40,776	2,504	17	1.0%	2.0%	0.7%

SOURCES: National Center for Health Statistics. Advance report of final natality statistics, 1988. Monthly vital statistics report; vol. 39, no. 4, supp. Hyattsville, Maryland; Public Health Service, 1990. National Center for Health Statistics. Advance report of final mortality statistics, 1988. Monthly vital statistics report; vol. 39, no. 7 supp. Hyattsville, Maryland; Public Health Service, 1990. New York State Department of Health, 1988, unpublished data, Vital Statistics, Bureau of Production Systems Management, Information Systems and Health Statistics.

NOTE: Number of births does not include cases missing maternal age.

*N.Y.C. foster care is a non-random sample of infants born in 1988 and placed in foster care prior to their first birthday.

TABLE 7.7

Number of Live Births by Birthweight, Age, and Onset of Prenatal Care: New York City Infant Foster Care Population, 1984–88 (in percent)*

	Percent				
Birthweight	1984	1985	1986	1987	1988
Total	100.0%	100.0%	100.0%	100.0%	100.0%
below 1000 gms	1.2%	0.9%	1.2%	2.2%	1.7%
1000 to 1499 gms	2.5%	4.1%	3.6%	4.1%	4.1%
1500 to 1999gms	4.3%	7.2%	8.8%	10.5%	9.6%
2000 to 2499 gms	16.9%	16.5%	20.1%	20.5%	21.4%
2500 gms and above	75.0%	71.3%	66.4%	62.8%	63.1%
Age					
Total	100.0%	100.0%	100.0%	100.0%	100.0%
Under 20	34.2%	25.0%	22.7%	15.4%	12.1%
20 to 24	23.3%	28.4%	31.2%	32.5%	32.7%
25 to 29	23.3%	24.6%	29.2%	31.6%	31.9%
30 to 34	13.4%	16.0%	12.8%	14.8%	17.1%
35 to 39	5.2%	4.8%	3.6%	5.2%	5.4%
40 and above	0.6%	1.1%	0.5%	0.5%	0.7%
Onset of Prenatal Care					
Total	100.0%	100.0%	100.0%	100.0%	100.0%
1st Trimester	17.6%	19.2%	15.1%	15.2%	27.0%
2nd Trimester	20.4%	23.2%	19.7%	19.3%	28.5%
3rd Trimester	24.1%	19.7%	14.5%	13.5%	14.6%
No Care	37.8%	37.9%	50.7%	52.0%	28.8%

SOURCE: New York City Department of Health, Bureau of Vital Statistics.

* New York City infant foster care population is a nonrandom sample of infants born between 1984 and 1988 and placed in foster care prior to their first birthday. Number of births does not include those cases missing data about birthweight, maternal age, or onset of prenatal care.

status that are consistent with the increase in admissions brought about by higher rates of substance abuse among pregnant women. Birthweight data, one of the most reliable vital statistics, indicate that one out of four infants admitted to foster care in 1984 weighed less than 2,500 grams compared to one in three in 1988 (see table 7.7). The data also suggest that a significant shift in the age of the mothers with an infant in foster care occurred over this five-year period. In 1984, 34% of the mothers were under the age of twenty, a figure that dropped to 12% in 1988. Infant foster children in 1986, 1987, and 1988 were much more likely to be born to a mother in her twenties than in previous years. About 66% of mothers in our 1988 sample were between the ages of twenty and twenty-nine compared with

46% in 1984. If substance abuse contributed to the increase in admissions, then the higher proportion of older mothers corresponds with reports that crack use was most prevalent among women in their twenties rather than among teenagers.

Although prenatal care utilization appears to have improved, it is difficult to sort out changes brought about by programs aimed at high-risk populations and changes attributable to reporting practices. Nonetheless, prenatal care utilization among mothers with infant foster children was far below the utilization rates reported for the general population of childbearing women. In 1988, 30% of the mothers with infants in foster care reported no prenatal care. When mothers of infants in foster care did seek prenatal care, the number of visits tended to be low; about 40% of the women reported fewer than six visits.

V. Birth Status and Placement Duration

Most of the state foster care tracking systems in place today do not contain detailed social or medical data, so it is not always possible to determine how the circumstances leading up to placement actually influence the time a child spends in foster care. With this in mind, the vital statistics link to New York's CCRS data offers a rare glimpse at the degree to which factors like birth status may affect placement duration. In light of the recent past, the ability to establish these connections is important for two reasons. First, infants typically remain in foster care longer than older children. Second, if birth status is linked to placement duration, then the fact that the birth status of infant foster children declined between 1984 and 1989 indicates that expectations with regard to length of stay should be adjusted upward.

When compared with that of children above the age of one at the time of admission, the movement of infants through the foster care system differs in two ways. The data for New York City found in table 7.8 show that fewer infants leave their first placement spell within ninety days, and more infants remain in care for two or more years. The data for the 1984 entry cohort illustrate these points most clearly. With respect to early discharge, about 18% of the 1,267 infants admitted to foster care in 1984 were discharged within ninety days.[7] The comparable figure for children above the age of one at the time of admission was 34%. The proportion of all children admitted to foster care who were discharged within ninety days increased in

TABLE 7.8

Children Placed, Still in Care, and Discharged by Length of Placement if Discharged. New York City, 1984–89

Age at Placement	Number						Percent					
	1984	1985	1986	1987	1988	1989	1984	1985	1986	1987	1988	1989
All Infants												
Number Placed	1,267	1,532	1,580	3,321	4,382	3,276	100.0%	100.0%	100.0%	100.0%	100.0%	100.0%
Still in care*	198	410	727	2,446	3,593	2,952	15.6%	26.8%	46.0%	73.7%	82.0%	90.1%
Number discharged	1,069	1,122	853	875	789	324	84.4%	73.2%	54.0%	26.3%	18.0%	9.9%
Length of placement												
90 days or less	234	382	312	353	465	260	18.5%	24.9%	19.7%	10.6%	10.6%	7.9%
91 to 180 days	101	124	92	142	138	55	8.0%	8.1%	5.8%	4.3%	3.1%	1.7%
181 to 365 days	107	124	91	130	132	9	8.4%	8.1%	5.8%	3.9%	3.0%	0.3%
1 yr to 18 mos	100	91	80	99	51	N/A	7.9%	5.9%	5.1%	3.0%	1.2%	N/A
18 mos to 2 yrs	91	86	88	96	3	N/A	7.2%	5.6%	5.6%	2.9%	0.1%	N/A
2 to 3 yrs	179	152	149	55	N/A	N/A	14.1%	9.9%	9.4%	1.7%	N/A	N/A
Above 3 yrs	257	163	41	N/A	N/A	N/A	20.3%	10.6%	2.6%	N/A	N/A	N/A
Children Older Than One Year												
Number Placed	7,744	9,289	10,069	12,484	13,173	9,223	100.0%	100.0%	100.0%	100.0%	100.0%	100.0%
Still in care*	963	1,465	3,018	6,866	9,089	7,449	12.4%	15.8%	30.0%	55.0%	69.0%	80.8%
Number discharged	6,781	7,824	7,051	5,618	4,084	1,784	87.6%	84.2%	70.0%	45.0%	31.0%	19.3%
Length of Placement												
90 days or less	2,660	3,941	3,792	2,953	2,523	1,492	34.3%	42.4%	37.7%	23.7%	19.2%	16.2%
91 to 180 days	712	903	845	710	673	263	9.2%	9.7%	23.7%	5.7%	5.1%	2.9%
181 to 365 days	864	888	781	740	651	29	11.2%	9.6%	7.8%	5.9%	4.9%	0.3%
1 yr to 18 mos	555	523	492	597	224	N/A	7.2%	5.6%	4.9%	4.8%	1.7%	N/A
18 mos to 2 yrs	464	476	401	421	13	N/A	6.0%	5.1%	4.0%	3.4%	0.1%	N/A
2 to 3 yrs	664	579	602	197	N/A	N/A	8.6%	6.2%	6.0%	1.6%	N/A	N/A
Above 3 yrs	862	514	138	N/A	N/A	N/A	11.1%	5.5%	1.4%	N/A	N/A	N/A

SOURCE: Department of Social Services, CCRS Event History File, September, 1989.
* As of September, 30, 1989.

1985. Among infants, nearly 25% of the 1985 admission cohort left foster care within ninety days or less; among older children, about 42% were discharged within ninety days. After 1985 the proportion of children discharged from placement dropped sharply. By 1988 fewer than 11% of the infants admitted left placement within the first three months compared with 19% of the children above the age of one.

The tendency of infants to remain in placement for lengthy periods is also depicted in table 7.8. About 34% of the infants who were admitted in 1984 and discharged prior to September 1989 stayed in placement for more than two years before being discharged. In addition, nearly 16% of the children admitted as infants in 1984 were still in care as of June 30, 1990; in other words, one out of two infants who entered placement in 1984 were in foster care for at least two years. The discharge patterns observed among older members of the 1984 cohort were substantially different. As of September 1989, 12% of the children above the age of one were still in care, and about 20% were in placement for two or more years before being discharged. In other words, about one of three children above the age of one at the time of admission remained in care for more than two years.

The fact that fewer members of the post-1985 cohorts were discharged within ninety days can be interpreted as a signal that children and the circumstances surrounding their placement were somehow becoming more difficult, a change that could have diminished the chances of early reunification. The first indication that this was true can be gleaned from table 7.9. These data describe the discharge patterns for five consecutive entry cohorts divided into groups based on normal and below normal birthweights. In general, the discharge patterns conform with previous results. Regardless of birthweight, about one of six infants placed in 1984 left placement within ninety days. This proportion increased in 1985 to about one in four, before declining from 1986 to 1988. During this latter period, differences between the experience of infants with normal birthweight and those whose birthweight was below normal did begin to emerge, as fewer and fewer infants in the latter group were discharged within ninety days. The same downward trend characterized the experience of infants with normal birthweight, but the downturn was not as sharp.

Infant foster children with birthweights below normal were also more likely to remain in care for two or more years. For example, including children still in care, about 58% of the 1984 cohort mem-

Table 7.9
Infants Placed in Foster Care by Placement Duration, Birthweight, and Year: New York City, 1984–88

Birthweight and placement duration	Number					Percent				
	1984	1985	1986	1987	1988	1984	1985	1986	1987	1988
Total*										
Infants Placed	355	703	826	1929	2420	100%	100%	100%	100%	100%
Still in Care*	55	198	386	1427	1966	15.5%	28.2%	46.7%	74.0%	81.2%
Number discharged										
90 days or less	53	161	148	208	279	14.9%	22.9%	17.9%	10.8%	11.5%
91 to 180 days	23	49	48	74	68	6.5%	7.0%	5.8%	3.8%	2.8%
181 to 365 days	31	61	52	75	77	8.7%	8.7%	6.3%	3.9%	3.2%
1 yr to 18 mos	32	47	47	54	29	9.0%	6.7%	5.7%	2.8%	1.2%
18 mos to 2 years	27	42	44	57	1	7.6%	6.0%	5.3%	3.0%	0.0%
2 to 3 years	62	71	84	34	N/A	17.5%	10.1%	10.2%	1.8%	N/A
Above 3 years	72	74	17	N/A	N/A	20.3%	10.5%	2.1%	N/A	N/A
Above 2,500 grams										
Infants placed	269	502	582	1211	1516	100%	100%	100%	100%	100%
Still in Care**	42	124	254	859	1218	15.6%	24.7%	43.6%	70.9%	80.3%
Number discharged										
90 days or less	40	114	114	150	182	14.9%	22.7%	19.6%	12.4%	12.0%
91 to 180 days	18	37	34	50	41	6.7%	7.4%	5.8%	4.1%	2.7%
181 days to 365	25	49	39	50	53	9.3%	9.8%	56.7%	4.1%	3.5%
1 yr to 18 mos	27	38	36	37	22	10.0%	7.6%	6.2%	3.1%	1.5%
18 mos to 2 yrs	21	33	33	42	N/A	7.8%	6.6%	5.7%	3.5%	N/A
2 to 3 years	47	54	60	23	N/A	17.5%	10.8%	10.3%	1.9%	N/A
Above 3 years	49	53	12	N/A	N/A	18.2%	10.6%	2.1%	N/A	N/A
Below 2,500 grams										
Infants placed	85	201	242	716	903	100%	100%	100%	100%	100%
Still in Care**	12	74	132	566	748	14.1%	36.8%	54.5%	79.1%	82.8%

Number discharged									
90 days or less	13	47	33	58	97	15.3%	23.4%	13.6%	8.1%	10.7%
91 to 180 days	5	12	14	24	27	5.9%	6.0%	5.8%	3.4%	3.0%
181 to 365 days	6	12	13	25	24	7.1%	6.0%	5.4%	3.5%	2.7%
1 yr to 18 mos	5	9	10	17	7	5.9%	4.5%	4.1%	2.4%	0.8%
18 mos to 2 yrs	6	9	11	15	N/A	7.1%	4.5%	4.5%	2.1%	N/A
2 to 3 yrs	15	17	24	11	N/A	17.6%	8.5%	9.9%	1.5%	N/A
Above 3 yrs	23	21	5	N/A	N/A	27.1%	10.4%	2.1%	N/A	N/A

*Total sample includes 8,147 infants with matching placement records and birth certificates.
Date for 1989 not included.
** As of September 1989.
N/A: Not applicable.

bers were in foster care for more than two years after placement. Among children with normal birthweights the comparable figure was 50%. The data in table 7.9 also suggest that the proportion of those staying in care long among infants with low birthweight increased after 1985. If children still in care are included with those children discharged after two years, roughly 66% of the 1986 entry cohort experienced a placement that lasted at least two years, provided the child weighed less than 2,500 grams at birth.

There are, of course, any number of explanations that can be used to link birthweight to slower movement through the foster care system. One assumption is that birthweight is highly correlated with complications during pregnancy and after childbirth. For example, low birthweight is often associated with drug exposure during pregnancy, and the association between the length of stay and birthweight may reflect the difficulties faced by caseworkers who must reunite children with parents who have a history of substance abuse. Postnatal complications could take the form of developmental delays that have to be addressed with intensive services in order to secure the best possible outcome. In turn, the time needed to deliver a more intense level of service may contribute to extended foster care placements. Alternatively, infants with low birthweight may stay in foster care longer because their teenaged mothers command fewer of the resources that make reunification possible.

An adequate test of the relationship between length of stay in foster care and birthweight (or any other variable) must simultaneously take into account the impact of several independent variables.[8] In the discussion that follows, I describe the results of two event history models that consider the joint effects of birthweight, placement type, prenatal care, mother's age, and sibling placements on the length of foster care placements. The first model (Model A), found in table 7.10, presents results for the infants admitted between 1985 and 1986 while the results in the second model (Model B) refer to the experience of infants admitted between 1987 and 1988. The influence each variable has on the length of stay is presented as a regressionlike coefficient measured in days. Coefficients preceded by a minus sign indicate that the corresponding variable is associated with shorter lengths of stay, and positive coefficients indicate characteristics that contribute to longer duration.

The variables themselves are joined in three substantively discrete categories: (1) placement history; (2) birth status; and (3) family

TABLE 7.10.

Event History Analysis of Length of Stay, Placement History, Birth Status, and Family Background

| Model A | | | Model B | | |
| 1985–1986 Admission cohorts | | | 1987–1988 Admission cohorts | | |
Independent variable	Estimate	S.E.	Independent variable	Estimate	S.E.
Intercept	732.00	103.27	Intercept	964.60	76.55
Placement History			Placement History		
Delay	195.01	47.79*	Delay	68.53	33.43*
Approved relative	1365.89	201.90*	Approved relative	654.28	50.79*
Congregate care	8.04	61.81	Congregate care	−149.31	37.49*
Birth status			Birth status		
Normal birthweight	−132.71	52.73*	Normal birthweight	−103.38	32.96*
1st trimester pnc	−182.05	69.6*	1st trimester pnc	−202.50	44.85*
2nd trimester pnc	−237.90	63.63*	2nd trimester pnc	−108.35	44.48*
3rd trimester pnc	−72.00	67.57	3rd trimester pnc	−129.13	50.39*
Family background			Family background		
Mother under 20	−220.20	69.77*	Mother under 20	−47.77	49.50
Mother 20 to 25	−77.80	64.33	Mother 20 to 25	−24.38	40.64
Mother 30 to 35	−42.48	78.17	Mother 30 to 35	−63.15	48.30
Mother above 35	110.47	123.58	Mother above 35	−92.58	75.69
Sibling in care	197.49	36.05*	Sibling in care	162.80	25.22*
Nonwhite	125.21	65.63	Nonwhite	61.78	54.59
Neighborhood	79.61	45.36	Neighborhood	−47.20	30.75
Scale	463.43	12.68	Scale	388.40	10.97

PNC: prenatal care

* Significant at or below .05.

background. Within placement history, the model controls for the effects of placement type and the time between birth and the recorded date of placement. Birth status indicators include birthweight and onset of prenatal care while variables that incorporate features of the child's background include the mother's age, whether or not siblings were ever in placement, race/ethnicity, and neighborhood. Neighborhood refers to whether the child resided in one of the New York zip codes found to be located among the lowest 20% of the income distribution.

The results found in Model A of table 7.10 show a strong positive relationship between placement duration and the placement of a child in the home of a relative, placement within ninety days of birth, and the presence of other siblings in care for infants belonging to the 1985 and 1986 birth cohorts. In particular, infants with a placement in a relative's home remained in foster care 1,366 days longer than children without such a placement.[9] That placements in the homes of relatives tended to be longer is substantiated by the fact that 92% of the infants placed with relatives in 1985 and 1986 were still in foster care in September of 1989. Infant placements also tended to be longer if the infant was admitted to foster care within ninety days after birth. Data for the 1985 and 1986 admission cohorts indicate that placement within the first three months added about 195 days to the placement duration when compared with children placed between the fourth and twelfth month after birth. Finally, whether an infant ever had siblings in foster care also contributed to the length of stay in placement. The findings suggest that infants with siblings in placement remained in foster care for approximately 197 days longer than infants with no recorded sibling placements.

For members of the 1985 and 1986 birth cohorts, the age of the infant's mother and the status of the child at birth tended to decrease the time spent in foster care. Of these factors, prenatal care seemed especially important. Infants whose mothers sought prenatal care in the first or second trimester experienced placements that were 132 to 182 days shorter than those of babies with no prenatal care. In addition to the impact of prenatal care, babies born at weights above 2,500 grams stayed in placements that were 103 days shorter than the placements experienced by babies with low birthweight. Model A further suggests that infants with teenaged mothers spent 220 days less in care than children born to women between the ages of twenty-five and twenty-nine, even after the presence of siblings in foster care is taken into account.

The results found in Model B of table 7.10 show how the relationship between the placement duration and placement history, birth status, and family background changed for infants who entered foster care between 1987 and 1988, years that coincided with the upheaval created by the crack epidemic. In short, children in placements with relatives and children with siblings in placement continued to remain in foster care for periods of time that were considerably longer than those experienced by their counterparts. In addition, children admitted soon after birth (within ninety days) remained in foster care longer although the effect of an early placement was less pronounced when compared with the results for the 1985/86 cohort.

Unlike the children who were admitted between 1985 and 1986, the children who entered foster care between 1987 and 1988 spent less time in foster care if their placement history included a congregate or group care facility. These findings suggest that placement histories that included a congregate care placement were about 149 days shorter, a result that is somewhat at odds with conventional wisdom but is consistent with efforts on the part of New York City to minimize the time children spend in congregate care facilities at the same time as the number of congregate care placements among infants was increasing. The results in Model B also show that no relationship between the mother's age and the length of placement could be established for the 1987/1988 cohort, a finding that coincides with the fact that fewer infants with teenaged mothers were reported in the 1987/1988 placement cohorts.

The analysis of the 1987 and 1988 cohorts does substantiate the strong relationship between birth status and placement duration. Prenatal care initiated at any time during pregnancy was associated with placements that were up to 202 days shorter than those of children born to mothers without the benefit of prenatal care. Even prenatal care in the third trimester was associated with infants who spent four months less in foster care than children with no prenatal care. The relationship between birthweight and placement duration further suggests that healthy babies tend to spend less time in foster care. The fact that a higher proportion of infants with low birthweights were admitted to foster care during the height of the crack epidemic does indeed mean that the impact of substance abuse goes well beyond the sheer number of children. The implications of these findings are discussed more fully in the final section of the paper.

VI. Implications

When crack cocaine first reached the streets of New York City in 1985, the foster care caseload in the City included slightly more than sixteen thousand children, its lowest level in more than ten years. Barely five years later, the foster care population numbered fifty thousand children. Of this total, children admitted as infants accounted for 34% of the placements, more than four times the number of one-year-olds, the next largest group. All told, the infants admitted to New York City's foster care system since 1984 have accumulated more than seventeen million days in foster care at a public cost well in excess of $600 million. Because the public's investment in health care, education, and social services for these children and their families can only go higher, it is important to sift carefully through the data for insights that can be used to structure policies and programs.

In this last section, I examine how the findings might be applied to child welfare policy and program development. By design, the review is limited. The utilization of prenatal care, infant placement patterns, and access to services vary widely from one community to the next, so any real interpretation of the findings is subject to the nuances of local circumstances. Since community leaders and practitioners are in a far better position to comprehend and apply the findings, the goal here is simply to identify basic themes.

Birth Outcomes, Child Placement, and Service Integration

Few measures of family stability capture the vulnerability of children better than the number of infant placements into foster care. In a single year, from 1986 to 1987, infant placement rates doubled. Between 1986 and 1989, the rate of infant placement nearly quadrupled, which means that 4.5% of the children born in New York City in 1989 spent some, if not all, of the crucial first year of life in foster care. In those communities where placements were most concentrated, the rate of placement exceeded 10%. From the health data, we also know that the problems posed by rising placement rates were compounded by a marked decline in the health status of the children admitted to foster care. Birthweight, prenatal care utilization, gestational age, and Apgar scores all declined between 1984 and 1988. Thus, the infants who entered foster care after 1986 arrived more vulnerable than ever before.

In view of the changes that have taken place, it is apparent that two relatively well-defined problems exist for which solutions must be found. First, there is the high rate of admission among infants. Steps must be taken to lower the overall likelihood that a baby will enter foster care. The emphasis on family preservation programs around the country provides the context within which targeted prevention programs, shaped to fit observed patterns of need, should be designed. In states where the impact of infants on the overall caseload was substantial, such as New York, Illinois, and Michigan, traditional notions of placement prevention must be augmented with services that are not ordinarily associated with mainstream child welfare services. As such, any mechanism that dissolves categorical distinctions between health care and traditional child welfare services and yields better access to prenatal care should have a positive impact on placement rates, not to mention on many other birth outcomes. In New York, the Neighborhood-Based Alliance offers community-based programs an opportunity to erase categorical eligibility, a framework that could be used to integrate family preservation with health care services both conceptually and financially. Medicaid case management, otherwise known as COBRA case management, may be another way to unify family preservation services with health care in the broader context of service integration.

Second, it is important to remember that discharge from placement is a clinically and programmatically unique phase of the placement process. Regardless of how far infant placement rates drop, there are nearly 25,000 New York City children under the age of six already in foster care who will need placement with families sometime in the next few years if not sooner. Helping children and parents adjust to reunification is a complex undertaking in its own right, especially for children who were separated from their parents at birth. Continuity of medical care, school readiness, and family counseling are just some of the services that must be bundled together for a population of preschool foster children if reentry into foster care is to be kept to a minimum. Again, the capacity to blend services according to the needs of families depends on how well agencies are able to maximize program flexibility. The HomeRebuilders program in New York addresses these issues in part by offering voluntary agencies in New York City the opportunity to invest foster care maintenance payments and administrative costs into services that will reduce the time spent in placement (Wulczyn 1992).

The Community Dimension of Permanency Planning

For the past two decades or so, child welfare policy and practice have been organized around the doctrine of permanency planning. In practice, permanency planning means that the placement of children should be avoided whenever possible. If separation cannot be avoided, then the child should be moved as quickly as possible from temporary living arrangements, such as foster care, to a permanent home, preferably with the natural family. Repeated, unplanned movements between a substitute caregiver and the natural family are undesirable because the disruptions adversely affect the attachments children form with their parents.

Because the primacy of parent-child relationships is central to the doctrine of permanency planning, it is hard to imagine child welfare practice drifting away from family preservation and reunification. Nevertheless, the data assembled for this study make it clear that permanency planning is an increasingly complex undertaking, especially in communities where the rate of infant placement reaches the levels observed in 1988. In essence, the separation of parents from their children and the conditions that lead to this disruption of the family are more widespread then ever before. The communities reporting high rates of infant placement are the same communities that will face the challenge of family preservation and reunification most squarely. Success will depend not only on the readiness of mothers and fathers to assume the responsibilities of parenthood but also on the capacity of community institutions to adjust to the needs of so many troubled families.

The vital role community institutions must play in the development of sound child welfare practice injects what might be called a community dimension into traditional notions of permanency planning. Whereas permanency planning now reflects a desire to keep children and families together that is motivated by our understanding of child development, the community dimension of permanency planning acknowledges the fact that communities are an essential source of esteem for families, especially for adults in the midst of raising children. If parents need supportive services to develop or sustain the capacity to nurture children, then communities that offer this support reinforce the value of family stability among their residents.

Policy abstractions are of little or no value if they cannot be translated into policies and programs that address the pattern of need. The strong relationship between birth status, placement history, and neighborhoods where poverty is common suggests that there must be a way to intensify service delivery in those areas were placement rates are highest. For example, what steps can be taken to build and coordinate local service capacity around the needs of the children leaving foster care and returning home to the same communities? Is it possible to identify common needs like day care, health maintenance, and school readiness so that institutions within the community can orchestrate a common response under the umbrella of child welfare so that family disruption is minimized?

Child Placement and Poverty

Before closing, it is important to call attention to the connection between child placement and poverty. Virtually all of the zip code areas (neighborhoods) listed as having the highest placement rates can also be found among the ones listed as having the lowest level of family income. In other words, children born into families who reside in the poorest communities are the children who face the greatest risk of placement as infants.

At the outset, I mentioned that child placement represents a fundamental break in the continuity of traditional parent-child relations much like the dissolution of two-parent families into single-parent families. When viewed as part of the changes transforming the family experience of American children, the placement trends observed in the past few years take on an added significance. The basic point to be made is that the proportion of children living in families not headed by either parent is increasing. According to 1970 census data compiled by the Center for the Study of Social Policy, approximately 4.6% of all children in the United States lived in households where neither parent was present. Twenty years later, the 1990 census data showed that the figure had increased to 6.2% (Center for the Study of Social Policy 1992).

While these are relatively small percentages when compared with the number of children living in single-parent families, the placement data reported in this chapter amplify the most recent census figures in two important ways. First, the rate of infant placement reported for New York City in 1990 suggests that the number of children who will ever live in households not headed by either biological parent has grown considerably in just the past few years.[10] For children born in 1989, the citywide rate of infant placement was 4.5%. By way of comparison, Sandra Hofferth's national estimate found that fewer than 1% of the 1980 birth cohort was born into a no-parent family (Hofferth 1990).[11] In addition, cumulative placement rates in New York City have been estimated to be in the range of 9% for all nonwhite children born between 1984 and 1988 (Wulczyn & Goerge 1990).[12] Second, the placement data clearly indicate that the number of children who spend some time living in a home headed by someone other than either biological parent is much higher in inner city areas characterized by concentrated urban poverty. Together, these data may serve as the first signal that the family experience of children is about to undergo a dramatic shift, much like the transition from two-parent to single-parent families.

NOTES

The research described in this chapter was made possible, in part, by a grant from the Foundaticn for Child Development. Mike Ellrot and Joan Cooney of the New York State Department of Health made the link with vital statistics possible. Polly Morrow and Paul Rojas helped prepare the foster care data, and John O'Donnell organized the tables and charts. The data base would not have come together without their help.

I am particularly grateful to the Department of Social Services for its support. James Purcell, Associate Commissioner of Family and Children Services, read and reread drafts of the paper. Each time, he helped to sharpen the programmatic implications of the findings. It has been my good fortune to work with colleagues who understand the relationships between public programs and who are willing to invest the resources needed to make the connection more visible.

1. One explanation for the increase in cocaine abuse during pregnancy cites the popularity of crack among women (Besharov 1989:6–12; Kuehne 1990; Howard, Beckwith, Rodning, & Kropenski 1989; Miller 1989).

2. It is important to remember that these counts refer to official statistics. The number of children living with relatives "unofficially" at the time the kinship policies went into effect is not known, but some estimates suggest that the figure may have been as high as seven thousand children.

3. Daniel P. Moynihan, "Children of the state: Welfare Reform, Congress, and Family Responsibility," *Washington Post*, November 25, 1990, Daniel P. Moynihan, *Congressional Record*, January 14, 1991, p. S-493. *New York Times*, Editorial, December 24, 1989.

4. This measure of the infant placement rate departs from measures I have used elsewhere. In previous papers, I used the number of infants placed in the calendar year of their birth, a measure that slightly understates the infant placement rate because children born in December in one calendar year and placed in January of the next year were not included in the placement rate calculation for the birth cohort.

5. In view of the discussion later in the paper, it is worth noting that according to New York State regulations, a positive test for in utero drug exposure is not sufficient grounds for a finding of abuse or neglect.

6. It is important to note that these comparisons do not take into account important population differences.

7. The data reflect a child's status as of September 30, 1989. These data include first admissions only. Readmissions are excluded from the analysis. Also, the data refer to spells of placement, meaning that the children may

have moved from one placement to another, provided the child was not returned to the home of the parent.

8. The approach best suited to the study of placement duration is an event history framework that incorporates the effects of several independent variables into a single statistical model. An appreciation for the utility of event history models in foster care research is building (Goerge 1990; Benedict & White 1991).

9. The relationship between placements in the homes of relatives and length of stay has been described elsewhere (Goerge 1990; Wulczyn & Goerge 1992).

10. In part, the differences described here are a result of the methodology used to generate the counts. The census figures are, of course, point-in-time counts and describe the prevalence. Cumulative placements reflect the experiences over time of all cohort members and more accurately reflect the full experience of a group of children.

11. In her chapter, Hofferth describes how family status at birth influences the amount of time spent in other family types. Children born into families with a mother only offer the best example. These children have only a small chance of living at some point in families headed by both natural parents. The question this analysis raises is how the family experience of children born into families with no parent will alter the prospects for living in families of other types.

12. Similar estimates for Cook County, Illinois, and Wayne County, Michigan, reveal a cumulative placement rate of approximately 4% of the nonwhite children born in 1984.

REFERENCES

Benedict, M. & White, R. B. (1991, January/February). Factors associated with foster care length of stay. *Child Welfare.*

Besharov, D. J. (1989, Fall). The children of crack: Will we protect them? *Public Welfare*, 6–12.

Center for the Study of Social Policy. (1992) *Kids count data book.* Washington D.C.: Author.

Gallagher, M. (1991, Summer). Foster care as welfare. *NY: The City Journal, 1*(4).

George, R. M. (1990, September). The reunification process in substitute care. *Social Service Review, 64*(3), 422–57.

Hofferth, S. (1990). Recent trends in the living arrangements of children: A cohort life table analysis. In J. Bongaarts, T. Burch, & K. Wachter (Eds.), *Family demography: Methods and their application.* Oxford: Oxford University Press.

Howard, J., Beckwith, L., Rodining, C., & Kropenski, V. (1989, June). The development of young children of substance abusing parents: Insights from seven years of intervention and research. *Zero to Three, 9*, 8–12

Kaye, K. et al. (1989, May). Birth outcomes for infants of drug abusing mothers. *New York State Journal of Medicine, 89*(5), 256–61.

Kuehne, E. (1990, June 6). Changing clinical profile of foster children. *Health Supervision of Children in Foster Care in the 90s: A Consensus Conference.* New York: The Children's Aid Society.

Link, M. J. (1990, October). *Kinship foster care: The double-edged dilemma.* Rochester, NY: Task Force on Permanency Planning for Foster Children.

Miller, J. (1989, June). Addicted infants and their mothers. *Zero to Three, 9,* 20–23.

New York State Senate Committee on Investigations, Taxation, and Government Operations. (1989). *Crack babies: The shame of New York.* Albany: The Senate of New York.

Phibbs, C., Bateman, D., & Schwartz, R. (1991, September). The neonatal costs of maternal cocaine use. *The Journal of the American Medical Association, 266*(11), 1521–26.

Wulczyn, F. H. (1991). *The concentration of infant placements in New York's boroughs.* Albany: New York State Department of Social Services.

Wulczyn, F. H. (1992, March). *HomeRebuilders: A family reunification demonstration proposal.* Albany: New York State Department of Social Services.

Wulczyn, F. H. & Goerge, R. M. (1992). Foster care in New York and Illinois: The challenge of rapid change. *Social Service Review, 66*(2), 278–94.

Wulczyn, F. & George, R. M. (1990). *Public policy and the dynamics of foster care: A multistate study of placement histories.* Albany: New York State Department of Social Services.

EIGHT

Factors Associated with Entrance into Group Care

Mark E. Courtney

For over a century there has been a debate about the appropriateness of group care for abused and neglected children (Lerman 1982; Wolins & Piliavin 1969). Controversy surrounding what types of children and youth, if any, should be cared for in these settings has never subsided though the roles of children's institutions have changed over the years both in response to this debate and as a result of market forces.

Research has contributed to our knowledge of the characteristics of group care settings for children (Cohen 1986; Dore, Young, & Pappenfort 1984) and of the characteristics of the children themselves (Berrick, Courtney, & Barth in press; Fitzharris 1985; Hulsey & White 1989; Wells & Whittington 1992; Whittaker, Fine, & Grasso 1989). A review of the literature, however, reveals that no previous research specifically addresses the question of what characteristics of child, family, and service affect the odds of placement into group care. In California, the setting of this study, the proportion of children in group care has not grown considerably over the past few years.[1] On the other hand, the age distribution of children in group care has changed. An appreciation of developments in the dynamics of the foster care system in California may help to put in context changes that have occurred in the group home population.

The most significant change in California's foster care population has been its tremendous growth. Between 1985 and 1990 the number of children and youth in foster care supervised by county welfare departments increased from around forty thousand to over seventy thousand. Adjusting for population growth, the number of welfare-supervised children in foster care per ten thousand California children under the age of eighteen increased from fifty-eight to ninety-three over this same period of time. Thus, the growth in the foster care population was not merely a reflection of an increase in the child population of California. This growth is consistent with trends observed in other large states (Wulczyn & Goerge 1992).

The growth in the foster care population accompanied a shift in the age distribution of foster children (County Welfare Directors Association of California 1990). Between 1985 and 1989 the number of children in foster care who were less than four years old increased by 165% from 7,060 to 19,000. However, the total number of children under four in California increased by only 4.5 percent during this time. Over the same period the number of infants (children under one year old) in foster care more than tripled from 1,300 to 4,370. Overall, the average age of children in foster care in California fell from 9.3 years in 1985 to 7.8 years in 1989 (Barth, Berrick, Courtney, & Albert 1992).

Parental substance abuse contributed to the increasing numbers of young children entering care, but the exact extent of this contribution is unknown. A comparison of the characteristics of families receiving placement prevention services in 1985 to a similar group receiving services in 1989 showed that the number of families reporting substance abuse problems increased from 55% of all families to 88% over this period of time (Barth, Berrick, & Courtney 1990b). Substance abuse is also likely to contribute to the large number of children in care with special medical needs. A survey of the social workers of a random sample of children in foster care in 1987 revealed that 34% of the children had special medical needs (Barth, Berrick, & Courtney 1990a). These children were more likely to be placed in group care than children without such problems.

The foster care system has not responded to the growing pressure of increasing placements and more troubled children through proportional increases in traditional placement resources. On the contrary, different types of placements (e.g., foster family homes, kinship homes, group homes, specialized or treatment foster homes) have grown at widely varying rates (County Welfare Director's Association of California 1990). For example, placements in the home of a relative more than tripled between fiscal year 1984–85 and 1988–89 from 10,000 to 30,200, far outstripping the overall increase in foster care. Similarly, placement in specialized or treatment foster care facilities more than doubled over this period. In contrast, placements into foster family care in general grew by 34% while placements into group care grew by 51%. Thus, the growth in the foster care population was accommodated more by a shift to kinship care and by the response of private sector providers (group care and specialized foster care are provided almost exclusively by private providers in California) rather than by a growth in licensed foster family care.

It appears that the foster care system in California has been unable to create enough familylike placement resources to accommodate the large recent influx of young children and children with special needs. This has happened in spite of the rapid growth of specialized treatment foster care in the state. The relative dearth of familylike placement settings has likely contributed to the shift in the age distribution of children in group care. The rapid increase in the number of infants and very young children entering the group care population, however, has added a new twist to the debate concerning the appropriate use of group care. The percentage of children under the age of five in group home care more than doubled over the five years between 1985 and 1990. During the same period the percentage of group home children who were infants (under one year old) grew by more than 50%.

In addition, the escalating costs of foster care in general give rise to understandable interest on the part of researchers, practitioners, and policymakers about this relatively expensive type of care setting for abused and neglected children. For example, in California, group care settings cost between two and sixteen times the as much as conventional foster care placement (Barth, Berrick, Courtney, & Albert 1992).

This study uses administrative data to explore the relationships between selected child, family, and service characteristics and the odds that a child will enter group home care. Additionally, special attention is paid to the experience of infants in group care.

Sample and Method

This analysis relies on the University of California at Berkeley Foster Care Database (UCB-FC Database) to examine the characteristics of children and families as they contribute to entry into group care. This database was derived from administrative data used by the state of California to create cross-sectional reports on its foster care population.

The UCB-FC Database currently includes data pertaining to approximately 88,000 children who entered foster care for the first time in California between January 1988 and May 1991.[2] For the purposes of this study, a random sample of 8,748 children (10%) was drawn from the larger group. For most purposes, analyses of this sample will provide results equivalent to the analysis of the overall sample. Data from the sample were organized into a framework that was amenable to longitudinal analysis. Variables were created to indicate entries into and exits from foster care as well as entries into and exits from particular foster care placements for each child in the sample. This allowed for an analysis of the discharge outcomes for children who left foster care during the three-year period and of the status of the children at the end of the study for those who remained in care. It also facilitates an examination of placement transitions including group home placements.

The UCB-FC Database suffers from some significant limitations that deserve discussion. First, the relatively short time frame of the database currently limits its usefulness in examining foster care outcomes that take longer to occur (e.g., adoption, emancipation). On the other hand, this time frame does allow for the examination of events (e.g., initial placement, reunification) that take place within, and for some time after, the permanency planning time line for California. Second, the administrative data that are the source of the database cover a relatively narrow range of child- and family-related factors.

Third, some of the items recorded in the database are of questionable reliability and/or validity for various reasons. It is unclear whether significant differences in the recorded usage of preplacement preventive services between Los Angeles County and the remainder of California are due to different reporting practices or actual differences in service provision. Social workers are required to report only the *primary* reason why a child is removed from the home, whether or not there are other reasons. Thus, a child who is known to be abused *and* neglected will be reported as one or the other but not both. It is generally the case, however, that when there is good evidence that a child has been abused *and* neglected, abuse will be listed as the removal reason since this is a more justifiable reason for removal under existing legal mandates. Thus, it is not clear whether reports of abuse and reports of neglect indicate different types of events, or different intensities of events, or both. Social worker reports of the health problems of children are believed to underestimate such problems, particularly since drug exposure has only recently been added to the list of recorded health problems. Similarly, reporting practices regarding the provision of other services to children and families (e.g., counseling, transportation, parenting training) and changes in the child's service plan are so inconsistent as to render them useless for analytic purposes.

In spite of these limitations, the UCB-FC Database is a rich source of information regarding child, family, and system characteristics that are pertinent to the study of children's paths through foster care. The longitudinal format of the data facilitates the creation of important new information on the dynamics of foster care placement in California. Nearly all of the items in the database are very reliable and valid either because of their simplicity (e.g., gender, age, region) or because their reporting is "money driven" in the sense that they are required from either the county or the provider for reimbursement for services rendered (e.g., placement type and placement dates). With the exception of the items measuring preplacement services, reason for removal, and health status, all of the variables used in this study are considered by state foster care officials to accurately reflect the reality of a child's situation at any point in time in foster care.

In order not to misconstrue the data, the variable "removal reason" is interpreted in this study as the primary reason for removal given by the social worker rather than as an objective measure of the child's prior experience. Similarly, "health status" serves only to indicate those children who have easily identifiable and relatively severe physical, mental, and emotional health problems.

The analysis is divided into two parts. The first part is a logit analysis describing the effect of certain variables (gender, health condition, reason for removal from home, who the child was removed from, age at entry into foster care, preplacement prevention services, and AFDC eligibility) on the odds that a child's *first* foster care placement will be in a group home. This analysis relies on the entire random sample of 10% of the larger group. The second part is a logit analysis describing the effect of these same variables on the odds that a child will be placed in a group home after his or her first placement.

To study this question, a sample of all children in the UCB-FC Database who entered care between January of 1988 and June of 1989 (*n* = 3,627) was selected. The members of this cohort were therefore exposed to the potential of entering group care for at least one and a half years in foster care prior to the time the data were entered into the database. Obviously, the relatively short time span of the current study (three years) limits the accuracy of the second part of the analysis to the extent that only children and youth who entered group care three years or less after placement into foster care can be accounted for. However, the analysis does provide a good picture of the process of group care entry for this time frame. The validity of this type of analysis will improve as the UCB-FC Database is updated over time.

First Placement in Group Care

Before constructing a logit model of the odds of initial placement into group care, bivariate relationships between selected explanatory variables and group home placement were examined.

Table 8.1 serves to illustrate these relationships. The bivariate analyses suggest the following conclusions. Approximately 7% of the children who entered foster care between 1988 and mid-1991 were initially placed in a group home. Gender, ethnicity, AFDC eligibility status, and preplacement preventive services seem to play little or no part in increasing or decreasing the odds that a child is initially placed in group care. Children who are labeled by their social worker as having an emotional disorder are more likely to be initially placed in group care than children with organic/physical disorders or no health problems. Children placed voluntarily or removed from their homes for reasons of emotional abuse or physical disability are more likely to be placed first in a group home than children removed from their homes for other reasons. Youths (ages thirteen and older) are more likely than other children to be initially placed in group care. Children removed from two-parent homes are least likely to enter group care first while children who come from the homes of relatives (children who were living with relatives but were not in foster care with them) other than a father or mother are most likely to be placed in group care first.

Logit models provide a useful method for examining the *unique* effect of each explanatory variable on a dichotomous dependent vari-

TABLE 8.1
First Placement in Foster Case vs. Group Care

	Foster care		Group care				
	N	%	N	%	X²	Phi	P
Gender							
Female	4365	93%	306	7%	4.99	.024	.03
Male	3757	92%	317	8%			
Ethnicity							
African-American	2537	93%	183	7%	3.08	.019	.54
Asian-American	103	92%	9	8%			
Caucasian	3355	92%	278	8%			
Latino	1981	93%	141	7%			
Other Ethnicity	149	93%	12	7%			
Health							
Emotionally Disordered	73	67%	36	33%	112.7	.114	<.01
No Health Problem	7790	93%	564	7%			
Organic or Physical	262	92%	23	8%			
Removal Reason							
Caretaker Absent	2131	92%	174	8%	119.0	.117	<.01
Disability Handicap	116	85%	21	15%			
Emotional Abuse	106	88%	15	12%			
General Neglect	1608	95%	81	5%			
Other Reason	76	89%	9	11%			
Physical Abuse	1283	92%	105	8%			
Severe Neglect	1722	94%	108	6%			
Sexual Abuse	865	94%	53	6%			
Voluntary Placement	218	79%	57	21%			
Removed							
(Removed from)							
Father	365	93%	29	7%	22.28	.050	<.01
Mother	6431	93%	492	7%			
Other Relative	177	85%	31	15%			
Parents	1152	94%	71	6%			
Age							
Four through six	1255	96%	50	4%	216.25	.157	<.01
Less than one	2054	95%	112	5%			
One through three	1646	95%	86	5%			
Seven through twelve	2020	93%	153	7%			
Thirteen or older	1150	84%	222	16%			
Poverty (AFDC Elig)							
AFDC Eligible	4082	93%	302	7%	.72	.009	.40
Not Eligible	4043	93%	321	7%			
Replacement Services							
ER	5815	93%	427	7%	4.20	.022	.12
ER & FM	782	93%	58	7%			
None	1528	92%	138	8%			

able while also taking into account *interactions* between variables. Examination of variables for inclusion in a logit model for initial placement into group care revealed that gender, ethnicity, AFDC eligibility status, preplacement preventive services, and the type of household from which the child was removed (e.g., single mother, parents) seem to play little or no part in increasing or decreasing the odds that a child is initially placed in group care, given the effect of more salient factors. On the other hand, child health problems, referral reason, and the child's age at entry into foster care all significantly influence the likelihood that a child will be placed initially in a group home. These variables were entered into the final model.

Table 8.2 is a summary of the parameter estimates for the final logit model of first placement into group care. The *chi-square* value and corresponding probability level associated with the model indicate that it fits the data from the sample well. This model illustrates the effects of several factors on the odds that a child will avoid initial placement in a group home. The table shows the log-odds parameter for each factor, the standard error of this parameter, the probability that this effect differs from zero, and the effect of this factor on the odds of placement in a group home. The intercept term refers to the predicted overall odds that a child will avoid group care on his or her first placement, all things being equal.

Of particular interest is the column showing the effect on the odds of group home placement since this is the most easily interpreted measure of association between the explanatory variables and the item of interest. At the most basic level, any factor with a value greater than one in this column increases the odds that a child is not placed initially in a group home, or, conversely, decreases the odds that a child will first be placed in group care. Similarly, any factor with a value less than one increases the odds of initial placement in a group home. In general, older children and youths (ages seven and over), children with health problems, and children who enter care for reasons other than abuse or neglect (particularly voluntary placements) are more likely to enter group care during their first placement.

The model also suggests that the referral reason interacts with both age and health problems in terms of the effects of these factors on the odds of placement in a group home. For the oldest youths, referral for reasons of physical or sexual abuse decreases the odds of placement in a group home even more than the overall effect of this factor. On the

TABLE 8.2

Parameters of the Logit Model for First Placement in a Group Home

Variable	Log odds co-efficient	Standard error	Approx. P-value[a]	Effect on odds[b]
Intercept	1.923	.140	.001	6.841
Age				
Less than 4	.919	.220	.001	2.506
4 through 6	.482	.206	.019	1.619
7 through 12	−.229	.140	.102	.795
13 or older	−1.171	.123	.001	.310
Health Problems				
Health Problems	−.617	.125	.001	.540
No Health Problems	.617	.	.	1.852
Referral Reason				
Abuse	.573	.198	.004	1.773
Neglect	.566	.165	.001	1.762
Voluntary	−.642	.352	.068	.526
Other Reasons	.497	.217	.022	.608
Interactions: Age by Referral Reason				
<4 by Abuse	−.653	.247	.008	.521
<4 by Neglect	−.686	.228	.003	.504
7–12 Neglect	.290	.158	.067	1.336
>13 by Abuse	.664	.156	.001	1.943
>13 by Voluntary	−.942	.288	.001	.390
Interactions: Health Problems by Referral Reason				
Problems by Abuse	.401	.184	.029	1.494
Problems by Neglect	.409	.149	.006	1.505
Problems by Other	−.399	.190	.036	.671
Goodness of Fit Statistics for the Model[c]				
Pearson *Chi-Square* = 5.98	DF = 12	p = .917		
Likelihood Ratio *Chi-Square* = 6.95	DF = 12	p = .861		

[a] Only those interaction parameters with $p < .1$ are shown.

[b] Odds that a child will have a first placement *other* than in a group home.

[c] Goodness of fit p-values closer to one shows a stronger likelihood that the model accurately describes the data.

other hand, for this older group, voluntary placement increases the odds of placement in a group home over and above the already powerful effect of this factor. Placement for reasons of neglect has a particularly strong effect in decreasing the odds of entrance into a group home for children between the ages of seven and twelve. Referral for abuse or neglect has a much different impact for younger children (under the age of four) than it does for all others. While referral for these reasons decreases the odds of placement in a group home for all other age groups, it has no such effect for young children. This interaction is largely responsible for the fact that slightly more very young children enter group care (about 5%) than do children in the age group of four to six (3.8%). Not surprisingly, older youths who are voluntarily placed in foster care and who have mental, emotional, or physical health problems are most likely to enter group care. In fact, they are more likely to enter group care initially than any other type of placement.

The interaction between referral reason and health problems is more straightforward. The effect of abuse and neglect on decreasing the odds of initial placement in group care is even greater for children who suffer from health problems. On the other hand, the interaction between referral the reason "other" and health problems increases the odds that children with these characteristics will enter group care over and above the main effects of these characteristics.

The odds model for placement in a group home is a *multiplicative* model. To find out the odds that a given foster child will enter a facility *other* than a group home, simply multiply the intercept term by each of the parameters for the characteristics of interest, keeping in mind any possible interactions. For example, table 8.2 shows the predicted odds that a thirteen-year-old youth voluntarily placed in foster care and suffering from health problems will be initially placed in a facility other than a group home. The model is: Predicted Odds of Initial Placement = Intercept (6.8421) × 13 Years Old (.3098) × Voluntary Placement (.5263) × Health Problems (.5398) × 13 Years Old *and* Voluntarily Placed Interaction Term (.3897) = .2346 to 1. Thus, the chance of this child entering a foster care setting other than a group home is only one in four!

One finding of particular concern that can easily be missed in analyzing the terms of the model is the surprisingly large number of very young children who are entering group care. Approximately 18% of the foster children who entered foster care in California during the study period and whose first placement was a group home were under one year of age when they entered care. Given the size of the sample, this suggests that more than one thousand infants were placed initially in an institutional setting within the foster care system of California over a three-and-a-half-year period starting in 1988.

The large number of infants being placed in group care might not be a cause for alarm if these placements were relatively brief transitional stays. However, a survival analysis of the data pertaining to the

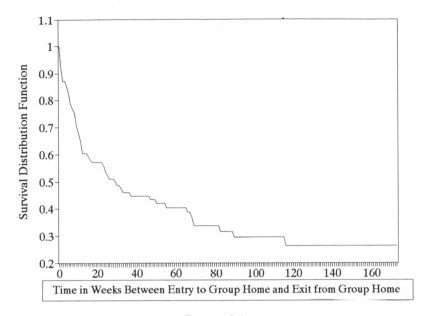

*Estimated Survivor Function for Initial Infant Placements
in Group Care Facilities*

infants who were initially placed in group care indicates that their stays were not brief. Figure 8.1 shows the Kaplan-Meier estimate of the survivor function for children initially placed in a group home (Lawless 1982). This survivor curve illustrates the estimated percentages of infants initially placed in group care who remain in those initial placements at various points in time after entering care. Although the data suggest that a large number of infants have relatively brief stays in care, approximately 40% remain in an initial group home placement more than one year, and about one-quarter of them remain there for over two years.

Later Placement in Group Care

Approximately 9% of the sample of children who entered care between January 1988 and June 1989 and who had initially been placed in a facility other than a group home entered group care at some point during the study period. Again, bivariate relationships were examined to provide guidance in constructing a logit model. Table

8.3 illustrates these relationships. Gender, AFDC eligibility status, and preplacement preventive services are not related to subsequent group home placement. Ethnicity, referral reason, and whose home the child was removed from are weakly related to a later placement in a group home at a bivariate level. Caucasian children and those in the category "other" appear slightly more likely to enter a group home. Physically and sexually abused foster children as well as those with disabilities are slightly more likely than others to enter group care. Children removed from the home of their single mother are slightly less likely to enter a group home after another placement. Age is strongly related to a later placement in a group home with the probability of such a placement increasing with the child's age at entry into foster care. Children with health problems (particularly those who have emotional disorders) are much more likely than other children to have a stay in group care after their first placement. Children initially placed in either a foster home or a shelter are more likely to be later placed in a group home than are children initially placed with relatives or a guardian.

The bivariate relationships to placement in group care do not account for relationships between the explanatory variables. When the effects of all these factors are tested simultaneously, gender, removal reason, AFDC eligibility status, ethnicity, and preplacement preventive services seem to have little or no effect on eventual entry into group care. On the other hand, age at entry into foster care, presence or absence of health problems, and the type of initial placement facility all remain as significant contributors to subsequent entry into group care.

Table 8.4 shows the parameter estimates for the final logit model (which tests for simultaneous and interactive relationships between variables) of placement into group care *after* initial placement in another facility. The *chi-square* value and corresponding probability level associated with the model indicate that it does not fit the data as well as the model for initial placement; however, there is no compelling evidence to reject the general conclusions of the model because p does not approach significance. The limited variables clearly do not account for as much of the variation in later placements as they do for initial placements. Nonetheless, the model illustrates some important contributors to the likelihood of placement in a group home. Like table 8.2, table 8.4 shows the log-odds parameter for each factor, the standard error of this parameter, the probability that this

TABLE 8.3
Later Placement in Foster Care vs. Group Care

	Foster care		Group care		X^2	Phi	P
	N	%	N	%			
Gender							
Female	1786	91%	172	9%	.02	.003	.88
Male	1520	91%	149	9%			
Ethnicity							
African-American	1091	93%	86	7%	14.43	.063	.01
Asian-American	55	90%	6	10%			
Caucasian	1346	89%	159	11%			
Latino	765	93%	61	7%			
Other Ethnicity	49	84%	9	16%			
Health							
Emotionally Disordered	17	53%	15	47%	58.59	.127	<.01
No Health Problem	3199	92%	295	8%			
Organic or Physical	90	89%	11	11%			
Removal Reason							
Caretaker Absent	857	91%	83	9%	25.63	.084	<.01
Disability Handicap	14	82%	3	18%			
Emotional Abuse	51	93%	4	7%			
General Neglect	679	92%	60	8%			
Other Reason	32	91%	3	9%			
Physical Abuse	497	90%	57	10%			
Severe Neglect	766	94%	50	6%			
Sexual Abuse	322	86%	54	14%			
Voluntary Placement	88	93%	7	7%			
Removed							
(Removed from)							
Father	163	87%	25	13%	9.50	.051	.02
Mother	2686	92%	239	8%			
Other Relative	77	89%	10	11%			
Parents	380	89%	47	11%			
Age							
Four through six	540	94%	33	6%	206.30	.238	<.01
Less than one	854	97%	27	3%			
One through three	714	96%	27	4%			
Seven through twelve	832	87%	125	13%			
Thirteen or older	366	77%	109	23%			
Poverty (AFDC Elig)							
AFDC Eligible	1685	91%	168	9%	.22	−.008	.64
Not Eligible	1621	91%	153	9%			
Placement Services							
ER	2369	91%	232	9%	.14	.006	.93
ER & FM	426	92%	39	8%			
None	511	91%	50	9%			
Facility							
Foster Home	1993	89%	241	11%	128.60	.188	<.01
Guardianship	116	97%	4	3%			
Kinship Home	1118	97%	40	3%			
Other	79	69%	36	31%			

TABLE 8.4

Parameters of the Logit Model for Placement in a Group Home After Placement in Another Type of Facility

Variable	Log odds coefficient	Standard error	Approx. P-value[a]	Effect on odds[b]
Intercept	1.417	.210	.000	4.125
Age				
Less than 4	1.008	.120	.000	2.740
4 through 6	.399	.145	.006	1.490
7 through 12	−.448	.098	.000	.639
13 or older	−.959	.106	.000	.383
Health Problems				
Emotionally Disordered	−.753	.193	.000	.471
Not Emotionally Disordered	.753	.193	.000	2.123
Facility				
Foster Home	−.051	.100	.613	.950
Relative/Guardian	1.109	.128	.000	3.031
Other Facility	−1.059	.155	.000	.347
Goodness of Fit Statistics for the Model[c]				
Pearson *Chi-Square* = 7.17 *df* = 12 *p* = .846				
Likelihood Ratio *Chi-Square* = 13.42 *df* = 12 *p* = .339				

[a] Odds that a child will avoid placement in a group home *after* placement in another type of facility.

[b] Goodness of fit *p*-values closer to one shows a stronger likelihood that the model accurately describes the data.

effect differs from zero, and the effect of this factor on the odds of placement in a group home. Again, the intercept term refers to the predicted overall odds that a child will avoid group care during at least the first one and one-half years of placement, all things being equal.

In general, as a child's age at entry into foster care increases, the likelihood increases that he or she will enter group care after the initial placement. Health problems also significantly increase the odds that a foster child will ultimately be placed in group care. A child or youth who is labeled as having an emotional disorder by his or her social worker is more likely than a child with organic problems, physical problems, or no health problems, to enter group care. The initial placement also plays a strong role. Placement in a relative's home significantly decreases the odds of later placement in a group home compared to placement in a foster home of nonrelatives. Initial placement in a small family home or county shelter has the greatest effect in increasing the odds of subsequent placement in a group home.

Like the model for initial placement in a group home, this model is multiplicative, allowing for easy estimation of the predicted odds of group home placement. The predicted odds that a given foster child (intercept = 4.125) who is thirteen years old (.383), has an emotional disorder (.471), and was initially placed in a county shelter (.347) will avoid subsequent placement in a group home for at least one and a half years are .258 to 1 (1.471 × .383 × .471 × .347 = .258 to 1). In other words, such a person would be nearly four times more likely than not to enter a group home during his or her first few years in foster care.

Summary

The explication of the characteristics of welfare-supervised children and youths that seem to increase the odds of placement in a group home is instructive.

Older children are still much more likely than young children to enter group home care. Children and youths suffering from health problems, particularly emotional problems, are more likely to be placed in group care. Emotional disorders are especially likely to result in placement in a group home even when the initial placement was in another facility.

The referral reason is strongly associated with an initial placement in a group home. Voluntary placement significantly increases the odds of initial placement in a group home, particularly for older entrants into foster care. Placement for reasons of abuse or neglect generally predicts the avoidance of placement in group homes, but oddly enough this is not as true for children under four as it is for all other children. For all children, placement due to abuse or neglect partially mitigates the effect of health problems in increasing the odds of placement in a group home while placement for "other" reasons interacts with health problems to sharply increase the likelihood of such a placement. This may indicate that children whose health problems are secondary to their reason for placement (i.e., abuse or neglect) are less likely to be placed in group homes while the health problems of children placed for "other" reasons (e.g., disability or handicap) have a greater impact on the initial decisions to place these children in a group home.

The logit models of entry into group care purposely exclude youths who enter group care through referral by county probation departments. This is important for two reasons. First, youths referred by probation departments to group home care may differ in significant ways from welfare-supervised group home children and youths. Court dependents are placed in group care and foster care in general because of parental abuse and/or neglect. Although probation youths also often suffer from exposure to these same experiences, they are not placed in group homes for these reasons. They are placed in care due to violations of the law. Furthermore, probation referrals to group home care are almost always older than twelve in contrast to the welfare-supervised group home population, which includes increasing numbers of young children. This implies that percentages of "young children" in group care actually refer to percentages of *court-dependent* young children in group care. The percentages of young children in the overall group home population are about half as high as those found in the welfare-supervised sample. Second, the issues involved in the debate surrounding the appropriateness of group home care differ for probation and welfare placements in group homes. Although there has been some discussion of the use of specialized foster care for court wards (Chamberlain 1991), and examples of this practice exist in California, the primary alternatives to group home care for court wards are county probation camps and institutions of the California Youth Authority. Both of these settings are more restrictive than group homes and generally more expensive. On the other hand, discussion of alternatives to group home care for dependents focuses primarily on less expensive and more familylike settings (i.e., treatment foster family care).

The most striking finding of the analysis of subsequent placement into group home care is the strong effect of initial placement. Nearly one-third of all children initially placed in county shelters will be placed in group homes within the following two to three years. The risk of placement in a group home is nearly three times higher for this group than it is for children and youths initially placed in conventional foster care and over nine times greater than that experienced by those initially placed with relatives (the group with the least risk of group home placement) regardless of a child's age or health problems.

Although the quality of the data is limited, these findings suggest areas of improvement in efforts to avoid unnecessary or inappropriate placements in group homes. If the mental and physical health needs of foster children can be met through the use of specialized familylike settings, it seems reasonable to expect that initial and subsequent group home placements can be decreased. Furthermore, it is not at all clear that the emotional and behavioral problems that are typical of children voluntarily placed in foster care can be met only in group care settings. Other research using the UCB-FC Database indicates that these children have a very good prognosis for reunification with their families (Courtney 1992). Specialized foster family care may be able to meet the needs of these children and return them to their homes without resorting to expensive institutional placement.

The effects of the initial placement setting on subsequent placement in group care are strong and provocative. The data cannot tell us for certain if children are initially placed in shelter care because they have emotional and behavioral problems, which are predictive of the need for later group home care, or if the initial placement in shelter care increases the need for later group home placement. The strong and independent effect of shelter care placement over and above that of health problems and age, however, suggests that it may be wise to increase efforts to avoid shelter care placement whenever possible. The strong effect of initial kinship care placement in decreasing the odds of group care placement (at least in the short run), indicates that these families may be more willing than other foster parents to cope with the types of emotional and behavioral problems that often result in a child's placement in group care. Alternatively, the overall stability of kinship care compared to other placements regardless of the characteristics of the child (Goerge 1990; Courtney 1992) may account for the decreased likelihood of group home placement.

One of the most noteworthy findings of this study concerns the changing age distribution of the group home population. An increasing number of very young children are being placed in group homes, and their stays in group care are not brief.

Put simply, group care is not the optimal environment for the care and development of very young children; the concept hearkens back to the orphanages and institutions of the nineteenth century and does not speak well of our current priorities. Group home care does not offer young children consistent parenting and should be used only briefly and as a last resort. In the past several years, however, the number of infants in group care in California has grown significantly. It is estimated that approximately eleven hundred of the infants who entered foster care during the study period were initially placed in group homes. More broadly, over two thousand foster children who were under the age of four at entry into foster care were initially placed in group homes during the study period.

A thorough examination of alternatives to group home care for young children is needed. Pilot programs to divert children and youths from shelter care into specialized foster care or kinship care may reduce later placements in group homes. However, in spite of increased efforts to avoid placement in group homes for children and youths who could benefit from more familylike settings, it is unlikely that the ongoing debate about the appropriateness of group home care will be resolved through its elimination. There still appears to be a large number of foster children who will continue to need the structured setting of a group home.

Many questions remain about California's continued use of group care. As the UCB-FC Database is updated over time, the longer follow-up period will provide for a much better overall picture of the entry process and the long-term costs associated with group care. At the same time, it will help to clarify the durability of the preventive effects that kinship care and treatment foster care have on entrance into group care. Longer follow-up will also allow the examination of the differences in the dynamics of entry and exit from group care between welfare and probation populations. In addition, it is hoped that the addition of more qualitative information about children and families to the database will enrich our understanding of group care and its outcomes for foster children and youths.

NOTES

The author gratefully acknowledges the support of the U.S. Department of Health and Human Services, Children's Bureau, and the California State Department of Social Services for their support of this study.

1. Unless otherwise cited, all statements regarding the foster care population in California are based on unpublished data from California's Foster Care Information System.

2. It is possible that some of the children in the sample had experienced one or more spells in foster care prior to their entry to care after January 1988, which would not be recorded in the database. This would happen if a

child's case had been closed for more than three years prior to that date, in which case all information regarding that child would be "purged" from the state database. Due to the purge procedure implemented by the state system, however, these episodes must have occurred prior to January 1985 and ended prior to that date. Thus, for the purposes of this study, any foster care stay that occurs three years or more after the end of a previous stay is considered a "first" foster care episode for that child.

REFERENCES

Barth, R. P., Berrick, J. D., & Courtney, M. E. (1990a). *A second snapshot of families, children, and child welfare services in California.* Berkeley, CA: Family Welfare Research Group.

Barth, R. P., Berrick, J. D., & Courtney, M. E. (1990b). *A third snapshot of California's children and families in the context of the external environment.* Berkeley, CA: Family Welfare Research Group.

Barth, R. P., Berrick, J. D., Courtney, M. E., & Albert, V. (1992, May). *Pathways through child welfare services: Final report.* Berkeley, CA: Family Welfare Research Group.

Berrick, J. D., Courtney, M. E., & Barth, R. P. (In press). Specialized foster care and group home care: Similarities and differences in the characteristics of children in care. *Children and Youth Services Review.*

Chamberlain, P. (1990). Comparative evaluation of specialized foster care for seriously delinquent youths: A first step. *Community Alternatives: International Journal of Family Care, 2*(2), 21–36.

Cohen, N. (1986). Quality of care for youths in group homes. *Child Welfare, 65*(5), 481–94.

County Welfare Directors Association of California (1990). *Ten Reasons to invest in the families of California.* Sacramento: County Welfare Directors Association of California.

Courtney, M. E. (1992). Reunification of foster children with their families: The case of California's children. Ph.D. diss., University of California, Berkeley.

Dore, M. M., Young, T. M., & Pappenfort, D. M. (1984). Comparison of basic data from the National Survey of Residential Group Care Facilities. *Child Welfare, 63*(6), 485–95.

Fitzharris, T. (1985). *The foster children of California: Profiles of 10,000 children in residential care.* Sacramento: Children's Services Foundation.

Goerge, R. M. (1990). The reunification process in substitute care. *Social Service Review, 64*(3), 422–57.

Hulsey, T. & White, R. (1989). Family characteristics and measures of behavior in foster and nonfoster children. *American Journal of Orthopsychiatry, 59*(4), 502–9.

Lawless, J. E. (1982). *Statistical models and methods for lifetime data.* New York: John Wiley.

Lerman, P. (1982). *Deinstitutionalization and the welfare state*. New Brunswick, NJ: Rutgers University Press.

Wells, K. & Whittington, D. (1991). *Characteristics of youths referred to residential treatment: Implications for program design*. Manuscript.

Whittaker, J. K., Fine, D., & Grasso, A. (1989). Characteristics of adolescents and their families in residential treatment intake: An exploratory study. In E. A. Balcerzak (Ed.), *Group care of children: Transitions toward the year 2000*. Washington, D.C.: Child Welfare League of America.

Wolins, M., & Piliavin, I. (1969). Group care: friend or foe? *Social Work, 14*(1), 35–53.

Wulczyn, F. H. & Goerge, R. M. (1992). Foster care in New York and Illinois: The challenge of rapid change. *Social Service Review, 66*(2), 278–94.

NINE

The Effect of Public Child Welfare Worker Characteristics and Turnover on Discharge from Foster Care

Robert M. Goerge

Introduction

The public child welfare caseworker has been a much maligned individual in the past decade. Many ills of the child welfare system have been attributed to the shortcomings of the caseworker. Whether it's the death of a child if left with an abusive parent or a child's drift in foster care due to a lack of planning and effort to have the child reunified with his or her parents or adopted, the worker is often the primary target of criticism. Workers have been prosecuted in criminal courts and have been dismissed as a result of negligence in their duties. Public child welfare administrators, while often blaming workers or supervisors, also provide explanations that caseworkers are overworked or underpaid and that retaining experienced workers is a persistent problem.

This paper focuses on the public child welfare caseworker because in the majority of cases he or she has primary responsibility and authority over the case. While a private agency caseworker may work most closely with the child or family and, as in recent years in Illinois, may actually be providing "full service" to the family, each case is still controlled by a public agency caseworker who must report to the juvenile court on the progress of the case.

Stone and Stone (1983) have argued that "the actions of the caseworker may be more important in determining if the child will experience unstable foster care than the problem(s) that brought the child into placement, the child's psychological characteristics, or the characteristics of the child's foster parents." While the research discussed in this paper does not test this hypothesis, it is a major assumption of the study. In an environment that has insufficient resources, where it is difficult to assess the child and family's individual needs, and where procedural goals are stressed, the activities of the service providers and the structure of the service system may determine the permanency outcomes for a particular child and family.

In the ideal service system, the worker assigned to the case should be the one that can obtain the best outcomes for that child or family. In other words, the needs of the child and family should match the skills of the caseworker and should determine what type of caseworker is assigned to the case. However, given the resource constraints and current condition of the service system, the popular perception is that there are not enough skilled caseworkers to provide the proper service to families, and workers are not assigned to cases in a manner that matches the needs of the case to the worker's skills.

A major assumption of this study is that the workers have significant influence on when the child returns to the home of the parents and that a significant level of effort is needed in order to return the majority of the children to their families. While there are other important factors, such as the characteristics of the child and parents and service provided to the child, the caseworker guides the child and family through service provision, case reviews, and the courts on a day-to-day basis. As the "street-level bureaucrat," the caseworker can maneuver through the system in a way that has the most direct effect on the clients (Lipsky 1980). Certainly, a judge or a supervisor can exert influence over a particular case, but in most instances it is likely that they follow the lead of the caseworker. One hypothesis for the recent growth in the aggregate caseload in many urban areas, including Chicago, New York, and Los Angeles, has been that an increase in the caseload of individual workers has resulted in workers having less time to work on reunification of individual children with their families, which in turn results in lower discharge rates (Wulczyn & Goerge 1992; Barth 1992).

While there have been a few studies that address the effect of caseworker's characteristics and workload on the experiences of children in foster care, there is a general lack of satisfactory research on the topic. Often it is difficult to collect complete and reliable information on the activities of caseworkers from the caseworkers themselves (Fein, Maluccio, Hamilton, & Ward 1983). The problems of timeliness of the research, sample size, and the appropriate use of statistics impede the pursuit for reliable information that could be helpful in the decision making involving the human resources in child welfare. This article attempts to initiate a new approach to these issues by presenting a method to study the effects of the characteristics of both the caseworker and caseworker turnover on the discharge of children from foster care. The method, event-history analysis, makes it possible to evaluate the influence of various time-dependent processes as they affect the eventual reunification of the child with his or her family. In this paper, the time paths of reunification, changes in living arrangements, and caseworker assignments and characteristics are analyzed simultaneously in order to understand how these processes may be dependent on each other.

This study includes indicators of the child's, caregiver's, and caseworker's activities. In particular, characteristics of the child, the number and timing of placement changes as well as caseworker turnover and level of experience are used to explain the timing of reunification of the child with his or her family. The use of time-varying independent variables addresses the number of placements and the number of workers a child has had.

Research on Caseworker Effects

Previous research on this topic has been quite limited. Shapiro's (1976) study of the effects of agency investment on 616 children in foster care and their families represents one of the most influential in the literature. The study revealed information about the role of the caseworker in foster care placements. For example, the study found that over the duration of the placement, families with children in foster care have progressively less contact with caseworkers. "These contacts are increasingly limited to the mother only, and these mothers are increasingly likely to be seen in an unfavorable light, accompanied by decreasing optimism about their ability to make homes for their children," according to Shapiro. This finding is relevant to reunification because, as Shapiro concludes, "whatever the problem that precipitates placement, the difficulty encountered by the workers in assessing maternal adequacy is the *key reason* for continuing placement." Further, Shapiro found that the caseworkers' "attitude toward the mother influenced the discharge rate at all times."

Shapiro also examined the caseworkers' level of experience and caseload size as well as the agencies' caseworker turnover rate in order to further assess the relationship among the caseworkers, the agencies, and the clients. Shapiro worked from the hypothesis that "the probability of the child's continuing in placement would be lower if he had a trained, experienced worker." She found that the more experienced the worker during the first year of placement, the more likely the child was to be discharged. However, this relationship did not hold as the child's stay in care lengthened. Caseload size was found to affect the discharge rate: "workers with either low or high case loads tended to discharge children more frequently than those with average loads." Furthermore, if the caseworker remained on a particular case, this fact "contributed to the discharge rate within the first two years of placement, but not later." Shapiro found that the more frequently the worker had contact with the child and his family, the greater the likelihood of discharge was within the first year. Finally, Shapiro concludes that "the agency's investment—reflected in the form of such assets as worker stability, experience, low case loads, and high frequency of contact—contributed significantly to the discharge rate in the first two years of placement but ceased to be important in later phases"(p. 76).

Shapiro noted that "caseworker turnover has a negative impact on the client because it may play a role in the replacement process." A fair amount of work has been done on this topic. Pardeck (1982, 1984, 1985) found that the instability of placements was strongly related to caseworker turnover. He suggests that the inability of a caseworker to build a rapport with the family, child, and foster parents may result in the placement's instability. He found that caseworker turnover had its greatest effect in the first three years of placement. He also found that the educational experience of a worker had no observable effect on the number of placements a child experienced.

Method

There are multiple processes occurring over time that interact. Caseworker activity is only one of them. Other processes include what is happening in the various living arrangements of the child and what is happening with the parents that may be affecting the process of the child going home. One reason why the effect of caseworker activity on placement outcomes has been studied rarely is that the techniques to study time-varying covariates and multiple outcomes have been foreign to child welfare and human services research until very recently. Techniques like multiple regression and other "static" analyses are inappropriate for studying the situation in which many variables change over the study period and when one does not know when the values of the variables will change (Tuma & Hannan 1984). This analysis builds on a previous analysis of reunification using event-history techniques (Goerge 1990). The *hazard rate,* which is the instantaneous probability of experiencing an event or making a transition at a particular time given that the event has not yet happened, is modeled. Unlike survival analysis, which is being used more often in human services research, this analysis allows for multiple transitions from and to multiple states (Flinn & Heckman 1982) instead of to only one terminal event. It also allows one to estimate the effect of other time-varying covariates, which may change at intervals different from the primary events of interest (Allison 1984), to be estimated.

This study of caseworkers' activities relies entirely on data from the Illinois Department of Children and Family Services (DCFS) management information system. The staff of the Chapin Hall Center for Children at the University of Chicago have developed this administrative case-tracking into the Chapin Hall Child Welfare Careers Database. This database follows the placement experiences of children in the Illinois child welfare system from 1976 through the present. These data were merged with administrative records of caseworker assignments and reassignments also from the DCFS information system, and a longitudinal file of caseworker changes was constructed. From these data the dynamics of the caseworker process were analyzed. These data were used to determine when a caseworker's career began and thus how much experience that worker had at the time he or she was assigned a particular case and when caseworkers were reassigned from a case.

The raw data are converted into episodes in which the variables are constant for that period of time. In this analysis, an episode is a specific placement/caseworker combination. A new episode begins when a child experiences a placement change or a caseworker change. Thus, a child can experience many episodes before a reunification. CTM (Continuous Time Models), a computer program developed by

TABLE 9.1
Number of Workers per Child

Number of workers	All children in sample		Reunified children		Children not reunified	
	N	%	N	%	N	%
0	1	0.1%	1	0.2%	0	0.0%
1	276	32.4%	256	58.9%	1	0.2%
2	176	20.7%	76	17.5%	100	24.0%
3	113	13.3%	49	11.3%	64	15.4%
4	95	11.2%	29	6.7%	66	15.9%
5	65	7.6%	11	2.5%	54	13.0%
6	59	6.9%	7	1.6%	52	12.5%
7	28	3.3%	5	1.1%	23	5.5%
8	16	1.9%	0	0.0%	16	3.8%
9	12	1.4%	1	0.2%	11	2.6%
10	8	0.9%	0	0.0%	8	1.9%
11	2	0.2%	0	0.0%	2	0.5%
Total	851	100.0%	435	100.0%	416	100.0%

James Heckman and George Yates of the Economics Research Center at NORC, University of Chicago, was used to estimate the parameters of the model.

Description of the Sample

The sample of 851 children was randomly selected from all children placed into foster care in Illinois during the calendar year 1988. The size of this sample was chosen because of the memory requirements of the computer program used. These cases were tracked through June 30, 1992. Slightly over half of these children (52%) were reunited with their parents within a mean time of fifty-one weeks. The remainder are still in care or have aged out of care with a mean time in care of 152 weeks. Lengths of stay were censored at the age of twenty-one if the child did not exit care.

Number of Workers. Table 9.1 shows the distribution of number of workers per child for all children, those reunified and those not reunified. The differences in the distributions between those reunified and those not reunified are dramatic, with most of the reunified children having had only one worker, and most of the children not reunified having had three or more. However, it is important to understand that those children not reunified by June of 1992 had been in care between three and a half and four and a half years while those children who were reunified could have been in care for any duration between one week and slightly over four years. Given the differences in the duration of care, it is difficult to determine whether the differences between the two groups are related to the differences in caseworker turnover. This is why an event-history analysis is necessary—allowing us to evaluate the likelihood of reunification throughout a child's foster care experience.

Those children who were reunified had a mean of nearly two workers. With a mean duration of one year, this suggests a turnover occurring on the average every six months. This means that there is little continuity for children from one six-month case review to another. For children who remained in care (a mean time in care of nearly three years), the average number of workers was nearly four, translating into a turnover on these cases of every nine months.

Workers' Level of Experience. Table 9.2 shows that most of the workers who were responsible for these cases had five or more years of experience when they were assigned the case. Only slightly over 25% had less than two years of experience. Workers with less than one year of experience are typically still in training and have lower average caseloads.

Number of Placements. Table 9.3 shows the distribution of the number of placements. While the differences are less dramatic than those seen for worker turnover in table 9.1, it is clear that most children who remain in care or who are not reunified experienced more than three placements. Two-thirds of the children who were reunified had less than three placements.

TABLE 9.2
Workers' Experience

Years	N	%
< 1	160	18.8%
1–2	66	7.8%
3–5	172	20.2%
5 +	453	53.2%
Total	851	100.0%

TABLE 9.3
Number of Placements per Child

Number of placements	All children in sample		Reunified children		Children not reunified	
	N	%	N	%	N	%
1	204	24.0%	176	40.5%	28	6.7%
2	210	24.7%	110	25.3%	100	24.0%
3	123	14.5%	62	14.3%	70	16.8%
4	91	10.7%	38	8.7%	53	12.7%
5	64	7.5%	18	4.1%	46	11.1%
6	41	4.8%	12	2.8%	29	7.0%
7	31	3.6%	10	2.3%	21	5.0%
8	17	2.0%	4	0.9%	13	3.1%
9	16	1.9%	5	1.1%	11	2.6%
10	9	1.1%	0	0.0%	9	2.2%
11	4	0.5%	0	0.0%	4	1.0%
12	7	0.8%	0	0.0%	7	1.7%
13	4	0.5%	0	0.0%	4	1.0%
14	5	0.6%	0	0.0%	5	1.2%
15	4	0.5%	0	0.0%	4	1.0%
16	2	0.2%	0	0.0%	2	0.5%
17	3	0.4%	0	0.0%	3	0.7%
18	2	0.2%	0	0.0%	2	0.5%
19	1	0.1%	0	0.0%	1	0.2%
20	1	0.1%	0	0.0%	1	0.2%
21	1	0.1%	0	0.0%	1	0.2%
22	1	0.1%	0	0.0%	1	0.2%
30	1	0.1%	0	0.0%	1	0.2%
Total	851	100.0%	435	100.0%	416	100.0%

Age at the Time of Placement. Table 9.4 shows the distribution of age at the time of placement. About half of the children enter care at five years of age or under and less than 15% enter after the age of fifteen. This distribution of ages in this sample taken from cases placed in 1988 falls between the distribution of the early to mid-1980s, when there were more adolescents entering care and the late 1980s to early 1990s when nearly 25% of the children entering care were infants compared to only 16% infants in 1988 (Goerge, Casey, & Grant 1992).

Race/Ethnicity. Nearly 60% of the sample were African-American children, 5% were Hispanic children, and the remainder were white. From the early 1980s to the early 1990s there was a large increase in Illinois in the percentage of African-American children entering foster

TABLE 9.4
Age of Placement

Years	N	%
< 1	121	15.98%
1–2	135	17.83%
3–5	139	18.36%
6–8	106	14.00%
9–11	77	10.17%
12–14	74	9.78%
15–17	98	12.95%
18–21	7	0.92%
Total	757	100.00%

care but only a small increase for Hispanic children and a slight decrease for white children.

Results: Effects on Reunification

The model in table 9.5 represents the effect of the covariates on the probability of reunification. A negative parameter means that this characteristic reduces the probability of reunification. When the estimate is two times the standard error, it is statistically significant at the .05 level; at 1.7 times the standard error, the estimate is significant at the .10 level.

The results of this model are also consistent with previous work (Goerge 1990). The probability of reunification decreases with time in care, indicating that many children are reunified soon after being placed.

The most striking finding from the final multivariate model (table 9.5) is that the coefficient for the number of workers is positive and statistically significant (*coeff/s.e.* >2). This means that as a child has experienced more workers over time or as caseworkers on a particular case turn over, there is a greater probability of a child being reunified with his or her parents.

Caseworker tenure did not have a particularly strong effect on the likelihood of reunification of the child. A moderate effect was seen in that children who had workers with between one and two years of experience at the time of placement were likely to stay in foster care longer. Workers with less than one year experience did not have a similar effect. It is possible that because inexperienced workers have

TABLE 9.5
Effects on Reunification

Variable Name	Estimate	S.E.	Est/S.E.
Intercept	−4.270	0.632	−6.756
Duration	−1.204	0.112	−10.731
Number of Workers	0.357	0.143	2.497
Years of Experience			
1–2	−1.228	0.712	−1.725
3–5	−0.586	0.437	−1.341
5+	−0.539	0.400	−1.348
Number of Placements	−0.181	0.102	−1.775
Place Type	0.275	0.335	0.821
Race			
African-American	0.183	0.385	0.475
Hispanic	−0.036	0.940	−0.038
Cook County	−0.953	0.439	−2.171
Age in Years			
1–2	−1.024	0.573	−1.787
3–5	−0.979	0.540	−1.814
6–8	0.055	0.447	0.123
9–11	−0.882	0.718	−1.228
12–14	0.024	0.528	0.046
15+	−0.351	0.501	−0.700

smaller caseloads, they are able to reunify cases more quickly, or they are assigned to cases that are more easily reunified.

This analysis also shows that as a child has more placements, there is a lesser chance that he or she will be reunified with his or her family. Children in Cook County (which includes Chicago) stay in care longer. In Illinois in general younger children stay in care longer than children older than six at the time of placement.

Discussion

To many the findings of this study will be contrary to the practice wisdom. The finding that more caseworker turnover on a particular child's case results in quicker reunification is counterintuitive to some. However, the more recent practice wisdom in public child welfare practice is that action on a particular case may only occur at some procedural or bureaucratic milestone. For example, a change in the living arrangement of a child may only occur at a six-months case review or at an eighteen-months dispositional hearing. Another point in time when a child may go home may be when a case is reassigned to a new caseworker who must reevaluate the case, and the previous caseworker has to justify why the case should remain open or why the child should remain in placement. The more caseworkers a child has, the more possibilities exist for review and for the consideration of reunification. It may be that our findings are consistent with previous research indicating that a caseworker's expenditure of time on a case is a strong determinant of the outcomes of a case in that the time of a change in caseworkers due to turnover may be when caseworkers spend the most time on a case.

Shapiro found that as a worker spent more time on a case, the worker was less likely to be inclined to return the child to his or her parents. In particular, the worker's evaluation of the mother was the key factor in determining the discharge of the case. Extrapolating to the current environment, changing caseworkers may "turn the clock back," so that the evaluation of the mother (and the case) is not yet affected by the amount of contact between the mother and the previous worker.

A large amount of caseworker turnover can be attributed to a specific reason. Particularly in Cook County, a considerable amount of staff transfer exists between the four administrative subregions of the county. The reasons for this are known only in an anecdotal fashion—some areas of the city are more desirable to work in than others. It is believed that this transfer from one office to another is not as great in the state outside of Cook County because there are fewer sites to which a worker can transfer within other regions of the state.

The fact that workers with a tenure of more than one year and less than two years show a tendency to return children to their parents more slowly is consistent with the belief that more experienced workers ensure better outcomes. The fact that workers with less than one year of experience show no difference from more experienced workers does not, however, support this argument. This finding may be an artifact of an incomplete analysis. It is much more likely that workers with less than one year of experience have smaller caseloads and are receiving more attention from supervisors. If we included the size of the worker's caseload in the analysis, the effect of experience would most likely become evident.

Future work

In many ways, this study is an exploratory study since we need to test whether the results of this study are true for other cohorts, and we need to continue to build in additional causal factors in order to understand the multidimensional nature of foster care. However, this sample does represent the children placed in 1988, and since nearly half of them are still in care, the results of these analyses are important for current policy and practice.

A number of additions and modifications should be undertaken as this work is developed further. As already mentioned, the model presented above should include characteristics of caseloads, such as size, types of cases, and service statistics for children in that worker's caseload (e.g., the "track record" of that worker). Caseworkers may spend more time on cases in which they can succeed, namely those that have been in foster care for a short period of time. If they have more cases of children staying in foster care very long, they may divert their energy from those to cases that can be successfully resolved (Stone & Stone 1983). Also, the types of cases a worker carries can affect outcomes. Specialization of worker caseloads has been found to be more effective in speeding up the process of reunifying children (Stein et al. 1977).

The findings of this analysis may also apply to adoption or placement disruption or aging out. The same type of analysis should be undertaken to build on previous work on the effect of caseworker and caseload variables on placement disruption. A study of the reasons for caseworker turnover should also be undertaken in order to identify strategies to promote the optimal dynamic for the best foster care outcomes.

NOTE

The author would like to thank John Van Voorhis, Stephen Grant, and Katherine Casey of the Chapin Hall Center for Children for their assistance.

REFERENCES

Allison, Paul D. (1984). *Event history analysis: Regression for longitudinal event data.* Beverly Hills, CA: Sage Publications.

Barth, R. P., Berrick, J. D., Courtney, M. A., & Albert, V. (1992). *Pathways through child welfare services.* Berkeley, CA: Family Welfare Research Group.

Fein, E., Maluccio, A. N., Hamilton, V. J., & Ward, D. E. (1983). After foster care: Outcomes of permanency planning for children. *Child Welfare, 62*(6), 485–558.

Flinn, C. J. & Heckman, J. J. (1982). Models for the analysis of labor force dynamics. In Basmann and Rhodes (Eds.), *Advances in Econometrics* (pp. 35–95). London: JAI Press.

Goerge, R. M. (1990, September). The reunification process in substitute care. *Social Service Review, 64*(3), 422–57.

Goerge, R. M., Casey, K. M., & Grant, S. H. (1992). Substitute care in Illinois: 1976–1991. Manuscript.

Lipsky, M. (1980). *Street-level bureaucracy.* New York: Russell Sage Foundation.

Pardeck, J. T. (1982). Multiple placement of children in foster family care: An empirical analysis. *Social Work, 29*(6) (November 1984), 506–9.

Pardeck, J. T. (1982). *The forgotten children: A study of the stability and continuity of foster care.* Washington, D. C.: University Press of America.

Pardeck, J. T. (1985). A profile of the child likely to experience unstable foster care. *Adolescence, 20*(79), 659–96.

Shapiro, D. (1976). *Agencies and foster children.* New York: Columbia University Press.

Stein, T. J., Gambrill, E. D., & Wiltse, K. T. (1977, May). Dividing case management in foster family cases. *Child Welfare, 56*(95), 321–31.

Stone, N. M. & Stone, S. F. (1983). The prediction of successful foster placement. *Social Casework: The Journal of Contemporary Social Work, 64*(1), 11–17.

Tuma, N. B. & Hannan, M. T. (1984). *Social dynamics: Models and methods.* Orlando, FL: Academic Press.

Wulczyn, F. H. & Goerge, R. M. (June 1992). Foster care in New York and Illinois: The challenge of rapid change. *Social Service Review, 66*(2), 278–94.

TEN

Explaining the Growing Number of Child Abuse and Neglect Reports and the Growing Foster Care Caseload

Vicky Albert

At both national and state levels, the substantial growth in California's foster care caseload causes concern. Among other consequences, this growth in the foster care caseload leads to increasing costs. It also suggests that changes are taking place in general population demographics, economic and social conditions, or in various child welfare system policies and practices. Specifically, increases in the size of the foster care caseload may reflect increases in the number of children in the general population, increases in child abuse and neglect incidences, or changes in other external developments, such as substance abuse, poverty, or homelessness.

This essay explains the growth in the number of child abuse and neglect reports as well as the growth in the size of the foster care caseload in California. The focus is on California's foster care children who constitute over 20% of the nation's foster care caseload. Close to 45% of the national foster care caseload that receives federal funding under Title IV-E of the Social Security Act is in California and New York.[1] Therefore, what happens to California's children has significant social and fiscal consequences not only for California but also for the rest of the nation. The results from the present research are interesting for what they tell us about California and also as a template for similar research in other states.

This study begins by describing trends in child abuse and neglect reports reflected in emergency response (ER) dispositions; that is, decisions regarding child abuse and neglect reports received during the month or in the previous month. Thereafter attention is paid to trends in the foster care caseload and to past related research. The analytic section of the study is devoted to modeling and simulations. A time-series model is developed for ER dispositions and for the foster care caseload during the period from 1985 to 1990. The model is used for determining the extent to which selected external developments impact the number of emergency response dispositions and the size of the foster care caseload. The model is also used to forecast the consequences of external developments for the foster care caseload. The results of these forecasting exercises and policy recommendations are presented in the last section of the study.

Trends in California's Emergency Response Dispositions

The emergency response program is responsible for the assessment of child abuse reports and for the determination of the disposition of those reports. In any given month, the total number of emergency response dispositions reported from counties to the state is the number of decisions made regarding child abuse and neglect reports received during that month or in the previous month. These decisions include the number of child abuse reports that result in cases subsequently transferred to family maintenance, family reunification, or permanent placement programs within the county and those transferred to other counties. Also included in monthly ER dispositions are the number of ongoing open service cases in the ER unit and the number of investigations closed without further action.[2] Some cases are closed because they have been determined to be inappropriate for in-person response, for example, because the call was for information purposes only. Cases also close because ER in-person response or services are provided, and no further action is deemed necessary to protect the children in the family.

Overall, the number of ER dispositions reflects the number of decisions made during the month regarding child abuse and neglect reports. This study explains growth in ER dispositions rather than growth in the number of child abuse or neglect referrals received during the month for two major reasons. First, counties record the number of families referred for abuse or neglect during a month rather than the number of children. This number of referrals does not

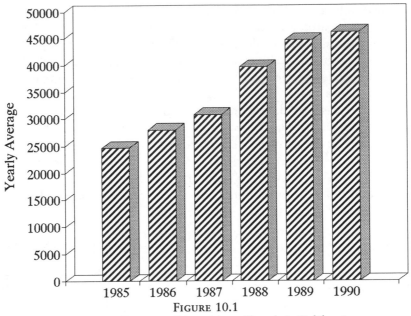

FIGURE 10.1

Emergency Response Dispositions: Trends in California

meet the needs of this study since its focus is on children rather than families receiving protective services. Second, the total number of referrals received during any given month includes those families for which insufficient information exists, and consequently these referrals are not investigated beyond the initial complaint. For example, some of the complaints are prank calls, and other do not provide any information about the location of the alleged abuse or neglect situation. Hence, the number of child abuse reports received during each month is erratic, including events that might not necessarily reflect the actual occurrence of child abuse or neglect in the population.

Yearly trends in California's total emergency response dispositions are shown in figure 10.1. When examined on a monthly basis, these trends reveal considerable seasonality: total ER dispositions peak in the summer months and dip in the winter months. Calculations show that the average number of total ER dispositions per month in 1985 was 24,672 whereas the corresponding number in 1990 was 46,149. This is an overall growth of 87%. The average monthly growth rate differed substantially between three periods. In every month between

January 1985 and December 1987 there were on average 130 more dispositions than in the previous month. Between January 1988 and December 1988 there were about 980 more dispositions every month; between January 1989 and November 1990 there were about 60 more dispositions every month. The growth rate in dispositions was very high during 1988.

Trends in California's Foster Care Caseload

California's foster care caseload comprises nearly one-fifth of the national foster care caseload; its growth needs description and analysis. Figure 10.2 represents California's welfare supervised foster care caseload from 1985 to 1990 and the incidence rate per ten thousand children. The caseload numbers are cases open during each quarter.[3] In this figure several salient features stand out. First, between December 1985 and December 1990 California's foster care caseload grew by about 83%, from 40,763 to 74,399 cases. This is a growth rate of about 10% per year. Second, the greatest increase in the caseload occurred between March 1987 and March 1990; in this interval the caseload grew by close to 61%, from 45,449 to 73,115 cases. This is

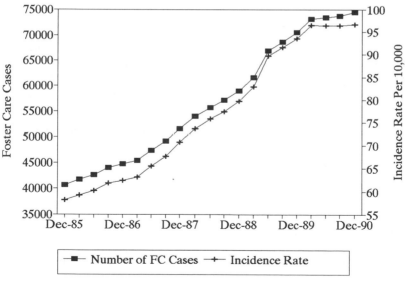

FIGURE 10.2
Foster Care Cases and Incidence Rate per 10,000 Children, 1985–1990

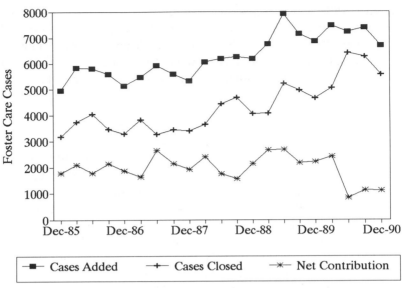

FIGURE 10.3
Number of Foster Care Cases: Reported Welfare Only

a quarterly growth rate of about 4%. Third, from March 1990 to December 1990 the caseload growth abated. Over this period, the caseload grew by a quarterly average rate of less than 1%. Fourth, every year a higher proportion of children under the age of eighteen from the general population has participated in the foster care system. Whereas in 1986 on average sixty-one per ten thousand children in California were in foster care, the figure for 1990 was ninety-seven per ten thousand children, an increase of almost 60%.[4] Overall, California's foster care caseload grew substantially between 1985 and 1990, as did caseloads in other parts of the country.[5] The extent to which this caseload growth resulted from increases in the number of openings or from decreases in the number of closings is addressed next.

Patterns of Change

Changes in the caseload from one period to the next are the result of adding new cases (admissions) and closing other cases (terminations). The difference between admissions and terminations during any month is the net contribution. Figure 10.3 presents the number of admissions, terminations, and the net contribution to the foster care caseload from 1985 to 1990.

Several observations from this graph play a role in the discussion that follows. First, from December 1985 to March 1990 the average net contribution was fairly constant at about 2,100 cases per quarter. Second, during the next three quarters the net contribution fell by about one-half to an average of 1,020 cases per quarter. Whether this drop is temporary or signifies a permanent abatement of the caseload growth is unknown. Third, foster care openings and closings show some cyclical sensitivity: both total admissions and discharges are higher during the summer months and lower in the winter months. Fourth, when the caseload was growing rapidly in 1987, 1988, and 1989, the growth appears to have been the result of different phenomena. During 1987, the rate of openings and the rate of closings were below their 1986 levels. The caseload continued to grow because closings decreased faster than openings did. Fewer children entered foster care, but even fewer children left foster care. During 1988 and 1989, both openings and closings grew, but openings grew faster than closings. In 1988 there were about 7,800 more openings than closings, and in 1989 the corresponding figure was about 9,800. In 1990 the number of admissions stabilized while the number of closings continued to grow.[6]

Explaining the Growing Foster Care Caseload or the Growing Incidence of Child Abuse and Neglect: Past Findings

The surge in the size of the foster care caseload in the latter half of the 1980s was not unique to California although California's caseload grew more than twice as fast as the national caseload. Between 1985 and 1990, U.S. child substitute care grew from 280,000 to 407,000 children: an increase of 45.4% (Tatara 1991). In recent years, several researchers have paid particular attention to the growth in foster care caseloads in Michigan, New York, and Illinois, noting that in the second half of the 1980s all three states experienced an increase in their foster care caseloads. In attempting to disentangle the causes of this growth, the researchers examined total admissions, discharges, and net contributions in each of the three states. They claimed that prior to the mid-1980s, when the caseloads were not growing at a rapid pace, levels of admissions were comparable to levels of discharges. After 1986, however, the foster caseload in each state grew due to increasing admissions and decreasing terminations (Wulczyn & Goerge 1990a). This phenomenon also occurred in California in 1988 and 1989.

Fairly recent research has demonstrated that, at least in New York State, reentry has played a significant role in exerting upward pressure on the foster care caseload (Wulczyn 1991). Wulczyn followed the movement of more than 83,000 children on and off the foster care caseload in New York State from 1984 to 1988. He was able to demonstrate that, for example, between 1984 and 1986 the number of admissions in New York City exceeded the number of the total discharged by 1,165. When admissions exceeded terminations and the caseload began to increase, reentrants to foster care were a major contributing factor in exerting upward pressure on the caseload. About 65% of these 1,165 children in New York City were reentrants in 1984 and the corresponding figure for 1987 was 75%. Wulczyn also found that select variables were associated with reentry, including the age of the child and the duration of the child's previous foster care placement. Children who were between the ages of ten and twelve when placed for the first time had the highest reentry rates. Moreover, children whose placement lasted less than ninety days had higher reentry rates than those who had initially stayed in care longer (Wulczyn & Goerge 1990b).

The surge in infant placements in the latter half of the 1980s may be one reason why exit rates have decreased in New York. Infants, especially those under the age of six months, were found to have longer foster care spells than older children. Researchers have emphasized the need for policies that result in the reduction of the length of spells in the foster care system in order to control the size and cost of the caseload (Wulczyn 1991).

While some research has been conducted in the area of foster care caseload dynamics, longitudinal studies that explain the increase in incidences of child abuse and neglect are scarce. One cross-sectional study, developed a structural regression model in order to estimate the abuse level in several counties. Select economic and social stress variables on the county level were used as predictors of each county's abuse and neglect levels. Two variables in particular were found to produce an estimate of the local abuse population with the least error: local density level or crowding and the number of arrests (Ards 1989). This study was informative since it provided an understanding of how changes in select external developments may affect local child abuse rates; yet, since it was cross-sectional, the study did not demonstrate how historical changes in external developments may affect changes in such rates. Moreover, it did not account for recent drug-related problems that undoubtedly have contributed to the rise in the incidence of child abuse and neglect.

Overall, past research in the area of foster care caseload dynamics has been confined to explaining the growth of the caseload by examining the roles that foster care admissions, terminations, or reentries have played in contributing to that growth. Researchers have not developed a mathematical model that simultaneously accounts for various external social developments and child welfare policies and practices that may explain the caseload growth. Similarly, a few researchers have examined trends in child abuse and neglect or estimated local child abuse rates using cross-sectional data, but they have not explained these trends by using a time-series analysis. Time-series analysis, however, has been used successfully in related social welfare fields and will help explain the increase in the foster care case load.

Using Time-Series Analysis in Income-Maintenance Research

Traditionally, time-series analysis has been a popular and widely used analytic technique in the field of economics. As of late, it has captured the attention of some social welfare policy analysts. For example, in the field of income-maintenance, increases in the caseload of Aid to Families with Dependent Children (AFDC) have been explained using time-series analysis. Plotnick and Lidman (1987), for instance, constructed a multivariate model for the AFDC caseload of single parents in Washington State using data for the years between 1974 and 1983. The objectives of their research were to specify a model that explains the growth in the AFDC caseload and to use this model to forecast the size of the caseload for fourteen months in the future. The dependent variable was the AFDC caseload, and the independent variables belonged to three classes: labor-market conditions, AFDC program characteristics, and demographics. Their model tracked the actual AFDC caseload quite well and selected variables explained about 99% of the variation in the caseload.

Whereas Plotnick and Lidman specified a single model for the AFDC caseload, Albert (1988) developed a model of the AFDC caseload by subdividing it into month-to-month changes in AFDC additions and AFDC terminations. Each component of the caseload is hypothesized to be a function of labor-market conditions, demographics, and welfare system characteristics. This work allowed for the calculation of the consequences of major national policy shifts brought about by the Reagan administration in 1981 for AFDC accessions, terminations, and the entire caseload. The impact of changes in welfare benefits and aggregate unemployment on the AFDC caseload and on additions and terminations were determined by engaging in several forecasting exercises.

Overall, time-series analysis has been used to explain the growth in the AFDC caseload or its components, additions and terminations, by incorporating three sets of variables: labor-market conditions, AFDC program characteristics, and demographics. Time-series analysis, however, has not been used to explain the growth in the foster care caseload or the increase in incidences of child abuse and neglect. The advantages of using this type of analysis are examined next.

Modeling ER Dispositions and the Size of the Foster Care Caseload

A model used to forecast child abuse and neglect reports or the foster care caseload must rest on some theoretical assumptions about the relationship between the dependent variables and external factors. Aside from theoretical expectations, a model also should be based upon what past research has concluded about the relationship between relevant variables. With a good model in hand, time-series analysis can be useful in child welfare in at least two major ways:

  • by making it possible to determine how and to what extent external developments, such as the number of drug-related arrests, affect the number of ER dispositions and the size of the foster care caseload;
  • by providing an opportunity to forecast the consequences for the foster care caseload under alternative assumptions about external developments.

An interesting forecasting exercise is determining the impact of changes in external developments by estimating what would have occurred in their absence and comparing these results with what actually did occur. In this study, such forecasting is performed in order to determine the impact of changes in the number of births and the impact of changes in drug-related arrests on the foster care caseload. Another interesting forecasting exercise would be to determine the impact of major child welfare policy changes by estimating what would have occurred in their absence and comparing these results with what actually did happen with the policy changes in effect. This type of exercise is left to future research.

In order to engage in the desired forecasting exercises, a monthly time-series model is constructed for analyzing and simulating California's foster care caseload. The model is also used for understanding the impact of external developments on the number of ER dispositions during the month. The lag structure of the model is presented in the subsequent section in table 10.1. Since a similar time-series analysis has not been conducted before, the modeling efforts relied on available descriptive information about the characteristics of foster care children and on the best judgment of the researchers.

Overall, two similar equations are developed using two different dependent variables. One dependent variable consists of the total number of ER dispositions per month, and the other is the monthly foster care caseload. The total number of emergency response dispositions each month is taken to represent the number of child abuse or neglect reports. The idea underlying the model is that month-to-month changes in the number of ER dispositions or in the foster care caseload result from changes in various independent factors. These independent factors are listed in figure 10.4.

As can be seen in figure 10.4, the model incorporates seven independent variables. The independent variables can be thought of as having both indirect and direct effects on the foster care caseload. These variables directly affect both ER dispositions and the caseload and indirectly affect the caseload via the ER dispositions. The following section discusses the possible effects of selected variables on the foster care caseload only since the theoretical effects on total dispositions would be expected to be similar.

Births

Between 1985 and 1989 California experienced a dramatic rise in the number of children under the age of one admitted into the foster care system. Nearly 4,400 infants were in foster care in 1989, an increase of 235% over four years. As demonstrated by other research, children

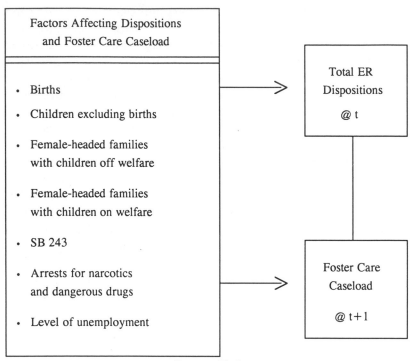

Factors Affecting Dispositions
and Foster Care Caseload

- Births

- Children excluding births

- Female-headed families
  with children off welfare

- Female-headed families
  with children on welfare

- SB 243

- Arrests for narcotics
  and dangerous drugs

- Level of unemployment

Total ER
Dispositions
@ t

Foster Care
Caseload
@ t+1

FIGURE 10.4
Model of ER Dispositions and Foster Care Caseload

who enter foster care as infants tend to remain there for longer periods of time than older children (County Welfare Director's Association 1990). All else being equal, this means that a surge in infant placements is bound to alter the dynamics of the foster care caseload and in turn have fiscal ramifications.

Given the recent upsurge in infant foster care placements, the number of births in California in any given month can be expected to partially explain the size of the foster care caseload. Therefore, the model contains the monthly number of births in California. From 1985 to 1990 this number shows considerable seasonality, with peaks in the summers and troughs in the winters. In 1985 the average number of live births in California was 39,235, whereas in 1990 the corresponding figure was 52,346; an increase of 33%.[7]

When babies are placed in foster care, they are often placed soon after birth due to parental abandonment or parental inadequacy. Nonetheless, the impact of births on the size of the foster care caseload may be delayed since some infants may not be placed right after birth and since some time may pass before the effect of births shows up in Foster Care Information System counts. A four-months lag structure starting with a one-month lag should account for most of the underlying effect of births on the foster care caseload. In other words, all else remaining constant, in any given month the size of the foster care caseload is a function of the number of births that occurred one, two, three, and four months previously. The extent to which the number of births influences the size of the foster care caseload is a question that can only be answered after a model controlling for other factors is tested.

Children

From July 1985 to July 1990 the total number of children in California's population increased by about 10%, from 6,896,284 to 7,701,025. Throughout this five-year period, Caucasian children constituted close to one-half of all children, while the corresponding figure for Hispanic children was about one-third. Corresponding figures for African-American and Asian children have been close to 9 and 10%, respectively. Over the same time interval, the proportion of Caucasian children has decreased slightly while the proportion of African-American and Asian children has remained virtually the same, and the share of Hispanic children in California grew slightly from 33% to 35%.[8]

Nearly two-thirds of children in out-of-home care in California are minority children. African-American children are disproportionately involved with the child welfare system. They represent 26% of new entrants into the foster care system. Hispanic children represent about 20% of new entrants while Asians represent about 4% (County Welfare Director's Association 1990). Therefore, an increase in the number of foster care cases can be predicted on the basis of an increase in the number of African-American and Hispanic children under the age of eighteen in California. Thus, the number of African-American and Hispanic children under eighteen, but excluding those under the age of one, is also included in the model.

Female-Headed Families: On and Off Welfare

Female-headed families with children have a high propensity of experiencing prolonged poverty and welfare dependence (Albert 1988).

Between July 1985 and July 1990, female-headed families constituted about 10 to 11% of all families with children in California. During these years, about 65 to 70% of all female-headed families received AFDC at some point.[9]

Close to four out of five children placed in foster care in 1990 came from single-parent families and close to two out of three of all foster children came from families eligible for AFDC. Thus, any changes in the proportion of either female-headed families or in the proportion of those receiving welfare may affect the number of child abuse reports and in turn the foster care caseload. The model, therefore, incorporates two variables that capture changes in these types of families. One variable represents the number of female-headed families with children who receive AFDC, and the other represents the number of female-headed families with children who do not. It would be expected that as the number of female-headed families with children, both on and off welfare, increases, the foster care caseload will also grow. A two-months lag structure starting with a one-month lag should account for most of the underlying effect of female-headed families on and off welfare on the foster care caseload.

Drug Abuse

Drug abuse by a parent or guardian has become a major factor associated with out-of-home placement. A survey by California's Senate Office of Research in 1988 (see County Welfare Director's Association 1990) and 1989 revealed that over 3,150 children under the age of one were made dependents of the court as a result of substance exposure.

The number of arrests for narcotic and dangerous drugs partially reflects the extent to which drug use or abuse occurs in California. This number is quite seasonal: increasing during the summer months and decreasing during the winter months. From January 1985 to August 1989 the number of arrests connected with narcotic and dangerous drug use climbed at a monthly rate of about two percentage points. Between August 1989 and December 1990 the number of such arrests declined at a monthly rate close to two and one-half percentage points. In January of 1985, the number of drug arrests was about 5,700. By August 1989 the number of drug arrests for narcotics and dangerous drugs hovered around 12,000. The corresponding figure in December of 1990 was 7,500.[10]

Since the number of drug-related arrests on the part of the parents may result in the need for more foster care placements, the model incorporates a variable representing the number of monthly arrests for narcotics and dangerous drugs in California. It is expected that as this number increases, the number of foster care cases will too. A two-months lag structure starting with a one-month lag should account for most of the underlying effect of drug-related arrests on the foster care caseload.

Emergency Response Dispositions

The number of ER dispositions is taken to be a predictor of the foster care caseload. Since ER dispositions do reflect the number of child abuse and neglect reports or incidents, this number is expected to change in response to the same demographic or social variables to which the foster care caseload responds. As can be seen in figure 10.4, the independent variables directly affect both ER dispositions and the caseload but indirectly affect the caseload via the ER dispositions. It also is expected that as the number of ER dispositions grows, so will the number of children placed in foster homes. A one-month lag should account for most of the underlying effect of this variable on the foster care caseload. This variable is also used as a dependent variable in one of the equations.

Senate Bill 243

Senate bill 243 (S.B. 243) passed in the fall of 1987 and was implemented in January 1988. This bill made major changes in the child welfare services (CWS) system. Of particular relevance to this study is that the bill narrowed the definition of abuse for dependency proceedings. Due to S.B. 243, the decision to remove a child from the home or terminate parental rights has to be based on the immediate danger to the child. Previously, the law was broader, not focusing on immediate danger to the child.

S.B. 243 has other provisions relevant to this study. Most important, S.B. 243 reemphasized the priority of foster care placement with relatives. S.B. 243 codified the public's intent that the foster care placement of choice should be with the child's relatives before other foster care placements are considered.

The way in which this bill has affected the size of the foster care caseload is indeterminate. On the one hand, it would be expected that because this bill narrowed the definition of child abuse, fewer children would be placed in foster care. On the other hand, it could be argued that one of the consequences of this bill would be to increase the foster care caseload since social workers were given more latitude in choosing relatives as alternative caregivers. In other words, given a somewhat ambiguous situation of child abuse or neglect, under S.B. 243 social workers and judges might be more inclined to remove a child from the parental home if relatives were available to care for the child. The upshot would be that more children who previously would have remained with their parents are placed in foster care under the present law. While this law was to be implemented in January of 1988, most likely March of that year is the earliest time this variable affected the size of California's foster care caseload.

Seasonality

Finally, the foster care caseload equation includes a set of seasonal monthly dummy variables. Although the variables discussed above cover some of the major influences on the foster care caseload, other social factors also may affect the caseload. To the extent that these factors systematically or seasonally change the caseload, a set of seasonal variables is appropriate. Since some of these social factors are unknown, the sign of the coefficient of each seasonal variable is difficult to hypothesize. The seasonal variables are included in an additive rather than proportional form since the model is in a linear functional form.

Summary of Variables

In the absence of any known previous time-series analyses in the area of foster care, the independent variables in the model were selected on the basis of available descriptive statistics or anecdotal evidence showing that children with certain characteristics and problems are more apt to be in foster care. Similarly, the lag structure of the equation was left solely to the judgment of the researcher. For the foster care caseload, a two-months lag structure seemed appropriate since it was thought it might take that long for particular changes in external factors to affect the dependent variable and for the data to be included in Foster Care Information System counts. A one-month lag structure seems more appropriate for predicting the incidence of child abuse or neglect by using total ER dispositions, since decisions

TABLE 10.1

Time Series Analysis

Regression results: dependent variable is ER dispositions			
Total observations 68		Degrees of freedom 46	
R**2 (adj) .953 see		1885.4230	

Variable name	Lag	Coefficient	Stand. error
Constant	0	− 33326.17	21902.28
Births	1	− .4595998	.3908286
Births	2	.9992546	.4482431
Births	3	.2670921	.4022536
Births	4	− .3329586	.4038228
Nonwhite	1	− .5516727E-02	.1815543E-01
Femfam	1	.3980236E-01	.1219135E-01
Unemploy	1	.3306490	5.590921
AFDCFG	1	.7755452E-01	.8070028E-01
SB243	0	5297.463	1585.203
Drugs	0	.9854913	.5970611

Regression results: dependent variable is foster care caseload			
Total observations 68		Degrees of freedom 46	
R**2 (adj) .977 See		1960.1516	

Variable name	Lag	Coefficient	Stand. error
Constant	0	− 93779.99	17737.70
Toterdis	1	.7073855E-01	.1584719
Births	1	.7972550	.4482475
Births	2	.4212361	.4302773
Births	3	.1054181	.4688207
Births	4	.2026894	.4185785
Nonwhite	2	.1181812E-01	.1613334E-01
AFDCFG	2	.5169182E-01	.8178539E-01
Femfam	2	.4072479E-01	.1389718E-01
SB243	0	997.4903	1890.458
Drugs	2	.6657315	.6134480

to transfer children to a program occur prior to foster care placements.

Results: Emergency Response Dispositions

The estimated equations for total ER dispositions and the foster care caseload are presented in table 10.1. The independent variables in the ER dispositions regression equation explain about 95% of the variance in monthly dispositions. In addition, the results reveal that most of the variables in the equation have the expected sign and have a large impact on the number of decisions regarding child abuse and neglect reports received either during the same month or in previous months.

It should be noted that the following key findings present all levels of statistical significance associated with each variable. The conventional statistical level of .05 for rejecting the null hypothesis is quite difficult to attain in time-series analysis since correlations between time and the independent variables often exist. A broader view of statistical significance is therefore needed. The following is a summary of key findings.

- The number of births, a highly seasonal variable, has a substantial impact on the number of child abuse and neglect reports finalized during a particular month. The sum of the coefficients' signs is positive, indicating that a monthly increase of 1,000 births results in about 470 additional ER dispositions. A joint F-test on the lagged set of births reveals a significance level of .20.
- The sign of the coefficient associated with African-American and Hispanic children in California is negative and unexpected ($p <$ .10). That is, as the number of African-American and Hispanic children in the population increases, the number of ER dispositions decreases.
- A monthly increase of one thousand female-headed families with children who are not on welfare results in about forty additional ER dispositions. The results show that this variable is statistically significant ($p < .0005$).
- The coefficient of the number of female-headed families on welfare (AFDC-FG) has the expected sign, but it is statistically insignificant ($p < .17$). Similarly, the coefficient of the unemployment level has the expected sign but is statistically insignificant ($p <$ .48).
- The number of arrests in California for dangerous or narcotic drugs has a great impact on the number of children in foster care each month. This variable indicates that if the number of drug-related arrests increases by 1,000, the total of the dispositions will increase by 990. This variable is statistically significant ($p < .05$).
- With the implementation of S.B. 243, total dispositions increased by about 5,300 per month. The coefficient is statistically highly significant ($p < .001$).

Results: The Foster Care Caseload

The estimated equation for the foster care caseload is also presented in table 10.2. As in the case of ER dispositions, the independent variables explain a noteworthy percentage of the variance in the dependent variable (98%). For the most part, these variables have the expected signs and a substantial impact on the dependent variable. Fewer of the coefficients in this equation have statistical significance levels that are as good as those found in the other equation. This may be due to greater autocorrelation found in this equation.[11] The following is a summary of key findings.

- The coefficient associated with the number of ER dispositions suggests that a monthly increase of one thousand dispositions results in about seventy-one additional foster care cases ($p < .33$).
- A joint F-test on the set of lagged births reveals a level of statistical significance of .06. At each lag, births have the expected positive sign. Their total magnitude is quite substantial: for every increase of one thousand newborns during a month, fifteen hundred additional children enter the foster care system. Plausible explanations for this finding are provided in subsequent sections.
- The coefficient associated with California's children of African-American and Hispanic descent suggests that a monthly increase in the number of African-American and Hispanic children by one thousand, but excluding infants, results in about ten additional foster care cases ($p < .10$).
- The coefficient of the number of female-headed families with children, excluding those on AFDC-FG, suggests that if that number increases monthly by one thousand, the number of foster care cases will grow by about forty. This result is statistically significant ($p < .005$).
- The coefficient of the number of female-headed families on welfare (AFDC-FG) suggests that a monthly increase of one thousand in that results in about fifty additional more foster care cases. In contrast to the coefficient of all non-AFDC-FG female-headed families with children, this is not statistically significant ($p < .26$).
- The impact of the number of arrests for narcotics and dangerous drugs is quite substantial. The coefficient for this variable suggests that a hypothetical increase of 1,000 arrests would result in about 665 more foster care placements each month ($p < .14$).

TABLE 10.2
Regression Results

| Variable | ER dispositions ($df = 46$) | | Foster care ($df = 46$) | |
| | T-Statistics significance | | T-Statistic significance | |
	Coefficient	Level	Coefficient	Level
Constant	−33326.17	—	−93779.99	—
Toterdis	—	—	.071	.33
Births	−.460	*	.797	**
Births	.999	*	.421	**
Births	.257	*	.105	**
Births	−.333	*	.203	**
Nonwhite	−.006	.10	.012	.10
Famfam	.040	.0005	.040	.005
Unemp	.331	.48	—	—
AFDC-FG	.078	.17	.052	.26
SB243	5297.46	.001	997.490	.30
Drugs	.985	.05	.665	.14

* A joint F-test for multiple lags revealed $p < .20$.
** A joint F-test for multiple lags revealed $p < .06$.
NOTE: Variable Definitions:
Births(t-1) = number of births in the state of California that occurred one month ago,
Births(t-2) = number of births in the state of California that occurred two months ago,
Births(t-3) = number of births in the state of California that occurred three months ago,
Births(t-4) = number of births in the state of California that occured four months ago,
Nonwhite(t-2) = total number of Latino and African-American children less than age 18 in California minus births two months ago,
Femfam(t-2) = number of female-headed families in California excluding those on AFDC, two months ago,
AFDCFG(t-2) = number of female-headed families on AFDC in California, two months ago,
Drugs(t-2) = total number of narcotic and dangerous drug arrests in California, two months ago.
DD(t) = dummy variable identifying the presence of SB 243 policies during month t.
Here, t-1 indicates a lag of one month, t-2 indicates a lag of two months, etc.

• As in the case of total ER dispositions, the impact of S.B. 243 on the foster care caseload is substantial. With the beginning of the implementation of this legislation, the foster care caseload increased by close to one thousand cases per month ($p < .30$).

Table 10.2 summarizes the impact of independent variables on ER dispositions and on the foster care caseload.

Summary and Implications

Overall, the selected independent variables explain a large percentage of the variations in the monthly number of ER dispositions or in the monthly foster care caseload.[12] Two variables in particular have a *substantial impact* on each of the dependent variables: the number of births and the number of arrests for narcotics and dangerous drugs during the month. The coefficient of the number of drug-related arrests in the foster care equation and the one of births in the disposition equation, however, should be viewed with caution because of their levels of statistical significance.

When births are lagged one to four months, their impact on dispositions or on the foster care caseload is sizable. On a cursory examination, in the case of foster care, the results suggest that 150% of any increase in the number of newborns wind up in the foster care caseload. There must be either substantial error in these birth coefficients or some other explanations for these rather surprising results.

Since the set of lagged births yield a statistical significance level of .06, the results do not appear to be in large error. The large impact of births may be explained in several ways. First, it may be that the arrival of a newborn triggers events for other children in the family. If one assumes that there are two children per family and that both children would be placed in foster care, the present results suggest that 75% of any increase in the number of newborns results in foster care placement. Even so, this figure is still quite high.

A second explanation may be that some other variables, unaccounted for in the model, fluctuate in a similar fashion to births and contribute to the rise in foster care placements. Another explanation may be that a rise in additional births in the population leads to problems in other families whose children then enter foster care. The more children in the population, the further existing social and educational services for children must be stretched.

The impact of the number of drug arrests on dispositions and on the foster care caseload confirms anecdotal evidence regarding the impact of drug abuse on foster care placements. The impact of this variable on ER dispositions is greater than that on foster care placements, indicating that drug arrests are associated more with incidences of child abuse and neglect than with foster care placements. Nonetheless, the figure of an increase of 1,000 drug related arrests resulting in 660 more foster care placements is quite substantial.

A positive and large relationship between S.B. 243 and total ER dispositions exists and the coefficient of this variable is statistically significant ($p < .001$). A plausible explanation is that S.B. 243 helped clarify the definition of abuse or neglect for dependent children, in turn letting more children be served in the system than otherwise would have been the case.

Overall, the model of ER dispositions and foster care caseload is designed to test hypotheses about the effects of independent variables, to simulate the total dispositions and foster care caseload, and to determine the impact of select variables on the foster care caseload through several forecasting exercises. The simulations and forecasting exercises are discussed next.

The Simulations

In time-series analysis, a model's ability to replicate actual data is not completely determined by the amount of variance explained by the independent variables in the regression equation nor by the statistical significance of its coefficients. The ability of the model to simulate actual series is very important. For a model to predict historical (actual) series well, the simulated series needs to track the historical series closely. A historical simulation, therefore, is performed in order to evaluate the present model's abilities to replicate historical data. The historical simulations begin in May 1985 and end in December 1990.[13] Two graphic representations of the simulated and historical time series are presented in figures 10.5 and 10.6. The dotted and the solid lines in the figures represent the simulated and historical time series, respectively.

Simulating ER Dispositions

Figure 10.5 shows that the simulated series of total ER dispositions replicates the historical series quite well. Every sharp increase or decrease is captured. The simulated independent variables oscillate through the historical values, and there is not much consistent overestimation or underestimation in the dependent variable.

Calculations show that from May 1985 to December 1990 the mean and standard deviations of actual and simulated series were quite similar. While the average monthly number of dispositions was 36,367, the corresponding figure for the simulated series was exactly the same. The standard deviation for the historical or actual series was 8,733, while the corresponding figure for the simulated series was 8,592. In absolute terms, the simulated series deviated from the actual series on the average by about 1,270 dispositions (or 3.5%) per month. Overall, the total simulated values for ER dispositions are

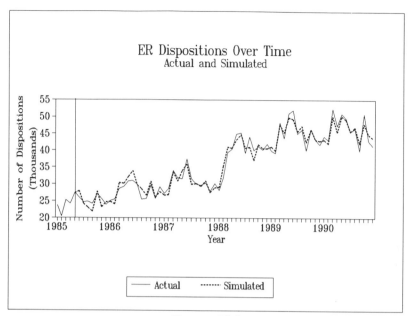

FIGURE 10.5
ER Dispositions Over Time, Actual and Simulated

close to the historical values, as further evidenced by the root mean square percentage error of about 4%.

Simulating the Foster Care Caseload

Figure 10.6 shows that the simulated foster care caseload replicates the historical caseload quite well although turns in the historical series are not captured as well in this case as they are in the case of total dispositions.[14]

As in the case of total dispositions, the average number of foster care cases from 1985 to 1990 is exactly the same: 54,780 foster cases per month. The standard deviations for both the historical and simulated series differ by less than 1%, 12,803 and 12,700, respectively. On the average, the simulated series deviated from the actual series by about 1,400 foster care cases per month. In relative terms and on average, the simulated values for the foster care caseload deviated less than the simulated values did in the case of total dispositions. The root mean square percentage error for the simulated foster care caseload is about 3%.[15]

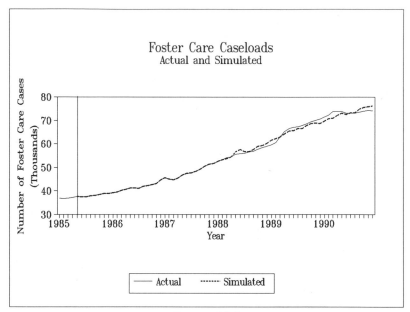

FIGURE 10.6
Foster Care Caseloads, Actual and Simulated

Thus, while the simulated series of total dispositions captures changes better than the simulated foster care series, in general the simulated foster care series stays closer to its historical series. Although the performance of the simulated foster care caseload series could be improved with further research, the model can be used to determine:

- the consequences for the foster care caseload if arrests for narcotics and dangerous drugs remained at their 1987–88 rate of increase; and
- the consequences for the foster care caseload if the number of births decreased by 20%.

The Consequences of Drug Arrests for Foster Care

In this experiment, the number of arrests for narcotics and dangerous drugs between October 1989 and December 1990 are kept at the yearly rates of increase that existed between September 1987 and August 1989. Since the model incorporates a two-months lag structure for the number of arrests for narcotics and dangerous drugs, the

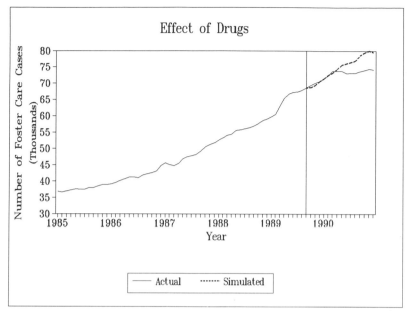

FIGURE 10.7
Effect of Drugs

simulation begins in October 1989 rather than in September 1989. Figure 10.7 shows the foster care caseload with the simulation starting in October 1989. As seen in figure 10.7, the caseload would have been higher beginning in April 1990. The reason it was not higher immediately is that the simulated series underestimates the historical series during 1989, and it takes some time to overcome the underestimation for this forecast.

Calculations reveal that the actual effects of the decrease in drug arrests starting in October 1989 was that the actual foster care caseload was about 3.5% lower than it would have been had drug-related arrests kept increasing at their previous rate. However, a caveat is in order. Since the statistical significance level of the coefficient associated with the number of drug arrests is not strong ($p < .14$), the results should be viewed with caution.

Changing Births: The Consequences for Foster Care

For this exercise, the number of births is lowered by 20% along with the resulting decrease in the number of children in California's

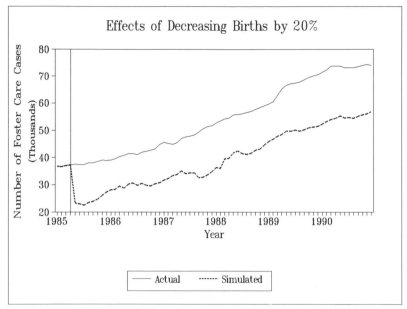

FIGURE 10.8
Effects of a 20% Decrease in Births

population.[16] This simulated series is compared to the historical series in figure 10.8. The results of this exercise illustrate the key role that changes in the number of births play in shaping the foster care caseload. It is estimated that decreasing births by 20% would result in a 27% decrease in the foster care caseload. As argued before, this figure must include the effects of more than one child in a family placed in foster care or perhaps the impact of other variables that are not accounted for in the model and that fluctuate similarly to births. Overall, the effects of births on the foster care caseload are powerful.

Summary and Policy Implications

This study examined the effects of changes in several external factors on California's foster care caseload. It also examined the impact of changes in external factors on reports of child abuse or neglect as measured by the number of monthly ER dispositions. Since California's share of the nation's foster care caseload is relatively large, the consequences of changing external factors for California's foster care caseload have both state and national ramifications.

Evidence from other studies indicates that child abuse may be more likely to follow unwanted births (Zuravin 1991). These data do not allow for the testing of such a hypothesis. The data, however, allow for the determination of the effects of total live births on ER dispositions or on the foster care caseload. All the findings from this study suggest that trends in the infant subpopulation strongly influence trends in the foster care caseload.

Similarly, the findings reveal that the number of female-headed families, often intertwined with poverty and welfare dependence, shapes ER dispositions and the size of the foster care caseload. In a similar vein, the findings show that the number of arrests for narcotic or dangerous drugs partially determines the incidence of child abuse and neglect and the number of children in foster care in any given month.

Thus, in part, the success of state or federal attempts to reduce the incidence of child abuse or neglect and the foster care caseload will depend on the success of programs that reduce the birth rate and the drug abuse rate in the general population. Their success also will depend on the extent to which problems accompanying single parenthood, poverty, and welfare dependence are alleviated. The relationship between these efforts must be understood. For example, strategies to combat drug use that involve the arrest and incarceration of parents must consider their impact on the incidence of child abuse or neglect reports and on the foster care caseload.

Three important policy implications may be drawn from the findings presented in this study:

- State and federal efforts should focus on preventing unwanted or unplanned births. Ample and affordable family planning should be provided to women who are likely to face poverty and other hardships after giving birth.
- State and federal efforts need to continue to focus on providing aid to families known to abuse drugs. Programs that address the needs of parents incarcerated for drug abuse need expansion. These include arrangements for mothers to receive drug treatment while residing with their children in group care, foster care, or residential treatment (Barth 1991).
- State and federal efforts need to focus on further assisting poor female-headed families with children so that fewer children from these families are placed in foster homes.

While the above objectives are broad and difficult to fulfill, child welfare policies are easier to alter. This research suggests that child welfare policy changes, such as S.B. 243, slightly alter the foster care caseload and should be viewed with caution due to the lack of statistical significance of the variable's coefficient. In contrast, the impact of S.B. 243 on the monthly number of ER dispositions is substantial and statistically significant. This result contradicts the expectation that ER dispositions would decline as a result of the narrowing of child abuse definitions. This finding may reflect the continued divergence of child abuse reporting and child welfare services structure. Additional reexaminations or clarifications of child abuse definitions within the child welfare system are still necessary.

Overall, in attempting to understand and deal with problems of foster care, the child welfare system needs to coordinate its intervention and research efforts with other public systems that aim to alleviate problems accompanying unwanted pregnancies, drug abuse, poverty, and welfare dependence.

NOTES

The author gratefully acknowledges the U.S. Department of Health and Human Services, Children's Bureau, and the California State Department of Social Services for their support of this study.

1. Under Title IV-E of the Social Security Act, federal matching funds are provided to states in order to assist foster care children who meet certain eligibility requirements. Caseloads and costs for the program vary significantly between states. For further information regarding the distribution of Title IV-E Social Security funds across the states see Congressional Budget Office Testimony before the Subcommittee on Human Resources, Committee on Ways and Means, U.S. House of Representatives (Washington, D.C.: March 19, 1991).

2. The number of ER dispositions each month was provided by the California State Department of Social Services.

3. For descriptive purposes the number of cases during each quarter was used. For the time-series analysis, the number of foster care cases at the end of each month is taken instead of the number of cases during each quarter. All foster care caseload numbers were provided by the California State Department of Social Services.

4. Yearly figures of the number of children under the age of eighteen were

provided by the California Department of Finance, Population Research Unit. Quarterly and monthly figures were derived by linear interpolation.

5. During the second part of the 1980s, foster care caseloads have grown substantially in other parts of the country. For details see the section that discusses past research.

6. Quarterly figures of foster care admissions and closings were provided by the California State Department of Social Services.

7. Monthly live births were taken from the California State Department of Health, Birth Records Division.

8. Yearly numbers of children under the age of eighteen by race were provided by the State of California, Department of Finance, Population Research Unit. These numbers were linearly interpolated to monthly values.

9. The yearly numbers of female-headed families were provided the State of California Department of Finance. These numbers were linearly interpolated to monthly figures. Monthly AFDC-FG caseload numbers were provided by the California Department of Social Services.

10. Monthly numbers of arrests for narcotics and dangerous drugs in California were provided by the State of California Department of Justice, Bureau of Criminal Statistics and Special Services.

11. The foster care caseload regression equation has a Durbin-Watson statistic that shows the presence of significant autocorrelation. In turn, the Hildreth-Lu *rho* correction procedure for first-order autocorrelation was applied. The *rho* corrected results did not significantly alleviate this problem of autocorrelation. Therefore, the initial equation is presented and used throughout the chapter. It is expected that further research will help alleviate this problem. In addition, since selected independent variables, such as births, affect foster care caseload directly and indirectly via dispositions, the predicted rather than the actual value for ER dispositions was tried for predicting the impact of this variable on the foster care caseload. The upshot was that the results obtained using the predicted value for dispositions did not differ much from those using the actual value. Therefore, the actual value for dispositions was used.

12. The variables in the total ER dispositions equation are much less correlated with one another than are those in the foster care caseload equation.

13. The historical simulation begins in May rather than in January of 1985 since the model has at most a four-months lag. For a detailed explanation of the simulation process see Albert 1988.

14. According to anecdotal evidence, the sharp increase in the foster care caseload in 1989 may be the result of accounting errors corrected by Los Angeles county in 1989. Since Los Angeles county's foster care caseload accounts for about 40% of the total foster care caseload in California, this accounting correction may have substantial impact on the total statewide caseload. However, since there is no guarantee that this is the reason for the

sharp increase, no other exogenous variable is incorporated into the model at this time.

15. The root mean square percentage error is analogous to the standard deviation. The actual historical value of a series is subtracted from its simulated value. But the measurement is in terms of the percentage of some deviation relative to the actual historical series value.

16. It is assumed that this decrease began in May 1984 and lasted until December 1990. Since the unborns do not become part of the population, the decrease in births also affects children aged one to eighteen in California's population. Consequently, the variable in the model capturing the number of African-American and Hispanic children was appropriately decreased.

REFERENCES

Albert, V. (1988). *Welfare dependence and welfare policy: A statistical study.* Westport, CT: Greenwood Press.

Ards, S. (1989, October). Estimating local child abuse. *Evaluation Review, 13*(5), 484–515.

Barth, R. P. (1991, Summer). Sweden's contact family program. *Public Welfare, 49*(3), 36–42.

County Welfare Directors Association. (1990). *Ten reasons to invest in the families of California: Reasons to invest in services which prevent out-of-home placement and preserve families.* Sacramento: Author.

Plotnick, R. & Lidman, R. (1987, Winter). Forecasting AFDC caseloads. *Public Welfare, 45*(1), 31–35.

Tatara, T. (1991, November). Some additional explanations for the recent rise in the U.S. child substitute care population. *Research Notes.* Unpublished Report. Washington, D.C.: American Public Welfare Association.

Wulczyn, F. & Goerge, R. (1990b, April). *A multi-state view of foster care system dynamics: Placement duration and foster care re-entry in N.Y. and Illinois.* Manuscript. New York Department of Social Services and Chapin Hall Center for Children at the University of Chicago.

Wulczyn, F. & Goerge, R. (1990a, December). *Public policy and the dynamics of foster care: A multi-state study of placement histories.* Washington, D.C.: U.S. Department of Health and Human Services, Office of Assistant Secretary for Planning and Evaluation.

Wulczyn, F. (1991, March). Caseload dynamics and foster care re-entry. *Social Service Review, 65*(1), 133–56.

Zuravin, S. (1991, July/August). Unplanned childbearing and family size: Their relationship to child neglect and abuse. *Family Planning Perspectives, 23*(4), 155–61.

PART FOUR

ADOPTION RESEARCH

Adoption research has a long and honored tradition within child welfare services. Ed Mech's (1965) presentation of perspectives on adoption research posed challenges that we continue to address: "The prospects of moving toward a scientific base for child placement appear bright, though at present the hiatus between the actual and potential contributions of research to practice is truly vast. . . . Effective methodological strategies have yet to be developed, and attempts to coordinate the conceptual efforts of practitioners and researchers have barely begun" (p. 7). The papers in this section narrow the vastness of the chasm between research and practice and enlist the rigorous methods Mech demands.

We have included an important study about adoption seeking in the United States because it addresses one of the most important issues in the field and does so with great sophistication. Bachrach, London, and Maza use data from the National Survey of Family Growth (Cycle IV) to collect data on adoption from a national probability sample of 8,450 women. They provide the first scientifically derived estimates of adoption seeking based on direct measures of the population. Although practitioners often report that research produces self-evident findings, this is not the case here. These estimates are nearly ten times lower than previous estimates. Like many of the investigations reported in this volume, the authors also find provocative racial differences in adoption seeking. A companion piece (Bach-rach, Stolley, & London 1992) considers the changing probabilities of relinquishing for adoption. Their findings from both studies will be further elaborated with questions added in Cycle V of the NSFG. Such national probability samples are much underused in child welfare research. For example, child welfare relevant studies could be developed from the National Longitudinal Study on Youth (NLSY) since it includes a probability sample of children born to young parents. These databases offer a rich source of information on providing comparison groups for future research.

In the last decades, adoption has had strong links to more formal child welfare services as the numbers of special needs adoptions has increased. Still, the great majority of both adoption seekers and children who are adopted never have contact with child welfare agencies. The diversity of adoption represents a great opportunity for the field and, at the same time, is a challenge to conducting and interpreting adoption research. Researchers must remember to differentiate the service context and the individual child and family characteristics that result in measurable outcomes. There is a tendency to overgeneralize conclusions about adoption outcomes from adoption samples that fail to differentiate between infant and older child adoptions; inter-country and domestic adoptions; and private agency, public agency, and independent adoptions.

Barth's paper on adoption of drug-exposed infants includes these distinctions and shows that parental self-reports of outcomes are significantly shaped by the adoption agency. Whether or not a child was drug-exposed had no significant impact on parental reports of the outcome of the adoption; yet, the type of adoptive placement (i.e., independent, private agency, or public agency) did. This study is the first to systematically consider outcomes of adoptions of drug-exposed infants—the early returns are promising; these children will also be followed across time. Following families just two years after the adoption, Barth's study has adequate power to conclude that the lack of differences between groups was not a function of inadequate sample size.

The future of adoption research will certainly include more standardized measures and longitudinal studies (Berry in press; Groze & Rosenthal 1991). Understanding of the need to ensure these features of important research is not new. In 1965 Henry Maas called for "longitudinal studies [which] may clarify for us crises that are common in the development and socialization of adopted children and perhaps, also, those points at which intervention in the family can most profitably provide preventive or remedial services" (p. 6).

Also badly needed is more comparative research (Barth 1991). We lack basic comparisons between the outcomes for adopted children, children in foster care (kinship and otherwise), and children remaining in marginal birth families. The next round of adoption research must help clarify the ways in which adoption is the same as and different from other family arrangements. Child welfare practitioners have widely varying views about the preferability of various family forms. Despite surprising research consensus about the low disruption rates, many child welfare workers continue to expect that adoptions of older children will yield little that is good or lasting. There is no justification in fact for such thinking. Speculation about the stability of kinship foster care and guardianship is more understandable since research in these areas is in its infancy. Comparative research on the lifetime outcomes of these forms of "permanent placements" must begin.

REFERENCES

Bachrach, C. A., Stolley, K. S., & London, K. A. (1992). Relinquishment of premarital births: Evidence from national survey data. *Family Planning Perspectives, 24,* 27–33.

Barth, R. P. (1991). Research on special needs adoption. *Children and Youth Services Review, 13,* 317–21.

Berry, M. (In press). Contributors to adjustment problems of adoptees: A review of the longitudinal research. *Child and Adolescent Social Work Journal.*

Groze, V. & Rosenthal, J. (1991). *Special needs adoption.* New York: Praeger.

Maas, H. (1965). Introduction. In H. Maas (Ed.), *Perspectives on Adoption Research* (pp. 4–6). New York: Child Welfare League of America.

Mech, E. (1965). Trends in adoption research. In H. Maas (Ed.), *Perspectives on Adoption Research* (pp. 3–32). New York: Child Welfare League of America.

ELEVEN

On the Path to Adoption: Adoption Seeking in the United States, 1988

Christine A. Bachrach, Kathryn A. London, and Penelope L. Maza

In recent years the popular press has given much attention to long waiting lists for adoption and the undersupply of healthy white infants relative to the number of couples seeking to adopt. This picture has been informed entirely by reports from adoption agencies, organizations representing adoption agencies, and anecdotal accounts from individuals seeking to adopt. Until now no reliable data existed to estimate the size of the population seeking adoption. Yet such information is important to inform federal and state policies relating to adoption and reproductive issues and to obtain a better understanding of adoption as a strategy for family formation among U.S. couples. This paper reports estimates of the population seeking to adopt collected in 1988 for women aged fifteen to forty-four by the National Center for Health Statistics.[1]

This paper also examines the correlates of adoption seeking among U.S. women. Our approach is grounded in previous research and theory pertaining to adoption and the propensity to adopt. We distinguish adoption seeking from both of these phenomena, however. Adoption seeking is defined as behavior that is intended to result in the adoption of a child. In this study this is defined in terms of contact with an adoption agency or lawyer. Individuals who have some interest in or propensity for adopting may not engage in adoption-seeking behavior for a variety of reasons explored later in the paper. Individuals who have sought adoption likewise may never adopt a child. Our focus on adoption seeking enables us to investigate the circumstances that lead individuals to explore this alternative means of family formation, independent of whether an adoption occurs.

Background

It is axiomatic that adoption provides an alternative to biological parenthood. Thus, couples who desire children but are unable to have them are typically viewed as the most likely ones to seek adoption. However, adoption and biological parenthood are different in important ways, and these differences may affect the likelihood that adoption will be pursued (Miller 1981; Daly 1988; Lasker & Borg 1987). The fundamental difference between adoptive and biological parenthood is the absence of biological relatedness, in the case of unrelated and stepparent adoption, and the existence of a lesser degree of relatedness in the case of adoption by other relatives. Biological relatedness carries with it the certainty of similarity in background and the likelihood of similarity in genetically transmitted characteristics; it also confers upon the child an unequivocal basis for integration into the family, an integration that must be achieved through other means in the adoptive family (Kirk 1959).

Certain experiences inextricably tied to biological parenthood are not or may not be experienced by adoptive parents: pregnancy, childbirth, breastfeeding, and early infant care. In contrast to biological parenthood, which may or may not result from rational choice, adoptive parenthood requires positive action, usually on the part of a couple who must agree on taking action toward adopting. Biological parenthood is achieved by most couples without outside intervention, whereas adoptive parenthood requires intervention by the courts and usually by an adoption agency or lawyer.

Finally, adoption offers possibilities that biological parenthood does not: the opportunity to expand kinship ties to a larger social group (Harbison 1983), to express humanitarian values in one's personal life, to obtain children with specific desired characteristics, such as a particular gender, or to extend responsibility for a known child, such as a relative or foster child. Such possibilities may account for what Feigelman and Silverman (1979) term "preferential adoption," the adoption of children by couples who are capable of biological childbearing.

Seeking to adopt may be viewed as the result of rational decision-making processes in which costs and benefits of alternative actions are weighed. In the case of adoption, benefits will consist of all those factors contributing to the motivation to have a child, whereas costs may include not only the financial costs of adoption but also barriers such as long waiting lists, agency requirements for certain parent characteristics, and uncertainty of success in adopting the type of child desired. To the extent that these cost factors are in part responses to limited supply, actual adoption-seeking behavior will reflect only the quantity of adoptions demanded under existing circumstances and may underestimate the "latent" demand that would be evoked by an increase in the supply of adoptable children and a reduction in the costs of adoption.

In view of these considerations, we posit three main factors that are likely to determine the probability of adoption seeking: (1) the desire for children, (2) the inability to have children, and (3) the resources available to meet the costs of adoption. Inability to have children may include the inability to conceive, to carry to term successfully, or even the experience of the death of children. Resources include not only financial resources needed to pay adoption expenses but also those resources needed to meet agency requirements (age, marital status, health) and to negotiate the procedures required for adoption. A diverse set of other factors may also be involved in bringing about adoption in some cases, e.g., in adopting a foster child or relative or adopting for humanitarian reasons.

Adoption seeking has received little attention in previous research. However, studies exist that examine the correlates of having adopted a child and the correlates of reported propensity to adopt among representative samples of the U.S. population. These studies can provide a reference point for studying adoption demand. In addition, a number of studies have provided qualitative information on the psychosocial processes that characterize couples seeking adoptive parenthood (e.g., Daly 1988; Miller 1981).

Research on the Correlates of Adoption

Social and demographic characteristics of adopting parents have been studied over a variety of time periods and for a variety of populations. Results have been remarkably stable over these diverse contexts, indicating that having adopted a child is primarily a function of age, childlessness, and the inability to bear children, and only secondarily a function of high socioeconomic status (Leahy 1933; Bonham 1977; Bachrach 1983, 1986; Poston & Cullen 1986). The two studies that examined adoption in a multivariate context concurred that the three factors of age, childlessness and impaired fecundity[2] each had both additive and interactive effects on the likelihood of having adopted a child. According to Poston and Cullen (1986), the highest rates of adoption occurred among childless women who were nonfecund. Socioeconomic factors appear to have different effects on adoptions of relatives and that of nonrelatives. Adoption of nonrelatives is substantially more common among white, well-educated, and high-income individuals, while adoption of relatives appears to be more common among those who are black, poor, or poorly educated (Bachrach et al. 1990).

Research on the Propensity to Adopt

Studies of women who actually adopt may give an incomplete picture of the demand for adoptable babies. First, and most important, are the direct effects of "barriers" to adoption such as the criteria used by adoption agencies for screening, or choosing among, would-be adopters (Freedman et al. 1987), the costs of adoption, whether pursued through an agency or independent channels, and the limited supply of babies placed for adoption. Stated simply, not all couples who seek to adopt are successful in doing so. Second, it may be that the perception of barriers discourages some potential adoptive parents from taking steps to adopt.

The propensity for adoption among U.S. women was examined briefly by Bonham (1977) and in more detail among white married women by Poston and Cullen (1989). This propensity was measured by a question included in the 1973 and 1976 NSFG, asked of nonsterile women who expected to have one or more additional children, "If it should turn out that you and your husband are unable to have the number of children you expect, would you adopt a child?" In both years, approximately seven in ten white wives exhibited some propensity to adopt, as indicated by a "yes" or "maybe" response. The propensity to adopt was greatest at the youngest ages and the lowest parity levels.

In 1973 sterile women were not asked about adoption propensity, but in 1976 women sterile for reasons other than contraception were asked if they intended to adopt. Only 11% of the women who were asked this question responded with yes, and 10% responded "maybe." The propensity to adopt among the sterile women varied most strongly by parity—it was highest for childless women—and was also higher for women in their late twenties and early thirties than at older or younger ages. The propensity to adopt tended to increase with increasing education and family income.

Previous Estimates of the Population Seeking To Adopt

Because direct information relating to adoption seeking has not been available previously, in the past those who sought to estimate the size of the population seeking adoption relied on the known association between adoption and impaired fecundity. In 1984 the National Committee for Adoption (NCFA), an advocacy group for adoption agencies and a clearinghouse for information about adoption, estimated that two million couples in the U.S. were seeking to adopt (NCFA 1984). This estimate was based on data referring to treatment for infertility among U.S. men and women. In 1989 the NCFA issued a revised estimate of "at least one million couples who . . . may wish to consider adoption." This estimate was based on data from the 1982 National Survey of Family Growth showing that 2.7 million U.S. couples had impaired fecundity and wanted a future birth. The new NCFA estimate incorporated the assumptions that half of these couples would achieve their desired fertility through infertility treatment rather than adoption, and an additional 11% would forego their fertility goals rather than adopt. The estimate did not include single adopters or those with no fecundity impairments and thus was thought to be conservative (NCFA 1989).

Data and Methods

Data are drawn from the National Survey of Family Growth (NSFG), Cycle IV, that was conducted in 1988 by the National Center for Health Statistics. This survey consists of interviews conducted with a national probability sample of 8,450 women between the ages of fifteen and forty-four on topics related to fertility, family planning, and reproductive health. In addition to ascertaining whether respondents had ever adopted children and the characteristics of those adoptions, the interview included questions about steps taken to seek adoption.[3] Specifically, the women were asked if they had ever contacted an adoption agency or lawyer about adopting a child, if they had formally applied to an agency or hired a lawyer, and if they were still actively seeking to adopt at the time of the interview. The women were asked if they were actively seeking to adopt only if they had either applied to an adoption agency or engaged a lawyer. Our estimates of the population *currently* seeking adoption thus represent only those who had taken some concrete step toward adoption. By contrast, we have estimated those who have ever sought to adopt more generously by including all those who ever contacted an agency or lawyer about adoption, regardless of whether the initial contact was followed by further steps.

In this paper, we present data on current adoption seeking in summary fashion and confine our detailed analyses to people who ever sought adoption, whether successfully or not.[4] We do this for two reasons. First, only thirty women in the NSFG sample were currently seeking to adopt, a number too small to permit reliable estimates by race. By contrast, the sample included 309 women who had ever sought adoption. Second, current seeking is affected not only by factors that bring about seeking but also by those that determine success or termination of the search. Those who adopt quickly (or give up quickly) are less likely to be captured in a measure of current seeking than those who take longer to adopt or persist longer in trying. Those who are missed are likely to differ from those who are included with respect to the type of child sought as well as in regard to other characteristics related to the adoption process.

Variables included in our analyses of the determinants of adoption seeking are listed in table 11.1 along with their means and standard errors. The desire for children is measured by the number of children the woman would most like to have in her lifetime. The ability to have children is measured by a categorical variable classifying women according to self-reported conditions that make it impossible or difficult to bear children (see note 2). This variable reflects current status and captures previous experiences with fecundity impairments only to the extent that these have persisted over time. Additional variables further measure previous obstacles to family formation: whether the woman has experienced one or more child deaths and whether she has experienced one or two or more miscarriages and stillbirths. Finally, a dichotomous variable indicating childlessness at the time of the interview provides a summary measure of lifetime fertility.

Two variables reflect the interactive effects of the desire for chil-

TABLE 11.1

Means (Standard Errors) of Variables Used to Predict Past and Current Adoption Seeking, by Race

Predictor	Nonblack	Black
Desired number of children	2.576 (0.023)	2.441 (0.021)
Fecundity status		
Contraceptively sterile	0.235 (0.007)	0.220 (0.011)
Noncontraceptively sterile	0.046 (0.003)	0.057 (0.006)
Nonsurgically sterile	0.013 (0.002)	0.018 (0.003)
Subfecund	0.059 (0.004)	0.043 (0.005)
Long interval	0.012 (0.002)	0.016 (0.003)
One or more child deaths	0.019 (0.002)	0.027 (0.004)
One pregnancy loss	0.174 (0.006)	0.181 (0.010)
Two or more pregnancy losses	0.064 (0.004)	0.070 (0.007)
Childless at interview	0.444 (0.008)	0.368 (0.013)
Ever sought infertility services?	0.121 (0.005)	0.086 (0.007)
Does woman desire more children than she expects to have?		
No, desires and expects same	0.555 (0.008)	0.510 (0.013)
Yes, 1 more desired	0.183 (0.006)	0.175 (0.010)
Yes, 2 more desired	0.087 (0.004)	0.081 (0.007)
Yes, 3 + more desired	0.040 (0.003)	0.047 (0.006)
Education attainment		
High school graduate	0.332 (0.007)	0.347 (0.013)
Some college	0.254 (0.007)	0.247 (0.011)
College graduate	0.192 (0.006)	0.098 (0.008)
Religious participation at age 14		
weekly or more frequently	0.682 (0.008)	0.720 (0.013)
Currently married	0.537 (0.008)	0.286 (0.012)
Previously married	0.125 (0.005)	0.185 (0.010)
Age at interview	29.46 (0.125)	28.43 (0.099)
Hispanic origin	0.105 (0.005)	0.035 (0.005)

NOTE: Omitted categories are: no children desired, fecund, no child deaths, no spontaneous pregnancy losses, one or more children ever born, never sought infertility services, desires fewer children than expected, less than high school education, religious participation at age fourteen less frequently than once a week, never married, and non-Hispanic.

dren and the ability to have children. The first of these is a dichotomous variable that takes the value of one if the woman ever visited a doctor or clinic for infertility treatment, implying both difficulty in conceiving or bearing children and a desire to overcome the difficulty. The second is a measure computed as the difference between the number of children desired over the woman's lifetime and the expected number of live births. Women with positive values on this variable desire more births than they expect to have. This variable was found to have a nonlinear relationship to adoption seeking in our multivariate analyses and is represented by four dummy variables, and those women who desire fewer children than they expect are treated as the reference category.

Two variables are included to measure the resources available for meeting the costs of adoption. Education is represented by three dummy variables and serves as an indicator of socioeconomic status as do skills, abilities, and other attributed qualities that may increase the success of an adoption effort. Marital status is represented by two dummy variables identifying currently and previously married women. Other variables include age (a measure of cumulative opportunity to initiate an adoption search), weekly or more frequent attendance at religious services (an admittedly poor proxy for humanitarian motives that might influence the decision to adopt), and Hispanic origin (included to assess the influence of membership in a minority group on adoption seeking). Because patterns of family formation and adoption differ markedly among black and white women, we have fit our models separately for black and nonblack women.

A major weakness of the available measures of women's characteristics is that most are measured as of the time of the survey whereas our dependent variable reflects efforts to seek adoption that may have occurred at any time in the past. Thus, although we have chosen our predictors from domains that causally precede adoption, the actual measures are not necessarily so, and the resulting model cannot be said to demonstrate causal links. The limitation of the NSFG to women is a second weakness. Most adoptions of nonrelatives involve couples and therefore a dyadic decision-making process. The NSFG captures only one side of that process.

A final weakness is that the available data do not differentiate between demand for adoptions of relatives and for those of nonrelatives even though the process leading to adoption seeking probably differs for these two types of adoption. We have based our model on a framework primarily relevant to adoption of nonrelatives, and we expect that most adoption seeking observed in this sample (at least among nonblack women) involves such adoptions. Our expectation is supported by data for actual adoptions reported by nonblack women in this sample, only 15% of which involved related children. By contrast, the proportion of actual adoptions reported by black women that involve related children is much higher (44%), suggesting that our framework may be less appropriate for explaining adoption seeking in this group.

Because the NSFG is based on a complex sample design, all esti-

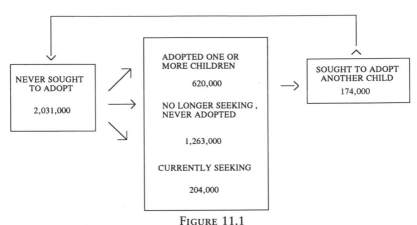

FIGURE 11.1
*Number of Women 15–44 Years of Age Who Have Ever Sought to Adopt,
by Outcome*

mates presented in this paper are based on weighted data. Use of
conventional statistical software with such data will result in overestimating the statistical significance of differences. For cross-tabular
comparisons, standard errors were computed using the balanced half
sample replication technique (see Judkins et al. forthcoming, for a
discussion of this technique applied to the NSFG); for multivariate
analyses weights were scaled back to approximate actual sample
sizes, and a conservative criterion ($p < .01$) was chosen to establish
statistical significance. Multivariate analyses are conducted using logistic regression because our outcome variables are dichotomous and
highly skewed.

Findings

Estimates of the Population Seeking to Adopt

As figure 11.1 illustrates, in 1988 slightly over two million women
between the ages of fifteen and forty-four had ever contacted an
agency or lawyer about adopting a child. Of these women, approximately six hundred thousand, or 31%, had actually adopted, and a
fraction of these had gone on to seek another adoptive child. At the
time of the interview, only slightly more than two hundred thousand
women were seeking to adopt. Over 1.2 million women had neither
adopted nor did they continue seeking adoption. Many of these
women never took formal steps toward adopting, either by applying

to an agency or by hiring a lawyer; others dropped out of the process after such steps were taken. We have no direct information on their reasons for dropping out. However, it is suggestive that 64% of those who ever sought to adopt gave birth themselves at some point in their lives. Many women may have abandoned their adoption seeking in response to such births. Others may have decided against adoption for a variety of reasons, including changes in life circumstances, unwillingness of one or both partners to adopt, or barriers to adoption. Still others, of course, will have been unsuccessful in obtaining a child.

Who Seeks to Adopt?

Percentages of women who have ever sought adoption are shown in table 11.2 according to race and other characteristics. At the time of the interview, only 3.5% of all women aged between fifteen and forty-four had ever sought to adopt. The percentage of nonblack women who had ever sought to adopt was highest among those women who desired three or more children, those who had fecundity impairments (particularly nonsurgical sterility), those who had experienced child deaths and/or fetal loss, those who had born children, those who had sought infertility services, those who desired more children than they expected to have, those who were currently or had previously been married, and among older women. With the exception of childlessness, all of these variables appear to affect adoption seeking in the hypothesized direction. The higher proportions having sought adoption among those who have born children may reflect the confounding effects of age, which affects the likelihood of achieving both types of parenthood positively. The proportion who ever sought adoption was related positively to educational attainment, but it was only slightly higher among those who attended religious services on a weekly or more frequent basis.

Black and nonblack women were equally likely to have sought to adopt. However, relationships between ever seeking adoption and factors measuring fertility desires and the ability to have children were less often significant among black women than among nonblack women even though the pattern of these relationships was generally similar for the two racial groups. This is due in part to the smaller sample size available for black women and also to the fact that many of the relationships appear to be weaker for this group. For example,

TABLE 11.2

Percentage of Women 15–44 Years of Age who Have Ever Sought to Adopt, by Selected Characteristics and Race: United States, 1988

Characteristic	Nonblack	Black
All Women	3.5 (0.3)	3.5 (0.5)
Desired number of children		
None	1.9 (.09)	5.3 (2.2)
One	2.6 (0.8)	1.6 (0.8)
Two	3.1 (0.4)	3.3 (0.7)
Three or more	4.4 (0.5)	4.2 (0.9)
Fecundity status		
Surgically sterile		
Contraceptive	4.9 (0.7)	4.9 (1.1)
Noncontraceptive	10.3 (2.1)	8.2 (3.0)
Nonsurgically sterile	24.4 (5.4)	4.0 (3.8)
Subfecund	10.6 (1.9)	7.8 (3.2)
Long interval	15.3 (4.8)	3.4 (3.7)
Fecund	1.2 (0.2)	2.2 (0.5)
Child deaths		
None	3.4 (0.3)	3.3 (0.5)
One or more	10.7 (3.3)	10.6 (4.8)
Miscarriages or stillbirths		
None	2.7 (0.3)	2.8 (0.5)
One	4.9 (0.8)	5.0 (1.3)
Two or more	10.0 (1.7)	6.7 (2.4)
Children ever born		
None	2.9 (0.3)	2.6 (0.2)
One or more	4.0 (0.4)	3.9 (0.8)
Ever sought infertility services?		
Yes	17.1 (1.6)	15.4 (3.2)
No	1.6 (0.2)	2.3 (0.4)
Does woman desire more children than she expects to have?		
No, desires fewer	1.8 (0.6)	4.0 (1.2)
No, desires same	1.6 (0.2)	1.8 (0.5)
Yes, 1 more desired	5.4 (0.8)	4.3 (1.3)
Yes, 2 more desired	10.1 (1.5)	9.2 (2.6)
Yes, 3 + more desired	12.8 (2.5)	7.0 (3.1)
Education		
Less than high school	2.0 (0.4)	1.3 (0.5)
High school graduate	3.6 (0.5)	3.2 (0.8)
Some college	3.7 (0.5)	5.3 (1.2)
College graduate	5.0 (0.7)	6.4 (2.0)
Religious participation at age 14		
Weekly or more	3.8 (0.3)	4.0 (0.6)
Less than weekly	2.8 (0.4)	2.1 (0.7)
Marital status		
Currently married	5.2 (0.5)	5.0 (1.1)
Previously married	4.5 (0.9)	6.1 (1.5)
Never married	0.5 (0.2)	1.7 (0.5)

Characteristic	Nonblack	Black
Age at interview		
15–24 years	0.5 (0.2)	0.5 (0.3)
25–29 years	1.5 (0.4)	1.9 (0.8)
30–34 years	4.4 (0.8)	6.0 (1.7)
35–39 years	5.8 (0.8)	6.9 (1.6)
40–44 years	8.4 (1.1)	6.3 (1.9)
Hispanic origin		
Yes	3.1 (0.8)	n/a
No	3.6 (0.3)	n/a

NOTE:Standard errors of percentages are shown in parentheses; n/a = not applicable.

among nonblack women 1% of fecund women and 5 to 24% of those with impaired fecundity had ever sought to adopt, whereas among black women 2% of the fecund and only 3% to 8% of those with impaired fecundity had done so. By contrast, variables such as age, marital status, and education had equally strong or stronger relationships with having sought to adopt among black as among nonblack women. Frequency of religious participation at age fourteen was significantly related to having sought adoption among black women but not among nonblack women.

Regression Results

Estimated coefficients for logistic regression models predicting the log odds of ever having sought to adopt are presented in table 11.3, along with estimates, obtained by calculating e^β, of the change in the odds of having sought to adopt associated with a unit change in each predictor variable. Among nonblack women, all but one of the predictors measuring difficulty in having children have statistically significant coefficients, indicating that each contributes independently to the likelihood of having sought to adopt. Compared with fecund women (the reference category), women with fecundity impairments are from 1.9 to 3.7 times more likely to have sought adoption, net of all other factors in the model. Women who had experienced one or more child deaths were 2.8 times more likely to have sought adoption than those without such experience, and childless women were 2.1 times more likely to have sought adoption compared to women who had borne children by the time of the interview.

The significant effect of having been sterilized for contraceptive

TABLE 11.3

Beta, Coefficients for Logistic Regression Models Predicting the Odds of Ever Having Sought Adoption, Women 15–44 Years of Age, by Race

Predictor	Nonblack beta	Nonblack odds	Black beta	Black odds
Intercept	−8.82***	0.00	−6.96***	0.00
Desired number of children	−0.06	0.94	−0.14	0.87
Fecundity status				
Contraceptively sterile	0.62**	1.86	0.03	1.03
Noncontraceptively sterile	0.98**	2.66	−0.11	0.90
Nonsurgically sterile	1.31***	3.71	−1.34	0.26
Subfecund	0.91***	2.48	−0.07	0.93
Long interval	1.24**	3.46	−0.44	0.64
One or more child deaths	1.03**	2.80	1.20**	3.32
One pregnancy loss	0.31	1.36	0.20	1.22
Two or more pregnancy losses	0.76**	2.14	0.27	1.31
Childless at interview	0.72**	2.05	0.17	1.19
Ever sought infertility services?	1.55***	4.71	1.56***	4.76
Does woman desire more children than she expects to have?				
No, desires and expects same	0.29	1.34	−0.29	0.75
Yes, 1 more desired	1.23***	3.42	0.22	1.25
Yes, 2 more desired	1.56***	4.76	1.11	3.03
Yes, 3 + more desired	2.13***	8.41	1.19	3.29
Educational attainment				
High school graduate	0.20	1.22	0.57	1.77
Some college	0.19	1.21	0.98**	2.66
College graduate	0.19	1.21	0.83	2.29
Religious participation at age 14				
weekly or more frequently	0.06	1.06	0.27	1.31
Age at interview	0.06**	1.06	0.07***	1.07
Currently married	1.46***	4.31	0.29	1.34
Previously married	1.21**	3.35	0.46	1.58
Hispanic origin	0.24	1.27	n/a	n/a
Modern *chi-square*	476.10***		149.23***	
n	5,565		2,736	

NOTE: "Odds" refers to the predicted change in the odds of ever having sought to adopt associated with a unit change in the predictor variable. Calculated by raising *e* to the (beta) power.

**$p<.01$. ***$p<.001$.

reasons is counterintuitive: the coefficient for this category suggests that the odds of having sought adoption are nearly twice as high for these women compared to fecund women, despite their having elected to terminate childbearing at some earlier point. This is an important finding, because it is a large group, comprising nearly one quarter of nonblack women of childbearing age. Adoption seeking in this group may reflect a variety of circumstances, including (1) contraceptive operations that were undertaken because pregnancy would endanger the woman's health and not because of a desire to avoid parenthood; (2) regret about the decision to terminate childbearing, perhaps in response to changes in life circumstances (such as remarriage); or (3) adoption motivated by factors other than the desire to have children.

Although the desired number of children is not significantly related to having sought adoption, women who desire more children than they expect to have are substantially more likely to have sought than women who desire fewer children. Furthermore, the odds of having sought adoption increase as the discrepancy between desired and expected numbers of children widens, to the extent that women who desire three or more children more than they expect to have are over eight times more likely to have sought adoption than women who desire fewer children than they expect to bear. The odds of having sought adoption are nearly five times higher for women who have sought treatment for infertility than for those who have not, indicating again that fecundity impairments coupled with the desire to overcome such barriers are associated with adoption seeking.

Variables measuring the resources available for adoption seeking are less consistently related to the odds of having sought to adopt. Age has a strong positive effect on the odds of having sought adoption, not surprisingly, and being currently or having previously been married is also associated positively with having sought to adopt. Educational attainment, Hispanic origin, and religious participation at age fourteen, however, have no significant effects on the odds of having sought to adopt.

Although the odds of having sought to adopt are similar among black and nonblack women, the correlates of adoption seeking appear to differ. Our model does relatively poorly in predicting the odds of having sought to adopt among black women. The model *chi-square* is lower, and the estimated coefficients are generally smaller and less often significant. Only four variables evidenced a significant association: (1) having experienced one or more child deaths, (2) having ever been treated for infertility, (3) having attended college, and (4) age. These four variables span the factors hypothesized as affecting adoption seeking (desire for children, inability to have them, and resources), suggesting that these factors are important in predicting adoption seeking among black as well as nonblack women. However, the absence of significant effects for fecundity impairments, pregnancy losses, childlessness, and desired versus expected fertility bespeaks a looser connection between fertility desires and capabilities and adop-

TABLE 11.4

Percentage (Standard Error) Who Ever Sought to Adopt, among Ever-married Women Aged 30–44 Years with No Living Children and Impaired Fecundity

Characteristic	Number of women, in thousands	percentage (se) who ever sought to adopt
Total	1,274[1]	32.0 (4.2)
Ever sought infertility services		
Ever	749	46.9 (6.0)
Never	525	10.6 (4.4)
Number of children desired		
None	139	3.9 (5.4)
One	184	26.1 (10.6)
Two	676	32.7 (5.9)
Three or more	248	49.8 (10.4)

NOTE: Women sterile for contraceptive reasons are excluded.

[1] These 1,274,000 women represent about 2% of all women between fifteen and forty-four years of age; of this group, those who have ever sought to adopt represent 20% of all women who have ever sought to adopt.

tion. Conversely the presence of an effect for educational attainment suggests that among black women, high socioeconomic status may play a greater role in permitting or even encouraging adoption than among white women.

The Role of Fecundity Impairments and Unmet Desire for Children

Results of the foregoing analyses indicate that, particularly among nonblack women, adoption seeking is primarily a function of the desire for children coupled with an inability to meet childbearing goals. We next pose the question whether these conditions are necessary and/or sufficient to initiate adoption seeking. To assess the sufficiency of these characteristics, we examine the proportion who have sought adoption within a population expected to have a high demand for adoption on the basis of these characteristics.

In table 11.4, we narrow our focus to women who have a fecundity impairment (other than a contraceptive sterilization operation) and who have no living children. We further eliminate women who are less than thirty years of age or never married, since such women may not have had the opportunity to learn of a fecundity impairment or to seek adoption. The resulting population consists of approximately

1.3 million women, or 2.2% of all women of childbearing age. Among these women, we expect that those who evidence high motivation for children should have the highest levels of adoption seeking. The absolute level of these estimates should be interpreted cautiously, for the standard errors are large. However, the results suggest that even among childless nonfecund women who evidence high motivation only about one half had taken any step toward adoption: 47% among the 749,000 who had ever been treated for infertility and 50% among the 248,000 who desired three or more children. For the other half, then, the desire for children and the inability to have them had not been sufficient conditions for adoption seeking.

The data in table 11.5 address the question of whether the desire for children and the inability to meet childbearing goals are necessary for adoption seeking. A large majority (87%) of the women who reported that they had ever sought to adopt reported a current fecundity impairment, current infertility (twelve months or longer of exposure to the risk of conception without conceiving[5]), or past infertility problems for which treatment was sought. About 66% of the women who had ever sought to adopt desired a larger number of children than they expected to give birth to themselves. All but 6% of the women who had ever sought to adopt had one of these two character-

TABLE 11.5

Women 15–44 Years of Age Who Ever Sought to Adopt, According to Fecundity (broadly defined) and Desire for Children, by Race

Characteristic	All who ever sought	Nonblack	Black
Number of women, in thousands	2,031	1,765	264
Total	100.0	100.0	100.0
Fecudity			
Evidence of past or present impairment [1]	87.1 (2.4)	89.6 (2.4)	70.5 (6.4)
All others	12.9 (2.4)	10.4 (2.4)	29.5 (6.4)
Desired number of children compared to number expected			
Desired greater	65.8 (3.4)	67.8 (3.6)	52.9 (7.0)
Desired same	25.9 (3.2)	25.8 (3.4)	26.8 (6.2)
Desired smaller	7.8 (1.9)	5.9 (1.8)	20.3 (5.6)
Past or present impairment or desired more children than expected	94.1 (1.7)	96.2 (1.5)	80.4 (5.6)

NOTE: Standard errors of percentages are shown in parentheses.

[1] Includes women who report a fecundity impairment, who are infertile (married women exposed to risk for twelve months or longer with no conception), or who have ever made a visit for infertility services.

istics. The impression that these characteristics are implicated in the vast majority of adoption seeking (and therefore may be "necessary" for adoption seeking to occur) is further reinforced by the fact that measures of past fecundity impairments and past attitudes toward children are not adequately captured by the NSFG. Some of those women in whom adoption seeking is not accounted for by fecundity impairments or an unmet desire for children may in fact have experienced these conditions in the past. Nevertheless, the presence of a small group of adoption seekers for whom these conditions do not appear to exist also suggests that while impairments and desire for children play important roles in driving the demand for children for adoption, these characteristics are not strictly necessary to bring about adoption seeking.

This conclusion gains further support when these results are examined by race. While the pattern for nonblack women is similar to that for all women, the results for black women indicate a substantial minority—nearly one-fifth—of women who ever sought adoption and for whom fecundity impairments and unmet fertility desires do not appear to have played a role. Thus, among black women these conditions appear important but by no means necessary for adoption seeking to occur.

The data presented in this paper are, to our knowledge, the first national estimates of the population seeking to adopt a child based on direct measures of this behavior. The estimates we have presented are substantially lower than previous estimates, which by necessity were based on assumptions regarding the relationship between fecundity impairments and adoption seeking. Our analysis of the determinants of adoption seeking underscores the importance of the inability to have children in motivating adoption seeking but clearly demonstrates the danger in assuming a one-to-one relationship between the two phenomena.

Although our estimate of the population seeking to adopt is low compared to previous estimates, it is nevertheless substantially higher than the estimated number of annual adoptions. The National Committee for Adoption (1989) estimated that 104,000 children were adopted in 1986, and 53,000 of these were adopted by relatives. In addition, approximately ten thousand children were adopted from abroad, bringing the total number of adoptions by nonrelatives to about 61,000. Because the majority of adoptions involving women are adoptions of nonrelatives, it is most appropriate to compare the 204,000 women currently seeking adoption at the time of the NSFG interview to the 61,000 adoptions by nonrelatives: a ratio of 3.3 seeking women for every annual adoption.

This ratio, which juxtaposes the number of women seeking adoption at a given point in time to the number of adoptions that occur over the course of a year, provides little information on such questions as average waiting times for adoption, because information on movement in and out of the population of adoption seekers is missing. Nevertheless, the ratio is roughly compatible with waiting periods of "at least two years" (NCFR 1984) for healthy white infants, given that not all seeking couples are successful or persist in the search and that not all adoptees who are nonrelatives are also healthy white infants. Our results confirm, therefore, the widely perceived shortage of babies free for adoption compared to the demand but suggest a much smaller imbalance than previous estimates have implied.

Our analyses indicate the central importance of the desire for children coupled with the inability or difficulty in having them as predictors of having sought to adopt a child. Measures of impaired fecundity, pregnancy loss, child deaths, and current childlessness are all strongly associated with adoption seeking among nonblack women, as is the desire for a larger number of children than the woman expects to give birth to herself. The importance of motivation to overcome barriers to childbearing is further indicated by the strong positive effects of having sought treatment for infertility as predictor for adoption seeking among women of all races.

The variables we have loosely termed resources are less consistently related to adoption seeking. Significant effects are found for age, which reflects the cumulative opportunity for adoption seeking to occur, and, among nonblack women, for marital status, which is closely linked to family formation and is also a common criterion for eligibility to adopt. Educational attainment was found to have no net effect on adoption seeking among nonblacks despite associations observed elsewhere between this variable and actual adoption (Bachrach et al. 1990). We considered the hypothesis that lacking the resources associated with high education may not deter nonblack women from seeking adoption, but it lowers the chances that they will be successful in adopting. However, adoption seeking is related positively to educational attainment before adjusting for other factors, and, in analyses not shown, we find that actual adoption is not related to educational attainment after adjustment for other variables. It appears more likely that the effect of education is confounded with and may operate indirectly through other variables included in our model.

The importance of fertility motivation coupled with an inability to achieve fertility desires in driving adoption seeking behavior is underscored by the finding that nearly all nonblack women who had ever adopted evidenced either some history of fecundity problems or expected to have fewer children than they desired. Thus, at least in this group, these factors appear to be necessary, or nearly so, for adoption seeking to occur. However, our results clearly demonstrate that these factors are not sufficient for adoption seeking to occur. Even of the women for whom these conditions seem to hold most strongly (and who have ever been married and are old enough to have begun the adoption search), only about half have ever sought to adopt.

Explaining this "failure" to seek adoption is beyond the scope of the NSFG data, but existing qualitative research on infertile couples suggests some likely answers. Adoption provides an alternative to biological parenthood but, as noted above, differs from it in various ways. These differences between biological and adoptive parenthood give shape to norms and attitudes about adoption, influence costs and benefits of adoption as perceived by prospective parents, and thereby affect adoption-seeking behavior. One recurrent theme in the existing literature on adoption is that adoption is viewed as second best to biological parenthood, and, in some cases, as a last resort (Kirk 1959; Daly 1988; Brodzinsky & Huffman 1988). The issues underlying these attitudes are varied and include loss of the pregnancy and childbirth experience, loss of the opportunity to continue one's own family line, fears about the unknown genetic endowment of the child and the child's prenatal development and care, fears about getting a child who was "damaged," and fears about how a child would cope with being adopted (Daly 1988; Miller 1981; Lasker & Borg 1987). Thus, adoption is viewed as risky compared to biological childbearing and as entailing the loss of certain valued experiences available only through biological childbearing.

Other factors that may deter prospective adoptive parents involve the process of adoption. Daly (1988) describes the uneven, "bumbling" process by which husband and wife may come to the decision to adopt and the delays in the transition to adoptive parenthood occasioned by the fact that both spouses may not relinquish the desire for biological parenthood and take on the identity of adoptive parent at the same pace. The availability of new technology for treating infertility may delay adoption seeking by extending the period over which infertility treatment is attempted (Lasker & Borg 1987). Like treatment for infertility, the adoption process is viewed by many infertile couples as time-consuming, intrusive, and beyond the control of the couple (Daly 1988). These psychic costs are of course accompanied by financial costs as well: the average agency adoption costs somewhat over $5,000 (NCFA 1989) although costs may vary widely depending on the type and circumstances of the adoption.

Another factor that may have an important deterrent effect on adoption seeking is the limited availability of healthy white infants that are freed for adoption. Given that most seeking couples want infants such as these (Kossoudji 1989; Westat 1986), the restricted supply acts to increase the costs of adoption. It does so in various ways: by lengthening the waiting period, by requiring a more intensive search to find a child, by increasing the rigor of agency screening practices, or by forcing the acceptance of a child with less desirable characteristics. Even couples who have not made an adoption-seeking contact are likely to be aware of such increased costs, either by word of mouth or through media reports, and may well be deterred by them.

Although it would be of great interest and of considerable importance for policy to know the relative importance of these factors in deterring couples from seeking adoption, existing research does not provide a guide. It seems likely that the demand is limited by both factors inherent in adoption—the differences between biological and adoptive parenthood and the procedural aspects of adopting—and factors resulting from a possibly temporary shortage of healthy white infants free for adoption. More nonfecund couples who desire children might seek adoption in response to a greater supply of children, but not all of them are likely to do so.

A final theme that has recurred throughout our analyses is the differences in the determinants of adoption seeking among black and nonblack women. Our models perform relatively poorly in predicting adoption seeking among black women, and although factors such as child death and infertility treatment have significant effects, the inability to have as many children as desired seems less closely linked to adoption seeking in this population. These results suggest, then, that the function of adoption among black women only partially overlaps the one it has among nonblack women. These differences may have their roots in the distinct family patterns of black women, in which childbearing is less closely associated with marriage, and child rearing is shared more widely among relatives and family friends. The role played by extended family members and friends in providing care for black children through informal adoption has been documented elsewhere (Hill 1977). This practice, which probably underlies the higher level of adoption of relatives among black than among nonblack women, is likely to be motivated by the need to provide for a known child as well as by circumstances of the adopting parent's life. Formal adoption, too, may occur in response to a greater level of need, not on the part of couples for children, but on the part of children for parents.

These suggestions are necessarily speculative, for the available data do not measure motivations for adoption nor even the type of child sought. Our analyses are constrained by these limitations and by the inability to relate adoption seeking to characteristics known to exist at the time adoption was sought as well as to characteristics of the adoptive father. We are unable to trace the seeking process over time, to assess how changes in life circumstances and delays in obtaining a child affect the decision to adopt and the type of child a couple is willing to accept. These limitations should be addressed by future research in order to move toward a more complete understanding of the adoption-seeking process.

NOTES

1. Support for collecting information on women seeking to adopt was provided by the Administration on Children, Youth, and Families, HDS through an interagency agreement with the National Center for Health Statistics (NCHS). General support for the NSFG is provided by NCHS, the National Institute of Child Health and Human Development, and the Office of Population Affairs.

2. The term "impaired fecundity" is used to describe conditions under which a woman or couple is either unable to bear a child or has some difficulty doing so. In the research reported here, fecundity impairments include sterilizing operations performed for contraceptive reasons (contracep-

tively sterile), sterilizing operations performed for other reasons (noncontraceptively sterile), other reported conditions that make it impossible to bear children (nonsurgically sterile), conditions that make it difficult but not impossible to bear children (subfecund), and difficulty evidenced by exposure to the risk of childbearing with no conception for at least three years (long interval). These women are collectively referred to as nonfecund in this paper. All other women are classified as fecund. The term *nonfecund* is used in preference to *infertile* because the latter term technically refers to women who have been exposed for twelve months with no conception (Mosher & Pratt 1990).

3. Because the NSFG is limited to women, our estimates of the population seeking to adopt will underestimate the true number to the extent that men seek adoption by themselves or in partnership with other men. Although this is known to occur, we believe it to be rare. Previous analyses show that 99% of all adopting women are currently married at the time of the adoption (Bachrach 1986). Our estimates will also exclude adoption seeking involving women (and men) over the age of forty-four. However, NSFG data (not presented here) indicate a sharp drop in current adoption seeking between the late thirties and early forties, again suggesting that few women may continue seeking beyond the age of forty-four.

4. Bivariate and multivariate analyses of current adoption seeking were conducted and results may be obtained from the authors. Results are generally consistent with those relating to ever seeking adoption, but the observed relationships are weaker and less often statistically significant.

5. Infertility is assessed for married women only.

REFERENCES

Bachrach, C. A. (1983). Adoption as a means of family formation: Data from the National Survey of Family Growth. *Journal of Marriage and the Family, 45,* 859–65.

Bachrach, C. A. (1986). Adoption plans, adopted children, and adoptive mothers. *Journal of Marriage and the Family, 48,* 243–53.

Bachrach, C. A., Adams, P. F., Sambrano, S., & London, K. A. (1990). Adoption in the 1980s. *Advance Data from Vital and Health Statistics, 181,* 1–7.

Bonham, G. S. (1977). Who adopts: The relationship of adoption and social-demographic characteristics of women. *Journal of Marriage and the Family, 39,* 295–306.

Brodzinsky, D. M. & Huffman, L. (1988). Transition to adoptive parenthood. *Marriage and Family Review, 3*(4), 267–86.

Daly, K. (1988). Reshaped parenthood identity: The transition to adoptive parenthood. *Journal of Contemporary Ethnography, 17*(1), 40–66.

Feigelman, W. & Silverman, A. R. (1979). Preferential adoption: A new mode of family formation. *Social Casework: The Journal of Contemporary Social Work, 60,* 296–305.

Freedman, B., Taylor, P. J., Wonnacott, T., & Brown, S. (1987). Nonmedical selection criteria for artificial insemination and adoption. *Clinical Reproduction and Fertility, 5,* 55–66.

Harbison, S. F. (1983). Defining and measuring the supply of children: Some anthropological considerations. *Social Biology, 30*(1), 32–40.

Hill, R. B. (1977). *Informal adoption among black families.* Washington, D.C.: National Urban League Research Department.

Judkins, D. R., Mosher, W. D., & Botman, S. (Forthcoming). National survey of family growth, cycle IV: Sample design, weighting, imputation, and variance estimation. *Vital and Health Statistics, 2.*

Kirk, H. D. (1959). A dilemma of adoptive parenthood: Incongruous role expectations. *Marriage and Family Living, 21*(4), 316–26.

Kossoudji, S. (1989). Pride and prejudice: Culture's role in markets. In S. Shulman & W. Darity (Eds.), *The question of discrimination: Racial inequality in the U.S. labor market* (pp. 293–314). Middletown, CT: Wesleyan University Press.

Lasker, J. N. & Borg, S. (1987). *In search of parenthood.* Boston, MA: Beacon Press.

Leahy, A. M. (1933). Some characteristics of adoptive parents. *American Journal of Sociology, 38,* 548–63.

Miller, W. B. (1981). *The personal meanings of voluntary and involuntary childlessness* (Final Report for Contract No. N01-HD-82853). Bethesda, MD: National Institute of Child Health and Human Development.

Mosher, W. D. & Pratt, W. F. (1990). Fecundity and infertility in the United States, 1965–88. *Advance Data from Vital and Health Statistics, 192,* 1–8.

National Committee for Adoption. (1984). *Adoption facts summary, 1984.* Washington, D.C.: Author.

National Committee for Adoption. (1989). *Adoption factbook.* Washington, D.C.: Author.

Poston, D. L., Jr. & Cullen, R. M. (1986). Log-linear analyses of patterns of adoption behavior: U.S. white women, 1982, 1976, and 1973. *Social Biology, 33,* 241–48.

Poston, D. L., Jr. & Cullen, R. M. (1989). Propensity of white women in the United States to adopt children. *Social Biology, 36,* 167–85.

Westat, Inc. (1986). *The study of adoption exchanges.* (Final Report for Contract No. 105-84-1804), Washington D.C.: DHHS, Office of Human Development Services, ACYF.

TWELVE

Adoption of Drug-exposed Children

Richard P. Barth

Substance abuse has been a primary reason for involvement in child welfare services for more than a hundred years (Gordon 1988), and drug use has been a key issue for at least a quarter of a century (Fanshel 1976). Sharp and recent increases in the number of children exposed to drugs before birth and in need of homes have been largely held responsible for the recent growth (after nearly a decade of decline) in the number of children in foster care in the U.S. (Feig 1990). Whereas family preservation is still the goal for families affected by drugs—as with other families—the capacity to prevent placement and to reunify children who have been exposed to drugs before birth with their parents is certainly compromised (Barth 1991; Berry in press). Relatives and strangers are increasingly becoming foster parents and adoptive parents of prenatally drug-exposed children. This study is the first to consider the adoption of drug-exposed children.

Because this study of adoptions of drug-affected children is set in California, data on the experience of child welfare services with drug-affected children are most relevant. California's experience closely mirrors national numbers (Feig 1990). California counties showed a combined 167% increase in referrals of drug-exposed babies to child welfare services between 1986 and 1989 (Senate Office on Research 1990). Of every one hundred drug-exposed infants referred to CPS, approximately twenty-seven are directly placed in family foster care, in relatives' homes, or in another out-of-home placement (others may require such placements in time). Among all drug-exposed children declared court-dependent in California in 1989, the rate of out-of-home placements is 60% (Senate Office on Research 1990); nationally, it was close to 80% in 1989 (Feig 1990). Whereas no clear estimates concerning reunification rates are available, it is safe to say that many of these children entering foster care will be candidates for adoption. Drug involvement is a poor predictor of reunification: "after birth of a drug-involved infant, most counties are finding that if the baby is not placed back with the mother almost immediately, the likelihood of that child ever being returned to that parent is quite low" (California Senate Office of Research 1990:5).

In California the number of children up to the age of three in long-term foster care without an adoption goal increased between 1987 and 1990 from 1,860 to 4,889 (Barth, Courtney, Berrick, & Albert in press). Between 1985 and 1990, the number of infants (i.e., children up to the age of age one) in group home care more than tripled, from 73 to 263. Young and drug-involved children seem to be excepted from permanency planning's goal of a permanent home for every child.

Whereas these astounding increases in long-term foster and group home care are likely to have arisen from the spread of debilitating drug use to women, they are compounded by considerable uncertainty about the appropriateness of adoption for these children. Concerns about the adoption of drug-affected babies are surfacing across the nation. The worries are for the children and for their adoptive parents. Concerns about the parents include the fear that they will not be able to manage the care of drug-exposed babies. California county administrators express the following concerns about the availability and ability of parents of perinatally drug-exposed children: "(their) parents need special training; they need respite; they have trouble dealing with medical professionals who themselves do not understand the needs/problems of drug-exposed infants" and "homes are difficult to secure for these infants . . . they are often difficult to comfort, cry excessively or have medical problems which require monitoring and frequent doctor or hospital visits" (California Senate Office on Research 1990).

All in all, there is considerable pessimism about the adoption of drug-exposed children. Charlotte McCullough (1991) of the Child Welfare League of America writes that adoption is rarely the option chosen for drug-exposed infants or for young children of drug-dependent parents. There are many barriers to adoption. Termination of parental rights is usually contested, and although the process can theoretically take place in eighteen months, in reality it usually takes three years. The infants become toddlers or older and the prospective parents become frustrated with the prolonged process. In addition, potential adoptive parents are fearful of the long-term effects of drug exposure and the possible need for expensive medical, educational, and psychological care. (p. 69)

Sandra Blakeslee's (1990) front page story in the *New York Times* is one of the few published discussions of prenatal drug exposure and adoption. She concludes that parents who adopt drug-exposed babies often find that rearing them is vastly more difficult than experts had predicted. Parents interviewed in her snowball sample, conclude that the children are often hyperactive, have difficulty getting along with peers, and have explosive tendencies. She reports that half of the members of a southern California support group for adoptive parents of drug-exposed children are planning to return custody of their children to the child welfare agency. Yet she does report on at least one child who, as one parent put it, "should have been one of the worst. She is one of the best" (p. 8). Another journalistic account describes the death by battering of a drug-exposed infant when the woman who was her foster mother and had planned to adopt her became exhausted and enraged (McFadden 1990).

Differing levels of pessimism about the future of drug-exposed children in general can be identified in the research of the nation's most eminent researchers. Judy Howard presented her findings to the Third Annual National Invitation Conference on Special Needs Children in late 1989 and indicated that the more data she gathers the more deviance she sees (keynote speech summarized in *Adoptalk*, Winter 1990). She predicted that these children are apt to wear out caregivers quickly both physically and emotionally. She indicated a possible need for orphanages as an alternative for drug-using parents who decide to take their child home to care for him or her. She did indicate, however, that results based on sound data on children exposed to drugs before birth are a decade away.

Barry Zuckerman (1991), on the other hand, emphasizes that "the mere presence, or even the degree, of a biologic insult are poor predictors of developmental outcome. Rather, children's development can best be understood by the dynamic interplay between the environment and the child, so that the child is shaped by the environment and the environment is actively modified by the child" (p. 34). He indicates that outcomes for the children in the first two years of life range from rare significant developmental problems to subtle behavioral or learning problems to normal development. Further, he clarifies how little we know about the relative impact of the caretaker's dysfunction and prenatal drug-exposure on the child's later functioning.

These concerns are leading some to believe that without drastic alternatives like orphanages children exposed to drugs before birth will experience the dual hardships of the physical effects of drug exposure and the transience and vulnerability of living in a family dominated by drugs. Yet orphanages are unacceptable on developmental and cost grounds (Ford & Kroll 1990). If feasible, adoption represents a more humane, less costly lifetime investment in these vulnerable children. There have been a few calls for a more affirmative adoption response. Kroll (1990) suggests that drug-exposed infants are "similar to other groups of disabled children—children who are successfully adopted as long as appropriate family preparation and follow-up support are in place" (p. 4). Yet even this assessment assumes that this is a "new disability," but the data upon which these hopeful comments stand are no stronger than those of their pessimistic counterparts.

The evidence certainly clearly indicates that, in general, handicapped children are not especially difficult children to adopt for families who are prepared for such an adoption. Recent evidence from a series of investigations into the adoption of handicapped children indicates that families that are properly prepared for and informed about their child's handicaps have excellent adjustment to the adoptions (Barth & Berry 1988; Nelson 1987; Glidden 1990). Indeed, a recent five-year follow-up study (Glidden 1991) indicates that the adoptive parents' satisfaction with parenting of handicapped children is very high and is more similar to the adjustment of birth parents with nonhandicapped children than it is to the adjustment of birth parents with handicapped children (which is the lowest of all). Perhaps drug-exposed children are categorically different from other children who have been adopted before them. Many are neither clearly handicapped nor normal. Blakeslee (1990) quotes a parent, "I don't know what to expect in the future. She may be a walking time bomb" (p. 8). Knowing that a child has Down Syndrome or spina bifida is accompanied by a far clearer view of the child's life course than is knowledge that a child has been exposed to drugs before birth.

Method

Sample

This paper reports on a cohort of drug-exposed children adopted in 1988–1989 and describes the first year to two years of the experience of their adoptive parents. The adoptive parents of 2,589 adoptive placements made in California from mid-1988 through mid-1989 were asked by their social workers about their interest in participating in a longitudinal study of adoptions. A total of 2,238 families (86%) agreed to participate. Questionnaires were mailed to all families ($n = 2,058$) with usable addresses and 1,268 families (62%) returned the completed questionnaires. Many of these families had adopted more than one child during the time frame of the study; the questionnaires described a total of 1,396 children. Respondents had adopted independently (that is, without the initiation but with the final approval of an agency) ($n = 563$), through a public agency ($n = 514$), a private agency ($n = 95$), or an intercountry agency placement ($n = 87$). Some 10% ($n = 135$) could not be classified because of missing or inconsistent data.

Overall, this study is the first prospective adoption study that can estimate the differences between the study sample and the sampling frame. Compared to all the adoptions in the state in the same year, our sample underrepresents relatives (10% in our sample and 21% in the overall sample) and underrepresents African-American children (13% versus 21%) in the general adoption population in California.

Measures

Case identification numbers were matched with state data files to provide background and demographic information on each of the adoptive families, including those families who did not wish to answer the questionnaire. This information covered the characteristics of the adopted child(ren), the birth parents, and the adoptive parents, with some extra information about the adoption, such as the type of adoption, whether a subsidy was provided, if the adoptive parents were also the foster parents, and if the child(ren) had any special problems.

In a mailed questionnaire, parents were asked a multitude of questions about the child and the adoptive family. The instrument tapped child and parent information (health, problems, demographics), family constellation and support, the decision to adopt, knowledge of the child's background, knowledge of the birth family, the adoption process, the child's placement (including services and preparation), the child's school performance (if of school age), the child's Problem Behavior Inventory (described below), foster parent adoptions, post-placement services, and satisfaction with the adoption.

Prenatal drug exposure. Several items asked parents for an indication of whether their child had been exposed to drugs before birth. These included: Before you agreed to the placement, were you aware that the child had been exposed to drugs before birth (yes, no, did not know but found out later, still unknown); before the placement were you aware that the birth parents had been using drugs at the time of the child's birth and before you agreed to the placement; what do you know of the birth mother's drug use during pregnancy (circle all that apply: don't know, mother smoked, mother drank alcohol, mother took drugs). Table 12.1 depicts the frequencies for these items.

Children were classified as drug-exposed if parental responses to all three of the questions resulted in an indication of known prenatal drug exposure (indications of prenatal smoking and alcohol use were not used). A total of 320 (24.7%) of the respondents were selected by this method. Another 456 (35.2%) of the children were classified as not exposed to drugs because their parents identified no such indicators. As a result of the stringent scoring of drug exposure, many children with one or more (but not as many as three) indicators of drug exposure were screened out of the category of those exposed to drugs. Children whose parents indicated at least once that they had been exposed to drugs or for whom parents indicated "still unknown" regarding their drug exposure were classified as "unknown." This group ($n = 620$) was larger (47.8%) than the other two groups. Differences between the adoption agency auspices were highly significant ($p < .001$), with the public agencies making the highest percentage of placements of drug-exposed children (37%) and having the lowest proportion of children in the unknown group (27%) (see table 12.2).

We also have data from the social worker's completion of an item for all agency adoptions that asked whether the child was "born

TABLE 12.1
Extent of Perinatal Drug Exposure by Adoption Type (in Percent)

	TOTAL (n = 1172)	Indep. (n = 563)	Public (n = 514)	Private (n = 95)
A. Before the placement, were you aware that the parent's condition involved drug-exposed at birth or prenatally (parent report)				
Yes	39%	34%	50%	25%
No, found out yes later	18	13	16	9
No	43	53	34	76
B. What do you know of the birth mother's drug use during pregnancy (parent report)				
Don't know (316A)	21	12	23	9
Mother smoked cigarettes (316B)	29	32	32	17
Mother drank alcohol (316C)	22	19	28	13
Mother used drugs (316d)	28	19	42	13
No apparent drug use (316e)	36	50	24	63
C. Before you agreed to the placement, were you aware that the child was exposed to drugs before birth (5–9A) (parent report)				
Not exposed	50	65	35	74
Was exposed	30	22	45	14
Still unknown	20	13	20	12
D. Born addicted to drugs (social worker report)				
Present	N/A*	N/A	6	0
Severe	N/A	N/A	1	0

NOTE: Agency auspices are unknown for 9.6% of all cases and 6.1% of all adoptions are intercountry; these are excluded from the table.

* Not available, because this data is not available for independent adoptions.

addicted to drugs" and allowed the social worker to indicate whether this condition was present or whether it was severe. The definition in the instructions to the social workers reads " 'born addicted to drugs' means that at or soon after birth, the child had symptoms which were caused by maternal use of controlled substances except when those controlled substances are used as part of a medically prescribed plan" (SDSS 1987). This item was completed only for agency adoptions. For informational purposes, we have included the frequencies on this item in table 12.1. A relatively small percentage of children were described as having been addicted at birth (7.3%). This compares to 13.8% in the sampling frame. The criteria of birth symptoms was considered too narrow and the coding on the category by social

TABLE 12.2
Adoption Type by Drug Exposure Classification*

	Not drug exposed		Drug unknown		Exposed	
	n	%	*n*	%	*n*	%
Independent	154	27	476	4	333	59
Public agency	159	31	189	37	168	27
Private agency	22	23	11	12	62	65
Intercountry	71	82	3	3	13	16
Unknown agency	50	37	41	30	44	33
Total	456	36	320	25	620	48

NOTE: Row percentages may not total to 100% due to rounding errors.
  ** p < .001$ for overall X^2

workers was considered too unreliable for our analysis. (All of these children are included in our subsample of drug-exposed children).

Problem Behavior Index (PBI). The PBI includes many items from the Achenbach Child Behavior Checklist (Achenbach & Edelbrock 1981) and additional items from other child behavior scales (Graham & Rutter 1968; Rutter, Tizard, & Whitmore 1970; Peterson & Zill 1986). The rating scale was developed for use in the National Longitudinal Survey of Youth (NLSY) and has been standardized on a random sample of more than six thousand children. The PBI is completed by the child's parent concerning six areas of problem behavior. The PBI was used for children ages two and older and the choice of the three items (none, somewhat, a lot) rates the child's antisocial, anxious/depressed, hyperactive, headstrong, immature/dependent, and social withdrawal/peer conflict behavior. Higher scores indicate more problems; older children generally have more problems (Center for Human Resources Research 1991). Cronbach's *alpha* on the total score is .89. *Alphas* on subscales range from .60 to .76. The PBI score is significantly correlated with the PIAT reading score.

Results

Family Characteristics

The educational and occupational characteristics of families adopting drug-exposed children are described and compared with those of families adopting children thought not to have been exposed to drugs.

Comparisons are made first regarding the family's preparation for adoption (see table 12.3).

Single-parent adoption. Single parent adoptions account for 11% of agency adoptions. Overall, single parents were less (p < .01) likely to adopt drug-exposed children. Single parents adopted 6.2% of all children. They adopted 9% of the children not exposed to drugs, 6.9% of the drug-exposed children, and only 3.7% of the children whose drug exposure was unknown.

Adoptions by relatives. Overall, adoptions by relatives amounted to about 10% of all adoptions and relatives were more likely (*p* < .05) to adopt drug-exposed children. In independent adoptions, more drug-exposed children were related to their adoptive mothers than were children not exposed to drugs (13% versus 6%, *p* < .03). Of the children not exposed to drugs, 3% were adopted by a grandmother and 3% by an aunt. Of the drug-exposed children, 7% were adopted by a grandmother, 4% by an aunt, and 2% by a cousin. In public agency adoptions, drug-exposed children were more likely to be adopted by relatives than were children not exposed to drugs (13% versus 7%, *p* < .05). There was a low rate of placements with relatives and no differences between groups for adoptions mediated by private agencies.

Foster-parent adoptions. Respondents who had adopted through public agencies indicated whether they had planned to adopt the child when the child came to reside with them as a foster child. A majority (81%) of the children adopted through public agencies were first cared for by their adoptive parents as foster children. Roughly half of the foster parents who became adoptive parents intended to become adoptive parents when they became foster parents; this percentage was similar for foster parents who adopted drug-exposed children and for those who adopted other children. There were no overall differences in the fost-adopt status depending on the drug exposure status.

Adoptive mother's employment. In all, 38% of the adopting mothers were employed. Nearly half (47%) of the mothers who adopted drug-exposed children were not employed at all versus 39% of those who had adopted children not exposed to drugs. There is no significant difference between adoptive mothers who are employed full-time, part-time, or not employed at all in relation to adopting drug-exposed children versus children not exposed to drugs. In public agency adoptions, 44% of the mothers adopting drug-exposed children worked full-time as compared to 38% of those adopting children without drug exposure. In independent adoptions, 31% of the mothers who adopted drug-exposed children worked full-time versus 39% of those who adopted children without drug exposure ($p < .05$).

Adoptive mother's education. Overall, adoptive mothers are highly educated with 62% having some college education or higher. In private agency and independent adoptions, adoptive mothers of drug-exposed children had received less formal education than adoptive mothers of children not exposed to drugs. Educational levels of mothers in private agency ($p < .01$) and independent adoptions ($p < .01$)—but not in public agency adoptions—were significantly lower if their child had been exposed to drugs before birth.

Preplacement Experience

Parents detailed their preplacement experiences. These are described next.

Preparation. Parents generally felt well prepared for their child's placement, indicating an average response of 3.4 (*s.d.* = .79) on a scale from one (very unprepared) to four (very prepared). Significant differences in preparation were experienced by parents according to their child's drug exposure. Whereas 60% of all the parents felt very well prepared overall, only 54% of the parents who indicated that their child was not exposed to drugs indicated being very well prepared whereas the parents of drug-exposed children indicated being very well prepared in 65% of the cases ($p < .01$). Families who adopted children not exposed to drugs were considerably more likely to report being very unprepared or unprepared (13.8% versus 8.5%) than other families.

Similarities and differences. On the whole, adoptive parents of drug-exposed children were no different than those of children without drug exposure in terms of their reports of similarities between the child they originally had in mind and the child they adopted. Only

TABLE 12.3

Demographics (in Percent) by Adoption Type and Drug Exposure

	Public agency (n = 514)		Private agency (n = 95)		Independent (n = 563)	
	Not DrugX	DrugX	Not DrugX	DrugX	Not DrugX	DrugX
Single Parent Adoption						
Mother	19	7**	5	0*	17	20
Father	1	0	0	0	0	0
No	80	93	96	100	83	80
Transracial						
No	83	76	95	5	90	87
Yes	17	22	91	9	107	114
Relative Adoption						
No	93	87*	96	94	94	87*
Yes	7	13	4	6	6	13
Birth Mother Education						
8th and under	18	10**	0	10**	0	17**
Some HS	46	55	36	20	80	50
HS grad	21	27	23	40	7	33
Some college	12	7	36	30	13	0
College grad or more	2	1	5	0	0	0
Adoptive Mother's Education						
8th and under	1	1	4	0	9	0
Some HS	6	4	14	30	4	11
HS grad	20	23	36	40	30	44
Some college	40	40	23	10	26	44
College grad or more	34	33	23	20	30	0
Adoptive Father's Education						
8th and under	0	1	0	0**	1	0
Some HS	6	4	0	14	2	2
HS grad	25	15	42	43	10	15
Some college	29	32	50	29	27	19
College grad or more	39	49	8	14	59	60
Adoptive Mother's Employment						
Full-time	38	44	35	36	31*	39
Part-time <25	15	13	16	18	16	15
Full-time at home	3	.6	3	2	0	2
Part-time at home	9	4	10	6	7	5
Not employed	38	37	36	38	47	39

* $p < .05$
** $p < .01$

one in five parents (*n* = 290) indicated that they adopted the child
even though the child was different from the one they had originally
had in mind. They identified reasons why they proceeded with the
adoption. Parents of drug-exposed children most often (62%) indicated that they adopted the child because they had a strong attraction
or attachment to the child. Only 26% of the adoptive parents of
drug-exposed children indicated that the social worker supported
their ability to care for a drug-exposed child. This is a significantly
lower (*p* < .05) percentage than reported by parents who adopted
children not exposed to drugs (43%). About 13% of the parents who
adopted a drug-exposed child indicated that they thought the child
functioned at a higher level than he or she actually did. This is not
significantly different from the group having adopted other children.
About four out of ten adoptive parents indicated that they feared that
the "child would be in a poor situation if not placed with me." This
was relatively constant regardless of drug exposure. About 11% of
the parents who adopted a drug-exposed child indicated that they had
"limited options to adopt the kind of child I preferred." This was
quite similar to other parents. Also, overall, 11% of the adoptive
parents indicated that they agreed to adopt this child because they
"worried about getting another child for adoption." There were no
differences by drug-exposure. On the whole, there are few differences
between the groups in this regard.

Expectations about caring for the child. Parents were asked how easy
or difficult they had thought it would be to care for the child—choices
ranged from one (very difficult) to four (very easy). Overall and on
the average, the parents' expectations were that it would be moderately difficult (*M* = 3.2; *s.d.* = .76). There were significant differences (*p* < .05) in expectations between groups, with parents of
drug-exposed children expecting it to be very difficult or moderately
difficult in 26% of the cases whereas parents whose child was not
drug-exposed expected a very difficult time in 20% of the cases. On
the other end of the scale, 27% of the adoptive parents of drug-
exposed parents expected a very easy time whereas the adoptive
parents of children not exposed to drugs expected a very easy time in
36% of the cases.

Arrangements with the birth mother. In independent adoptions, birth
mothers had help choosing the adoptive parents more often when

their child had not been exposed to drugs than in cases of drug-exposed children (88% versus 74%, *p* <.01). That is, only 12% of these arrangements were made without the assistance of a mediator. In independent adoptions, the adoptive parents were more likely to pay the birth mother's expenses for a child not exposed to drugs than in cases of a drug-exposed child (74% versus 50%, *p* < .001). Birth mothers who have used drugs appear to get less support from adoptive families (they may receive more governmental support).

Parent Satisfaction

Adoptive parents were, on the whole, quite satisfied with their adoptions (see table 12.4). Because of the very different paths that families follow to adoption, significant differences in satisfaction were anticipated depending on the type of agency. This was true. Overall, private agency placements were the most satisfactory, and public agency placements the least, with independent placements falling in between (*p* < .01). After controlling for the type of placement, however, fifteen different tests of satisfaction with the adoption yielded no significant difference at the *p* < .05 level between parents who had adopted drug-exposed children and those who had adopted children not exposed to drugs. Among the parents having adopted drug-exposed children, 84% were very satisfied and 12% were satisfied; a proportion quite similar to that for couples. All single parents reported that they definitely would adopt the same child again, a rate slightly higher than that for couples (90%, *p* < .10).

Children's Characteristics

Gender. For the total sample, the number of male and female adopted children is almost equal, 657 males (50%) and 649 females (50%). There was no significant difference between the genders of drug-exposed children and those without drug exposure for either agency or independent adoptions. For independent adoptions, however, the gender ratio is slightly tilted toward females (drug-exposed: 42% male versus 58% female, not exposed to drugs: 49% male versus 51% female) but still not statistically significant at the level of *p* < 10. Females exposed to drugs before birth may be somewhat more adoptable than drug exposed males.

Age and time in the home. At the time of completing the questionnaire, children in the drug-exposed group were on the average 5.21

TABLE 12.4
*Parent Self-Reports of Satisfaction with Adoption by Type
and Drug Exposure*

	Independent		Public agency		Private agency	
	Not DrugX	DrugX	Not DrugX	DrugX	Not DrugX	DrugX
Overall Satisfaction						
Very dissatisfied	1%	5%	1%	2%	0%	0%
Some dissatisfied	3%	1%	5%	4%	0%	0%
Satisfied	7%	13%	22%	13%	0%	0%
Very satisfied	88%	80%	72%	81%	100%	100%
Vis á Vis Your Expectations						
Much worse	1%	4%	4%	2%	0%	0%
Worse	7%	9%	6%	11%	0%	0%
Expected	30%	36%	45%	38%	18%	9%
Better	23%	19%	19%	23%	27%	18%
Much better	40%	32%	26%	25%	55%	73%
Adopt again?						
Definitely not	1%	0%	2%	1%	0%	0%
Likely not	0%	1%	3%	2%	0%	0%
Likely would	3%	8%	11%	9%	0%	0%
Definitely would	96%	91%	85%	88%	100%	100%
End adoption						
No	93%	89%	84%	89%	100%	100%
Not seriously	5%	11%	11%	9%	0%	0%
Not to agency	1%	0%	0%	2%	0%	0%
Discussed with agency	1%	1%	1%	1%	0%	0%
Have ended	0%	0%	2%	0%	0%	0%
Effects on marriage						
Not married	5%	11%	17%	7%*	5%	0
Weakened	4%	3%	3%	4%	0%	0
No change	32%	38%	37%	40%	25%	50
Strengthened	59%	48%	43%	50%	70%	50

NOTE: All columns add up to 100% because of rounding errors.
* $p < .05$

years of age whereas the children not exposed to drugs were 4.85 years of age (n.s.). The children in the group whose drug exposure was not known were significantly younger—on the average, 3.29 years, $p < .001$. The groups were somewhat different ($p < .06$) in their length of time in the home at the time the parents completed the questionnaire, with the drug-exposed group in the homes 2.9 months and the group without drug exposure in the home 2.7 months.

Health problems. Over a third (39%) of the adoptive parents who participated in an agency adoption reported one or more health problems in their adopted child. Of the adoptions that reported health problems ($n = 540$), the drug-exposed children were significantly overrepresented in several categories as compared to the children not exposed to drugs. Of the children who were reported to have health problems, a medical condition was present in 18% of the drug-exposed children but in only 10% of the children without drug exposure ($p < .001$). According to social worker reports at the time of placement, drug-exposed children also experienced developmental delays somewhat more often than children without drug exposure (15% versus 10%, $p < .08$).

Problem Behavior Inventory. There were no significant differences between the groups in the Problem Behavior Inventory regardless of whether the subscales or the summary score were used (see table 12.5). Although each score was nominally higher for the drug-exposed sample than for the group without drug exposure, no single score nor the summary score approached statistical significance. The variances were nearly as high as the mean scores, indicating the possibility that the instrument was not well suited to assess the behavior of this relatively young sample. Cronbach's *alpha* ranged from .60 to .71 for individual subscales and was .90 for the summary score.

Temperament. A single item from the NLSY temperament scale was used. The item asked all parents who were caring for the child after

TABLE 12.5
Problem Behavior Inventory Scores by Drug Exposure

	Not DrugX (n = 307)		DrugX (n = 267)	
	M	SD	M	SD
Antisocial	.37	(.39)	.38	(.30)
Anxious/depressed	.36	(.31)	.37	(.29)
Stubborn/parent conflict (Head)	.56	(.32)	.59	(.33)
Hyperactive	.47	(.31)	.49	(.32)
Immature	.41	(.32)	.47	(.32)
Peer	.25	(.33)	.26	(.32)
SUMMARY	.41	(.29)	.45	(.24)

NOTE: No *t*-tests or X^2 were significant at $p < .05$

birth whether the child: (1) almost never cried, (2) cried less than average, (3) cried about average, (4) cried more than average, or (5) almost always cried. The mean score was 2.3 (*s.d.* = .91). There were no significant differences between the groups.

Education. Children in the study were generally preschool age, although one hundred children not exposed to drugs and sixty-four drug-exposed children were in first grade or higher. There was no significant difference in grade level, with approximately 50% in either first or second grade. Roughly 10% of each group were in "all special education classes," 4% were in "mostly special education classes," and 86% in "mostly regular education." There were also no differences in parent's reports of children's enjoyment of school, with 4% disliking school, 74% liking school, and 22% disliking and liking school in equal measure.

Cost

The average cost of the adoption to the families (this includes the adoption fee and adjunctive costs) was $3,722. This differed significantly depending on the type of placement, with the average for private placements running as high as $5,439 and for public agency adoptions amounting to $1,394. Among adoptive parents who had previously been foster parents, the average foster care rate was $396 per month. Among foster parents who adopted children, there was no significant difference between drug-exposed children and those not exposed to drugs in the likelihood of receiving a "difficulty of care" rate as foster parents (about 23%) or in the average rate. Yet adoptive parents of drug-exposed children were far more likely to receive adoption subsidies than were adoptive parents of children not exposed to drugs (52% versus 33%; $p < .001$). Drug-exposed children also received significantly higher adoption subsidies ($p < .001$), averaging $178 per month as compared to $116 for children not exposed to drugs. The average adoption subsidy was $250 per month lower than the average foster care rate for drug-exposed children.

Follow-Up

Four years after placement (and two years after the data presented above were collected) the sample was surveyed again. The return rate was 88% ($n = 1099$); the average age of the children at this follow-up was about seven years. Preliminary results are available (Barth, Needell, & Berry 1993). Comparisons between children's outcomes and parental satisfaction for prenatally drug-exposed and not prenatally drug-exposed children at four years after placement were largely consistent with the two-year findings. The results for drug-exposed children and parents who adopted drug-exposed children continue to be highly positive and virtually indistinguishable from those for parents adopting other children not exposed to drugs.

Conclusions

The difficulties of research on prenatal drug-exposure are great (Kronstadt 1991). At this time, this study cannot answer fundamental questions about what will happen to drug-exposed children if given the enriched environments typical of adoptive homes. The research does not precisely specify whether drug exposure had actually occurred or what its extent was. Experience indicates that some parents see that their children are not acting as they had hoped or expected and then deduce perinatal drug-exposure (Barth 1990). The research did not query parents or social workers about how they knew what they said they knew. There is reason for particular concern that the older children identified as drug-exposed may have been labeled this way in a post hoc fashion, as there was less testing and recording of perinatal drug-exposure prior to 1987. Still, we cannot rule out the possibility that exposure to cocaine or heroin did in fact occur earlier. Indeed, inclusion in the category of those exposed to drugs required that parents indicated that they knew of this drug exposure before the placement.

Perhaps the best this study can claim is that it clarifies the initial adoption experience of parents who believe that their children were exposed to drugs before birth. It almost goes without saying that revisiting these families on this issue is essential. Even so, early expectations can have a strong influence on parental behavior, and expectations of the outcomes of adoption have a strong influence on the likelihood of becoming an adoptive parent. Moreover, initial satisfaction may help increase the development of close relationships that buffer later stresses.

The consistency of the findings of no differences between the drug-exposed group and the one without drug exposure is rather remarkable. Whenever the null hypothesis is not rejected, problems in power must be considered. Given the large sample size, inadequate power is not a real threat to confidence in these findings. Indeed, given the large sample size, nonmeaningful but statistically significant differences are more of a concern for interpretation.

On almost all indicators of satisfaction, parents of drug-exposed children were highly satisfied, and their satisfaction was equivalent to that of parents who adopted children not exposed to drugs. Only one difference emerged—couples adopting independently had somewhat lower satisfaction if they adopted a drug-exposed child—and that difference was small. Overall, the idea that drug-exposed children are significantly different than those without drug exposure and that adopting them is less satisfying is not supported by these data.

Adoptive parents of children whose drug exposure was unknown expected the easiest time of all in caring for their child. They may have been less likely to expect a hard time because their children were adopted when younger than the group not exposed to drugs and because they did not have convincing evidence that their child was born affected by drugs. Only time will tell whether they are right, and whether adopting a young child with uncertain drug exposure is easier than adopting an older child of any type or a young child with drug exposure.

Parents of drug-exposed children also indicated being better prepared than parents of children without drug exposure. The reasons for this are not clear. It may result, however, from the greater likelihood of adopting a drug-exposed child after providing foster care to him or her. This preparation may have helped offset initial effects of the parents' uncertainty about their child's future.

Many adoptions by foster parents involved drug-exposed children. These parents know their children very well. If they had been fearful of the uncertainties of adoption, they would probably have retained the less committed status of foster parents. Their commitment speaks well of their children and their positive expectations of them.

Adoption of drug-exposed children appears to save money. An Oregon study (Zimmerman 1990) of eleven children born drug-exposed in 1986 and subsequently adopted revealed total costs of $39,000 per child for casework, foster care, medical expenses, and adoption and legal costs over a four-year period (i.e., $9,750 per year). The $39,000 in adoption-related costs are roughly equivalent to eighteen months of residential drug treatment programs for women and children together (California Department of Alcohol and Drug

Programs 1990). The adoption of these children is estimated to save the agency a minimum of $50,000 over the cost of long-term foster care (Roberts 1993). Our findings indicate that adoption assistance payments are nearly $3,000 less per year than the foster care rate families were receiving for the same children. These savings are increased because of the low administrative costs of adoption subsidies (i.e., there are no social worker visits or court reviews). Overall, savings may exceed $5,000 per year or as much as $100,000 per child over the duration of the child's minority years. Savings over the child's lifetime will be still greater.

That drug-exposed children and those not exposed to drugs are more similar than different and that their parent's experience is roughly equivalent should be understood by adoption social workers. This does not mean that the adoption of a drug-exposed child is not without challenges, but it does indicate that those challenges can generally be met. Certainly, the information from this study provides a contrast to journalistic appraisals based on interviews with families who were dissatisfied with their adoptions. There is no question that this study may underrepresent adoptive parents who are unhappy with their adoptions; we did not get responses from the entire sample of adoptive families or even from our entire sampling frame of parents asked to participate in the study. Still, with a 62% response rate and a sample that is the largest by far of any study of this population, these conclusions are relatively sturdy. They hold up at four years.

Although it may concern some potential adoptive parents that such a high percentage of children available for adoption have probably been or possibly been exposed to drugs before birth, the mitigating news is that these children and the experiences of their parents do not appear to be significantly different from the norm. The children's significantly more fragile health and the uncertainty about their developmental future makes them more like special needs adoptees than like traditional newborn adoptees. At this point, however, it appears that many drug-exposed children can and will be adopted without substantial special services.

This initial success does not minimize the importance of making ongoing services available as needed. Although parents reported faring very well in satisfaction, they may need additional resources, as will many other adoptive parents, when their children grow older. Now, in the aftermath of the recent drug epidemic, is a good time to improve services to all adoptive parents and their children.

NOTE

This study was partially funded under an award to the Berkeley Child Welfare Research Center from the U.S. DHHS, Administration on Children and Families, Children's Bureau. A Lois and Samuel Silberman Senior Faculty Fellowship Award to the author greatly facilitated this work. The State of California Department of Social Services, Adoption Branch has provided invaluable assistance. An earlier version of this paper appeared in Children and Youth Services Review (1991).

REFERENCES

Achenbach, T. M. & Edelbrock, C. S. (1981). Behavioral problems and competencies reported by parents of normal and disturbed children aged four through sixteen. *Monographs of the Society for Research in Child Development.* Serial No. 188, 46(1).

Adoptalk. (Winter 1990). The addicted child: Summary of Judy Howard's presentation (pp. 4–5). Minneapolis: North American Council on Adoptable Children.

Baker, P. C. & Mott, F. L. (1989). *NLSY child handbook 1989: A guide and resource document for the national longitudinal survey of youth 1986 child data.* Columbus, OH: Center for Human Resource Research.

Barth, R. P. (1991). Educational implications of prenatally drug-exposed children. *Social Work in Education, 13,* 130–36.

Barth, R. P., Courtney, M., Berrick, J. D., & Albert, V. (In press). *Pathways to permanency planning.* New York: Aldine de Gruyter.

Barth, R. P. & Berry, M. (1988). *Adoption and disruption: Risks, rates, and responses.* Hawthorne, NY: Aldine de Gruyter.

Barth, R. P. & Berry, M. (This volume). Implications of research on the welfare of children under permanency planning. In R. Barth, J. D. Berrick, & N. Gilbert (Eds.), *Child Welfare Research Review.* New York: Columbia University Press.

Barth, R. P., Needell, B., & Berry, M. (March, 1993). Adoption of drug-exposed children four years after adoptive placement. Paper presented at the Third Annual Children's Bureau Grantees Meeting, Washington, D.C.

Berry, M. (1992). An evaluation of family preservation services: Fitting agency services to family needs. *Social Work, 37,* 314–21.

Blakeslee, S. (May 19, 1990). Parents fear for future of infants born on drugs. *New York Times,* p. 1, 8–9.

California Senate Office on Research. (1990). *California's drug-exposed babies.* Sacramento: Author.

California Department of Alcohol and Drug Programs. (1990, June). Preliminary fact sheet on perinatal drug and alcohol use.

Center for Human Resource Research. (1991). *Children of the NLSY: 1988 tabulations and summary discussion.* Columbus, OH: Author.

Fanshel, D. (1975). Parental failure and consequences for children: The drug-using mother whose children are in foster care. *American Journal of Public Health, 65,* 604–12.

Feig, L. (1990). Drug-exposed infants and children: Service needs and policy questions. Washington, D.C.: U.S. DHHS.

Ford, M. & Kroll, J. (1990). *Challenges to child welfare: Countering the call for a return to orphanages.* St. Paul: North American Council on Adoptable Children.

Glidden, L. M. (1990). The unwanted ones: Families adopting children with mental retardation. In L. M. Glidden (Ed.), *Formed families: Adoption of children with handicaps* (pp. 177–205). New York: Haworth Press.

Glidden, L. M. (1991). Adopted children with developmental disabilities: Post-placement family functioning. *Children and Youth Services Review, 13,* 363–77.

Gordon, L. (1988). *Heroes of their own lives.* New York: Viking.

Graham, P. J. & Rutter, M. L. (1968). The reliability and validity of the psychiatric assessment of the child, II: Interview with the parent. *British Journal of Psychiatry, 114,* 581–92.

Kroll, J. (Winter 1990). U. S. Congressional committee projects dramatic growth in out-of-home care. *Adoptalk,* 1–3, 5.

Kronstadt, D. (1991). Complex developmental issues of prenatal drug exposure. *The Future of Children, 1*(1), 36–49.

McCullough, C. B. (1991). The child welfare response. *The future of children, 1*(1), 61–71.

McFadden, R. (1990). Tragic ending to the adoption of a crack baby. *New York Times,* June 19.

Mott, F. L. & Quinlan, S. V. (1991). *Children of the NLSY: 1988 tabulations and summary discussion.* Columbus, OH: Center for Human Resource Research.

Nelson, K. (1987). *On adoption's frontier.* New York: Child Welfare League of America.

Peterson, J. L. & Zill, N. (1986). Marital disruption, parent-child relationships, and behavioral problems in children. *Journal of Marriage and the Family, 48*(2), 56–73.

Roberts, D. (1993). Child welfare services for drug-exposed newborns and their families. In R. Barth, J. Pietrzak, & M. Ramler (Eds.), *Social and health services to drug and AIDS-affected families* (pp. 253–71). New York: Guilford.

Rutter, M., Tizard, J., & Whitmore, K. (1970). *Education, health, and behavior.* London: Longman.

Senate Office of Research. (1990). *California's drug-exposed babies: Undiscovered, unreported, underserved.* Sacramento: Author

State Department of Social Services (SDSS) of California. (1987). *Adoption regulations.* Sacramento, CA: Author.

Zimmerman, J. (1990). Drug-exposed infants: Preliminary cost tracking. Unpublished paper #18. Salem: Oregon Children's Services Division.

Zuckerman, B. (1991). Drug-exposed infants: Understanding the medical risk. *The Future of Children, 1*(1), 26–32.

PART FIVE

OUTCOMES OF CHILD WELFARE SERVICES

Child welfare services entered the permanency planning era in 1980. The passage of a dozen years of permanency planning calls for an assessment of the impact of these efforts on children and families and for forecasting its future. Some child welfare scholars (i.e., Fein & Maluccio 1992) are suggesting that "permanency planning may have become another remedy in jeopardy" (p. 335). Others (e.g., Pelton 1990) are calling for radical transformations of the child welfare system. Indeed, permanency planning as we know it seems to have few defenders. At times this disdain for the condition of the child welfare system in 1992 is attributed more to the failure of child welfare services funding to keep pace with the need rather than to faulty program design (Pecora, Whittaker, Maluccio, Barth, & Plotnick 1992). The current challenge is to use the limited resources available most effectively while pursuing improvements in the conceptual, statutory, and service delivery framework. Information about the outcomes of the current system is critical to that effort.

The permanency planning movement intended to change child welfare services mainly on the front end (i.e., making reasonable efforts to prevent placement) and at the tail end (i.e., the emphasis on permanent placements, especially adoption). Yet, foster care remains the core service for many children (Fein & Maluccio 1992). Widom's unique follow-up study of a cohort of children placed in foster care more than twenty years earlier uses criminal justice histories as an outcome measure. She shows that foster care offers a protective environment for physically abused, neglected, and sexually assaulted children if the placement is early, stable, and lasting. Children placed because of abuse or neglect *and* delinquency had strikingly worse outcomes.

Researchers using foster care management information system data (see the articles by Goerge, Wulczyn, and Courtney, this volume) will be able to replicate these results when they are able to achieve data matches with other management information systems for adults (e.g., higher education, criminal justice, mental health services). This is the basis for Bohman's (1985) remarkable study of the adult outcomes of children adopted in Sweden. Although none of these longitudinal efforts are free of major methodological flaws, Widom's findings are consistent with other findings reviewed in Barth and Berry (this volume) indicating that children in foster care achieve developmental benefits. These benefits are clearly limited by the degree of problems the children bring into foster care (Fanshel, Finch, & Grundy 1989) and by the level of service they receive.

Much of the newer evidence about the outcomes of child welfare services is drawn from recent efforts to understand caseload dynamics (such as the studies by Wulczyn and Goerge in this volume). These studies provide the basis for making inferences about outcomes when certain assumptions are made, especially: (1) that a child's return home is safe and most developmentally advantageous; (2) that multiple placement moves are harmful; (3) that the briefer the time spent in foster care the better; and (4) that less restrictive out-of-home care arrangements are developmentally preferable to more restrictive arrangements. Another assumption they often make is that children are victimized by only one kind of abuse; Albert (this volume) shows that this is certainly not the case and that children who experience multiple types of abuse have different services experiences than other children.

A research review of the outcomes of child welfare services provides a rough picture of what is known about how well children are protected by the system. In 1987 Berry and Barth reviewed the evidence on the outcomes of child welfare services in *Social Service Review*; this paper won the Frank Bruel Prize for excellence in child welfare services research. Over the last few years, there has been an explosion of research on family preservation activities; these works include, most notably, Nelson and Landsman (1992), Fraser, Pecora, and Haapala (1991), and Yuan, McDonald, Wheeler, Struckman-Johnson, and Rivest (1990). These studies have been competently reviewed in Rossi (1991) and are not reviewed in great detail here. Much of the research reported in this volume also contributes to a contemporary assessment of the outcomes of permanency planning for children in the domains of placement stability and reabuse. Only a few new studies, however, include information about consumer satisfaction and developmental outcomes. Although the potential of management information systems research is great, interviews with children, parents, and social workers for assessing critical outcomes are critically needed.

REFERENCES

Barth, R. P. & Berry, M. (1987). Outcomes of child welfare services since permanency planning. *Social Service Review, 61,* 71–90.

Bohman, M. & Sigvardsson, S. (1990). Outcome in adoption: Lessons from longitudinal studies. In D. M. Brodzinsky & M. D. Schechter (Eds.), *The psychology of adoption* (pp. 93–106). New York: Oxford University Press.

Fein, E. & Maluccio, A. N. (1992). Permanency planning: Another remedy in jeopardy. *Social Service Review, 66,* 335–48.

Fraser, M., Pecora, P. J., & Haapala, D. (1991). *Families in crisis: The impact of intensive family preservation services.* Hawthorne, NY: Aldine de Gruyter.

Nelson, K. & Landsman, M. (1992). *Family preservation services.* Springfield, IL: Charles Thomas.

Pecora, P. J., Whittaker, J. K., Maluccio, A. N., Barth, R. P., & Plotnick, R. D. (1992). *The child welfare challenge: Policy, practice, and research.* New York: Aldine de Gruyter.

Rossi, P. M. (1991). *Evaluations of intensive family preservation programs.* New York: Edna McConnell Clark Foundation.

Yuan, Y. Y., McDonald, W. R., Wheeler, C. E., Struckman-Johnson, D., & Rivest, M. (1990). *Evaluation of AB 1562 in-home care demonstration projects, volume I and II.* Sacramento, CA: MacDonald and Associates.

THIRTEEN

The Role of Placement Experiences in Mediating the Criminal Consequences of Early Childhood Victimization

Cathy Spatz Widom

The disposition of a large sample of early childhood abuse and neglect cases was followed up via criminal records. The majority of the children had been placed outside the home, primarily in foster care. The kinds of placement and factors affecting placement decisions were examined. Differences in arrest rates were found between children placed solely because of abuse or neglect and those placed for abuse or neglect in conjunction with delinquency. Similar results were found for foster care placement. Placement alone did not appear to increase the risk of criminal behavior.

Abused and neglected children are generally at high risk for social problems. However, recent findings have demonstrated that not all abused and neglected children grow up to become delinquents, adult criminals, or violent criminal offenders (Widom 1989b). What are some of the possible mediating variables that act to buffer or protect abused and neglected children from the developmental deficits and later delinquent and adult criminal behavior characterizing so many of these children? Garmezy (1981) has called them "protective" factors: those dispositional attributes, environmental conditions, biological predispositions, and positive events that act to mitigate against early negative experiences. Although one can speculate on a number of reasons why child abuse and neglect lead to various outcomes (Widom 1989c), it is possible that certain life experiences act as buffers against long-term negative consequences.

One of the factors that may act to protect abused and neglected children from more serious long-term consequences is placement outside the home. Proponents of such out-of-home placements as foster care point to the potential for serious future harm in leaving these children in the home. On the other hand, critics of placement outside the home have stressed the need to maintain biological family ties and to minimize government intervention in family life. They have expressed concern that, notwithstanding the potential risk for continued abuse and neglect, foster care may actually be worse for children than staying in the home (Hubbell 1981; Wald 1976). Critics also point to the financial cost of out-of-home placements. In addition, it can be argued that out-of-home placement may act to exacerbate the stress of children from abusive and neglectful families.

Difficult ethical and practical dilemmas are associated with decision making in cases where removal from an abusive or neglectful home is being considered. Critics have argued against taking cases of child abuse and neglect to court, against taking children out of their homes and away from their families, and against exposing them to multiple and serial placements. However, decision making is often hindered by the lack of solid empirical evidence even though public policy ultimately depends on value judgments by the community and the broader society. To understand outcomes, it is also important to understand selection factors that influence placement decisions and the characteristics of experiences in placement outside the home.

The existing literature concerning the impact of placement experiences on abused and neglected children suffers from methodological problems that detract from its scientific validity and, ultimately, from its relevance to policy. These problems are not reviewed here since Wald, Carlsmith, and Leiderman (1988) have already provided an excellent review. However, some of the background literature on the following three issues will be reviewed briefly: (1) on factors influencing placement decisions; (2) on the length and type of placements experienced by abused and neglected children; and (3) on outcomes for abused and neglected children placed outside the home.

Placement Factors

Influences on Decision Making

Studies of court decisions have suggested that some characteristics of parents, such as substance abuse or criminal involvement, tend to increase the likelihood that children will be placed outside the home

(Aber 1980; Weinberger & Smith 1970). In one study, which examined 425 cases of families whose children were placed in foster care in New York City, Jenkins and Sauber (1966) reported five major categories of reasons for the placement of children: (1) physical illness or incapacity of the child's caregiver (29%); (2) mental illness of the mother (11%); (3) personality or emotional problems of the child (17%); (4) severe neglect or abuse (10%); and (5) family problems (33%). Runyan, Gould, Trost, and Loda (1982) examined the records of the North Carolina registry of child abuse and neglect to determine which of a large number of social, family, and child characteristics influenced the decisions to place children in foster care. Using confirmed reports of maltreatment received between June 1978 and June 1979, Runyan and his colleagues found that children from about 15% of the families had been placed in foster care. Parental characteristics (such as substance abuse or an employed mother) and the type of abuse (burns and scalds) significantly increased the likelihood of foster care placement; however, the referral source (law enforcement agencies) and geographic area were also important factors. Race, income, and education were not significant predictors of placement.

In a retrospective study of case records of a protective services agency, Ross and Katz (1983) found that even after controlling for the nature of abuse families receiving welfare or those perceived by the agency as having a family member with a mental health problem, a child with behavioral problems, and an ineffective parent, were more likely to have a child removed. In a later study, Katz, Hampton, Newberger, Bowles, and Snyder (1986) reviewed the hospital records of 185 children and found that children with physical injuries were more likely to be placed in a foster home or in residential care if they were from poor families. Children with nonphysical injuries were more likely to be removed for such placements if their families were more affluent. In sum, decision making about placements for abused and neglected children appears to be based on judgments about selected characteristics of the families and the children.

Placement Length and Type

Historically, foster care has been viewed as a temporary solution to a crisis situation, to be used only until the child's home situation could be made safe and relatively stable. The reality frequently appears to be quite different. In one study, the average length of time spent in foster care in some cities was found to be five years (Fanshel 1981). Wiltse and Gambrill (1973) examined a sample of 772 foster children in San Francisco and found that the average length of time in care for these children, too, was nearly five years; almost two-thirds of the children (62%) were expected to remain in care until they reached their maturity. Thus, many children remain in foster care for a substantial period, and some of these children experience even more extended stays in foster care (Tatara 1989).

One of the common criticisms of placement experiences, and of foster care in particular, is its instability. According to Knitzer and Allen (1978), the majority of children who remain in foster care for at least six months are subject to multiple placements and are thus deprived of stable, continuous caregiving. In their five-year longitudinal study of over six hundred children entering foster care in New York in 1966, Fanshell and Shinn (1968) carefully traced all moves their subjects made while in foster care (these moves included interagency and intraagency transfers, and reentries into foster care of previously discharged children). About 42% of the children had experienced only one placement, 30% had two, 18% had three, and 10% had experienced four or more moves (p. 139). Thus, a substantial proportion of these children had experienced turnover (or more than one placement) while in care; however, the extent to which turnover and the number of placements are related to long-term consequences is not known.

Outcomes

It has frequently been asserted that social intervention strategies in cases of child abuse and neglect are at best ineffective and destructive and at worst harmful to the child. Palmer (1979), for example, referred to the "myth that placement experience is somehow good for the child" (p. 262). Some examinations of foster care experiences have described the inadequacies, failures, and high costs of the system (Gruber 1978; Schor 1982) whereas others have reported a high rate of behavior problems (Bohman & Sigvardsson 1980; Bryce & Ehlert 1971; Frank 1980; Littner 1974) and school problems (Canning 1974) among foster children. However, none of these studies compared the rates of such behaviors to those in children not in foster care nor did they present information about the foster children prior to their placement.

On the other hand, other studies of adults who grew up in foster homes have found no evidence of greater criminality, mental illness, or marital failure than in the general population (Fein, Maluccio, & Kluger 1990; Festinger 1983; Maluccio & Fein 1985; Meier 1965; Theis 1924). Kent (1976) examined case records of a large group of court-supervised abused and neglected children in Los Angeles and found that children who had been in foster care for at least one year were rated by their social workers as being better off (physically and socially) than they were at the time they entered foster care.

Fanshel and Shinn (1978) found that after a six-month period in foster care the well-being of the majority of the children had improved in terms of physical development, IQ, and school performance. They did not find that the more time a child spent in foster care, the more likely the child was to show signs of deterioration. Most children maintained their improvement over the five-year period of the study: "Our findings do not show that children who remained in foster care fared less well with respect to intellectual abilities, school performance, and personal and social adjustment compared to those who returned to their own homes" (p. 479).

In a retrospective study using case records of two hundred children in the long-term care of two welfare agencies, Palmer (1979) reported a decrease in behavior problems in foster children between the time of placement and their discharge. The outcome was not related to the children's age at admission to foster care. Leitenberg, Burchard, Healy, and Fuller (1981) compared school attendance and police contacts of 187 neglected and "unmanageable" children and found that the children in foster homes showed the lowest levels of problem behavior compared to other children in different living situations (group homes, a state reform school, or their natural home, living with their biological parents). For children aged between eleven and thirteen and for those between the ages of fourteen and sixteen in the study by Leitenberg and associates, school attendance was lower and police contact higher when the children were living in an alternative placement.

Other studies have found that children in foster care did not have especially high rates of delinquency. After interviewing a large sample of adults who had previously been in foster care in New York City, Festinger (1983) concluded that they were not so different overall from their peers in their activities, feelings, and aspirations. Using a matched historical cohort design with children who had been maltreated, Runyan and Gould (1985) studied the impact of foster care on the subsequent development of juvenile delinquency. They compared 114 foster children between the ages of eleven and eighteen who had been in foster care for three or more years with a group of 106 victims of child maltreatment, similar in terms of age, sex, race, and year of diagnosis who had remained with their own families. Children for whom there was evidence of severe or moderate mental retardation were excluded from both of the study groups. Cohort differences in maternal education, type of abuse, history of prior maltreatment, sex, and race were controlled for in statistical analyses. Runyan and Gould concluded: "Overall, there appears to be no support for the idea that foster care is responsible for a significant portion of later problems encountered by victims of maltreatment" (p. 562).

After the age of eleven, the foster care children committed 0.050 crimes per person per year, in contrast to the home care children who committed an average of 0.059 crimes per person per year—a nonsignificant difference although foster care children were significantly more likely to have committed an assaultive crime.

In a more recent study involving thirty-two white children over a two-year period, Wald, Carlsmith, and Leiderman (1988) found that the foster care children had a somewhat better adjustment socially and emotionally than did those in the comparison group and that foster care had not harmed the children.

In two studies of children in care in England, Quinton and Rutter (1988) found that serious parenting problems (as evidenced by parenting breakdowns) very seldom occurred when the parents had not themselves experienced poor parenting or marked family disruption in childhood: "What evidence there is tends to suggest that most adversities that are strictly restricted to infancy have relatively few long-term sequelae provided that later environments are consistently good" (p. 204).

At present, there is a mixed picture of the impact of placement on abused and neglected children. Very little is known about the role of placement experiences as mediators of long-term criminal consequences, and the methodological limitations in many of the studies reviewed make it difficult to draw firm conclusions.

This paper describes the placement experiences for a large sample of juvenile court cases of child abuse and neglect from approximately twenty years ago and examines the role of these placement experiences in relation to delinquent, adult criminal, and violent criminal outcomes. It focuses exclusively on the juvenile court cases ($n = 772$) contained within the larger sample, for which a complete description of the design and subject selection criteria can be found elsewhere (Widom 1989a). The extent and type of placement experiences for the juvenile court children are described, and some of the factors influencing their placement are examined. Aspects of the placements are then related to long-term criminal consequences (delinquency, adult criminality, and violent criminal behavior). This analysis is based exclusively on official records.

Method

Design

Children who were physically abused, sexually abused, or neglected approximately twenty years ago were followed up through an examination of official criminal records. The data for the present analysis are based on 772 cases of abuse and neglect processed through the county juvenile court in a metropolitan area in the Midwest between 1967 and 1971. This time period was chosen (1) to maximize the likelihood that the cases are currently closed, and (2) to allow for the maturing of the individuals concerned while avoiding the problems associated with much older files.

To insure that the order of the temporal sequence was clear (because we did not want to include cases where delinquency may have preceded abuse or neglect or may have been the cause of the abuse or neglect), abuse and neglect cases were restricted to those in which children were eleven years of age or younger at the time of the incident.

This design has limitations because of its exclusive reliance on official records. Much child abuse and neglect that occurs does not come to the attention of welfare departments, the police, or the courts. This fact especially applies to official data from the late 1960s and early 1970s when it is generally believed that only a fraction of all maltreatment cases was reported. The abuse and neglect cases studied here are those in which agencies have intervened and those processed through the social service systems (Groeneveld & Giovannoni 1977). These cases were dealt with before most states had adopted mandatory child abuse reporting laws and before the Federal Child Abuse Treatment and Prevention Act was passed. In addition, because of exclusions from the initial sample, these findings are not generalizable to abused and neglected children who were adopted in early childhood (Widom 1989a).

During the period from 1967 to 1971, cases of physical abuse, sexual abuse, or neglect could be referred to the county juvenile court by a police officer or any other person. The court was required to make a preliminary inquiry and then determine whether further action should be taken. When possible, the inquiry was to include a preliminary investigation of the home and environmental situation of the child, his or her previous history, and the circumstances of the condition alleged. On the basis of this information, a probation officer would then file a petition. The Department of Public Welfare (DPW) could also file a petition with the court concerning a dependent or neglected child and request that the child be made a ward of the court or a ward of the county welfare department.

Physical abuse cases referred to "cruelty to children," with allegations that a specific individual had "knowingly and willfully inflicted unnecessarily severe corporal punishment" or "unnecessary physical suffering" upon the child or children. These cases included injuries such as bruises, welts, burns, abrasions, lacerations, wounds, cuts, bone or skull fractures, and other evidence of physical injury to the child.

Sexual abuse cases covered a variety of charges, ranging from relatively nonspecific charges of "assault and battery with intent to gratify sexual desires" to more specific, detailed ones of "fondling or touching in an obscene manner," sodomy, incest, and so forth.

Neglect cases were those in which the court had found a child (or children) to have no proper parental care or guardianship, to be destitute, homeless, or living in a physically dangerous environment. The neglect petition reflected a judgment that the parental deficiencies in child care were beyond acceptable community and professional standards at the time. These cases represented extreme failures to provide adequate food, clothing, shelter, and medical attention to children. Neglect petitions were generally filed by the county DPW with the request that the child be made a ward of the DPW. A variety of placement options was available and pursued, including foster care, Guardian's Home, and facilities for physically or emotionally handicapped or mentally retarded children.

Subjects

In this sample of 772 juvenile court cases, there are about equal numbers of males (53%) and females (47%) and more whites (67%) than blacks (33%). The mean current age of these abused and neglected subjects is 25.69 years (*s.d.* = 3.53). Most of them (85%) are currently between the ages of twenty and thirty, with about 10% under the age of twenty, and about 5% older than thirty (the youngest is sixteen and the oldest thirty-two). The current age distribution of this sample indicates that our design has allowed sufficient time for most of these subjects to come to the attention of authorities for delinquent, adult criminal, and violent criminal behavior (Hartstone & Hanson 1984; Rojek & Erikson 1982; Strasburg 1978; Wolfgang, Figlio, & Sellin 1972).

Data collection

Detailed information from the files of the juvenile court and probation department (which processed the cases of abused, neglected, or dependent children) was recorded. This information typically included a description of the original abuse or neglect incident and the disposition of the case (e.g., wardship, foster care, or other types of out-of-home placements). Information about characteristics of the parents and families is based on case worker records and thus may reflect underestimates of characteristics that were not noted in these official records.

Information on delinquency and adult criminality in this paper is also based exclusively on official records. Year-by-year delinquent activity information (including disposition of each charge and associated detentions or institutionalizations) for all subjects was recorded and coded from files in the juvenile probation department. Adult criminal histories for all subjects were researched at local, state, and federal levels of law enforcement. Bureau of Motor Vehicle records were searched to find social security numbers for the subjects to assist in tracing criminal histories. Marriage license bureau records were also searched to find married names for all females.

Delinquency and adult criminality are categorized as follows: (1) any juvenile arrest refers to any arrest occurring prior to age eighteen; (2) any adult arrest refers to any arrest after age eighteen, excluding arrests for traffic offenses; (3) both juvenile and adult arrests refer to arrests for robbery, assault, assault and battery, battery with injury, aggravated assault, manslaughter/involuntary manslaughter or reckless homicide, murder/attempted murder, rape, sodomy, and robbery and burglary with injury.

Results

The results are organized into two parts. In the first, the extent, type, and length of placement experiences of children who were abused and/or neglected are described and the issue of who gets placed is considered. The second part examines the role of placement experiences as potential mediators between childhood victimization and long-term criminal consequences—delinquency, adult criminality, and violent criminal behavior.

The vast majority of these 772 juvenile court cases had experienced some form of out-of-home placement during their childhood and/or early adolescence. Approximately 14% ($n = 106$) had no record of having been placed by age eighteen; for thirty-two children (4.1%), it is not known whether they were placed; an additional thirty-one (4%) children were made wards of the Department of Public Welfare but were apparently not removed from their homes. Because of such ambiguities, these sixty-three cases were excluded from the analyses, leaving a total of 709 children upon whom the analyses are based.

Placement Factors

Types of placement. More than half of these abused and neglected children were placed in foster care (54.8%, $n = 423$), and about one-quarter (25.5%, $n = 197$) spent time in the Guardian's Home. A few of the children were placed in a psychiatric facility (2.2%), a home for the mentally retarded (1.1%), a facility for emotionally disturbed or physically handicapped children (1.0%), or a medical facility (0.4%). Approximately 7% of the sample were placed with another relative at some point during childhood. These percentages represent the proportion of children out of the total juvenile court sample who had been placed in that type of facility at any point in their childhood (up to the age of eighteen).

Number of moves. A common perception about placement experiences of abused and neglected children is that they suffer frequent

TABLE 13.1
Age Upon Entrance and Duration of All Placements

Type of Placement	Age at Entrance			Length (years)			
	N	M	S.D.	N	M	S.D.	MD
Medical	8	3.11	2.28	3	.04	.07	.01
Foster care	410	6.88	3.41	379	5.17	4.22	4.41
Guardian's home	184	7.45	3.86	137	.66	1.36	.16
Relative's home	45	7.95	4.22	33	5.85	4.69	5.91
Home for the retarded	8	12.28	6.23	8	5.40	5.62	2.37
Other facility[a]	8	12.84	2.60	4	1.74	.50	1.76
Psychiatric	14	15.12	2.39	8	.75	.52	0.79

[a] Other facility for the emotionally disturbed or physically handicapped.

moves from one placement situation to another. To examine this issue, moves have been defined as any change in residence for the child. This means that a move from one foster care situation to another is one move. Similarly, transfers from the Guardian's Home to foster care to a second foster home would be counted as three moves. The mean number of moves in our sample was 1.75 (*s.d.* = 1.59) and the range was from zero to fifteen moves. About half (50.4%) had only one placement outside the home, 15.5% had two moves, 12.4% had three to five moves, and only 3.5% had six moves or more.

Initial placement. Very few (5.9%) of the abused and neglected children in this sample of juvenile court cases of abuse and neglect were placed before the age of one, less than one-fifth (17.8%) were placed before the age of two, and the majority (56%) were placed between the ages of six and eleven. Not surprisingly, the age at first placement correlates very highly ($r = .87$) with the child's age at the time of the abuse or neglect petition.

Start and length of placements. Table 13.1 presents the average age upon entrance into each type of placement and the average amount of time spent in various placements. While the earliest mean age of placement concerned placement in a medical facility, this entailed very few of the children and lasted only a very short time. With this exception, the earliest mean age of placement ($M = 6.88$ years) was for placement into foster care for an average of 5.17 years. This is consistent with previous work on the length of time children spend in foster care (Fanshel 1981). Placement in the Guardian's Home was at a later age ($M = 7.45$ years) and was apparently intended as a temporary placement only ($M = 3$ months). Interestingly, children were on the average older when placed in homes for the mentally retarded ($M = 12.84$). Psychiatric facilities were entered at the latest age ($M = 15.12$). In terms of the time spent in placements, placement in foster care, in a relative's home, or in homes for the mentally retarded averaged over five years whereas in facilities for the emotionally disturbed or physically handicapped, it averaged less than two years.

It is commonly assumed that abused or neglected children are first placed in temporary facilities (e.g., the Guardian's Home) for a short period and subsequently moved to a foster home. Since it was possible to examine the sequence of placements beyond the age at entrance presented above, the probability of a first placement in the Guardian's Home followed by one in foster care was tested against the opposite sequence, from foster care to the Guardian's Home. Of the 159 children who had been placed in the Guardian's Home, about 43% ($n = 68$) were subsequently placed in foster care. In contrast, of the 337 children whose first placement was in foster care, only 3.8% ($n = 11$) had a second placement in the Guardian's Home. Thus, while placement in the Guardian's Home was often followed by foster care, the majority of abused and neglected children placed outside the home went directly into foster care.

Who Gets Placed?

Child characteristics. More males (87.7%) were placed than females (81.9%) and more white (86.9%) than black children (81%). The age at which the abuse or neglect incident occurred did not influence the likelihood of being placed, but the type of abuse or neglect made a significant difference. Children who experienced both physical abuse and neglect were most likely to be placed (98.1%); those suffering either abuse or neglect had lower placement rates (from 73% to 85%). Children who were sexually abused only were least likely to be placed. Children with indications of behavior problems noted in the juvenile probation department records ($n = 51$) were significantly more likely to be placed than children without behavior problems (98% versus 84%, $X^2 = 71.15$, $df = 2$, $p < .001$).

Family characteristics. Parent and family characteristics also influenced the placement decisions. An alcoholic parent (mother or father) increased the likelihood of the child being placed, as did a mother with mental problems. All children with an alcoholic mother (or one with alcohol problems) were placed (*n* = 120), and of the children with an alcoholic father (*n* = 47), all but one were placed. It should be kept in mind that many of these were female-headed single-parent households.) Similarly, 95% of the children whose mothers had mental problems were placed. Family variables reflecting general disorganization and disruption also played a role in placement decisions. Children from families with such characteristics were more likely to be placed than were those from families without them, as follows: parents separated, 92% versus 79%; mother unknown, 95% versus 82%; father unknown, 91% versus 84%; no relatives willing or able to care for the children, 97% versus 66%. Interestingly enough, having a mother or father who was noted as criminal in the records was not associated with differences in placement decisions.

Parental characteristics were also related to the amount of time children spent in various placements. Separate regressions were computed predictive of the total time spent in any type of placement, in any nondelinquent placement, and in foster care with a variety of parent and child characteristics as independent variables. Table 13.2 presents the regression coefficients for these equations. Mental illness of the parent(s) and maternal alcoholism or criminality were highly significant predictors for the amount of time in all three placement options, as was the child's race. Having a parent whose whereabouts were unknown was a significant predictor for any type of placement and for placements for reasons other than delinquency and approached significance for foster care. Being a child with behavior problems was predictive of the total time in any type of placement and in nondelinquent placements (although this last was not significant).

Arrest Outcomes

Since one of the purposes of this paper is to examine the role of placement as a mediator between childhood victimization and later delinquent and adult criminal behavior, it is important that placement experiences associated with abuse and neglect be distinguished, if possible, and treated separately from placements associated with delinquency.

TABLE 13.2

Regression Coefficients Predictive of Total Time in any Placement,
Nondelinquent Placements, and Foster Care

Variable	Total placement time					
	Any		Nondelinquent		Foster care	
	β	SEβ	β	SEβ	β	SEβ
Parent mental illness	2.91	.47****	2.89	.47****	2.96	.50****
Race	1.55	.43****	1.50	.43****	1.33	.46***
Mother alcoholic or criminal	1.16	.45***	1.12	.45**	1.17	.48**
Parent unknown	1.15	.43**	1.08	.43**	.93	.48*
Child behavior problem	1.82	.76**	1.44	.75**	.68	.76
No relations	−.81	.44*	−.80	.44*	−.82	.52
Father alcoholic or criminal	.71	.57	.71	.57	.57	.62
Sex	−.07	.39	−.11	.39	.11	.43
Child age at 1st placement	−.28	.20	−.28	.20	−.10	.22
Multiple R	.35		.34		.35	
Multiple R²	.12		.12		.12	
No. of cases	488		488		376	
F	7.22		6.79		5.67	

NOTE: All *F* values are significant at <.001.
*p<.10; **p<.05; ***p<.01; ****p<.001.

In examining the role of placement experiences, it was apparent that whereas some children were placed outside the home because of delinquency, others were placed only in response to their abuse or neglect. While few children were placed for delinquency alone (*n* = 16), 12.5% (*n* = 96) were placed for both delinquency and abuse or neglect. With few exceptions, delinquent placements occurred after the initial placement for abuse or neglect.

For these reasons, in the following analyses, which focus on outcome, the placement variable is divided into three categories: (1) children never placed, (2) children whose placement was related only to abuse or neglect, and (3) children placed in relation both to delinquent behavior and to abuse or neglect. Omitted from this analysis are the children placed in delinquent or detention facilities for reasons other than abuse or neglect.

Placement Experience and Arrest Outcomes

Table 13.3 represents a comparison of the proportion of the sample who had juvenile arrests, adult arrests, and violent arrests in terms of

TABLE 13.3
Juvenile and Adult Arrests as Function of Placement Experiences

		Arrest %			
Type of placement	N	Any juvenile (N = 209)	Any adult (N = 217)	Both juvenile & adult (N = 115)	Any violent (N = 93)
None	106	15.1	29.2	6.6	10.4
Abuse/neglect only	489	17.8	23.3	8.6	8.4
Delinquent plus abuse/neglect	96	92.7	60.4	55.5	34.4
X²		234.51	54.75	145.75	50.68
p (df = 2)		<.001	<.001	<.001	<.001

the cause and nature of their placement experience, if any. The results reveal an interesting pattern. Abused and neglected children who were not placed and those placed for abuse or neglect only had similar arrest outcomes (juvenile, adult, both juvenile and adult, and violent crimes), but both were strikingly different from children placed for a combination of delinquency and abuse or neglect. Children with no placements and those with placements because of abuse or neglect only were six times less likely to have arrests as both a juvenile and an adult and three times less likely to be violent than were those children placed for abuse or neglect and delinquency. These findings suggest that the fact of placement is not itself associated with an increased risk for delinquency or adult criminal behavior.

Table 13.4 presents a similar breakdown and analysis using outcomes for children in foster care. Abused and neglected children who had experienced foster care were divided into two groups, one whose placement was only in foster care and the other whose placement experiences included both foster care and some other form of placement. (The group "All Others" in table 13.4 refers to children placed out of their home but not in foster care facilities.) Inspection of the table reveals a pattern similar to that presented in table 13.3 for placements in general. That is, children with no placements or with foster care placement only had lower rates of any type of arrest at any age than did the other groups of abused and neglected children, but the two groups were otherwise relatively indistinguishable from one another. Thus, what has often been viewed as negative outcomes of foster care may be due to the confounding influence of a small frac-

TABLE 13.4
*Juvenile and Adult Criminal Behavior as Function
of Foster Care Placement*

Type of placement	N	Arrest %			
		Any juvenile (N = 209)	Any adult (N = 217)	Both juvenile & adult (N = 115)	Any violent (N = 93)
No placement	106	15.1	29.2	6.6	10.4
Foster care only	263	15.2	21.3	6.5	7.6
Foster care plus other	160	50.6	41.3	27.5	18.8
All others	180	40.0	35.6	26.1	17.8
X^2		80.31	21.44	53.57	15.60
p ($df = 3$)		<.001	<.001	<.001	<.001

tion of children placed in foster care who have early involvement in delinquent activity.

Placement characteristics and arrest outcomes. Table 13.5 presents arrest outcomes as a function of age at the first placement, time in the first placement, and the number of placement moves. To control for the effects of age in this analysis, the percentages for any adult arrest, for both juvenile and adult arrests, and for any violent arrest were calculated only for those subjects twenty-one years of age or older at the time of the criminal history data collection (March 1988).

Few of the children placed before the age of one had arrest records, and none of them had arrests for violent crimes. The percentage of subjects arrested for delinquency increases significantly with the child's age at the first placement ($X^2 = 14.04$, $df = 4$, $p < .01$), as it does for adult criminality ($X^2 = 15.47$, $df = 4$, $p < .01$), and for violent crimes ($X^2 = 10.72$, $df = 4$, $p < .05$). Children placed for the first time at a later age had higher rates of delinquency and adult criminality. This is consistent with the results presented earlier for children placed for abuse and neglect only, whose mean age of placement was lower and who had lower arrest records. It is possible that results such as these form part of the basis for the common belief that it is more difficult and risky to take older children into foster care.

Another factor examined in relation to delinquent and adult criminal outcomes is the amount of time spent in the first placement. At least one version of common sense suggests that the more time the child spends in that first placement, the better off he or she will be.

This is based on the assumption that in the context of stable caretaking relationships the child would have the opportunity to develop attachments and thus a stronger sense of self and greater self-esteem.

As expected, children who spent more than ten years in their first placement had the lowest overall rates of arrests in all categories of arrest. However, significant differences were found for delinquency ($X^2 = 16.39$, $df = 4$, $p < .01$) and for violent offenses ($X^2 = 11.62$, $df = 4$, $p < .05$) though not for adult arrests or for both juvenile and adult arrests. Children who spent four to six years in their first placement had the highest overall rates of arrests in all arrest categories.

Separate regression analyses were conducted using total time in placement, total time in nondelinquent placements, and total time in foster care only (with the current age as a covariate in each equation) as predictive of arrests in each arrest category. None of these total time predictors was significant.

Table 13.5 also presents results on the relationship of the number of placement moves and long-term criminal consequences. The assumption is that the more moves a child makes, the more stressful and negative these experiences will be and that this, in turn, will result in more negative consequences (that is, in more delinquent or adult criminal behavior). In table 13.5 a clear relationship is revealed between the number of moves made by the child and later arrests as a juvenile ($X^2 = 155.87$, $df = 3$, $p < .001$), as an adult ($X^2 = 30.40$, $df = 3$, $p < .001$), as both juvenile and adult ($X^2 = 88.44$, $df = 3$, $p < .001$), and for violent crimes ($X^2 = 26.54$, $df = 3$, $p < .001$).

This analysis, however, does not address the issue of the direction of causality. That is, do more moves hurt the child or does the child with more problems make more moves? In an attempt to examine this question more carefully within the constraints of the existing data, further analyses were conducted on the abused and neglected children in this sample who had made numerous moves. First, it is clear that males made more frequent (defined as three or more) moves than did females (11.5% versus 6.3%), whereas black and white children did not differ in that regard.

Second, children with indications of behavior problems in their records were more likely to have made frequent moves than those without such indications (37.2% versus 6.8%). Children with indicated behavior problems also made significantly more moves than those without ($M = 4.04$ versus $M = 1.37$ moves, $t(706) = 11.63$, p

TABLE 13.5

Differences in Arrest Outcome as Function of Placement Characteristics

		Arrest %			
Placement variable	N	Any juvenile (N = 209)	Any adult (N = 217)[a]	Both juvenile & adult (N = 115)[a]	Any violent (N = 93)[a]
Age at First Placement					
<1 year	34	14.7	14.3	14.3	0.0
1–3 years	103	22.3	15.9	13.0	5.8
4–6 years	137	29.9	27.6	12.7	9.7
7–11 years	292	32.5	38.0	20.2	17.8
>11 years	15	60.0	26.7	20.0	13.3
p-value		<.01	<.01		<.05
Time in first Placement					
<1 year	172	26.7	28.5	13.9	6.6
1–3 years	116	27.6	33.0	18.6	16.5
4–6 years	73	45.2	34.3	24.3	18.6
7–10 years	97	33.0	34.7	15.8	18.9
>10 years	47	12.8	22.9	5.7	8.6
p-value		<.01			<.05
Placement Moves					
None	106	15.1	34.1	7.7	12.1
One	390	16.4	25.9	8.7	9.6
Two	121	35.5	34.3	20.0	13.3
Three or more	123	72.4	53.9	45.2	28.7
p-value		<.001	<.001	<.001	<.001

[a] Analyses restricted to subjects age twenty-one and older in March 1988.

< .001). This difference persists even after controlling for moves related to delinquency. That is, children with behavior problems also had more moves for reasons other than delinquency than children without such problems ($M = 2.31$ versus $M = 1.2$ moves, $t(706) = 7.06$, $p < .001$). Finally, of the 124 children in this sample who made three or more moves, 65.3% ($n = 81$) were in the group characterized by both delinquency and abuse or neglect. This is a much higher percentage than would be expected to occur by chance, given that they represent only 13.1% of the entire sample.

Best outcomes. Children who appeared to have the best outcome in terms of delinquency and adult criminality (that is, the lowest arrest rates for delinquency, adult criminality, and violent criminal behavior) were those (1) who were youngest at the time of their first placement (those under one year of age did best); (2) for whom the first placement was for more than ten years; and (3) who did not make frequent moves.

Recognizing that there might be substantial overlap among children with these characteristics, outcomes were examined for the children who were less than one year old at the time of their first placement and who spent more than ten years in that placement. Only seven children in the sample met these joint criteria, and none of them had an official record of arrest for delinquency, adult criminality, or violent criminal behavior. Outcomes were also examined for children who were less than one year old at their first placement, spent at least seven years in that placement, and had only one subsequent move. Of the nineteen children who met these three criteria, two (10.5%) had arrests for delinquency, and none had arrests for adult criminality or violent crimes. The prognosis for children meeting this second set of joint criteria appeared to be quite favorable.

Discussion

The context of this study is important in interpreting the findings. These are cases of abuse and neglect from a midwestern juvenile court during the late 1960s and early 1970s. Thus, these cases occurred before the passage of the federal child abuse reporting laws and before the tremendous increase in reported child abuse cases. These findings are based on within-group analyses of children from families with multiple problems who are at high risk for a number of social problems. Given the early trauma they experienced because of the initial abuse or neglect incident and the subsequent processing through the juvenile court, there are probably few children in this group who are not at high risk. In addition, children in foster care and other kinds of placement are a particularly vulnerable group in that they have experienced both a disturbed family situation and separation from their natural parents. The majority of the children under study were placed outside the home.

The characteristics of their families were found to influence the placement decisions. Mothers and fathers with recorded problems (alcohol, mental, or physical) had the highest likelihood of having their children placed. Families who were the most disorganized (mother or father unknown or dead, no known relatives willing to care for the children, etc.) were also more likely to have children taken from the home. It is interesting to note that these findings are consistent with those of researchers from different periods (Jenkins & Sauber 1966) and different parts of the country (Runyan et al. 1982). Out-of-home placement of children is more likely to occur when the courts determine that potential supervision and guidance of the children is inadequate, when the mother is thought to be incapable (mental illness or alcohol problems), when the child has behavior problems, and when there are no other family members willing or able to care for the child. A certain logic thus appears to exist among decision makers.

In simple descriptive terms, the current findings regarding the amount of time in placement and the most frequent placement experiences may seem surprising. While many have assumed (or hoped) that foster care placements would be short-term and temporary, these findings indicate that, as much as twenty years ago, foster care was often a long-term placement (another result consistent with earlier research). The average amount of time spent in placement was about five years and sometimes lasted through childhood and adolescence.

One of the important findings from this research is the need to distinguish children who are placed because of abusive or neglectful home situations from those placed in part because of abuse or neglect but also as a result of their own delinquent behavior. Aggregating placement information for all abused and/or neglected children appears to obscure important differences in outcome. The small group of abused or neglected children with behavior problems noted in early childhood (sometimes as early as age five or six) and those abused or neglected children who experience frequent placement moves (from placement to placement or from foster home to foster home) must be distinguished from the majority of children, who may experience one relatively stable placement. The present results reveal the importance of looking beyond the issue of placement versus no placement, particularly in conjunction with the frequently described cyclical nature of foster care placements. One needs to differentiate between placements related to abuse or neglect and placements that are a function of behavior problems, of adolescent delinquency, and of associated detentions.

Mnookin (1973), for example, commented that the frequency of moves may depend on the child's adjustment before he or she enters foster care and cited Wiltse and Gambrill (1973): "A disturbed child who enters foster care is more likely to experience more numerous placements, and his symptoms increase accordingly." Similarly, commenting on the relationship between the number of foster home placements and subsequent delinquency, Runyan and Gould (1985) did not attribute causality to the association but pointed rather to the role of early behavior problems. In their study, children whose own behavior resulted in removal from their first foster home were 2.36 times more likely to become involved in delinquency than their peers in foster care who were moved for other reasons. Of the forty-two children in that study who moved from a second foster home, seven of the eight who were in legal difficulty had moved subsequently because their behavior was a problem for the foster parents.

In future research, it will be important to take into account the role of factors that influence placement decisions (family strengths or weaknesses) as well as characteristics of the child that may influence the success or lack of success of placement experiences. In their discussion of parenting breakdown, Quinton and Rutter (1988) noted that poorer outcomes may have resulted from genetically based vulnerabilities: "It cannot be assumed that institutional experiences would have had an equally deleterious effect if children's backgrounds were free of biological or psycho-social risks" (p. 204).

Scholars and practitioners have often criticized out-of-home placements, and foster care in particular, for deleterious consequences. The current findings suggest that, under certain circumstances, out-of-home placement experiences do not necessarily lead to negative effects. It is important to determine the characteristics of children who may benefit from out-of-home placement and those of children for whom these experiences may not be beneficial. There appears to be a small group of abused and neglected children who have behavior problems, which may in turn lead to frequent placement moves. The presence of these children may account for the high rates of delinquency, adult criminality, and violent criminal behavior often associated with children in foster care. Whether frequent moves reflect an early predisposition to antisocial behavior or are in part a response to it, children with numerous placements are in need of special services. Policies are needed that provide resources for this subgroup of abused and neglected children.

In this sample, the vast majority of abused and neglected children were placed outside the home during some part of their childhood. At present, it is unclear what proportion of children in foster care in the United States return home (Tatara 1989; Gershenson 1984). However, if it is determined that stability in placement is important, or that early placement under certain conditions is beneficial, then it may be necessary to make changes in the legal process to insure a greater degree of stability for the child. At the same time, there may be certain conditions under which children are better served by remaining at home.

The purpose of this analysis was to discover whether certain life experiences act to buffer or exacerbate earlier childhood experiences. While these findings offer some insight into the role of placement as a mediator, given the exclusive reliance on official records for both the independent and dependent variables, the time period investigated, and the geographic restrictiveness of this sample, caution is urged in interpreting and generalizing from these findings. Present-day foster care children may differ from the sample of children studied here in being older at the age of entry, staying in care for shorter periods because of the implementation of P.L. 96-272, and coming from families that may be more dysfunctional because of substance abuse, domestic violence, and homelessness.

The subjects in the present study are currently between the ages of eighteen and thirty-three, with the majority in their twenties. Since age is a predictor of adult criminal behavior (Widom 1989b), subjects under twenty-one were eliminated in analyses where age was an important factor. This restriction reveals a limitation of the current results. In a few years, it will be important to update the criminal history information: (1) to determine if overall rates of criminality and violence have increased in the sample as a whole; and (2) to determine whether the role of placement and foster care remains the same. It is clear that further research is needed to unravel the linkages among early childhood victimization, intervening variables, and later criminal and violent criminal behavior.

REFERENCES

Aber, J. L. (1980). The involuntary child placement decision: Solomon's dilemma revisited. In G. Ger, C. Ross, & E. Zigler (Eds.), *Child abuse: An agenda for action*. New York: Oxford University Press.

Bohman, M. & Sigvardsson, S. (1980). Negative social heritage. *Adoption and Fostering, 3*, 25–34.

Bryce, M. E. & Ehlert, R. C. (1977). 144 foster children. *Child Welfare, 50*, 499–503.

Canning, R. (1974). School experiences of foster children. *Child Welfare*, 53, 582–87.

Fanshel, D. (1981). Decision-making under uncertainty: Foster care for abused or neglected children? *American Journal of Public Health*, 71, 685–86.

Fanshel, D. & Shinn, E. B. (1978). *Children in foster care: A longitudinal investigation*. New York: Columbia University Press.

Fein, E., Maluccio, A. N., & Kluger, M. (1990). *No more parting: An examination of long-term foster family care*. Washington, D.C.: Child Welfare League of America.

Festinger, T. (1983). *No one ever asked us: A postscript to foster care*. New York: Columbia University Press.

Frank, G. L. (1980). Treatment needs of children in foster care. *American Journal of Orthopsychiatry*, 50, 256–63.

Garmezy, N. (1981). Children under stress: Perspectives on antecedents and correlates of vulnerability and resistance to psychopathology. In A. I. Rabin, J. Aronoff, A. M. Barclay, & R. A. Zucker (Eds.), *Further explorations in personality*. New York: John Wiley.

Gershenson, C. P. (1984). *Child welfare research notes*. Washington, D.C.: DHHS, Administration of Children, Youth and Families.

Groeneveld, L. P. & Giovannoni, J. M. (1977). The disposition of child abuse and neglect cases. *Social Work Research and Abstracts*, 13, 24–30.

Gruber, A. R. (1978). *Children in foster care*. New York: Human Sciences Press.

Hartstone, E. & Hansen, K. V. (1984). The violent juvenile offender: An empirical portrait. In R. A. Mathias (Ed.), *Violent juvenile offenders: An anthology* (pp. 83–112). San Francisco: National Council on Crime and Delinquency.

Hubbell, R. (1981). *Foster care and families: Conflicting values and policies*. Philadelphia: Temple University Press.

Jenkins, S. & Sauber, M. (1966). *Paths to child placement (family situations prior to foster care)*. New York: The Community Council of Greater New York.

Katz, M. H., Hampton, R. L., Newberger, E. H., Bowles, R. T., & Snyder, J. C. (1986). Returning children home: Clinical decision-making in cases of child abuse and neglect. *American Journal of Orthopsychiatry*, 56, 253–62.

Kent, J. T. (1976). A follow-up study of abused children. *Journal of Pediatric Psychology*, 1, 25–31.

Knitzer, J. & Allen, M. L. (1978). *Children without homes: An examination of public responsibility to children in out-of-home care*. Washington, D.C.: Children's Defense Fund.

Leitenberg, H., Burchard, J. D., Healy, D., & Fuller, E. J. (1981). Nondelinquent children in state custody: Does type of placement matter? *American Journal of Community Psychology*, 9, 347–60.

Littner, N. (1974). *Some traumatic effects of separation and placement.* New York: Child Welfare League of America.

Maluccio, A. N. & Fein, E. (1985). Growing up in foster care. *Child and Youth Services Review, 7*(2/3), 123–34.

Meier, E. (1965). Current circumstances of former foster children. *Child Welfare, 44,* 196–206.

Mnookin, R. H. (1973). Foster care: In whose best interest? *Harvard Educational Review, 43,* 599–638.

Palmer, S. E. (1979). Predicting outcomes in long-term foster care. *Journal of Social Service Research, 3,* 201–14.

Quinton, D. & Rutter, M. (1988). *Parenting breakdown: The making and breaking of inter-generational links.* Aldershot (England): Avebury.

Rojek, D. & Erikson, M. (1982). Delinquency careers: A test of the delinquent career escalation model. *Criminology, 20,* 5–28.

Ross, C. & Katz, M. (1983). Decision-making in a child protection agency. Manuscript, Yale University, New Haven.

Runyan, D. K. & Gould, C. L. (1985). Foster care for child maltreatment: Impact on delinquent behavior. *Pediatrics, 75,* 562–68.

Runyan, D. K., Gould, C. L., Trost, D. C., & Loda, F. A. (1982). Determinants of foster care placement for the maltreated child. *Child Abuse and Neglect, 6,* 343–50.

Schor, E. L. (1982). The foster care system and health status of foster children. *Pediatrics, 69,* 521–28.

Strasburg, P. (1978). *Violent delinquents: A report to the Ford Foundation (Vera Institute of Justice).* New York: Monarch Press (Simon and Schuster).

Tatara, T. (1989). Characteristics of children in foster care. *Division of Child, Youth, and Family Services Newsletter (American Psychological Association), 12*(3), 16–17.

Theis, S. V. S. (1924). *How foster children turn out.* New York: State Charities Aid Association.

Wald, M. S. (1976). State intervention on behalf of neglected children: Standards for removal of children from their homes, monitoring the status of children in foster care, and termination of parental rights. *Stanford Law Review, 28,* 625–706.

Weinberger, P. & Smith, P. (1970). The disposition of child neglect cases referred by caseworkers to a juvenile court. In A. Kadushin (Ed.), *Child welfare services: A sourcebook.* London: Macmillan.

Widom, C. S. (1989a). Child abuse, neglect, and adult behavior: Research design and findings on criminality, violence, and child abuse. *American Journal of Orthopsychiatry, 59,* 355–67.

Widom, C. S. (1989b). The cycle of violence. *Science, 244,* 160–66.

Widom, C. S. (1989c). The intergenerational transmission of violence. In N. A. Weiner & M. E. Wolfgang (Eds.), *Pathways to criminal violence* (pp. 137–201). Newbury Park, CA: Sage Publications.

Wiltse, K. T. & Gambrill, E. D. (1973). Decision-making processes in foster care. Unpublished paper, School of Social Welfare, University of California, Berkeley.

Wolfgang, M. E., Figlio, R. M., & Sellin, T. (1972). *Delinquency in a birth cohort.* Chicago: University of Chicago Press.

FOURTEEN

Implications of Research on the Welfare of Children Under Permanency Planning

Richard P. Barth and Marianne Berry

Child welfare policy has long endeavored to provide a permanent, safe, and familylike living situation for every child. Public Law 96–272, the Adoption Assistance and Child Welfare Act of 1980, stridently expresses the intent to ensure that "each child achieve placement in the least restrictive (most family-like) setting available and in close proximity to the parents' home, consistent with the best interests and special needs of the child" (Public Law 96–272 of 1980). Preventing foster care placement through family maintenance services and reunifying children in foster care with their birth or extended families are the foremost goals of permanency planning. If a child cannot remain with his or her birth or extended families, adoption is believed to provide the most permanent of homes. Guardianship is considered the next most preferable arrangement and permanent placement in long-term foster care the least preferable. This analysis considers the use and success of these child welfare services since national permanency planning legislation and presents recommendations for reform.

Whereas the priority of "permanent" placements is defined by law, the use and success of placements has other determinants. The risk that a child will be *reabused* in any placement is a specter that hangs over all child welfare planners and practitioners. The *stability* of "permanent" placements also deserves consideration in the assessment of preferred placements. Since placement moves are often costly to children, families, and communities, the true "permanence" of placements affects their desirability. A more neglected aspect of permanence involves the lasting legacy of the placement on the child's *development*. The influences of child welfare services on a child's developmental outcomes are often overlooked as a critical indicator of the success of their programs. The child's and family's *satisfaction* with the placement is a fourth indicator of the suitability of placement. This paper first reviews trends in the delivery of each service program for children and then considers the evidence concerning the relationship of placement prevention, reunification, adoption, guardianship, and long-term foster care to these four outcomes. Given the paucity of national data, we also draw on state data—especially data from California, which has nearly one of eight of the nation's children.

Child Welfare Service Programs

Placement Prevention

Federal child welfare legislation mandates that in each case, reasonable efforts be made (a) prior to the placement of a child in foster care to prevent or eliminate the need for removal of a child from his or her home, and (b) to make it possible for the child to return to his or her home (1986). "Reasonable efforts" are yet to be adequately defined, but even the most generous interpreters would not argue that reasonable efforts are made in each case prior to placement (Seaberg 1986; Ratterman, Dodson, & Hardin 1987). Reasonable efforts to reunify children with their birth parents are expected by the judiciary, but agencies are rarely held accountable for failing to provide reasonable efforts to prevent placement (Ratterman, Dodson, & Hardin 1987). The U.S. Supreme Court's recent decision rejecting the right of private citizens to enforce their right to receive reasonable efforts may undermine efforts to expand services in the area of placement prevention.

Although reasonable efforts can assume many forms, *intensive family preservation service* programs (IFPS) are one type of preventative service increasingly employed. These programs are based on the proposition that efforts to prevent placement should include prompt, comprehensive in-home services to improve family relations and keep the family together. This commitment is often expressed in round-the-clock availability of workers, application of a wide range of behavior-changing skills and community resources, and the ability to work to strengthen the family's ecological system. Unlike conventional child welfare services, intensive family preservation programs are short-term and labor-intensive, with workers serving only a few families at a time and cases typically closing within a few months. Intensive family preservation services differ from each other in theoretical orientation and format (Barth 1990a; Nelson, Landsman, & Deutelbaum 1990).

The extent of reasonable efforts is partially determined by the availability of these intensive placement prevention services (Hunner 1986; Seaberg 1986). Intensive placement prevention programs have become more widely available since the 1980 child welfare reforms. The *Directory of Family-Based Services* (National Resource Center on Family Based Services 1987) lists 131 "intensive family services" programs in 37 states. A full 34% of these programs were, however, located in Iowa, Minnesota, New York, or Wisconsin. Thirteen of the remaining states had only one program serving a caseload of only sixty to one hundred families per year. In 1991 alone, more than 5,000 staff in over 150 programs were trained in the Homebuilders model (*On the Line* 1992). A recent review of selected family preservation legislation enactments (National Conference of State Legislatures 1989) finds that state legislated programs in eight states are serving a large number of families yearly (e.g., 904 families in Iowa, 325 families in Illinois). Taken together, however, the total number of families receiving IFPS is probably less than thirty thousand each year. Given the roughly 1,000,000 substantiated cases of child abuse each year and the 224,000 new entries into foster care in 1991 (see Tatara this volume), family preservation services are still not available for the vast majority of families in need.

Family Maintenance and Reunification from Foster Care

Family maintenance services are voluntary or involuntary services delivered by public child welfare agencies to children and families in their own homes. Placement prevention services are a component of family maintenance and can be used to facilitate family reunification following temporary foster care; we discuss *placement prevention* separately from *family maintenance and reunification* here because the research about them is quite distinct. Family maintenance services are typically comprised of case management plus referral to a standard menu of services—especially parenting classes, alcohol and drug treatment, and employment counseling. Although good national data on family maintenance services are scarce, they appear to be brief. A recent survey of states (Tyler 1990) found that families receive placement prevention or reunification services for an average of four months. In 1989 in California, less than half of the family maintenance recipients received more than 3 months and the average was 5.6 months (State Department of Social Services 1990) of services. When family maintenance services are not appropriate or successful, efforts to reunify children who have been placed in foster care are now limited to eighteen or twenty-four months (Barth 1986).

The current directory of the National Resource Center on Family-Based Services (1987) describes thirty-nine home-based or family-centered programs in twenty states specifically aimed at reunifying families as part of their service. Intensive family reunification programs are also increasingly common (Albert, Bruer, Rutsch, Schmidt, & Zaro 1992). Most of these are private agencies who contract with county agencies. Of course, every county or state also serves reunified families under its own auspices.

The number of children in foster care has risen by 19% in the last nine years (U.S. Select Committee, November 1989). Recent increases in the number of children in foster care at any time must be considered in perspective. Figure 14.1 shows the respective changes in child abuse reports and foster care entries since 1982. Placement in foster care is not a reflex response by social workers to child abuse. It is certainly more difficult now to enter into foster care than at any time since 1980. Children in foster care continue to go home. Of the 178,000 children who left substitute care during fiscal year 1983 alone, over 100,000 (56%) were discharged to their biological families (Tatara 1989). Yet leaving foster care is becoming slower and less likely (Tatara this volume; Wulczyn & George 1992).

Adoption

If reunification cannot be achieved, adoption is the preferred alternative since it provides a substitute family that society accepts and that requires minimal surveillance or support from the state. The 1980s have brought a reduction of obstacles to the adoption of older children, such as the cost for special medical, educational, and psycholog-

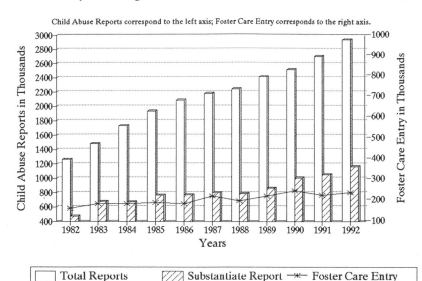

Child Abuse Reports correspond to the left axis; Foster Care Entry corresponds to the right axis.

FIGURE 14.1
Abuse Reports, Foster Care Entries, and Foster Care Entries per 10,000
Abuse Reports 1982–92

ical services; policies against adoptions by foster parents; and the automatic ruling out of children as adoptive candidates because they had failed in previous adoptive placements, are handicapped, or are adolescents.

Adoption of older children was intended to be a major contributor to the recent reduction of long-term foster care under permanency planning (Fein, Maluccio, Hamilton, & Ward 1983; Lahti et al. 1978). Recent concerns about the stability of adoptive placements of older children indicate only the slightest retrenchment from agency interest in promoting adoptive placements (Barth, Berry, Goodfield, Carson, & Feinberg 1986). Increased use of federal adoption subsidies partly indicates those efforts—they rose from $442,000 in 1981 to $132 million in 1990 (U.S. Select Committee on Finance 1990).

Yet, despite the stated preference for adoption in the law, in 1984 adoption was the planned placement goal for only 14% of the children in substitute care in the United States while long-term foster care was planned for 16% of the children in care. Only 11% were actually adopted (Maximus, Inc. 1984).

Adoption as a placement outcome depends both on adoption workers' perceptions of which children are adoptable and on the availability of adoptive homes. Many children have indeed been freed for adoption but continue to wait for an appropriate home. There are many other children also waiting who do not show up in these statistics, because adoption workers often wait until a specific home is available before freeing the child for adoption. Many children in foster care will never be freed or adopted. Adoption is unlikely for children who are in adolescence, and it is especially unlikely for black male children of any age (Maximus, Inc. 1984). In California the number of black children who are three years old or younger and in foster care without an adoption plan has tripled since 1989 and is approaching three thousand (Barth, Courtney, Berrick, & Albert in press).

Guardianship

Three exceptions to the preference for adoption are: (1) the parents have regularly visited the child and the child would benefit from continuing the relationship; (2) the child is twelve years old or older and does not wish to have her or his relationship with his parents legally severed; (3) the foster parents are unwilling to adopt, but the child would suffer if removed from their custody and placed for adoption. In such cases—which most often involve caregivers who are relatives of the child—guardianship is considered the preferred option. Guardianship is established by court order but does not require the termination of the birth parents' rights (Dodson 1984; Leashore 1984). Guardianship differs from state to state (and is not available to all foster children), but in general it provides guardians with the authority to make decisions about parenting without intervention of the child welfare agency. Guardians can authorize medical care and enter into other legal agreements for a child. Legal guardians generally cannot, however, obtain the financial assistance available to long-term foster and adoptive parents. In most states, guardians must have their own counsel and must initiate the guardianship petition. Such hindrances, in addition to the recency and ambiguity of the law, would suggest a relatively infrequent use of guardianship dispositions in permanent plans for children. Yet the importance of placing children with relatives is widely recognized and is an impetus for guardianship. In some states the percentage of cases with guardianship as the permanent plan is roughly equivalent to that of adoptions (State of California Legislative Analyst 1985); in California, guardianship has been planned for 9% of the children in foster care in recent years (Barth & Berry 1989).

Long-term Foster Care

Long-term foster care is not a preferred option. Reducing the extensive use of long-term foster care was a clear reason for the Adoption Assistance and Child Welfare Act. Various studies prior to 1980 basically agreed that stays in foster care were too long. Maas and Engler (1959) found that 31% of the children in foster care had been there for ten years; Fanshel and Shinn (1978) found that 36% of the children in foster care were still in foster care five years later; and Magura (1981) reported that 22% of the children in boarding foster family care had been there for six years or more. These stays have been reduced. By 1984 only 10% of the children in foster care had been there for six years or more, and by 1988 this percentage was close to five years (Tatara 1989; Tatara this volume). Nationally, the median length of time in foster care declined from 2.4 years in 1977 to 1.4 years in 1988 (Tatara in this volume).

Placement of children with relatives has begun to dominate reunification foster care in the last few years. In many large states, nearly half of the placements are in such kinship homes, and because reunification is less expedient from "kinship" foster homes, more than half of all children in foster care may soon reside in kinship foster care. How many of these children will later be redesignated as long-term foster care children is unclear, but the percentage is likely to be very high given the low likelihood of reunification or adoption by relatives. Due to these developments, we are seeing a reversal of the decline in the ages of children in foster care and the length of stay that characterized the last decade.

Foster placement is, of course, influenced by the success of placement prevention and reunification efforts, and these efforts are more successful with families of younger children. As a result, about half of the 276,000 children in foster care in fiscal year 1985 were thirteen years old or older; about 50,000 were aged sixteen or seventeen (Maximus, Inc. 1987). In 1985, 9.4% of the children in placement "aged out" of foster care, but by 1989 that percentage was reduced to 5.9% (this 37% decline is partly attributable to the 18% decline in children aged fifteen to eighteen in the population during those years). Large numbers of teens will continue to age out of foster care to live on their own, and these teens need to be equipped with the necessary skills and resources to facilitate independent and productive living upon discharge.

Passage of 99–272, the Independent Living Skills Initiative, has been instrumental to the improvement of services to youth who will emancipate from foster care. Services typically include life skills training and employment preparation. The extent to which these interventions address the serious challenges facing youths emancipated from foster care is only beginning to be assessed.

Service Outcomes

The child welfare reform provided many new mandates that have been accompanied by a modicum of new resources. Whereas most evaluations critique compliance with regulations and procedures, the most critical research questions concern outcomes: are children safe or reabused, in stable or transient situations, achieving developmental outcomes or falling further behind, and satisfied or dissatisfied with the services they receive?

Abuse During Care

Child welfare services aim to protect children from reabuse but, at best, only reduce it. The likelihood of reabuse varies with the type of placement; reabuse is most likely when the children are returned home and least likely when they are adopted.

The effectiveness of intensive family preservation programs in reducing reabuse is difficult to determine because these programs are not limited exclusively to abusive families. Whereas the majority of families served suffers from interaction problems, which can include abuse and neglect, the services may also be aimed at reducing running away or other family conflicts. The number of families still intact at termination can be used as an approximate indicator of the reduction of abuse during treatment with some caution about its validity as the only indicator of the programs' effectiveness.

The sample sizes of placement prevention program evaluations vary, with many studies evaluating fewer than one hundred families. One larger evaluation of the Homebuilders program in Washington reports a placement prevention rate of 82% at termination among

216 families (Pecora, Fraser, Haapala, & Bartlome 1987). Overall, family preservation programs report termination success rates of 55% to 94%.

Another large study of 367 families served by the In-Home Family Care programs in San Francisco and Oakland, California, indicates that only 6% of the families evaluated had been reported by Family Care workers to child protective services because of abuse or neglect either while in treatment or soon afterward (Berry 1992). In this program, the largest gains during treatment were made in the parents' child care skills, particularly in disciplining. These skills, on the average, continued to improve after the services had ended, as judged by workers at one-month, six-months, and one-year follow-up visits. Children were especially likely to remain in the home when the parents' disciplining skills continued to improve after the service.

Studies comparing the outcomes of intensive family preservation services to control groups receiving traditional placement prevention and family maintenance services are scarce. The best of these studies cannot yet demonstrate whether intensive services are more successful at preventing placement.

Feldman (1990) reports on a New Jersey experiment for youths at risk of entering out-of-home care. The approach was fairly faithful to the Homebuilders model. At the follow-up after one year, the treatment group (54% of families had a child enter placement) had slightly outperformed the controls (58% had a child enter placement) although the differences were not statistically significant. Differences between groups continued to be sharpened eighteen months after services, and the groups were significantly different by 1992 (L. Feldman, personal communication, October 1992).

Fraser, Pecora, and Haapala (1991) evaluated intensive family preservation services (IFPS), focusing on Homebuilders-based programs in Washington and Utah. Their case outcome data show that 67% of the children served were at home at the twelve-months follow-up, and the remainder spent at least two weeks in a more restrictive setting, with 28% in foster care or a more intensive placement, and 8% were with friends or had run away. A subpopulation of families who were on a case overflow list and a matched group of IFPS families showed that the comparison group (59% placement rate) fared considerably worse than the IFPS families (15% placement rate). Among the 427 reasons for placement identified by IFPS therapists and supervisors in the larger study, 24 reasons (6%) described either emotional abuse, sexual abuse, or neglect. The most rigorous family preservation study to date assessed the impact of Family First family preservation initiative in Illinois during the first four years of the program (Schuerman, Rzepnicki, Littell, & Chak 1993). The service model involved delivery of services by community-based agencies, with teams of social workers and paraprofessional for three-month periods. The evaluation designed involved random assignment of approximately sixteen hundred clients to treatment and control. Overall, the Family First program resulted in no reduction in the placement rate for children receiving placement prevention services above the 7% placement rate in the regular services control group. When placement did occur, there was no difference between Family First and control group clients in the length or type of placement. Overall, the program had no impact on confirmed subsequent reports of maltreatment for children who remained at home. At one year after case assignment 25% of families experienced a confirmed report of abuse or neglect and within two years 34% experienced reabuse. The most positive outcomes from the study indicated that parents reported a greater sense of control in their families and that child behavior problems were somewhat reduced (Rzepnicki this volume).

The evidence is mounting that family preservation programs may not have a substantial impact on foster care placement rates. These services may offer their greatest benefit by providing families with a positive experience as a child welfare service client and, thereby, encouraging help seeking or help using when they are again at risk of breaking up.

Family Maintenance and Reunification. Conventional family maintenance services reach a growing proportion of children who receive some form of child welfare services. Yet, their capacity to prevent abuse is still unclear. A follow-up of families ($n = 389$) given intensive placement prevention or family reunification services five years after these services provides another estimate of reabuse rates (Jones 1983). Among the families provided with such services, 17% had charges of maltreatment brought against them. In contrast, families who had received standard services had a 22% reabuse rate. In only a third of the cases were families functioning adequately at the time the case was closed. The other cases were closed for other reasons.

Another important five-year study of a pilot permanency planning project (Wald, Carlsmith, & Leiderman 1988) compared nineteen five- to ten-year-old white children remaining at home and receiving extensive family maintenance services and thirteen children of similar ages and circumstances who were placed in foster care rather than given services at home. The reabuse rates for the children given services at home were high: two were sexually abused; five continued to be hit severely although not injured enough to receive medical treatment; and four continued to be neglected. Of six other children who were returned home after an initial period of foster care, two were abused again, and two were neglected again.

A study in North Carolina compared abused children between the ages of eleven and eighteen who were subsequently moved into foster care ($n = 114$) to those who received services in their own homes ($n = 106$) (Runyan & Gould 1985). These children were matched on age, race, sex, time of abuse, relationship to abuser, and services provided. Children remaining in their own homes suffered a reabuse rate of 25% whereas 11% of children in foster care were abused, and half of these were abused by their birth parents during reunification visits. When excluding reabuse by birth parents of children in foster care, the risk for children at home was nearly five times higher than for children in foster care. Recent California data indicate that 40% of the cases provided with family maintenance services in 1989 had previously been terminated from child welfare services—this was up from 29% in 1985 (State of California Department of Social Services 1986, 1990). Of those, only a small group (3%) had first received out-of-home care; the majority had previously been given in-home services.

Adoption. Most studies of adoptive families find extremely low rates of abuse. Sack and Dale found that not one of twelve children (with an average age of five and one-half years) with histories of physical abuse prior to adoption were reabused despite the difficulties of an adoption breakdown (Sack & Dale 1982). Of the eighty-two disruptions studied by Boneh, 20% resulted from the agency's request for the child's removal, but fewer than 10% involved abuse by the adoptive parents (Boneh 1979). Barth and Berry (1988) found reabuse an even rarer reason for disruption. Since adoption disruptions occur in about 11% of all adoptions of older children (Barth et al. 1988), abuse of adoptive children would be about 1%. National studies of child abuse and neglect confirm this estimate indicating that adoptive parents are alleged perpetrators in 1.0% of all reports despite their representation of approximately 3% in the population at large, indicating that adoptive placements are unusually safe (Russell & Trainor 1984).

Guardianship. Rates of reabuse in guardianship cannot be reliably estimated from available data. Given that most guardians have been foster parents or relatives with close ties to the children, the rates may fall between those for adoption and long-term foster care.

Long-term Foster Care. McFadden's (1985) review of abuse in foster care in twenty-seven states found that complaints were filed against 0.3% to 6.7% of foster homes, and substantiated complaints ranged from 0.2% to 2.7% of the homes. The reabuse rates per child could be considerably less than that since foster homes typically have more than two children, and abuse allegations do not always involve all children. The national studies on child abuse and neglect confirm that foster parents are alleged abusers in 0.5% of all child abuse reports (Russell & Trainor 1984). A study of child abuse in Arizona concluded that about 7% of the foster child population is allegedly abused by foster parents (Bolton, Laner, & Gai 1981). One of the thirteen children placed in foster care in the study by Wald and colleagues was exposed to excessive physical punishment and one to emotional abuse (Wald et al. 1988). An effort to estimate abuse rates in *residential care* yielded a complaint rate of 0.4% among 1,000 children and a confirmed complaint rate of 0.9% among more than 69,000 children in care (Rindfleisch & Rabb 1984). Given that children in group care are more than twice as likely to be identified as difficult to control as are children in foster care, these abuse rates in group care are predictably higher than those for foster care (Fitzharris 1985). Fanshel, Finch, and Grundy (1990) found that 24% of girls and 8% of boys reported that someone in their foster family had tried to take advantage of them sexually. The responses do not indicate whether this person was an adult or peer. A quarter of the youths indicated they had experienced severe physical punishment in the foster home.

The Stability of Permanent Placements

A "permanent" placement is one that is intended, but not guaranteed, to last forever. Even though the law seeks permanence for children, whether in their own homes or with other families, permanence cannot be legislated. Replacement is inevitable in responsible child welfare services. Overall, while all types of placements are subject to disruption, adoption appears to be the most stable of outcomes and long-term foster care the least stable.

Family Maintenance and Reunification

A comparative study of eleven family-based preplacement prevention programs in six states (National Resource Center on Family Based Services 1988) found placement rates of 4% to 25% in the eleven programs, with an average placement prevention rate of 84%. Another study of fourteen placement prevention programs in Wisconsin (Landsman 1985) found a prevention rate of 82%.

Family preservation programs are intensive and time-limited, usually serving clients within a one- to two-month period. Despite this short service time, the numbers of families deemed at risk of placement who continue to remain intact after leaving services are quite high. Homebuilders reports preservation rates of 94% to 97% at three months following treatment and 88% at one year after treatment. The Oregon Intensive Family Support program has a 73% success rate at one year after treatment (Showell 1985). The Children's Home Society In-Home Family Care program reports an 88% success rate one year after completion of services (Berry 1992).

A study of forty-two adolescents (Wells & Whittington 1993) and their families who received family preservation services found that by twelve months after the intervention 41% of the children moved from their birth parents' home (either returning to foster care, living with relatives, or living on the streets). Of all the children in the study, 20% returned to a formal child welfare placement.

Evidence on children who are placed in out-of-home care, go back to their own homes, and then return to foster care suggests an increase in recidivism since permanency planning. Fanshel and Shinn (1978) assessed 624 children three times over five years. The children had been in foster care at least ninety days and either remained there ($n = 227$) or returned home ($n = 350$) and had a 16% recidivism rate. Lahti and associates (1978) conducted a study of many foster children, comparing foster care cases in Oregon who were served by a three-year project "Freeing Children For Permanent Placement," ($n = 259$) and a control group of children in care ($n = 181$). They reported that 20% of the children in their project were returned to out-of-home care following reunification efforts. Block and Libowitz (1983) found that 27% of children who had been reunified were subsequently placed again in foster care. Fein and her colleagues (1983) indicate a repeat placement rate of 32%. Two years after reunification, 70% of the children in foster care in the study of Wald and associates were still living in a permanent home—a percentage roughly equal to that of the children given in-home services (Wald et al. 1988). A study of 779 children who had been in foster care at least two years in Connecticut at the beginning of 1985 indicates that most placements were stable; two-thirds of the children had had only one or two placements; a quarter of the foster parents were planning to adopt their foster children; and three quarters of the youngsters were expected to remain indefinitely with their foster parents (Fein, Maluccio, & Kluger 1990).

Recent findings based on data from twenty-three states indicate that 49% of the children in foster care at the end of 1985 had more than one placement during the preceding three years. Including the current placement, 26% of the children had experienced three or more placements during the preceding three years (Tatara et al. 1987). A full 25% of the children who entered foster care during 1985 had been in the system before—within the preceding twelve months alone. Just as children moved from foster home to foster home in the 1970s, it has been posited that they may now be moving from foster care back home and then back into foster care (Pelton 1989).

A study by Goerge, Hartnett, Testa, and Wulczyn (1986) followed case histories of all the children in foster care in Illinois between July 1, 1976, and May 31, 1984. Their numbers reflect the differences in the reentry rates between the 1970s (before permanency planning) and the 1980s. Nearly one-third of the children admitted to foster care in 1976 were discharged in fiscal year 1977 and later readmitted. In 1978 the reentry rate was 30% and in 1979 it was 29%. Data also showed that the reentry rates during those years were highest for children whose stay in foster care was less than ninety days and for children between the ages of ten and fourteen at the time of their first placement. These findings appear stable and generalizable. From 1984 to 1986, the current decade and other settings, the total number of cumulative admissions (new plus reentrants) in New York City was higher by 1,165 children than the total number of children discharged. Of this surplus, reentrants made up 64% in 1984, 100% in 1985, and 75% in 1986. New admissions had only a marginal effect on the New York City caseload over the three-year period before 1987.

Longer stays in placement are associated with more stable reunifications. Between 1984 and 1985 in New York state, nearly twenty thousand white, black, and Hispanic children were discharged from the foster care system. Of these, 22% were later returned to foster care. Regardless of age or ethnicity, children who were between the ages of ten and twelve at the time of their first placement had the highest reentry rates. One-third of these children returned to care. Once again, children who experienced placements lasting less than ninety days had the highest rates of reentry. More than one-third of the 1984 and 1985 cohort members who were discharged within ninety days of their placement later returned to foster care. Reentry rates drop to between 29% (1984) and 28% (1985) among children who were in their first placement between 91 and 180 days. For children in placement between six months and one year, the reentry rate was 19% for the 1984 cohort and 18% for 1985. Lower return-to-care rates were observed in California with 13% of children returning at one year and 17% and 18% returning at two and three years, respectively (Courtney, Needell, & Barth 1993). The lower rate may be partially attributable to different sampling strategies. the California study involved a cohort of children who entered care in one six-month period and, therefore, oversamples children who stay longer (Wulczyn, personal communication, July 20, 1993). An evaluation of the Michigan family preservation program, know as Families first, contrasted the placement rates for children receiving family preservation services with those of children who had recently been released from foster care (Berquist, Szwejda, & Pope 1993). Children receiving family preservation services had a 24% placement rate over twelve months after the intervention, whereas 35% of children in the latter group were returned to foster care within twelve months of their return home.

Adoption

As a result of P. L. 96–272 and allied changes in child welfare policy, larger numbers of older and special needs children are entering adoptive placements. The rate of adoption disruptions has apparently risen since the advent of recent permanency planning reforms. The disruption rate in Kadushin and Seidl's study of adoptions of older children before permanency planning was less than 3% (Kadushin & Seidl 1971). Boneh (1979) reported ninety-six disruptions from 1970 to 1979 in the Massachusetts Department of Public Welfare, with the caveat that this is a low estimate due to the lack of systematic reporting of disruptions. Fein, Davies, and Knight (1979) found that 31% of adoptions were disrupted by the end of their five-year follow-up period; this rate was equivalent to the recidivism rate for children returned home.

Cohen (1984) reported a disruption rate of 7% per year for adoptions of older children in Canada. Boyne and colleagues (Boyne, Denby, Kettenring, & Wheeler 1984) reported a 23% disruption rate in their study of adoptive placements. Older children had still higher rates: 47% of the adoptions of children aged between twelve and seventeen were disrupted, compared to 25% of those involving children aged between nine and eleven, 15% of those involving children aged between six and eight, and 7% of those with children up to age five. California data suggest a modest increase in disruption rates since permanent planning began to be implemented, showing a rather stable rate of 8.7% throughout the 1970s and of 11% between 1980 and 1984 (Barth & Berry 1988).

Block and Libowitz (1983) alternately found all thirty-two adoptees in their study who had been discharged from foster care remaining in their initial adoptive homes at the end of the two-year study period. The Oregon Project's policy of "aggressive adoption" resulted in sixty—four adoptions and only two disruptions in the following fourteen months (Lahti 1982). Festinger's (1986) study of 897 adoptive placements in New York found an 8.2% disruption rate. Another large study of 235 adoptions of older children found a disruption rate of 9.4% (Partridge, Hornby, & McDonald 1986). Groze's (1986) study of ninety-one adoptions of children with special needs reports a 14% disruption rate. Since none of these studies followed the adopted children to adulthood, they consistently (but, we think, modestly) underestimate the true disruption rates.

Intensive adoption preservation programs may be able to reduce the disruption rate still further. In one pilot program, 92% of the families who were at the point of disruption and received intensive in-home services were preserved at the end of therapy (Prew 1990); no follow-up data are reported. In a second pilot project with similarly positive initial findings, a one-year follow-up found that nearly 50% of the adoptions had been disrupted (Barth 1991). This may still exceed base rates, as prior research shows that roughly 80% of the families considering disruption and contacting the agency for help, will later disrupt the adoption (Barth & Berry 1989).

Guardianship

Guardianship may allow the child to live in a familiar environment (e.g., in a foster home where he or she has lived for the past few years or with relatives) without terminating contact with his or her original family. This allows a compromise between severance of ties to either family and may add stability to the foster placement (Derdeyn, Rogoff, & Williams 1978). No probability samples of the permanency of guardianships are available. Anecdotal evidence suggests that guardianships are not vulnerable to breakdown—of nine guardianships developed in San Mateo County in California between 1978 and 1981, four had ended by 1987—and that the commitments of foster parents who agree to become guardians of young children may wither when those children reach adolescence (Ten Broeck & Barth 1986).

Long-Term Foster Care

Long-term foster care is intended to be permanent. However, for many children it is not. Fein and colleagues (1983) reported a 50% repeat placement rate among their fourteen children in permanent foster homes. All repeat placements involved children aged nine or older. Stone and Stone (1983) found a breakdown rate of 49%; Block and Libowitz (1983) reported a recidivism rate of 28%. More than 20% of youths who left the Casey Family Program (Fanshel, Finch, & Grundy 1989) foster care returned to their biological or adopted families, 37% emancipated at age eighteen, and 18% emancipated before age eighteen. One quarter ran away or were returned to agency or court jurisdiction at exit—these were the least successful outcomes. Recent reports are far more sanguine about the likelihood that a child will not move more than once during his or her tenure in foster care, perhaps because long-term foster care is now reserved for older children with no other placement options (Lawder, Poulin, & Andrews 1985).

Taber and Proch (1987) studied fifty-one teens in foster care and found that they had a median of nine foster placements with a range from three to thirty-three. The likelihood of repeat placement increased as the foster children got older, and their stays in foster homes grew shorter with each new placement. Long-term foster care for teens is often a contradiction, with each placement more of a trial for foster parent and child. Many foster children also run away before they age out of foster care; a full 20% of the children leaving substitute care in California in 1984 ran away (Maximus, Inc. 1984).

Measurable Developmental Outcomes

Although the "best interest of the child" is not the sole determinant of a placement, this concept continues to influence placement decisions. Perhaps the outcomes most closely aligned with this standard are the child's health and educational and social growth. Measurable developmental outcomes seem to be least favorable for children returned home. This section reviews measurable child welfare services effects on children.

Placement Prevention

The evaluation of fourteen placement prevention programs in Wisconsin (Landsman 1985) found that, overall, families achieved significant improvement, as rated by caseworkers, in mental health, reduction of child abuse and neglect, substance abuse, social isolation, and law violations. Children significantly improved in school performance, mental health, and behavior.

In an evaluation by Nelson and colleagues (National Resource Center on Family Based Services 1988) of eleven family-based placement prevention programs in six states, family preservation was associated with the following changes during services: improvements in behavior, material resources, family structure, family dynamics, emotional climate, perceptions of problems, community perceptions of the family, informal support network, and community involvement. Those families who had children removed had made significant declines in behavior, family dynamics, emotional climate, community perception of the family, and community involvement. Overall, the largest numbers of families made gains in behavior (70%), family relationships (65%), and emotional climate (64%), and the fewest made improvements in material resources (21%), and use of services (47%). Given the short-term nature of these preventive programs, this study does not answer the nagging question of the longevity of these families' gains, particularly since the greatest gains were made in the more intangible and elusive skills.

One evaluation of Homebuilders reports that the majority of families improved in the child's school attendance, hyperactivity, delinquent acts, and peer problems as judged by the parent or a therapist at the end of treatment (Kinney, Haapala, Booth, & Leavitt 1989). However, all families were judged to have remained the same regarding medical problems or physical handicaps, and the majority of families made no improvements regarding alcohol abuse or learning disabilities.

Another evaluation of Homebuilders looked at school adjustment, delinquent behavior, home-related behavior, and cooperation with the agency (Pecora, Fraser, Haapala, & Bartlome 1987). Except for cooperation, children in the program made significant positive improvements during service. Parents also made significant improvements in their supervision of younger children, their parenting of older children, their attitudes toward preventing placement, and their knowledge of child care. In the Utah Family Preservation program (Fraser & Haapala 1991), children made significant gains in school adjustment and behavior, and parents improved in parenting behavior, attitudes, and knowledge.

The families served by the Illinois Family First program, when interviewed sixteen months after random assignment to the program or control group, had (after controlling for their higher levels of problems at intake) fewer problems in physical child care, children's academic adjustment, and parental coping (Schuerman, Rzepnicki, Littell, & Chak 1993). In each of these domains, Family First parents reported more problems at the time of referral and fewer problems at the follow-up interview than regular services cases. In six other domains (i.e., housing, economic conditions, discipline, children's conduct, children's symptoms, and victimization of children) the mean proportions of problems were unchanged over time, and there was no difference between groups.

Family Reunification

Studies consistently show that children who are returned home from foster care have significant developmental vulnerabilities. Children returned home did not achieve as high IQ scores as those who remained in foster care over a five-year period in Fanshel and Shinn's study (1978). Those authors do caution, however, against overreliance on measured outcomes rather than on the unmeasurable characteristics of the child's emotional experience. Nor did children returned home score as high on adjustment as children in out-of-home placements (Lahti et al. 1978). Another study of 187 children either in foster care or at home found that older children (aged between eleven and sixteen) in their birth homes had significantly lower school attendance than their counterparts in foster homes or group homes (Leitenberg, Burchard, Healy, & Fuller 1981). Older dependent children returned to their birth homes also had significantly more police contact than foster children. Kinard found that having mothers with emotional problems, as indicated by psychiatric referrals, had detrimental consequences to emotional development of children while being placed away from home did not (Kinard 1982). Compared to children given services in foster care, children served at home in the study by Wald and colleagues (1988) received worse physical care, attended school less frequently, and achieved less in school. Self-esteem improved for both groups whereas social behavior with teachers and peers at school deteriorated for in-home children but not for foster children. Nearly half of the children in both settings still seemed at substantial risk at the end of two years. Even after a caveat that younger children might benefit even more from foster care than the school-age children in their study, Wald and associates conclude that unless interventions significantly improve parental functioning, children left at home remain at substantial risk (Wald et al. 1988).

Adoption

Although most adoptions resulting from permanency planning involve older children, the bulk of adoption research is about infant adoptions. Recent writings based on interviews with adult adoptees who are searching for their birth parents emphasize the difficulties rather than the benefits of adoption (e.g., Deykin, Campbell, & Patti 1984). The studies vary in sophistication and tend to rely on adoptee samples who are seeking treatment, an obviously skewed group. These studies are too numerous and generally unrepresentative to completely consider here—see Brodzinsky (1987) for a review—but suggest that adjustment to adoption is usually neither simple nor traumatic.

Evidence that adopted children have higher educational achievement than foster children is indirect but persuasive. Bachrach (1983) found that compared to children living with biological parents, adopted children are more likely to live in two-parent homes, enjoy a higher household income, have fewer siblings, and have an older, more highly educated mother not working outside the home. The latter predicts the likelihood of the child's successful education and employment. Rosenthal, Motz, Edmonson, and Groze (1991) found that 99% of the adopted children with special needs aged between six and seventeen were attending school even though 28% of the parents reported that their children had some learning disabilities. The typical (modal) adopted child had a B average.

In a longitudinal study of transracial adoptees (generally black children growing up in white homes) and their families, Simon and Alstein (1987) found that of the 111 transracial adoptees (median age: 14.9) in the study 82% graduated from college, were in college, or planned to continue on to college, and 13% planned to go on to some other type of school. The respondents expressed various occupational goals, but the most frequently cited fields were law, business, teaching, and computers. The median grade point average for the transracial adoptees in the study was 2.5. In light of the fact that students with a B average are five times more likely to finish school than students with a D average (*The Condition of Education* 1986), it follows that most of these youths will graduate. Roughly 20% of Americans aged eighteen and older completed a degree beyond high school in 1984 (U.S. Bureau of the Census 1984). Yet, even if only one-third of those adoptees who aspired to go to college or vocational/technical school will succeed in completing a degree beyond high school, the rate becomes 28% for the adoptees in the study. In the general population in 1985, the participation rate of high school graduates between the ages of eighteen and twenty-four in postsecondary institutions was 21.8%. Thus, adoption seems to promote educational attainment.

The educational achievement of adopting parents is high. More than one-fifth of the adoptive mothers of children with special needs who adopted through public agencies in California in 1990 and 1991 had a college degree or postgraduate education; more than half had some college or higher; adoptive fathers were still more educated. The academic performance of adopted children is, therefore, likely to be above the national norms. Indeed, Scarr and Weinberg (1976) found that children adopted into homes of parents with high educational attainment showed considerably higher IQ scores than their birth parents and the mean of the general population. These advantages for adopted children are particularly significant given that the typical occupations of the birth mothers were office worker, nurse's aide, and student—a rather well-positioned comparison group with the modal educational attainment of high school graduation. This is approximately the current educational level of foster parents in California and may be considerably higher than that of the birth parents whose children now enter the child welfare system. A recent study found that 84.1% of the foster parents in California had at least a high school diploma; 18.1% had attained a college degree (Berrick, Needell, & Barth in press). Among the adoptive parents who used public agencies in California, 36% had some college education and an additional 25% were college graduates or had postgraduate education. This suggests that the educational outcomes for children adopted by foster parents would be as substantial as the foster parents' educational advantages over the birth parents. In support, a little known French study (Dumaret 1985) is one of a kind in comparing children born to the same mother who either remained with their mothers, were adopted as infants, or resided in foster or group care. When compared to either control group (or the national norms for the general population), the adopted group surpassed all other comparison groups in school performance and IQ. Scarr and Weinberg (1976) conclude that adoption is a comprehensive ecological system to promote the welfare of a child. Rutter (1980) concurs that adoption is the one intervention that clearly makes a major, positive, long-term difference in the life of a child.

Other evidence on the outcomes of adoptions of older children is sparse. Among thirty children placed at two years of age or older (Tizard 1977), 84% showed satisfactory progress and attachment capacity more than two years later. In a study involving much older children (placed between the ages of five and twelve), 85% of the children made successful adjustments, and 73% of the parents were much more satisfied than dissatisfied with their adoption (Kadushin 1970). McRoy and colleagues (1982) found no differences in self-esteem between transracially and inracially adopted children—and when they compared them to the norm. The sample's mean age at the time of the study was 13.5 years and ages at the time of placement ranged from one to fourteen years. Lahti (1982) found that children placed in adoptive and fost-adopt placements fared better in family adjustment and emotional and developmental functioning than did children returned home or placed in long-term foster care. Children in adoptive placements did especially well in school functioning. However, 62% of the adopted children were less than three years old when placed.

Guardianship

To date, developmental outcomes for children in guardianship have not been investigated. In general, however, guardianship status may facilitate development by protecting a child against the return of custody to the birth parents when this would harm the child's development and by providing a stable environment.

Long-term Foster Care

Studies of children who have grown up in foster care provide guidance for policymakers and program planners concerned with the welfare of children who remain in foster care until discharged to their own care. Harrari's (1980) study of thirty-four adolescents who had left foster care within five years of entry and were not returned to their foster homes found their self-reports on a personality inventory to be indistinguishable from those of the general population. Kraus's (1981) investigation of almost five hundred former foster children found that time in placement and placement continuity were unrelated to later law violations; no comparisons to children raised in their own homes were drawn. Triseliotis and Russell (1984) found that children raised in foster or residential care grew up to have higher social class than their birth families. Contrary to other studies, Runyan and Gould (1985) found that foster parents reported more behavioral problems of their foster children than did natural parents for children maintained in their own homes (39% versus 12%). The authors caution, however, that these rates may be higher because of the foster parents' increased sensitivity to, and awareness of, behavioral difficulties.

A follow-up study of sixty-one former foster children from New Orleans who were between the ages of nineteen and twenty-nine at the time of the interview found that their educational achievement was lower than that of the general population in New Orleans or than that of a group matched according to minority status (Zimmer-

man 1982). More than half of the foster children had dropped out of
school. The students in foster care, on the average, had dropped
out before the eleventh grade. Those with the poorest educational
preparation had the most problems as adults. Most (75%) members
of the sample were self-supporting, but slightly more than one-third
lived at or below the poverty line. More than 10% were incarcerated
at the time of the study. Nearly half reported needing or seeking
mental health services. About 5% of the sample had been hospitalized
for mental illness at some time after foster care. A majority of the
youths appraised their lives as currently satisfactory or hopeful. Consistent with other research (Shostack & Quane 1988) youths discharged from foster care after a longer stay were found more likely to
be in the group that was functioning better.

Festinger (1983) found no differences between the outcomes for
her ex-foster children from New York City (and now adult respondents) and the population at large on most characteristics including
arrests, self-esteem, and happiness. Former foster children did have
significant shortcomings in educational and employment success.
Continued contact with the foster parents or ongoing contact with
the birth parents during the tenure in foster care were again associated with better outcomes.

A large study of former foster children in West Virginia shows that
young people who have aged out of foster care after an average of
five years in the system have rates of marriage, broken marriages,
incarceration, parenthood, and marital satisfaction that are comparable to those for the general population (Jones & Moses 1984). Former foster children lagged behind their peers in education by one year
and often had problems with alcohol (20%). The study also found
that 19% of the sample's own children were or had been in foster
care; this is an exceptionally high rate not found in other studies.
Overall, 62% were at least "mostly satisfied" with their lives. Most
(75%) of the former foster children were living with family, including
a spouse or partner, foster or adoptive parents, birth parents, other
relatives, such as grandparents or siblings, or their own children.

A follow-up study of fifty-five youths (average age of twenty-one)
who left foster care between 1980 and 1988 found numerous other
difficulties in living (Barth 1990b). More than half had not graduated
from high school before leaving foster care, and 38% had not obtained high school equivalency diplomas at the time of the study;
almost one-third had gone through a time when they either had no

home or moved weekly; about two-thirds reported that they sometimes or often worried about running out of money and food; 44%
indicated a serious illness, and 24% reported a hospitalization since
leaving foster care, but just 33% had health insurance; 33% drank
four or more drinks a day or used street drugs more than once per
day. The youths in the study reported high levels of depression, and
13% had been hospitalized for mental illness since leaving foster care.
Nearly half had been on AFDC or GA or often had problems paying
for food or housing.

Fanshel, Finch, and Grundy (1989) reported on children who had
on the average left the exemplary Casey Family Foster Care Program
seven years earlier. Their findings indicate that one-third of them were
below their age-appropriate school grade levels when entering their
care, and that this proportion was unchanged at the time of departure.

Discharged foster youths do not fare as well as the general population. They resemble individuals living below the poverty line with
respect to educational status, childbirth, and reliance on welfare.

In a study of independent living services for 291 adolescents between the ages of sixteen and twenty-one (mean age: eighteen) discharged from the care and custody of public child welfare agencies,
only 28% had completed high school at the time of discharge (Westat
1986). In a subsequent study of adaptation after leaving foster care
(Westat 1991), 810 youths were interviewed two and one-half to four
years after their discharge from foster care. At the time of their
discharge from foster care, 35% of the youths had completed high
school; 54% had finished high school by the end of the study as
compared to 78% of the general population at a similar age. This
54% figure closely resembles the high school completion rate of
children living below the poverty level (53%) and is significantly
lower than the 74.6% high school completion rate for the general
population (Westat 1991). One of the major findings of the study was
that "High school completion prior to discharge led to better outcomes, regardless of skills training" (Westat 1991:xiii). (This sample
had also received services that most foster youths do not receive.)
Only 4.9% of the youths in the Westat study had some college or had
completed college. This is half the rate of the adoptees in the Simon
and Alstein (1987) sample—even though the median age of the
adopted sample was nearly three years less.

Conclusions from studies on foster care outcomes can be cautiously drawn. Continued contact with foster parents and birth parents improves outcomes for youths in foster care. Educational and employment deficits are apparently most troublesome to adults who were previously foster children. Housing is a significant problem in many urban areas; an estimated 7,500 youth who were discharged from foster care were homeless in New York City (Demchak 1985). More than one out of four (27%) children who grew up in foster care and were then questioned as young adults reported severe or moderate housing problems (Triseliotis & Russell 1984). Criminal behavior and substance abuse are less common but possibly overrepresented in adults who were foster children. Whereas exposure to foster care does not doom a child to a distressed adulthood—and may provide the child with beneficial developmental experiences not found in his or her birth home—foster children are still at risk of short-changed futures.

Children and Families' Satisfaction

The satisfaction of children and families should be weighed in decision making. If other outcomes of permanent placements are equal, children's satisfaction becomes particularly salient. Although too little is now known about children's preferences, some data are available.

Placement Prevention

One of the underlying assumptions of permanency planning legislation and practice is that the child's development and emotional well-being is usually best served when he or she can remain with his or her biological family (with assurance of minimal safety and parenting standards). Therefore, children and parents are assumed to be most satisfied within such arrangements. However, few studies have actually addressed satisfaction with placement as an outcome. Many family preservation programs have measured client satisfaction with the services received, and many report high client satisfaction levels (Kinney et al. 1989; Lawder, Poulin, & Andrews 1984). Whether this translates into long-term satisfaction with the child remaining in the home after services are withdrawn is unknown.

Pecora, Bartlome, Magana, and Sperry (1991) provide findings from interviews with the 396 primary caretakers served by intensive family preservation units in Utah and Washington. From the primary caretakers's perspective, IFPS improved family relationships, anger management, the child's behavior, and family communication skills. The interviews focused on what clients (primary caretakers) thought were the most important treatment goals, what was most helpful about the service, comparisons of family functioning between now and before services were provided, and satisfaction with specific aspects of the therapist's behavior and with the service itself. A limitation of the study is that secondary caretakers were interviewed regarding consumer satisfaction only if the child was placed (in other words, when IFPS was unsuccessful). Children were not interviewed regarding client satisfaction. Nearly nine out of ten of the respondents were happy with the children concerned living at home. Clients generally reported high ratings on how they got along with the IFPS workers and how helpful the workers were. In addition, two other components were also rated positively: clients felt that it was important that the therapist went to their house for appointments, and clients valued the new skills and ways of doing things they had been taught. More than 90% of the primary caretakers would recommend home-based services to other families in similar situations.

Family Maintenance and Reunification

Families receiving child protective services (CPS) in Iowa were surveyed to determine their perceptions of the worker's performance and whether their family life had been made better or worse by the activities of the CPS worker (Fryer, Bross, Krugman, Denson, & Baird 1990). Over half of the respondents awarded workers the highest possible rating on each of the scales of seven items indicating positive worker qualities (e.g., helpful, efficient, knowledgeable). At least two-thirds of families rated workers positively on indicators of child welfare worker performance. Almost three out of four clients (72%) believed their family's lives were better due to the worker's efforts.

In the Oregon permanency planning study, all but one of the children returned home preferred their present home to their foster home (Lahti et al. 1978). Most children preferred whatever setting they were in at the time of the interview over their previous setting. A child's perception of permanence in any setting was, however, highly associated with his or her satisfaction across settings. It is not clear whether the child's perception of permanency results in a successful adjustment to the placement. Such a positive adjustment may be independently associated with satisfaction.

Adoption

In Proch's (1982) study of fifty-six children adopted by their foster parents, only eight of the twenty-nine children interviewed could distinguish between foster care and adoption. Most of these children were old enough to remember living in other foster homes. The essential difference between the two types of placements was stated as foster care being temporary and adoption permanent. Therefore, to those children who had multiple placements and sought a sense of belonging, adoption was preferable. In the study by Lahti and colleagues (1978), 22% of adopted (formerly foster) children defined foster children as not being treated as well as other children.

Kowal and Schilling (1985) report that 17% of adult adoptees (who had been placed as infants and later contacted an adoption agency or search group) were embarrassed or felt uncomfortable about the fact of adoption, and 25% reported feeling worried or insecure about being adopted. Still, 21% reported feeling differently from nonadoptees but no better or worse; 22% reported feeling no different, and 35% reported feeling "chosen" or "special." The vast majority (80%) of the children adopted between the ages of two and ten reported a "fairly positive" to "very positive" response to being adopted (Triseliotis & Russell 1984).

Guardianship

Legal guardianship may be a preferable alternative for older children who have lived with a foster family or relatives for a long time and do not want to be adopted and cannot go home. Otherwise, children's preference for guardianship has not been studied.

Long-term Foster Care

Long-term foster care can be preferred by children. In Bush and Gordon's (1982) study of 136 foster children, of 111 children judged unlikely to return home, half did not wish to be adopted. Most of these were older children removed at an older age. These children regarded adoption as destructive to their ties with their original families. The remaining half were more positive about the prospects of adoption, citing the security of their tenure in placement and the wish to belong to a real family.

Fewer than half (43%) of the children in the West Virginia study reported that they were treated differently from other children because they were in foster care (Jones & Moses 1984). In Fanshel's (1982) study, social workers rated foster children—who had been in care for at least one year and for an average of five years—as significantly more attached to their foster homes than to their birth homes. Few younger children experienced a conflict in attachments—more older children did. Children living in institutions felt less comfortable, not as happy, less loved, less looked after, less trusted, and less cared about than children in other forms of surrogate care or than children reunified with their families (Bush 1980). Children who had some choice in their foster placement were significantly more satisfied in their placements than were children with no choice (Bush & Gordon 1982). Fanshel's study of youths who left the Casey Family Foster Care Program (Fanshel et al. 1989) concluded that "the vast majority of subjects reported that they were treated kindly and accepted as family members in their Casey home of longest stay" (p. 92). The aforementioned sample of fifty-five young adults who left foster care in Northern California between 1980 and 1988 generally indicated that foster care was a positive experience, and 78% reported that their lives were *somewhat* or *much better* as a result of having been in foster care (Barth 1990).

The mandated priority for family maintenance and reunification over adoption over guardianship over long-term foster care clearly reflects society's respect for the abused and neglected child's right to have a family life that most closely approximates that of other children. Child welfare service providers generally concur that the ideal family life is one that is free from abuse, is lifelong, generates developmental advantages, and is desirable to the child. Intensive family preservation services and special needs adoption appear to be the most promising developments of the last decade, but the emergence of homelessness and drugs as two of the major influences on families entering the child welfare system suggest that these two programs face great challenges in preserving birth and adoptive families. The difficulties in meeting these challenges are expressed by the growth of the foster care population in the last two years. The difficulties that adoption agencies will increasingly face in making adoptive placements for drug-affected children are just beginning to be apparent.

Of all placement options, conventional family maintenance services or reunification with birth families, as they presently operate, fail most often to be free from abuse and to yield developmental well-being. The right of children to receive the care of their biological parents and the right of parents to have custody and control of the children born to them is nonetheless basic to the organization of American society. No amount of research can or should alter society's commitment to the parent's right to care for his or her children. Given that commitment, the policy implication of the findings that family maintenance and reunification too commonly risk children's well-being is to provide more intensive and lasting support to children in their own homes. Family preservation has been the ideal of child welfare services for a century. Yet ironically we provide only a few months of in-home services to families who have clearly shown long-term difficulties in meeting the challenges of parenting.

Placement Prevention

Current evidence on the efficacy of intensive family preservation consistently shows that the vast majority of families served experience no placement into foster care and that parents can make substantial gains in parenting skills and environmental conditions for the family. Such gains are impressive, given that services are provided for only eight to twelve weeks and that families are usually at high risk for child placement. Most families are still intact one year after services. Evaluations of family preservation programs stop short, however, of showing their long-term benefits for children, their ability to greatly improve outcomes beyond what can be expected of conventional services, or the lasting stability of family units where placement was averted. Parents who do receive family preservation services appear, at least, to report somewhat more success in parenting one year after services than do parents who received conventional services (Rzepnicki in this volume). Efforts to prevent placements among violent and drug-using families may promise as much danger to the welfare of children as benefit. Continued research on the ability of such efforts to produce change in the child's environment that lasts over the years is needed. So are innovations that combine various lengths and intensities of family preservation with less intensive family maintenance follow-up services.

Intensive family preservation services have witnessed an enormous growth in the last decade and in their research base (e.g., Fraser, Pecora, & Haapala 1991; Schuerman, Rzepnicki, Littell, & Chak

1993). A more comprehensive review of the limits of research on family preservation programs is available in Rossi (1991) although his treatment of three randomized studies fails to describe accurately the nature of the California projects, and his conclusion that we should focus future research efforts on a mega-randomized trial of family preservation services is very likely mistaken. The Rossi review fails, as all others have also, to indicate the level of reabuse that resulted from the use of intensive family preservation services. It appears the IFPS has met the test of "first do no harm," but the literature repeatedly fails to indicate what the result was for the 20% or more of the children who are initially retained at home because of IFPS and were later placed.

Family Maintenance and Reunification

Given the data on the difficulties experienced by children who are reunified with their birth parents or who are cared for in their own homes, interventions that only prevent reabuse for the brief time that such cases are open are inadequate. To lower the number of children in foster care by moving children who cannot go home into other permanent situations and by returning children to homes that are safe and will remain safe are two humane and efficient solutions to foster care drift. However, leaving children in homes that are not safe or returning children to homes that are not safe or will not be safe is neither humane nor efficient. Instead, child welfare services should move quickly to seek policy and program changes to reallocate their resources and provide additional services for families beyond mere placement prevention. Intensive family preservation service evaluations are informing policymakers that it is comprehensive and concrete services that often contribute to real gains in parenting skills and household safety in abusive and neglectful families. Conventional family maintenance and reunification programs can utilize this knowledge in their less intensive format by also focusing on skill-building and the mobilization of concrete resources rather than on referral to therapeutic options for many families.

More intensive and lasting services to children at home are indicated. The time limits developed for P. L. 96–272 to govern child welfare services were primarily established to reduce foster care drift by forcing child welfare agencies to decide on a permanent placement in a timely way. The time limits were chosen with guidance from research showing the drop off in reunifications after eighteen months. The use of such time limits for in-home supervision has no equivalent empirical basis and merely corresponds to those for out-of-home care. Indeed, the justification for such time limits appears to arise from concerns about the agencies' resources and the families' rights to privacy. The data presented in this review argue for extended time limits for cases that are supervised in-home or that involve the return of children from foster care. Available data suggests that preplacement services are often inappropriately brief, given the tenacity of family problems and the high reabuse rates. The weak and even inverse relationship between the time of case closing and improvements in family functioning fail to justify such brief preplacement services. Other evidence also indicates that services to children who have been reunified are often inadequate and end prematurely (Ten Broeck & Barth 1986). Ferleger and colleagues (Ferleger, Glenwick, Gaines, & Green 1988) found that reabuse was more likely when parents had received fewer than six months of treatment. The findings of Johnson and L'Esperance (1984) and those of Jones (1977) suggest that greater provision of services to families that are reunified will help prevent abuse and repeat placement. Current permanency planning time limits work against such efforts and make reunification a risky business for children by returning more children home with shorter periods of less supervision and service.

Reunification services not only refer to family support efforts made when the child is returned from placement but also to services provided to the parents and the child while separated in preparation for reunification. Lindsey's (1991) finding before the implementation of permanency planning that services to parents diminished greatly once a child was removed has not been refuted by research done after the advent of permanency planning. Little is known about the content and form of conventional maintenance and reunification services from state to state. A more detailed analysis of the contributors to program efficacy, beyond that of the duration of services, has been performed in family preservation services, and efforts can fruitfully be extended to family maintenance and reunification programs.

Longer service periods—two and even three years, for example— of supervision and in-home services for reunified families deserve more testing. Administrative or statutory changes will be needed. Semiannual administrative and judicial placement reviews might be required for two years after the placement. After two years, the agency would have to demonstrate the need for continued supervision at six-months reviews. Such support may help some families avoid reabuse. Clinical research from other endeavors to help troubled families indicates that changes in the behavior of children and parents do not last unless supported by changes in family skills and social environments (Wahler & Dumas 1984; Whittaker 1985). Some evidence indicates that simply keeping reunified cases open longer with limited services may lessen reabuse (Johnson & L'Esperance 1984). Such services would be less costly than foster care.

Critical to the implementation of the longer service period is addressing policymakers' concern about the family's right to resume its roles without state interference once the state acknowledges that the child is temporarily safe at home. The evidence from Iowa that clients appreciate agency efforts to prevent placement should allay such concerns. This notion neglects the evidence that children who have been injured or endangered are very often not safe at home even after reunification and closing of the case. Such a position endangers the rights of both the child and the birth parent(s) by giving too little recognition to the steep cost to birth families and children if reabuse leads to a permanent loss of custody.

Other service changes are needed. As Wald and colleagues have argued, children who are court dependents—whether at home or in foster care—deserve full psychological, physical, and educational assessments (Wald et al. 1988). These assessments can guide the delivery of services during the extended service and supervision period. Child welfare services would endeavor to contribute to families' capacities to fulfill and remediate children's deficits as identified in the assessments. Recent trends away from the use of foster care underscore the seriousness of reassessing in-home services and reunification. Children who have been abused or neglected and remain at home or are returned home after a brief time in foster care are the next great challenge in child welfare. Given that services to families in their own homes are less costly than out-of-home care and more precisely targeted than child abuse prevention programs, funding for additional and extended in-home services should be a priority. This is not the same as increasing intensive placement prevention services. Each is necessary.

Adoption

The adoption of older children under permanency planning appears to be a highly favorable form of placement. Fears that adoption disruption rates are skyrocketing under permanency planning are unfounded. The positive developmental outcomes of adoption and children's satisfaction with it seem, on the whole, consistent with current impressions and policies. Improved assessments and reconceptualized postplacement services may further these positive outcomes (Spencer 1985).

As preparation for adulthood becomes more complex and the period of dependency on adults lengthens, the benefits of adoption over temporary foster and group care arrangements are augmented. A child adopted at the age of eight may depend on assistance with housing and education for twenty years—the comparable foster child has only half that long to benefit from parental support. The difference in financial investment of the family on behalf of a child adopted at the age of three by a foster family versus a similarly situated foster child approaches $150,000 over their lifetimes (Barth in press). Although the total expenditures are only marginally different, the adopted child has a far higher percentage invested in his or her well-being and far less in administrative costs. This familial investment in a child yields a significant return to society as well and deserves promotion through considerably more support for recruitment and placement. Subsidies have also proven to help stabilize high-risk placements (Barth 1993). All parties to a special needs adoptions invest great hope and effort—this investment warrants the protection of intensive adoption preservation services.

Guardianship

So little is known about guardianship that potential changes are difficult to evaluate. Though research is obviously needed, simple and immediate strategies need not wait. To start with, more general access to guardianship subsidies is warranted (Leashore 1984). Without subsidies, some jurisdictions are granting guardianship while maintaining dependency to ensure adequate financial resources for the child. This contradiction may weaken a guardian's commitment to provide permanent placement. Subsidies help foster and adoptive parents to manage the daily and special expenses of caring for children who are hard to place; guardians deserve no less. After such adjustments are made, the stability and durability of guardianship beyond adolescence should be assessed. Several years ago we predicted that the use of guardianships would decline as child welfare agencies reduce the numbers of children with long relationships to foster parents in accordance with recently instituted time limits, use foster parent adoptions and legal-risk adoptions, and become more familiar and comfortable with terminating parental rights. Instead, guardianship is a much used and discussed option—particularly as the planned end result of kinship foster care.

Long-Term Foster Care

Permanency planning legislation has reduced the most flagrant problems of child welfare—children unnecessarily resigned to long-term and unstable placements. Until 1988 the number of children in out-of-home care had risen only 2% per year since 1980. The great increases of 1988 and 1989 have reached a plateau, and a modest annual rise has resumed. Yet, the likelihood of obtaining the desired outcomes of reunification and adoption decreases as children get older. Some children "grow out" of the primary options of reunification and adoption. For older children, particularly adolescents, guardianship and long-term foster care may provide the least restrictive alternatives because they allow more ready access to their birth families.

Foster care, the recent whipping boy of child welfare services, appears to offer considerable developmental advantages to children and is often regarded favorably and as sufficiently permanent by them. Our review reinforces the conclusions of the early Oregon Permanency Planning Project: "Generally we have not found foster care to be characterized by instable placements affording children limited chance for satisfactory adjustments" (Lahti et al. 1978:570). Unless additional efforts—especially higher care payments and more supportive services, such as respite care—are made to recruit and maintain quality foster parents, however, the risk of poor placement outcomes will increase.

Research on the outcomes of permanency planning is slowly gaining in sophistication, and the last few years have witnessed a growth in the availability of longitudinal data from administrative databases (e.g., Barth, Courtney, & Berry in press; Goerge in this volume;

Wulczyn in this volume). These data will, in a relatively short time, provide reliable answers to questions about recidivism and placement moves. Considerably more time must elapse before they can help answer more fundamental questions about developmental outcomes; linkages to health, mental health, and criminal justice databases will provide a great benefit in assessing adult outcomes resulting from our children's programs (see Bohman & Sigvardsson 1990 for discussion of the potential of these methods).

Future analyses must also allow for greater differentiation of services. The quiet revolution toward providing kinship foster care and the growing effort to increase the availability of treatment foster care clamor for caution about overgeneralizing the results to more conventional foster care. We know, for example, that children in kinship foster care have significantly slower transitions to the home of the parent and to group home care and to adoption—indeed, to any other placement at all (Courtney in press). We also have some evidence that children in kinship care receive fewer services from social workers and from education and other human service providers (Berrick, Barth, & Needell in press; Goerge, Van Voorhis, Grant, Casey, & Robinson 1992). What remains far less clear is whether the children in the two kinds of care are basically the same at intake (as found in Needell et al. in this volume), or whether more troubled children are likely to reside in care with nonrelatives (as suggested by Goerge et al. 1992). By the time this review warrants an update, we expect sufficient research of kinship care to emerge to warrant a more thorough treatment.

The notion that long-term foster care is antithetical to permanence must also be considered further (Fein & Maluccio 1992). If permanency planning is intended to provide lifelong families, then reunification and adoption seem to be by far the most preferred options. Yet, the evidence strongly suggests that long-term foster care—and especially kinship foster care—does not preclude lifelong attachments. Jones and Moses (1984) demonstrated that more than half the children who left long-term foster care before the age of eighteen relocated their birth parents and lived with one of them during their first placement following foster care. One out of three who left after the age of eighteen continued to live with the foster parents. Only a fourth of the children reported that one or both birth parents were dead or could not be located. Many foster children maintained contact with their siblings. Children who have been in foster care for several years are still likely to turn to their birth families or relatives after their discharge from foster care (McDermott 1983). Before we can ascertain the lifelong permanence of placements, additional and longer follow-up studies on children who entered long-term foster care under permanency planning are necessary.

Child welfare policy makers must insist that permanency planning's primary goal is to create living situations that endure for a lifetime. Maluccio and Fein (1983) have argued that permanency planning is designed "to help children live in families that offer continuity of relationships with nurturing parents or caretakers and the opportunity to establish *lifetime relationships*" (p. 197, italics added). A more limited, and too widely accepted, perspective is that permanency planning is intended to secure for each child "*a caring, legally recognized, continuous family in which to grow up*" (Cole 1985:1, italics added). Because permanency planning should be viewed as a set of services and options to provide "lifetime relationships" rather than a "continuous family in which to grow up," the weighing of service options must correspond to the goal. With greater support for long-term foster care and guardianship, these placement options can provide stable, safe, and beneficial places in which to mature; long-term group and residential care are less desirable. All these options pale in comparison with family maintenance and adoption. These choices stand the best chance of securing lifetime relationships—the goal of permanency planning. The second half of the 1980s has witnessed a backing away from adoption with far greater interest by funders and service providers in developing family preservation models. At the beginning of the 1990s, the rate of children entering foster care appears to be declining but the rate of children leaving foster care is declining even faster. Although reducing foster care is not a singular goal of permanency planning (and short-term foster care clearly provides substantial benefit to most children), an optimally functioning child welfare system requires effective efforts to sustain lifetime families through family preservation services and to create them through adoption.

The time-limited and meager services now available for special needs adoption, guardianships, and family preservation and reunification can only be viewed as the outcome of unmistakably short-sighted policies. Every policymaker and professional who considers compromising a child's chance for a permanent family in order to meet short-term exigencies should think again.

NOTE

This chapter is an expanded, revised, and updated version of a paper published by the authors as "Outcomes of Child Welfare Services Under Permanency Planning," Social Service Review, 1987, 61, 71–90. Support was provided by a grant from the Children's Bureau of U.S. D.H.H.S. to the Berkeley Child Welfare Research Center.

REFERENCES

Ahart, A., Bruer, R., Rutsch, C., Schmidt, R., & Zaro, S. (1992). *Intensive foster family reunification programs.* Washington, D. C.: Macro International.

American Humane Association. (1989). *Highlights of official child neglect and abuse reporting.* Denver: AHA.

AuClaire, P. & Schwartz, I. M. (1986). *An evaluation of the effectiveness of intensive home-based services as an alternative to placement for adolescents and their families.* Minneapolis: Hubert H. Humphrey Institute for Public Affairs, University of Minnesota.

Barth, R. P. (1986). Time limits in permanency planning: The child welfare worker's perspective. *Children and Youth Services Review, 8,* 133–44.

Barth, R. P. (1988). Theories guiding home-based intensive family preservation services. In J. K. Whittaker, J. Kinney, E. M. Tracy, & C. Booth (Eds.), *Reaching high-risk families: Intensive family preservation services.* Hawthorne, NY: Aldine de Gruyter.

Barth, R. P. (1990). On their own: The experiences of youth after foster care. *Child and Adolescent Social Work Journal, 7,* 419–40.

Barth, R. P. (1991). Adoption preservation services. In E. M. Tracy, D. A. Haapala, J. Kinney, & P. J. Pecora (Eds.), *Intensive family preservation services: An instructional sourcebook.* Cleveland: Mandel School of Applied Social Sciences.

Barth, R. P. (1993). Fiscal issues and stability in special needs adoption. *Public Welfare, 51*(3), 21–28.

Barth, R. P. (In press). The value of special needs adoption. In D. Mont & R. Avery (Eds.), *Special needs adoption policy.* Westport, CT: Greenwood Press.

Barth, R. P. & Berry, M. (1988). *Adoption and disruption: Rates, risks and responses.* Hawthorne, NY: Aldine de Gruyter.

Barth, R. P. & Berry, M. (1989). Child abuse and child welfare services. In M. Kirst (Ed.), *Conditions of children in California.* Palo Alto: Policy Analysis for California Education, Stanford University.

Barth, R. P., Berry, M., Goodfield, R., Carson, M. L., & Feinberg, B. (1986). Contributors to disruption and dissolution of older child adoptions. *Child Welfare, 63,* 359–71.

Barth, R. P., Courtney, M., Berrick, J., & Albert, V. (In press). *Pathways to permanency planning*. Hawthorne, NY: Aldine de Gruyter.

Barth, R. P., Courtney, M., & Berry, M. (In press). Timing is everything: An analysis of the time to adoption and legalization. *Social Work Research & Abstracts*.

Barth, R. P. & Pizzini, S. (1990). *A snapshot of California's families and children pursuant to the child welfare reforms of the 1980s*. Sacramento: State Department of Social Services.

Barth, R. P., Yoshikami, R. Y., Berry, M., Goodfield, R., & Carson, M. L. (1988). Predicting adoption disruption. *Social Work, 33*, 227–33.

Behavioral Sciences Institute. (1987a). *Summary of King, Pierce, Snohomish, and Spokane County homebuilders services, September 1, 1986–August 31, 1987*. Federal Way, Washington: Author.

Behavioral Sciences Institute. (1987b). *Homebuilders cost effectiveness with various client populations, 1974–1986*. Federal Way, WA: Author.

Berquist, C. Szwejda, D., & Pope, G. (March 1993). *Evaluation of Michigan's Families First program: Summary report*. Lansing, MI: University Associates.

Berrick, J. D., Barth, R. P., & Needell, B. (In press). A comparison of kinship foster homes and foster family homes: Implications for kinship foster care as family preservation. *Children and Youth Services Review*.

Berry, M. (1992). An evaluation of family preservation services: Fitting agency services to family needs. *Social Work, 37*, 314–21.

Berry, M. & Barth, R. P. (1989). Behavior problems of children adopted when older. *Children and Youth Services Review, 11*, 221–38.

Block, N. M. & Libowitz, A. S. (1983). *Recidivism in foster care*. New York: Child Welfare League of America.

Bohman, M. & Sigvardsson, S. (1990). Outcomes in adoption: Lessons from longitudinal studies. In D. Brodzinsky & M. Schechter (Eds.), *The psychology of adoption* (pp 23–44). New York: Oxford University Press.

Bolton, F. G., Laner, R. H., & Gai, D. S. (1981). For better or worse? Foster parents and foster children in an officially reported child maltreatment population. *Children and Youth Services Review, 3*, 37–53.

Boneh, C. (1979). Disruptions in adoptive placements: A research study. Manuscript. Massachusetts Department of Public Welfare.

Boyne, J., Denby, L., Kettenring, J. R., & Wheeler, W. (1984). *The shadow of success: A statistical analysis of outcomes of adoptions of hard-to-place children*. New Jersey: Spaulding for Children.

Bribitzer, M. P. & Verdieck, M. J. (1988). Home-based, family-centered intervention: Evaluation of a foster care prevention program. *Child Welfare, 67*, 255–66.

Brodzinsky, D. M. (1987) Adjustment to adoption: A psychosocial perspective. *Clinical Psychology Review, 7*, 25–47.

Bush, M. (1980). Institutions for dependent and neglected children: Therapeutic option or last resort? *American Journal of Orthopsychiatry, 50*(2), 239–55.

Bush, M. & Gordon, A. C. (1982). The case for involving children in child welfare decisions. *Social Work, 27,* 309–14.

Callister, J. P., Mitchell, L., & Tolley, G. (1986). Profiling family preservation efforts in Utah. *Children Today, 15*(6), 23–25.

Cohen, J. S. (1984). Adoption breakdown with older children. In P. Sachdev (Ed.), *Adoption: Current issues and trends* (pp. 129–39). Toronto: Butterworths.

Cohn, A. H. & Daro, D. (1987). Is treatment too late? What ten years of evaluative research tell us. *Child Abuse and Neglect, 11,* 433–42.

Cole, E. (1985). Permanency planning: A better definition. *Permanency Report, 3*(3), 5.

Courtney, M. (In press). Reunification from foster care. *Social Service Review.*

Courtney, M., Needell, B., & Barth, R. P. (July 1993) Preliminary results of outcome indicators development project. Unpublished paper available from Child Welfare Research Center, School of Social Welfare, University of California, Berkeley, CA 94720

Demchak, T. (1985). Out of foster care; into the streets: Services ordered for homeless youth. *Youth Law News, 6*(5), 12–15.

Derdeyn, A. P., Rogoff, A. R., & Williams, S. W. (1978). Alternatives to absolute termination of parental rights after long-term foster care. *Vanderbilt Law Review, 31*(2), 1165–92.

Deykin, G. Y., Campbell, L., & Patti, P. (1984). The postadoption experience of surrendering parents. *American Journal of Orthopsychiatry, 54,* 271–80.

Dodson, D. (1984). *Comparative study of state case review systems phase II—Dispositional hearings: Legal issues and state statutory survey (vol. 3).* Rockville, MA: Westat and American Bar Association.

Dumaret, A. (1985). IQ, scholastic performance, and behavior of siblings raised in contrasting environments. *Child Psychology, 26,* 553–80.

Fales, M. J. (1985). Adoption assistance: How well is it working? *Permanency Report, 3,* 3.

Fanshel, D. (1982). *On the road to permanency: An expanded data base for service to children in foster care.* New York: Child Welfare League of America & Columbia University School of Social Work.

Fanshel, D. (1972). *Far from the reservation: The transracial adoption of American Indian Children.* Metuchen, NJ: Scarecrow Press.

Fanshel, D., Finch, S. J., & Grundy, J. F. (1990). Modes of exit from foster family care and adjustment at time of departure of children with unstable life histories. *Child Welfare, 68*(4), 391–402.

Fanshel, D., Finch, S. J., & Grundy, J. F. (1990). *Foster children in life course perspective.* New York: Columbia University Press.

Fanshel, D. & Shinn, E. B. (1978). *Children in foster care: A longitudinal investigation.* New York: Columbia University Press.

Fein, E., Davies, L. J., & Knight, G. (1979). Placement stability in foster care. *Social Work, 24,* 156–57.

Fein, E., Maluccio, A. N., Hamilton, J. V., & Ward, D. E. (1983). After foster care: Outcomes of permanent planning for children. *Child Welfare, 62,* 485–562.

Fein, E., Maluccio, A. N., & Kluger, M. (1990). *No more partings: An examination of long-term foster family care.* Washington, D.C.: Child Welfare League of America.

Feldman, L. (1990). *Evaluating the impact of family preservation services in New Jersey.* Trenton: New Jersey Division of Youth and Family Services.

Ferleger, N., Glenwick, D., Gaines, R. R. W., & Green, A. H. (1988). Identifying correlates of reabuse in maltreating parents. *Child Abuse and Neglect, 12,* 41–49.

Festinger, T. (1983). *No one ever asked us.* New York: Columbia University.

Festinger, T. (1986). *Necessary risk: A study of adoption and disrupted adoptive placements.* New York: Child Welfare League of America.

Fein, E. & Maluccio, A. N. (1992). Permanency Planning: Another remedy in jeopardy? *Social Service Review, 66,* 335–48.

Fitzharris, T. L. (1985). *The foster children of California: Profiles of 10,000 children in residential care.* Sacramento: Children's Services Foundation.

Fraser, M., Pecora, P. J., & Haapala, D. (1991). *Families in crisis.* New York: Aldine de Gruyter.

Fryer, G. E., Bross, D. C., Krugman, R. D., Denson, D. B., & Baird, D. (1990). Good news for CPS workers. *Public Welfare, 48,* 38–41, 47.

Goerge, R. M., Wulczyn, F., Hartnett, M. A., & Testa, M. *State of the child.* Unpublished manuscript. Chicago: Chapin Hall Center for Children.

Goerge, R. M., Van Voorhis, J., Grant, S., Casey, K., & Robinson, M. (1992). Special education experiences of foster children: An empirical study. *Child Welfare, 71,* 419–38.

Groze, V. (1986). Special needs adoption. *Children and Youth Services Review, 8,* 363–73.

Harrari, T. (1980). Teenagers exiting from foster family care: A retrospective look. Ph.D. diss., University of California.

Hunner, R. J. (1986). *Active and reasonable efforts to preserve families: A guide for delivering services in compliance with the Indian Child Welfare Act of 1978 and the Adoption Assistance and Child Welfare Act of 1980.* Seattle: Northwest Resource Associates.

Johnson, W. & L'Esperance, J. (1984). Predicting the recurrence of child abuse. *Social Work Research & Abstracts, 20,* 21–31.

Jones, C. O. (1977). A critical evaluation of the work of the NSPCC's battered child research department. *Child Abuse and Neglect, 1,* 111–18.

Jones, M. A. (1983). *A second chance for families—Five years later: Follow-Up of a program to prevent foster care.* New York: Child Welfare League of America.

Jones, M. A. & Moses, B. (1984). *West Virginia's former foster children: Their experience in care and their lives as young adults.* New York: Child Welfare League of America.

Kadushin, A. (1970). *Adopting older children.* New York: Columbia University Press.

Kadushin, A. & Seidl, F. (1971). Adoption failure: A social work postmortem. *Social Work, 16,* 32–37.

Kinard, E. M. (1982). Experiencing child abuse: Effects on emotional adjustment. *American Journal of Orthopsychiatry, 52,* 82–91.

Kinney, J., Haapala, D., Booth, C., & Leavitt, S. (1988). The Homebuilders model. In J. K. Whittaker, T. Kinney, E. M. Tracy, & C. Booth (Eds.), *Reaching high-risk families: Intensive family preservation services.* Hawthorne, NY: Aldine de Gruyter.

Kinney, J. M., Madsen, B., Fleming, T., & Haapala, D. A. (1977). Homebuilders: Keeping families together. *Journal of Consulting and Clinical Psychology, 45,* 667–73.

Kowal, K. A. & Schilling, K. M. (1985). Adoption through the eyes of adult adoptees. *American Journal of Orthopsychiatry, 55,* 354–62.

Kraus, J. (1981). Foster children grown up: Parameters of care and adult delinquency, *Children and Youth Services Review, 3,* 99–114.

Lahti, J. (1982). A follow-up study of foster children in permanent placements. *Social Service Review, 56,* 556–71.

Lahti, J., Green, K., Emlen, A., Zadny, J., Clarkson, Q. D., Kuehnel, M., & Casciato, J. (1978). *A follow-up study of the Oregon Project.* Portland: Portland State University, Regional Institute for Human Services.

Landsman, M. J. (1985). *Evaluation of fourteen child placement prevention projects in Wisconsin, 1983–1985.* Iowa City: National Resource Center on Family Based Services.

Lawder, E. A., Poulin, J. E., & Andrews, R. G. (1984). *Helping the multiproblem family: A study of services to children in their own homes.* Philadelphia: Children's Aid Society of Pennsylvania.

Lawder, E. A., Poulin, J. E., & Andrews, R. G. (1985). *185 foster children five years after placement.* Philadelphia: Children's Aid Society of Pennsylvania.

Leashore, B. R. (1984). Demystifying legal guardianship: An unexplored option for dependent children. *Journal of Family Law, 23,* 391–400.

Leeds, S. J. (1984). *Evaluation of Nebraska's intensive services project.* Iowa City: The National Resource Center on Family Based Services.

Leitenberg, H., Burchard, J. D., Healy, D., & Fuller, E. J. (1981). Nondelinquent children in state custody: Does type of placement matter? *American Journal of Community Psychology, 9,* 347–60.

Lindsey, D. (1991). Factors affecting the foster care placement decision: An analysis of national survey data. *American Journal of Orthopsychiatry, 61,* 272–81.

Lyle, C. G. & Nelson, J. (1983). *Home-based vs. traditional child protection services: A study of the home based services demonstration project in the Ramsey County community human services department.* Oakdale, IA: National Resource Center on Family Based Services.

Maas, H. & Engler, R. (1959). *Children in need of parents.* New York: Columbia University Press.

Magura, S. (1981). Are services to prevent foster care effective? *Children and Youth Services Review, 3*(3), 193–212.

Maluccio, A. N. & Fein, E. (1983). Permanency planning: A redefinition. *Child Welfare, 62,* 195–201.

Maximus, Inc. (1984). *Child welfare statistical fact book, 1984: Substitute care and adoption.* Washington, D.C.: Foster Care Information System.

Maximus, Inc. (1987). *State child welfare abstracts, 1980–1985.* Washington, D.C.: U.S. DHHS/Administration for Children, Youth, and Families.

McDermott, V. (1983). Life planning services for older children project. Manuscript. St. Paul: Children's Home Society of Minnesota.

McDermott, V. (1987). Life planning services: Helping older placed children with their identity. *Child and Adolescent Social Work Journal, 4,* 245–63.

McDonald, T., Lieberman, A., Poertner, J., & Hornby, H. (1989). Child welfare standard for success. *Children and Youth Services Review, 11,* 319–30.

McFadden, E. J. (1985, November). Abuse in family foster homes: Double jeopardy for victimized children. Paper presented at the National Association of Social Workers Symposium, Chicago, Illinois.

McRoy, R. G., Zurcher, L. A., Lauderdale, M. L., & Anderson, R. N. (1982). Self-esteem and racial identity in transracial and inracial adoptees. *Social Work, 27,* 522–26.

Metro-Dade, Department of Youth and Family Development. (1989, December). *Intensive family services program: Statistical information, 1988–1989.* Miami: Author.

Moore, B. (1989). *In-home services for crack-using mothers in Detroit.* Washington, D.C.: DHHS.

National Conference of State Legislatures. (1989). *Selected state family preservation enactments.* Denver: Author.

National Resource Center on Family-Based Services. (1987). *Annotated directory of selected family-based service programs.* Oakdale, IA: Author.

National Resource Center on Family-Based Services. (1988). *Family-based services: A national perspective on success and failure.* Iowa City: Author.

Nelson, K. E., Landsman, M. J., & Deutelbaum, W. (1990). Three models of family-centered placement prevention services. *Child Welfare, 69,* 3–21.

On the Line. (1992). Program notes. *1*(2), 3. Tacoma, WA: Behavioral Sciences Institute.

Partridge, S., Hornby, H., & McDonald, T. (1986). *Legacies of loss, visions of gain.* Portland, ME: University of Southern Maine.

Pecora, P. J., Fraser, J. W., & Haapala, D. (1990). Intensive home-based family preservation services: Client outcomes and issues for program design. In D. E. Biegel & K. Wells (Ed.), *Family preservation services: Research and evaluation.* Newbury Park, CA: Sage Publications.

Pecora, P. J., Fraser, M. W., Haapala, D., & Bartlome, J. A. (1987). *Defining family preservation services: Three intensive home-based treatment programs.* Salt Lake City, UT: University of Utah Social Research Institute.

Pecora, P. J., Bartlome, J. A., Magana, V. L., & Sperry, C. K. (1991). How consumers view family preservation services. In M. W. Fraser, P. J. Pecora, & D. A. Haapala (Eds.), *Families in crisis: The impact of intensive family preservation services* (pp. 226–73). New York: Aldine de Gruyter.

Pelton, L. (1989). *For reasons of poverty: An evaluation of child welfare policy.* New York: Praeger.

Prew, C. (1990, Fall). Therapy with adoptive families: An innovative approach. *The Prevention Report,* p. 8.

Proch, K. (1982). Differences between foster care and adoption: Perceptions of adopted foster children and adoptive foster parents. *Child Welfare, 61, 259–68.*

Ratterman, D., Dodson, G. D., & Hardin, M. A. (1987). *Reasonable efforts to prevent foster placement: A guide to implementation.* Washington, D.C.: American Bar Association.

Reid, W. J., Kagan, R. M., & Schlosberg, S. B. (1988). Prevention of placement: Critical factors in program success. *Child Welfare, 67, 25–36.*

Rindfleisch, N. & Rabb, J. (1984). How much of a problem is resident mistreatment in child welfare institutions? *Child Abuse and Neglect, 8, 33–40.*

Rosenthal, J. A., Motz, J. K., Edmonson, D. A., & Groze, V. (1991) A descriptive study of abuse and neglect in out-of-home placement. *Child Abuse & Neglect, 15, 249–60.*

Rossi, P. H. (August 1991). *Evaluating family preservation programs: A report to the Edna McConnell Clark Foundation.* Unpublished monograph available from Edna McConnell Clark Foundation, New York, NY.

Runyan, D. K. & Gould, C. (1985). Foster care for child maltreatment: Impact on delinquent behavior. *Pediatrics, 75, 562–68.*

Russell, A. B., & Trainor, C. M. (1984). *Trends in child abuse and neglect: A national perspective.* Denver: American Humane Association.

Rutter, M. (1980). *Changing youth in a changing society.* Cambridge, MA: Harvard University Press.

Sack, W. H. & Dale, D. D. (1982). Abuse and deprivation in failing adoptions. *Child Abuse and Neglect, 6, 443–51.*

Scarr, S. & Weinberg, R. A. (1976). IQ test performance of black children adopted by white families. *American Psychologist, 31, 726–39.*

Schuerman, J. R., Rzepnicki, T. L., Littell, J. H., & Chak, A. (1993, June). *Evaluation of the Illinois Family First placement prevention program: Final report.* Chicago: Chapin Hall Center for Children.

Seaberg, J. R. (1986). "Reasonable efforts": Toward implementation in permanency planning. *Child Welfare, 65, 469–79.*

Showell, W. H. (1985). *1983–85 biennial report of CSD's intensive family services.* Salem, OR: State of Oregon Children's Services Division.

Showell, W. H. (1988). Personal communication. February 29, 1988.

Shostack, A. L. & Quane, R. M. (1988). Youths who leave group homes. *Public Welfare, 46*(4), 29–36.

Simon, R. J. & Alstein, H. (1987). *Transracial adoptees and their families: A study of identity and commitment.* Westport, CT: Greenwood Press.

Smith, S. E. & Howard, J. A. (1991). A comparative study of successful and disruptive adoptions, *Social Service Review, 65,* 248–65.

Spencer, M. (1985). Meeting the need for comprehensive post-legal adoption services. *Permanency Report, 3*(4), 5.

State of California Legislative Analyst. (1985). *Child welfare services: A review of the effect of the 1982 reforms on abused and neglected children and their families.* Sacramento: Author.

State Department of Social Services. (1986). *Preplacement preventive services, emergency response, and family maintenance programs.* Sacramento: State of California Department of Social Services.

State Department of Social Services. (1990). *Preplacement preventive services, emergency response, and family maintenance programs.* Sacramento: State of California Department of Social Services.

Stein, T. J. (1985). Projects to prevent out-of-home placement. *Children and Youth Services Review, 7,* 109–21.

Stone, N., M. & Stone, S. F. (1983). The prediction of successful foster placement. *Social Casework, 64,* 11–17.

Szykula, S. A. & Fleischman, M. J. (1985). Reducing out-of-home placements of abused children: Two controlled field studies. *Child Abuse and Neglect, 9,* 277–83.

Taber, M. A. & Proch, K. (1987). Placement stability for adolescents in foster care: Findings from a program experiment. *Child Welfare, 66,* 433–45.

Tatara, T. (Ed.). (1987). *National roundtable on CPS risk assessment and family systems assessment: Summary of highlights.* Washington, D. C.: American Public Welfare Association.

Tatara, T. (1989). Characteristics of children in foster care. *Newsletter of the Division of Child, Youth, and Family Services, 12*(3), 3–16, 17.

Ten Broeck, E. & Barth, R. P. (1986). Lessons from implementing a pilot permanency planning program. *Child Welfare, 69,* 281–94.

Tizard, B. (1977). *Adoption: A second chance.* New York: Free Press.

Triseliotis, J. & Russell, J. (1984). *Hard to place.* Exeter, NH: Heinemann Educational Books.

Tyler, M. (1990). State survey on placement prevention and family reunification services. Iowa City: National Resource Center on Family Based Services.

U.S. Bureau of the Census. (1989) *What's it worth? Educational background and economic status: Spring 1989.* Current population reports, Household economic studies, series R 70, no. 11. Washington, D. C.: Author.

U. S. Select Committee on Children, Youth, and Families. (1989, September). *U. S. Children and their families: Current conditions and recent trends, 1989.* Washington, D.C.: U.S. House of Representatives.

U. S. Select Committee on Children, Youth, and Families. (1989, November). *No place to call home: Discarded children in America*. Washington, D.C.: U.S. House of Representatives.

U. S. Senate Committee on Finance. (1990). *Foster care, adoption assistance, and child welfare services*. Washington, D.C.: Government Printing Office.

VanMeter, M. J. S., Haynes, O. M., & Kropp, J. P. (1987). The negative social network: When friends are foes. *Child Welfare, 66*(1), 69–75.

Wahler, R. G. & Dumas, J. E. (1984). Changing the observational coding styles of insular and noninsular mothers: A step toward maintenance of parent training effects. In R. F. Dangel & R. A. Polster (Eds.), *Parent training* (pp. 379–416). New York: Guilford.

Wald, M., Carlsmith, C. M., & Leiderman, P. H. (1988). *Protecting abused and neglected children*. Palo Alto, CA: Stanford University Press.

Wells, K. & Whittington, D. (1993) Child and family functioning after intensive family preservation services. *Social Service Review, 67*, 55–83.

Westat, Inc. (1986). *Independent living services for youth in substitute care*. Washington, D. C.: Department of Health and Human Services.

Westat, Inc. (1991). A national evaluation of Title IV-E foster care independent living programs for youth. (Phase 2: vol.1). Rockville, MD: Author.

Whittaker, J. K. (1985). Group and institutional care: An overview. In J. Laird & A. Hartman (Eds.), *A handbook of child welfare: Context, knowledge, and practice* (pp. 617–37). New York: Free Press.

Wulczyn, F. H. (1991). Caseload dynamics and foster care reentry. *Social Service Review, 65*, 133–96.

Wulczyn, F. H. & Goerge, R. M. (1992). Foster care in Illinois: The challenge of rapid change. *Social Service Review, 66*, 278–94.

Wulczyn, F. H. (July 20, 1993). Personal communication.

Zimmerman, R. B. (1982). *Foster care in retrospect*. New Orleans, LA: Tulane University.

Zwimpfer, D. M. (1983). Indicators of adoption breakdown. *Social Casework, 64*, 169–77.

Contributors

Helen Noh Ahn, Ph.D.
Lecturer
Seoul Women's University
Seoul, Korea.

Vicky Albert, Ph.D.
Research Specialist
Child Welfare Research Center
Family Welfare Research Group
School of Social Welfare
University of California, Berkeley.

Christine A. Bachrach, Ph.D.
Chief, Demographic and Behavioral Sciences Branch
Center for Population Research
National Institute of Child Health and Human Development
Bethesda, Maryland.

Richard P. Barth, Ph.D.
Hutto Patterson Professor
School of Social Welfare
University of California, Berkeley.

Jill Duerr Berrick, Ph.D.
Director, Child Welfare Research Center
Family Welfare Research Group
School of Social Welfare
University of California, Berkeley.

Marianne Berry, Ph.D.
Associate Professor
School of Social Work
University of Texas, Arlington.

Amy Chak, M.S.W.
Research Assistant
Chapin Hall Center for Children
University of Chicago.

Mark E. Courtney, Ph.D.
Assistant Professor
School of Social Work
University of Wisconsin, Madison.

Neil Gilbert, Ph.D.
Milton and Gertrude Chernin Professor
of Social Welfare and Social Services
School of Social Welfare
University of California, Berkeley.

Robert M. Goerge, Ph.D.
Assistant Director
The Chapin Hall Center for Children
at the University of Chicago.

Elizabeth Hutchison, Ph.D.
Associate Professor
School of Social Work
Virginia Commonwealth University, Richmond.

Julia Littell, Ph.D.
Research Fellow
Chapin Hall Center for Children
University of Chicago.

Kathryn A. London
National Center for Health Statistics
Family Growth Survey Branch
Hyattsville, Maryland.

Marva Lopez
Survey Professional
Abt Associates.

Penelope L. Maza
Administration for Children, Youth and Families
Children's Bureau
Washington, D.C.

Kristine E. Nelson, D.S.W.
Professor
School of Social Work
Portland State University.

Tina Rzepnicki, Ph.D.
Faculty Associate
Chapin Hall Center for Children and
Associate Professor
School of Social Service Administration
University of Chicago.

John Schuerman, Ph.D.
Faculty Associate
Chapin Hall Center for Children and
Professor
School of Social Service Administration
University of Chicago.

Toshio Tatara, Ph.D.
Director, Research and Demonstration Department
American Public Welfare Association
Washington, D.C.

Clarice Dibble Walker
Social Services Commissioner
Washington, D.C.

Cathy Spatz Widom, Ph.D.
Michael J. Hindelang Criminal Justice Research Center
School of Criminal Justice
University of Albany, New York.

Fred Wulczyn, Ph.D.
Assistant Professor, Columbia University and Policy Analyst
New York Department of Social Services, Albany.
Patricia Zangrillo
American Public Welfare Association
Washington, D.C.

Index

Aber III, J. L., 7, 10, 15, 16, 20, 22, 300
Achenbach, T. M., 280
Achenbach Child Behavior Checklist, 280
Adams, P. F., 253, 267
Adolescents, 21, 98, 147, 335
Adoption of drug-exposed children, California study, 273–91; Achenbach Child Behavior Checklist, 280; adoption assistance payments, 291; adoptive families, characteristics of, 280–84; birth mother, arrangements with, 284–85; child care expectations, 284, 290; children, characteristics of, 285–88, 291; children, labeling of, 289; costs, 280, 288, 290–91; education, adoptive mother's, 282; employment, adoptive mother's, 281–82; follow-up studies, 288–89; foster-parent adoptions, 281; media reports of, 275; methodology, 277–80; National Longitudinal Survey of Youth (NLSY), 248, 280, 287; NLSY temperament scale, 287; nondrug-exposed children, compared to, 282, 284; parent satisfaction with, 285, 290; prenatal drug exposure in, 278–80; preparation for placement, 282, 290; Problem Behavior Index (PBI), 280, 287; by relatives, 281; research, previous, 275–77; single-parent adoption, 281; social workers, 279, 291; type of agency and, 248, 281, 282, 284, 285, 288, 290; see also Parental drug abuse study, African-American children in foster care

Adoption Assistance and Child Welfare Act of 1980 (PL 96-272) 83, 118–19, 123, 139–40, 319, 323, 329, 337

Adoption: adoption seeking, 250–71; adult adoptees, 342; "aggressive adoption," 338; as alter-